Health Services Planning

Richard K. Thomas

Health Services Planning

Third Edition

 Springer

Richard K. Thomas
Public Health Research Institute, University of Tennessee Health Science
Center Health and Performance Resources, LLC
Mississippi State University (Social Science Research Center)
Memphis, TN, USA

ISBN 978-1-0716-1078-7   ISBN 978-1-0716-1076-3   (eBook)
https://doi.org/10.1007/978-1-0716-1076-3

This Springer imprint is published by the registered company Springer Science+Business Media, LLC
part of Springer Nature.
The registered company address is: 1 New York Plaza, New York, NY 10004, U.S.A.

Preface

When *Health Services Planning* was originally published in 1999, it was intended to fill a void that existed in the literature on the planning of health services. Its publication was also a response to developments in the US society in general and healthcare in particular that created an urgent need for the pursuit of at least some level of health planning. The 1990s witnessed continued fragmentation of the public healthcare system and the introduction of new challenges such as the reemergence of long-dormant communicable diseases. The growing number of uninsured individuals threatened to severely damage our ability to provide care. The closure of numerous hospitals and a large number of bankruptcies among healthcare organizations provided further evidence of the lack of planning for future exigencies.

Since that time, the situation in the United States has further deteriorated in many ways, making the need for health planning even more urgent. Serious shortcomings in the public health arena have been identified, and "safety net" hospitals have increasingly lost their ability to handle the overwhelming demand for their services. The Medicaid program is facing serious challenges, and the ability of Medicare to sustain itself for the long run has been questioned. Add to this the emergence of various communicable diseases that have long been thought eradicated, and the need for a systematic approach to health planning challenges is obvious.

Increasingly, the success stories spawned by the US healthcare "system" are offset by reports of the inefficiencies and lack of effectiveness that continue to characterize it. Much of the confusion, wheel spinning, and missteps characterizing our healthcare system can be attributed to a lack of planning both system-wide and on the part of individual organizations. In an environment that is undergoing constant evolution and experiencing rapid change on many fronts, decision makers require a framework for action. Without a plan in place, it is difficult, if not impossible, to make rational decisions.

Responsible parties in both the public and private sectors have come to realize that a systematic approach to the issues faced by healthcare is essential, and the 1990s witnessed a surge of interest in health services planning. Now, well into the twenty-first century, the growing demand for community-based solutions to critical health problems has begun to create an environment more supportive of public sector planning. Many daring individuals are even beginning to use the "p" word again. In the private sector, increasing competition, declining reimbursement, and a variety of other market forces are encouraging healthcare organizations to consider a planning-oriented response. The industry trend toward data-driven decision-making is providing additional impetus for this movement. While there is still some resistance to "planning" per se, planning activities are emerging under the heading of "strategic initiatives," "business development," or some other moniker.

Three major developments have prompted the need for a revised edition of *Health Services Planning*. First, the passage of the Patient Protection and Affordable Care Act (ACA) represented a major reform effort for the financing of healthcare. This act called for unprecedented restrictions on the health insurance industry and created a mechanism through which additional tens of millions of Americans would be able to acquire health insurance coverage. Importantly, it mandated that not-for-profit hospitals conduct community health needs assessments at least every 3 years in order to maintain their tax-exempt status. These assessments were not to be limited to the organization's patients but must consider the entire community. Such assessments, of course, represent the basic foundation for health services planning.

Second, the entities that are paying for most health services—insurance companies, Medicare, and Medicaid—are introducing programs for value-based or pay-for-performance reimbursement. Spearheaded by the federal Centers for Medicare & Medicaid, these efforts are forcing healthcare providers to take a more global approach to the management of their patient panels or health plan members. These initiatives require that healthcare providers become much more knowledgeable about their patients and prospective patients, requiring them to actually *plan* for the provision of services.

Third, the twenty-first century has witnessed the emergence of the population health movement, a movement that threatens to turn healthcare on its head. There is growing evidence that the US population is getting sicker and that the healthcare system as currently structured can do nothing about it. This situation has led to efforts to rethink our approach to "sick care" and develop a systematic approach to addressing not just the symptoms of health problems but the underlying causes. This development is so significant that a separate chapter in the book has been devoted to it.

One final consideration as this book goes to press is policies fomented by the Trump administration that appear to represent threats to the health of the public. Arguably, attacks on the health of the population are being waged along a number of fronts—from efforts to dismantle the ACA to the lessoning of environmental protections to resisting efforts to address climate change to reducing funding for the Centers for Disease Control and Prevention and other healthcare organizations. These actions are clearly "anti-planning" in their effect in that they represent one-off efforts to reduce the healthcare "safety net" while at the same time reflecting an across-the-board assault on the health of the public. These efforts will have significant implications for the future of health services planning.

This third edition of *Health Services Planning* retains the basic structure of previous versions. However, its contents have been systematically updated to reflect developments that have occurred in healthcare and health planning since 2003.

Some sections have been expanded and others contracted based on reader feedback and developments in the field. The "additional resources" lists at the end of each chapter have been expanded to include relevant websites. Additional exhibits have been added to provide more in the way of case studies.

If anything, the audience for a book such of this should be larger than for previous editions. The needs have become greater and the search for solutions more frantic. Health planning is increasingly seen as an issue not just for health professionals and government bureaucrats, but for people in many sectors of society who are affected by the deficiencies in the US healthcare system. The emergence of the population health movement has meant that communities have had to consider their role in community health improvement for the first time. Hopefully, this revised work will provide the foundation for the approach to health services planning for a wide range of concerned individuals.

The publication of this third edition of *Health Services Planning* reflects the input of a wide range of experts inside and outside of healthcare who, each in their own way, have contributed to the advancement of the field of health services planning. This includes those individuals in public sector environments who doggedly pursue the aims of health planning, often against overwhelming odds. It also includes those in healthcare organizations within the private healthcare sector who have pioneered the use of planning approaches in their particular domains. The experiences of individuals who are concerned over the state of the US healthcare system and see planning as a means for addressing many of these concerns have provided useful material for this book. In view of the broader scope now accorded to health services planning, the perspectives of those in other sectors beyond healthcare have increasing value. Their input in the form of anecdotes, suggestions, citations, and directions to resource materials has been invaluable.

Hopefully, this book will encourage a new generation of health professionals to come to understand the important role that planning can play in creating a more efficient and more effective healthcare system. If this book can make some small contribution toward creating the type of healthcare system that Americans want and deserve, it will have been well worth the effort.

Memphis, TN   Richard K. Thomas

Contents

About the Author

Richard K. Thomas, PhD is vice president of Health and Performance Resources in Memphis, Tennessee, and author, speaker, and consultant. He has been involved in healthcare market research, planning, and business development with hospitals, clinics, health plans, and other healthcare organizations in both the public and private sectors for more than 40 years. Dr. Thomas holds master's degrees in sociology and geography from the University of Memphis and a PhD in medical sociology from Vanderbilt University. He has held faculty appointments at several universities and medical schools and is currently a research affiliate with the Social Science Research Center at Mississippi State University and affiliate faculty with the University of Tennessee Health Science Center. Dr. Thomas is active in publishing and has authored or coauthored over 20 books on health-related topics, including works on health services planning, healthcare market research, and the demography of health and healthcare. He has authored dozens of articles on healthcare and given numerous presentations, seminars, and workshops on related subjects. He previously served as the editor of *Marketing Health Services*, the healthcare journal of the American Marketing Association.

Chapter 1
Introduction to Health Services Planning

"Health services planning" is a term that most health professionals are increasingly familiar with. However, the term means different things to different people. In some cases, it may refer to a vague notion of social engineering applied to healthcare. In others, it may refer to an activity as specific as the operation of a certificate-of-need process or the design of a health facility. A review of the planning literature reveals a variety of definitions in use as well as cases in which the author does not even offer a definition. Indeed, there is little consensus among experts as to the definition of health services planning and the concept is continuously being redefined as planning tries to "find itself" in the new millennium.

Health services planning has not been applied as extensively in the United States as it has in other developed countries, and even many health professionals do not understand the concept. For that reason, it is appropriate to start from the beginning and present the basic concepts used in the field. The sections that follow review the nature of planning in general and health services planning in particular. These sections are followed by a discussion of the issues surrounding health services planning in the contemporary healthcare environment.

What Is Planning?

Let us begin with a basic definition of planning and work toward a more healthcare-specific version. A useful working definition would read as follows:

> Planning is a process whereby a coordinated and comprehensive mechanism is developed for the efficient allocation of resources to meet a specific goal or goals.

Regardless of the context, the various components of this definition can be applied. First, planning represents a process. In fact, the process may be viewed by some as more important than the outcome. Planning implies that attempts are being made to coordinate the various aspects of the system being addressed. Further,

R. K. Thomas, *Health Services Planning*,
https://doi.org/10.1007/978-1-0716-1076-3_1

planning activities are comprehensive in their approach in that they consider all relevant variables. Ultimately, the intent of the planning process is to achieve certain identified goals and to do this through the efficient allocation of available resources.

The planning process itself has substantial merit, even in the absence of a completed plan. In fact, it could be argued that a true plan is never completed. Completion implies the creation of a static document within the context of a dynamic environment. The plan should always be evolving, and, in fact, it is virtually always the case that a plan is revised even before it is published. Further, it is often the case that certain objectives specified in the plan are met either partially or fully prior to the plan being finalized.

Another reason for focusing on the process (planning) rather than the outcome (the plan) is the benefits that accrue from the process itself. The very act of going through the planning process forces a community or organization to examine who they are, what they are doing, and why they are doing it. Often, the by-products of the planning process are more important to the organization than the plan itself. This notion is summarized in a quote attributed to the British statesman Benjamin Disraeli who contended: "The plan is nothing; planning is everything."

What Is a Plan?

Given this definition of planning, how, then, would a plan be defined? The plan is obviously the concrete product of the planning process, but this definition oversimplifies the significance of a plan. The printed product that results from the planning process should represent the formal codification of the plan. It provides the context in which planning should take place and should serve as a blueprint for reaching a specified goal or goals.

More importantly, the plan should serve as a context for decision-making. Within the framework of the plan, administrators, planners, and business development staff should be able to systematically propose and implement any type of project. The plan provides the "criteria" for decision-making by laying out the goals and objectives of the community or organization and specifying the point at which the community or the organization would like to be at some specified time in the future.

What Is Health Services Planning?

Having defined planning in a generic sense, how, then, should we define health services planning? Health services planning might be described as follows:

> Health services planning is a process that appraises the overall health needs of a geographic area or population and determines how these needs can be met in the most effective manner through the allocation of existing and anticipated future resources.

As will be seen, this definition probably fits the notion of community-wide planning better than it does organization-level planning. Yet, the same concept applies to both. Ultimately, all planning comes down to identifying the needs of the target population (however defined) and then determining the best means for meeting those needs.

One consideration related to health services planning that does not necessarily affect the planning process in other industries is the fact that for an existing healthcare organization services continue to be provided during the planning process. A manufacturing enterprise, for example, can shut down a plant or eliminate a product line until the planning process is completed. However, a hospital cannot refuse to treat heart patients or perform gallbladder surgery until the plan is completed. The fact that health services planning typically takes place "on the fly" complicates the process.

How Is Health Services Planning Different?

Healthcare as an institution in the US society is unique in many ways. This uniqueness creates a special situation for the industry with regard to planning. Elasticity in the level of demand presents a challenge for health planners, and the fact that health services providers are often dealing with life-and-death situations adds an emotional dimension to the planning of health services not found in other arenas.

Healthcare is also set apart by the manner in which the industry is organized. The industry involves literally hundreds of thousands of essentially autonomous entities operating in a virtually uncoordinated manner. The various providers have limited incentives with regard to the coordination of efforts and are seldom constrained by any centralized agent of control. Most operate independently of most of the other organizations involved in the provision of care. Even within an organization such as a hospital, the number of separate "kingdoms" is astounding. Many of these internal departments actually work at cross-purposes with each other. Relationships within the organization are complex, and this alone creates a difficult planning environment.

Healthcare is also characterized by a wide variety of customers whose nature varies from industry segment to industry segment. Patients represent only one group of customers, and an entity like a large hospital may have a dozen different customer groups with which to contend. Further, the various players in the industry have diverse objectives, some of which may be contrary to the objectives of other players.

The financial characteristics of healthcare also set it apart from other industries, with healthcare representing an exception to just about every "law" of economics. The role played by third-party payors is certainly unique, and the consequent indirectness of the decision-making process confounds the planning process. The fact that the end user may not make the consumption decision or pay for the service provided certainly creates a challenging context for health services planning.

The Diverse Functions of Healthcare

Perhaps the most important factor that differentiates healthcare from other industries is the diversity of functions that often characterize healthcare providers. Not only do different entities perform different functions, but a single entity like a hospital will perform multiple often conflicting functions simultaneously. For example, how does a church-sponsored hospital reconcile its mission of service and caring with the need to generate revenue above and beyond its expenses?

The obvious function of the healthcare system and its component organizations is to provide for the healthcare needs of the population. This is carried out most directly through patient care, and patient care is what comes to mind when we envision the healthcare system. However, there are thousands of healthcare organizations that are not involved in patient care. Even those who do provide care often serve a variety of functions. Many see themselves primarily as providing a community service; others see their role as essentially humanitarian. Some entities see themselves as contributing to the safety of the public, perhaps best exemplified by the various public health programs. Some organizations are clearly interested in the furtherance of certain religious perspectives, and others see themselves performing a social welfare role.

These examples do not include the economic functions that the healthcare system and its component organizations perform. Certainly, the redistribution of resources and the creation of wealth and jobs are important. On the other hand, teaching and research are specifically designated functions of the healthcare system.

Beyond these overt functions of the system, there are "latent" functions identified by observers. The healthcare system serves in many ways as a mechanism of social control, defining the characteristics of individuals that are considered by the society to be "normal" and "abnormal." In all societies, the healthcare system serves as an integrating mechanism for the society, bringing the population together in response to illness and implicitly enforcing group values. The system also plays a role in explaining the "why" of sickness and death.

From any perspective, healthcare is not the typical industry. As an industry it has unique characteristics that make the direct application of planning techniques from other industries difficult. Even at the organization level, the variety of types of organizations creates a challenge for any health services planner.

The Political Nature of Planning

Ideally, planning should be an objective process driven by technical considerations. In actual practice, though, planning inevitably involves *someone's* idea of the way things should be. Even when the plan represents group consensus, it is still a product of this group and not some other group. Thus, plans are never going to be completely objective in their formulation or implementation. They are likely to represent a compromise among vested interests in the community or competing forces within the particular organization. In fact, the broad participation that is currently encouraged at both the community and organizational planning levels assures that the process will be at least partially political.

One reason that planning inevitably has a political dimension is that plans are seldom just for the sake of planning. Some *thing* virtually always serves to initiate the planning process. At the community level, it may be a crisis related to publicly funded care, a communicable disease epidemic, or the runaway costs of care. At the organization level, it may be a crisis within the organization, changes in the external environment, actions of competitors, or any number of other developments. The process may be driven by the interests of a particular group or even an individual with a specific agenda. Indeed, some proponents of planning may have a preconceived notion of what the organization should do and will attempt to use the planning process to reach *their* goals.

It should be remembered that *most* healthcare decisions are political. The decision of a hospital to offer a particular service or add a new technology, the decision of a medical group to affiliate with hospital A rather than hospital B, and the decision to locate a clinic in an affluent suburb rather than the inner city are all made based on political, social, and economic considerations as well as clinical ones. Any health services plan reflects the influence of the political, social, and economic considerations that come into play in that particular healthcare environment, and the plan that results always reflects the environment that spawned it. The challenge for the planner is to balance the objective and technical dimension of planning with the realities of the context in which planning is taking place.

Who Needs Health Planning?

There are few healthcare organizations in today's environment that could not benefit from planning. In fact, virtually every organization is going to have to rely on planning to assure its continued viability in the future. The environment has become much too unstable and unpredictable to allow the capricious forces therein to control the destiny of a healthcare organization or health system. The industry maxim has become control or be controlled.

In the public sector, every community clearly needs to plan for its healthcare needs. Resources for the provision of health services are limited and are likely to become more limited in the foreseeable future. The cost involved in providing care continues to rise, and a persistent legion of uninsured Americans will continue to place a strain on the system. The continued maldistribution of services makes access to care a growing problem, and increased demands for accountability contribute to a need for health services planning at the community level. Indeed, a tenet of the emerging population health model is that community health improvement is a community responsibility and not something that can be left to the healthcare system.

At the organization level, it is difficult to imagine any healthcare organization being able to position itself for the future without a plan in place. From the largest national hospital chain to the one-person clinician's office, every entity must be able to control its future to the extent it can. Multipurpose organizations like hospitals must develop plans that allow them to adapt to the changing environment and coordinate the various and diverse components of their systems. Conglomerates that are the product of a merger of previously independent organizations face a particular challenge in meshing the organizational structures and corporate cultures of disparate entities.

Health professionals such as physicians, therapists, and other clinicians also face the need to lay out a systematic road map for reaching the future. Any number of examples can be provided of practitioners who found themselves in one kind of a difficulty or another for failing to plan for various contingencies. Other institutional providers, such as nursing homes, home health agencies, and assisted living facilities, must similarly be able to chart a well-thought-out course.

Health insurance plans, including managed care plans, must be able to determine their future direction and implement a plan for reaching their goals. No success in the future is going to come through happenstance; every organization must take an active role in "inventing" its future. Health plans face the same challenge confronting healthcare providers; they must control their destinies or be controlled by an unpredictable environment. The emergence of predictive modeling as a methodology utilized by health planners reflects the importance of understanding the current *and* future characteristics of the target population.

Planning for Whom?

The parties for whom the plan is being developed depend on the nature of the plan and the parties involved in the planning process. In community-wide planning, the plan ostensibly benefits the entire healthcare system and, by extension, all citizens of the community. In theory at least, the community health plan should represent the greatest good for the greatest number. The goals should be the provision of better access to care for all citizens, more efficient operation of the system, and more effective outcomes from the expenditure of public and private funds.

For organization planning, the objectives are much narrower. At this level, the self-interests of the organization are clearly the issue, and organization-level plans focus on the future needs of the organization (and by extension its customers) independent of the needs of the community. Inevitably, certain departments or individuals may benefit more than others, but, presumably, the intent of the plan is to enhance the effectiveness of the organization in reaching its corporate goals. With the introduction of the Affordable Care Act, planning was identified as a mandatory function of not-for-profit hospitals.

While community-wide planning and organization-level planning may appear to have mutually exclusive constituents, it is unrealistic to assume that they can be implemented totally independent of each other. Community-wide planning must take into consideration the needs of all entities involved in the provision of care, including for-profit healthcare organizations. Indeed, one of the constraints imposed on the federally mandated health planning of the 1960s and 1970s was that plan development could not interfere with established practice patterns. On the other hand, no healthcare organization operating in a local context can afford to ignore the concerns of the local community and the health plans that they formulate. Even today, certificate-of-need requirements and other regulations constrain the actions of private-sector healthcare organizations in some communities. Ultimately, community-wide plans must incorporate the perspectives of all players in the healthcare arena, and organization-level plans must accommodate themselves to the broader plans formulated for the community.

Why Is Health Planning Needed?

A number of reasons can be cited to justify the development of health services plans, although there is an ongoing debate over the appropriateness of some of these. Ultimately, it could be argued that planning is a virtue in its own right and that this should be enough reason in itself. The benefits derived from going through the planning process are multiple, even if no formal plan ever materializes. Yet this fact alone would seldom justify the initiation of the process.

Planning serves to engender coordination among the various components of a system or the subunits of an organization. Coordination is understandably required to implement a plan, but it is just as important to the planning process. Planning further serves to instill discipline into the operation of the system or organization. By drawing attention to the processes that are involved, planning serves as a force for efficiency.

The plan provides a powerful means for the allocation of resources. Indeed, the *raison d'etre* for planning is to assure the appropriate allocation of resources for future needs. There are always more demands for resources than there are available resources, and, in today's environment, there are certainly more opportunities than there are resources to exploit them. While a plan may not directly determine the manner in which resources are to be allocated, it can provide the framework within which decisions on resource allocation can be made.

Planning also serves the purpose of getting issues "out on the table" that would not otherwise be discussed. Any community assessment supportive of the planning process is likely to identify heretofore unknown problems, issues, and/or challenges. The process provides a venue for raising issues that might otherwise be ignored in the press of day-to-day operations. It allows the presentation of these issues in a context where they can be given thoughtful consideration and viewed within a framework in which other, perhaps competing, issues are being considered.

Another important function of the planning process is the setting of priorities, whether at the community or organization level. Priority setting is an inherent task within the planning process and one that impacts all other aspects of the organization. There are always too many worthy projects and too few resources to go around. Only within the context of a systematic plan is it possible to prioritize the various tasks that need to be performed.

Another function of planning, particularly in today's environment, is cost control. The knowledge base generated as a result of the planning process can become a tool for cost containment. The growing interest in pay for performance on the part of third-party payors has required healthcare providers to develop the ability to manage utilization and control costs. The emphasis on coordination, efficiency, and accountability inherent in every plan provides the opportunity to introduce measures that are more cost effective than existing practices.

The plan also serves as a mechanism for introducing accountability at both the community and organization levels. Indeed, this is one of the attributes that generates the most resistance to the planning process. Not only will the background research for the plan thoroughly examine existing community or organizational practices, but the implementation schedule adopted as part of the plan will clearly lay out the necessary tasks and assign responsibility. In this manner, it introduces a measure of accountability not otherwise present.

Another important function of the planning process relates to the collection of data. It could be argued that 80% of the planning process is devoted to the compilation of the necessary data and 20% is devoted to actual planning. More than 50 years of planning experience suggests that the process of identifying sources of data, reviewing existing data on the community or the organization, and ultimately using these data as a foundation for planning activities provides an opportunity for both planners and managers to examine issues from a perspective not previously available. During the heyday of community-wide planning in the 1960s and 1970s, the data that were available to health professionals were better than they have ever been before or since. By the same token, the data generated through the organization planning process produces information that might not otherwise be available. This author has never participated in an organization planning process in which some of the information collected did not elicit surprise and/or grave concern from the organization's staff.

One final reason for planning, and one that perhaps overrides all of the others, is the need to establish a framework for decision-making. In the final analysis, most healthcare decisions are made in a vacuum or at least under conditions involving less than optimal information. Because of this vacuum, it has been argued that hospital administrators are historically characterized by one of two modes of activity: paralysis or impulsiveness. The number of "wrong" decisions made by healthcare organizations whether representing the community or their own self-interests are too numerous to recount. Without a plan for guidance, the chances of making an inappropriate decision multiply.

In many cases, the failure to make a decision is worse than a wrong decision. Many communities have failed to take appropriate action to address a looming crisis. Organizations have lost market share or important referral relationships due to their failure to take decisive action. Paralysis results from not having a framework within which to make decisions or the criteria with which to evaluate the options. When confronted with a choice, decision makers must have a context within which to assess the situation. They must be able to determine how the proposed initiative fits into their overall plans and contributes to the specified goals and objectives of the community or the organization. A great opportunity is not really an opportunity if it does not contribute to the ultimate ends being pursued. The plan helps establish the criteria necessary for evaluating any such opportunity. These criteria may relate to the organization's mission, its revenue targets, the strategic initiatives that it is pursuing, or any number of other factors. What is critical is that criteria be in place so that timely and informed decisions can be made.

Why the Resistance to Planning?

The merits of planning for a function as important as the provision of health services should be obvious, and every other developed country has significant health planning capacity. Yet resistance to planning in general and to health services planning in particular reflects a prevailing—yet paradoxical—attitude within the US society. Americans may even be accused of "plan phobia." Even though we pride ourselves in our investments in research and development, the planning horizons for most US corporations are typically the next quarter. Long-term benefits are often sacrificed to bolster short-term gains. Although healthcare is not quite as short-sighted as some other sectors of the economy, this neglect of planning is nevertheless present in healthcare.

Why, we have to ask ourselves, are we as a society so opposed to planning? One would think that, with the values that permeate American society, we would be obsessed with planning. As a society, we emphasize *control* of our environment, *prediction* of future developments, operational *efficiency*, and *coordination* of activities. It is difficult to see how any of these conditions can be achieved without planning. Americans also emphasize *activism* (or the taking of a proactive approach to the situation), and a *future orientation* that encourages them to make investments that will pay dividends in the future. If these values were not enough to encourage a planning mindset, we could all agree that, as a society, we are obsessed with the economic bottom line. If nothing else, this emphasis on *profitability* should mandate a strong planning orientation. How else can one assure control of the factors that are likely to affect long-term success? While other societies publish 5- and 10-year plans for economic development, social programs, and other society-wide initiatives, no such federal planning activity takes place in the United States. While foreign corporations are developing 20-year plans, American corporations are obsessed with quarterly earnings.

Given the dominant traits of American society, how can we explain this phobia when it comes to planning? At the federal level (and down the governmental hierarchy to the community level) there is an almost irrational apprehension about the participation of government in the coordination of society's activities. The dominant philosophy in the economic system stems from a belief in the power of the "market" to drive institutions in the appropriate direction. Because of the influence of the economic system on the US society, this philosophy spills over into other areas including healthcare. Centralized planning is often equated with socialism and, at best, is thought to interfere with the operation of established patterns of service delivery. This perspective is reinforced by a widespread distrust of government on the part of the American people.

US society is controlled for the most part by coalitions of special interest groups, and these groups greatly influence the operation of American institutions. Systematic attempts at planning run counter to the notion of "deal-making" that drives everything from national politics to corporate decision-making to the development of health services. At the same time, the introduction of planning raises the specter of accountability for many groups that would rather toil in anonymity.

Nowhere is the lack of planning in the United States more obvious than in healthcare. In no other industry have the extant problems been so directly attributed to problems of coordination, communication, and cooperation. Virtually all of the problems that have dogged the healthcare industry—from fragmentation to duplication of services to ineffective data management—can be attributed to a failure to plan. Most importantly, the high cost of healthcare can also be attributed in great part to a lack of planning.

The healthcare industry is clearly characterized by some of the same apprehensions as the US society in general when it comes to planning. Certainly there is resistance to centralized coordination of activities that might be viewed as government "meddling." There is insistence that the market be left to drive the system, despite the general failure of this approach to appropriately direct the healthcare system in the past.

In healthcare, this concern over interference and accountability is magnified. In no other industry does one find so many autonomous entities with different agendas ostensibly attempting to contribute to a common goal. Within the hospital alone, there are many entities more concerned about their own welfare than they are about what should be the common goals of the organization.

Healthcare is also unique in that it is the only institution run essentially by "technicians." These technicians are clinicians—particularly the physicians who make most of the decisions—who argue that bureaucrats and administrators are not competent to make decisions and set policy for the healthcare system. Clinicians are "doers" who have little patience for drawn-out planning processes. Further, clinicians are inherently conservative in their approach; while ostensibly welcoming innovations in healthcare, they often resist any changes in practice patterns. This inherent conservatism works against the development of plans that carry the risk of upsetting the status quo.

One of the presumably beneficial functions of planning, the introduction of controls, has also been cited as a basis for resistance. The development of a plan implies the intention to control the future actions of members of the community or the organization. This not only applies to underlings who are expected to operationalize the plan (and perhaps radically change their day-to-day lives) but to top management as

well. Corporate executives are, in effect, being directed by virtue of the plan to follow a particular course. Even if the plan offers very general guidelines for the future
direction of the organization, management may see this as an infringement on their
authority and a limitation on their ability to make midcourse adjustments in the
operation of the organization.

Finally, there is the concern over the costs involved in planning health services.
This concern exists with regard to both community-wide and organization planning.
The planning process is expensive in terms of both direct costs and indirect costs.
Yet, at the same time, the costs of *not* planning have been found to be even greater,
when the implications for efficiency and effectiveness in the absence of planning are
quantified.

What a Plan Is Not

Whenever the issue of planning arises, the inevitable initial response is that "the last
plan is gathering dust on the shelf." This reaction reflects a general failure to recognize what a plan is and is not. Even planners have not always appreciated this distinction, and it is understandable that many plans have remained unimplemented in
the past.

A true plan should not be a static document. In fact, it should not be a document
at all but the embodiment of a process. A plan is not a plan if it is not dynamic,
evolving with the changing environment. Similarly, a true plan is not rigid but is
extremely flexible. After all, the intent is not to anticipate and plan for every potential development, but to create a framework in which new developments can be
addressed. A true plan is not a cookbook with step-by-step instructions for reaching
a specified point in the future. It should embody the principles necessary for achieving the goals of the community or the organization.

Perhaps the best analogy compares planning to water safety. A plan should not
be a life preserver to save a drowning swimmer but the swimming lessons that prepare the swimmer for any exigency. Thus, the plan does not provide the ultimate
solution but offers the mechanism for finding that solution.

The Planning Time Horizon

The question arises as to how far into the future one should peer when developing a
plan. There is no one answer to this question, and for any type of planning it probably makes sense to think in terms of short-range, intermediate-range, and long-
range planning. At a minimum, 5 years should be considered as the planning time
frame. If a community health system is being planned, a 20-year plan may be appropriate for systematically addressing the long-term development of the system,
although from a pragmatic perspective that type of time horizon may not be practical

in today's healthcare environment. Further, one is not likely to have adequate data for projecting more than 5 or 10 years into the future.

In any case, a plan should be flexible enough to adapt to shifts in the environment, a factor that often encourages a shorter time horizon. However, the 1- or 2-year planning horizon typical of the industry is probably too short to adequately introduce the infrastructure changes necessary for advancing the state of the healthcare system. And it is clearly too short to assess the impact of any planning initiative. The issue of time horizons is discussed further in the respective chapters on community health planning and organization-level planning.

The Changing Environment for Health Services Planning

What is it about today's healthcare environment that is encouraging an interest in planning not witnessed for 20 years? Why is this happening at this point in time? There are numerous factors that could explain the growing urgency surrounding the planning of health services at all levels, but perhaps the most compelling reason is the increasing instability and lack of predictability pervading today's healthcare system.

The primary impetus for planning can be summed up by reference to the paradigm shift that is occurring in the US healthcare. Most of the developments in recent years in healthcare can probably be attributed to the shift that has been occurring from an emphasis on "medical care" to a new emphasis on "healthcare." Medical care is narrowly defined and refers primarily to those functions that are under the influence of medical doctors.

This paradigm shift has been boosted by the growing appreciation of the nonmedical aspects of healthcare and a new appreciation of the connection between lifestyle and health status. More than any other factor, however, has been the realization that mainstream American medicine built upon the old disease theory system is increasingly unsuited for the management of the new and different health problems that emerged during the last quarter of the twentieth century.

Three other major developments have prompted the need for a revised edition of *Health Services Planning*. First, the passage of the Patient Protection and Affordable Care Act (ACA) represented a major reform effort for the financing of healthcare. This act called for unprecedented restrictions on the health insurance industry and created a mechanism through which additional tens of millions of Americans would be able to acquire health insurance coverage. Importantly, it mandated that not-for-profit hospitals conduct community health needs assessments at least every 3 years in order to maintain their tax-exempt status. These assessments were not to be limited to the organization's patients but must consider the entire community. Such assessments, of course, represent the basic foundation for health services planning.

Second, entities that are paying for most health services—insurance companies, Medicare, and Medicaid—are introducing programs for value-based or pay-for-performance reimbursement. Spearheaded by the federal Center for Medicare and

Medicaid, these efforts are forcing healthcare providers to take a more global approach to the management of their patient panels or health plan members. These initiatives require healthcare providers to become much more knowledgeable about their patients and prospective patients, requiring them to actually *plan* for the provision of services.

Third, the twenty-first century has witnessed the emergence of the population health movement, a movement that threatens to turn healthcare on its head. There is growing evidence that the US population is getting sicker and that the healthcare system as currently structured can do nothing about it. This situation has led to efforts to rethink our approach to "sick care" and develop a systematic approach to addressing not just the symptoms of health problems but also the underlying causes. (Some of these developments have been of such significance that Chap. 4 is dedicated to their discussion.)

Justifying the Planning Effort

In the final analysis, the historical lack of planning in healthcare itself provides the best justification for future planning. When one considers the level of expenditures for health services and the fact that much of this is a result of inefficiencies in the operation of the system, it is hard to argue against a systematic approach to the challenges facing the industry. It could be argued that the United States spends enough money to provide "Cadillac" care to every man, woman, and child in the country, if the funds were appropriately managed and allocated. Yet, many citizens do without treatment or medication, millions of Americans do not have a personal physician, and the number of medically uninsured is in tens of millions.

By the same token, the importance of healthcare to our society—and our economy—would seem to make careful planning mandatory. To paraphrase a familiar quote, "Healthcare is too important to be left to clinicians." While clinicians should not be excluded from the process, the planning perspective calls for a much wider view of the situation than has historically prevailed. When one considers the percentage of the population involved in the system and the cost of providing health services, the absence of a planning process seems totally unacceptable.

Healthcare is undergoing such rapid change that every new wave of reorganization leads to a different set of needs. The emergence of managed care alone spawned the need for a completely different set of planning agendas. Who would have thought that hospital administrators would ever say: "The only good bed is an empty bed"? Or that marketers would be asked to find the healthiest patients and not the sickest? Healthcare professionals in all types of organizations are faced with understanding an environment that is increasingly foreign to the industry.

Faced with the exigencies of the twenty-first century, most healthcare organizations are at a critical juncture. Their success depends increasingly upon their ability to adapt to a new environment. The situation calls for adopting a completely different mindset, a mindset in keeping with the anticipated industry developments of the new millennium. Adapting to changes of this magnitude "on the fly" will not be a viable approach in the future. The rapidity of change and the significance of the decisions that must be made mandate a well-conceived framework for decision-making in the form of community-wide and organizational level plans.

There is an immediate need to reeducate healthcare professionals on the theories, methods, and data used in health services planning, and this represents another reason for developing a planning agenda. Just as the hospital must be reengineered for the new environment, health professionals must be reeducated in order to continue to contribute to the planning process.

All of these factors make the revitalization of health services planning particularly appropriate. The problems extant in healthcare discussed in this chapter suggest a need for a new approach. The significance of decision-making for the organization is much greater than in the past. It is one thing to be able to plan for the provision of health services in a stable, predictable environment. It is quite another matter to develop plans in the midst of an unstable, unpredictable environment. These activities raise the importance of planning within the healthcare organization several notches. The consequences of a wrong decision can be fatal for a healthcare organization. Both the demands being placed on the health services plan and the consequences of the actions of planners are reaching unprecedented levels.

The good news is that the capabilities to carry out planning activities within healthcare have greatly improved. After a faltering start, some sound methodologies for health services planning have finally been established. Health-related data are becoming more readily available to support decision-making by healthcare executives. Appropriate technology is increasingly available for application to the challenge of planning.

Chapter 2
An Overview of Health Planning

It is appropriate to start our discussion of health services planning by providing an overview of this function as carried out in the past and present. In Chap. 1 the nature of planning was discussed and this chapter introduces the reader to various types of planning that might be considered under the general heading of health services planning. It summarizes the history of health services planning in the United States and provides an overview of the current status of this activity in this country.

For our purpose, health services planning will be divided into planning that takes place at the societal, community, or organization level. This distinction between community-wide planning and organization-level planning will be maintained throughout the book, with limited attention devoted to societal level planning. While the actual process of planning is quite similar, the objectives, players, and beneficiaries are quite different.

Nationwide Health Planning

Nationwide (or societal level) planning involves comprehensive planning for an entire nation. Various countries vary widely in terms of their societal level planning activities. These range from countries (including the United States) with virtually no national-level planning initiatives to countries (mostly with centralized health-care systems) that attempt to micromanage planning for that nation. Clearly, the approach to health planning reflects nationwide attitudes toward planning in general and governmental involvement in particular.

At the national level, health services planning is generally the responsibility of the central government. In most societies, in fact, health planning starts at the national level and is imposed downward through the healthcare system. In the United States, however, the ability of the central government to participate in health planning activities is seriously restricted. There are few powers granted to the

© Springer Science+Business Media, LLC, part of Springer Nature 2021
R. K. Thomas, *Health Services Planning*,
https://doi.org/10.1007/978-1-0716-1076-3_2

federal government in this regard, leaving the central government much less involved in health planning activities than is the case in other industrialized nations.

Countries with national health systems have a vested interest in planning for the operation of programs that affect the entire population. To the extent that the national system manages hospitals and other institutions and employs physicians and other clinicians, it behooves the national bureaucracy to implement well-thought-out plans. Indeed, it is not unusual for national health systems to indicate implicitly or explicitly that the primary goal of the system (and hence the planning) is efficient resource management rather than a health-related goal.

Community-Wide Health Planning

Community-wide planning involves the development of a health services plan that focuses on the total healthcare system that serves a designated geographic area. The starting point and the emphasis is the community and not the organizational players within that healthcare environment. This type of planning is called by a variety of names, most frequently comprehensive planning or system-level planning. The term "system level" is confusing since it has come to be used in relation to large healthcare organizations that have structured themselves as "systems." Thus, the term "community-wide planning" will be used to refer to this type of planning activity.

A number of characteristics can be ascribed to community-wide planning. This form of planning is ostensibly comprehensive in its approach. The total system of care, defined in its broadest sense, should be considered in this process, with the "comprehensive health planning" initiatives of the 1960s and 1970s prototypical of this approach. At the same time the total population is ostensibly the target of this process, and all citizens are the intended beneficiaries of the planning effort. To this end, the success of the community planning process is more often measured in terms of the overall health status of the community than in terms of individual health status or its impact on specific healthcare organizations.

Community health plans tend to be relatively long range with regard to their time frame, typically in the 5- to 10-year range. The more generalized the goal (e.g., raising the overall health status of the community), the greater the time required for plan implementation. This is not to say that short-term objectives are not addressed but that changing the course of a community's healthcare system will take a considerable amount of time.

Historically, community-wide planning typically has been sponsored by some branch of government. The planning initiatives of the 1960s and 1970s were initiated at the federal level and implemented through state and local governmental or quasi-governmental agencies. It is often thought of as "public sector" planning, although the impact of the planning activities often falls more directly on private sector organizations than on public entities. To a certain extent, community-wide planning does emphasize a "public health" approach to identify problems within the community. These activities often include a regulatory component and may be intended to "control" utilization, costs, and/or facilities development. Given the comprehensive nature of community-wide planning, it could be argued that only a government agency would be in a position to manage such a process. However, this has often created the uncomfortable situation whereby public ends are pursued by public agencies through attempts to control the behavior of private sector entities.

In the new community-wide planning environment that emerged during the 1990s, there was resistance to the type of "top-down" planning that characterized the comprehensive health planning era. In fact, most current planning initiatives have originated at the local level. While governmental agencies may play a role, these new planning initiatives are not necessarily seen as governmental functions. Community groups and private sector healthcare organizations are being joined by business leaders in many communities to create a true public/private approach to resolving community-wide health problems.

The focus of community health planning has historically been on facilities and personnel, reflecting to a great extent the benchmarks traditionally utilized in assessing the status of the healthcare system. In the absence of more relevant status measures of the appropriateness of the system, health planners have determined the extent to which shortages or surpluses exist with regard to such tangible features of the system as hospital beds and physicians. Thus, the "health" of the system might be evaluated in terms of the number of hospital beds per 1000 population or the physician-to-patient ratio.

Because of its comprehensive approach, community-wide planning often addresses topics or issues that would never be broached by most organizations involved in health planning for their own narrow purposes. These topics include public health, charity care, environmental concerns, and nonmedical factors that affect health status. Community-wide planning initiatives take into consideration the needs of the medically indigent and the extent to which the community's healthcare "safety net" operates effectively. Environmental pollution is often an issue in community-wide planning initiatives, but one that would seldom be addressed at the organization level of planning. Nonmedical issues such as crime, housing, and domestic violence must be taken into consideration in developing a comprehensive understanding of the healthcare needs of the population. For these reasons the United States has witnessed the emergence of community-based initiatives that are nongovernmental in nature.

Defining the "Community"

The "community" component of community-wide planning can be conceptualized at a number of geographic levels. These levels generally correspond to a particular governmental or administrative level. Ideally, an integrated planning process involving all levels of government would be in place, as is the case in most European countries with centralized planning functions. This type of hierarchical structure is notably absent in the US healthcare arena, however.

Community-wide planning can occur at the regional level although this stretches the concept of "community." In most centrally planned systems, regional planning encompasses designated geographic subunits of the national government. During the days of federally sponsored comprehensive health planning in the United States, the entire nation was divided into planning regions. Today, however, there are no formally designated administrative "regions," leaving no level of authority between the federal and state governments. However, certain "ad hoc" regions have been designated for which health services planning may occur. These would include regional authorities established to plan for the Appalachian and Mississippi Delta cultural regions. To the extent that health planners identify "unofficial" health services areas (e.g., the multicounty service area for a major medical center), the benefit of regional planning is recognized. These regions may reflect the catchment area for a hospital for a group of hospitals and can serve as a basis for rational service delivery planning.

A third level at which planning can occur is the state level. In the United States and many other countries, the state or province has specified responsibilities (often including health services) and maintains a budget for carrying out these activities. In the United States, the state is the next level of government below the national level. As a practical matter, most health planning that occurs in the United States today takes place at the state level.

The federal government has established "health service regions" in an effort to bring some organization to our understanding of patterns of health services utilization. These regions may reflect the catchment area for a hospital for a group of hospitals and can serve as a basis for rational service delivery planning.

The lowest level of government (and health services planning) in the United States is local government in the form of counties and municipalities. At this level, health planning authorities may be established to plan, regulate, and/or monitor the activities of the healthcare organizations within their jurisdiction. Cities may also establish health planning authorities, particularly if they contain large numbers of health facilities. Planning organizations at the local level typically have limited authority and often exist as voluntary associations. There are a few exceptions where local health planning authorities have significant power, however. This is nevertheless an important sphere for planning since most healthcare is "local."

Time Horizons for Planning

Health plans may be distinguished in terms of their time horizons. They are typically categorized as short range, intermediate range, or long range. A single plan, in fact, may include phases that relate to each of these time horizons. Short-range planning typically involves a time horizon of 1–2 years, while long-range planning typically covers 5 or more years. Intermediate-range planning, of course, falls in between.

Community-wide plans have typically been long range by national planning standards, with a 5-year horizon being common. For many, this appears to be a reasonable time frame since it allows adequate time to bring about what are often significant changes but, at the same time, does not appear to alter existing practice patterns too rapidly. While planning activities should observe the 5-year planning horizon, looking beyond 5 years in the current healthcare environment is considered risky by many observers.

With intermediate-range plans, typically extending less than 5 years into the future, the goals are understandably more modest. In community-wide planning, this may involve such activities as restructuring the local health authority board or establishing a community health information system. Radical changes in the health-care delivery system, however, are not likely to be achieved in this time frame.

Short-range planning is inconsistent with the community-wide planning concept. Little can be accomplished toward system-wide change in a 1- or 2-year planning time frame. Some short-term activities that are supportive of longer term goals may be implemented but not be seen as ends in their own right. The recruitment of a primary care physician for an underserved area or the establishment of a new health-care clinic, for example, may be accomplished in this time frame.

Organization-Level Planning

Organization-level planning refers to planning that occurs for and within a specific healthcare entity, and the majority of what could be considered health services plan-ning today takes place within healthcare organizations and not at the community level. Although planning on the part of healthcare organizations has not been totally embraced, recent years have seen a surge in planning activity (although it may be referred to by some other term than "planning"). In fact, the scope of planning has expanded and the planning emphasis has become refocused.

Organization-level planning differs from community-wide planning in a number of important ways. Where community-wide planning is broad and comprehensive, organization-level planning is relatively narrow and focused. Where community-wide planning is intended to serve the needs of the total community, organization-level planning is focused on the specific benefits to be derived by the organization involved in the planning. While community-wide planning seeks to encourage "system-wide" change, organization-level planning seeks to transform the individ-ual organization independent of the community's delivery system.

While the goal of community-wide planning ideally is to improve the health status of the overall population, that of organization-level planning is to advance the interests of the organization. While community health planning has historically been a public function, with all that implies, organization-level planning is usually restricted to private sector healthcare organizations. This last distinction has begun to blur as some not-for-profit organizations have started adopting corporate planning techniques and as public/private healthcare coalitions have emerged in certain communities.

Some of the new impetus for planning in healthcare has been generated by the rise of the for-profit national healthcare corporation. These entities are, for the most part, businesses first and healthcare organizations second. Among the business practices that these entities brought to healthcare are strategic planning and business planning. The need to plan is typically considered more urgent for private sector organizations in that their very survival has become increasingly dependent upon their ability to control their destinies.

Who Should Perform Organization-Level Planning?

From the largest national hospital chain to the one-person clinician's office, every healthcare organization must attempt to control its future to the extent possible. Developing a plan does not assure that the organization will control its fate, but it provides an advantage over those organizations that are operating without a plan. Clearly, multipurpose organizations like hospitals must develop plans that allow them to adapt to their changing environments and coordinate the various and diverse components of their systems. Other providers—physicians, therapists, and other clinicians—also face the need to lay out a systematic road map to the future. Other institutional providers, such as nursing homes, home health agencies, and assisted living facilities, must similarly be able to chart a well-thought-out course.

Health insurance plans, including managed care plans, must be able to determine their future direction and implement a plan for reaching their goals. No success in the future healthcare environment is likely to come through happenstance, and every healthcare organization must take an active role in "inventing" its own future.

For-profit corporations not involved in direct patient care have perhaps a longer history with various types of planning. Pharmaceutical companies and medical supply and equipment companies have historically operated more like traditional private sector corporations than healthcare organizations and have a long history of sound business operation. Medical laboratories and other support services also require planning input to determine the appropriate corporate direction.

Planning at What Level?

The most visible planning activities among healthcare organizations take place at the corporate level, with hospital-level planning being probably the representative example. In some cases, planning may be performed at the system level, involving perhaps several hospitals and other subsidiary components of the system. This might involve a national for-profit chain of hospitals or nursing homes, a home health organization with many subsidiary agencies, or a regional hospital network. However, planning at the health system level is particularly challenging due to the complexity and, often, geographical spread of the system components. At the same time, the need to merge various systems and corporate cultures mandates at least some level of planning at the system level.

At the facility level, planning is performed for a single facility and its associated services, even if the facility is part of a larger system. Historically, organization-level planning has centered on the hospital, at least among organizations involved in patient care. Clinics, specialty practices, nursing homes, and residential treatment centers are other entities that might develop plans at this level.

At the subsidiary level, planning is performed for a unit that is a distinct subsidiary of a larger facility. For example, a hospital may own a home health agency and choose to plan for its development separately. In fact, licensure regulations may require that planning for the home health agency be carried out independent of hospital planning.

Planning can also occur at the division level within the organization, with the various divisions ideally combining to form an organization-level plan. In a large organization, it may be difficult to carry out strategic planning, for example, for the entire organization without relying upon division-level plans. While these may ultimately be merged under the umbrella of the corporate structure within a large organization, much of the planning must occur at the divisional level.

Planning may also occur at the department level within the organization. Traditional organization-level planning that focuses on budgets, facilities, and human resources generally occurs at this level. As the concept of strategic planning has become more accepted, departments are becoming more integrated into the enterprise-wide planning process. The ultimate plan is ideally an amalgam of departmental plans.

Finally, planning may occur at the unit level. This may involve a strategic business unit (SBU) or a product line. In this case, the planning activities may cut across some of the other levels (e.g., departments, divisions). The hospital service line has come to be seen by many as an appropriate unit for planning, since its success typically depends upon its ability to coordinate activities in a number of functional and specialty areas. The service line lends itself to the types of organizational planning that are becoming increasingly common, such as strategic planning, marketing planning, and business planning.

The nature of the planning process, the approach, and the technical implementation are determined by the size, structure, and culture of the organization. A national healthcare organization may be structured as a monolithic corporate entity with tight management controls throughout the organization. Or it may involve a number of loosely affiliated companies under a holding company umbrella. Certainly, private sector organizations are going to approach planning differently from public sector entities. Organizations involved in direct patient care are going to have a different perspective from those involved in support services. Organizations selling products will require a somewhat different approach from those providing services.

At different levels within the organization as well, different types of planning are likely to be emphasized. The higher the level, in general, the more likely the planning will be strategic in nature. The lower the level, the emphasis is more likely to be on operational planning.

Geographic Focus for Organization-Level Planning

The geographic focus for organization-level planning, as with community-wide planning, can reside at any level. Large medical supply companies may be international in their scope and carry out corporate planning at the global level. Even here, however, such organizations are likely to think in terms of national markets and, like domestic corporations focusing on the US market, conduct planning at the national level.

While there are few strictly regional healthcare organizations in the United States, many national corporations divide their operations into regions and plan accordingly. Some large local systems may in effect constitute regional operations, and their planning activities may reflect this broader scope. Planning at the state level may occur with organizations that are licensed to operate on a state basis or otherwise conduct business strictly within a particular state. Health insurance plans are typically licensed by an agency of the specific state. This may mandate planning at the state level for these organizations.

Most healthcare providers are local in their orientation. In this context, "local" may refer to a single neighborhood or to a multicounty service area. It is at this level, however, that the typical organization-level planner is likely to be working today. Thus, most of the organization-level planning that takes place focuses on the local level.

Functional Emphasis

Perhaps the best way to categorize the various types of organization-level planning is to think in terms of their functional emphasis or the purpose the planning activity serves within the organization. Taking that approach, the following types of planning might be identified:

- *Strategic planning* involves matching organizational resources with organizational capabilities to position the organization to take advantage of opportunities in the market.
- *Marketing planning* involves a determination of the target for marketing activities and the appropriate "market mix" for achieving market-related goals.
- *Business planning* involves the coordination of resource allocation to achieve the business goals of the organization.
- *Financial planning* involves planning for the management of the organization's resources.
- *Facility planning* involves planning for the development, acquisition, and management of the bricks and mortar of the organization.
- *Technology planning* involves planning for the acquisition and management of equipment, computer resources, and other technology-based assets.
- *Policy planning* involves high-level planning for the development of policies that will guide the direction of the organization in terms of mission, relationships, etc.

- *Program planning* involves planning for the development and management of the constellation of programs and services characterizing the organization.
- *Human resources planning* focuses on the recruitment and management of personnel.
- *Operations planning* involves planning for the management of day-to-day instrumental activities of the organization.

Time Horizon

As with community-wide plans, organization-level plans may be distinguished in terms of their time horizons. Plans are typically categorized as short range, intermediate range, or long range. A single plan, in fact, is likely to include phases that relate to each of these time horizons, although with organization-level planning, the time horizon will reflect the type of plan. Strategic planning by definition is longer range in its scope, while operations planning is much more restricted in terms of time horizon. Short-range planning typically involves a time horizon of 1–2 years, while long-range planning typically covers 5 or more years. Intermediate-range planning, of course, falls in between. As with community-wide planning, there is a reluctance to develop plans that extend more than 5 years into the future.

At the organizational level, the rapidly changing nature of healthcare has, perhaps inappropriately, led to an emphasis on short-range planning. In addition, the entry into the field of publicly held national corporations who have to account to their shareholders every quarter has led to a more short-term orientation. As a result, long-range goals and even the organization's mission may be subservient to short-term concerns.

Health Planning in the United States: Past and Present

National Planning Initiatives

The United States has never established a national health policy nor developed health planning initiatives at the societal level. The closest we have come to nationwide health planning in the United States is often traced to the enactment of the Hill-Burton Act of 1946. This Act called for a national survey of hospital facilities and ultimately resulted in government funding for the establishment and oversight of hundreds of hospitals. It was the first federal initiative of any magnitude directed toward healthcare, an arena that was not on the federal radar screen until the 1950s. While not a planning initiative per se, the implementation of the provisions of the legislation required the initiation of a number of planning-type activities (e.g., needs assessment, site selection, resource allocation).

Formal healthcare planning in the United States is traced to the Comprehensive Health Planning Act of 1966. This planning initiative was in response to the discovery in the 1960s of large segments of the population that did not have access to mainstream healthcare, as well as to concerns over perceived inequities in the provision of services to different segments of the population. This act called for the establishment of a federally funded and coordinated planning initiative for assuring access to adequate healthcare for every American. Although the Act involved nationwide initiative, the emphasis was on the establishment of health service regions. This shifted the focus from national priorities to a focus on community-wide planning.

Community-Wide Planning

Although the Health Planning Act of 1966 was promulgated by the federal government, it was not intended to support a society-wide planning effort. Instead, the program established statewide and area-wide (i.e., sub-state) planning agencies for the implementation of the planning process. These agencies were charged with the development of state plans and were assigned responsibility for coordinating healthcare activities within the geographic areas under their jurisdiction. Planning agencies established guidelines for the development of facilities and programs. The primary means of control was through the review of projects that were proposed. However, these agencies could only make recommendations with regard to proposed projects and had limited power to affect change.

The Regional Medical Program (RMP) was another federal initiative established in the mid-1960s with the responsibility for coordinating and promoting health services within a health service area. RMPs blanketed the nation and were charged with facilitating the diffusion of medical technology and other breakthroughs from major medical centers to surrounding areas. While planning was not a stated responsibility of these programs, a certain level of planning was required in order for the RMPs to successfully disseminate medical knowledge throughout their regions. The health focus of the Regional Medical Programs was categorical, addressing a small number of disease entities rather than the entire healthcare system. In many parts of the country, the RMPs coordinated their activities with existing health planning agencies (established under the health planning legislation of 1966). Even this collaboration was problematic since the two types of organizations often did not share the same geographic boundaries.

Another landmark development of this period was the establishment of the Medicare and Medicaid programs. While neither Medicare nor Medicaid involved any substantial planning responsibilities, it has often been noted that the operation of these two programs had a major impact on medical practice patterns and, in that sense, served as a force for changing the nature of the healthcare system. Healthcare providers were forced to "plan" for the implications of these new programs.

Planning activities were revitalized nationwide in 1974 with the enactment of the National Health Planning and Resources Development Act. This act was prompted by growing concern over the lack of uniformly effective methods of healthcare delivery, the maldistribution of healthcare facilities and personnel, and the increasing cost of care. With a better financial footing than the 1966 planning initiative, this act called for the creation of statewide health coordinating councils and the establishment of local health systems agencies.

To remedy the lack of authority characterizing earlier planning efforts, the new planning act introduced the certificate-of-need process (CON) as a means of controlling the development of facilities and services. The CON process required any healthcare provider seeking to build additional facilities or add or change a service to demonstrate that the project was needed. The intent was to assure that any new project fit within the planning framework that had been developed at the state level. It was also intended to limit the duplication of services and equipment that was contributing to rising costs. (See Box 2.1 for a discussion of the certificate-of-need process.)

Box 2.1: The Certificate-of-Need Process

During the era of nationwide "comprehensive health planning" beginning in the mid-1960s and extending into the early 1980s, health planning agencies attempted to control the utilization of health services and ostensibly healthcare costs through restrictions placed on the establishment and expansion of health facilities and services. The primary tool for implementing these restrictions was the certificate-of-need (CON) process. Eventually written into federal regulations, the CON process has been used (and abused) by various states as a means of controlling the building of facilities, the development of services, and the acquisition of expensive equipment on the part of healthcare providers.

The CON concept is relatively straightforward. It mandates that a certificate-of-need application be filed that justifies the proposed facility, equipment, or service based on certain criteria that reflect community needs. The underlying notion is that objective parties would review any proposal and either approve or disapprove its implementation. Under the aegis of comprehensive health planning this decision was made at the local level and subsequently reviewed at the regional (sub-state) and state levels.

Under federally sponsored comprehensive health planning programs, uniform standards for the implementation of the CON process were enacted. Thus, the respective states followed similar guidelines and used similar criteria for reviewing applications. Each state was required to prepare a state health plan that adhered to federal standards. Further, each state was to establish local standards to supplement federal standards as a basis for evaluating the adequacy of a proposal. Thus, there were guidelines that specified the appropriate number of hospital beds or physicians per 1000 residents or the

(continued)

Box 2.1 (continued)

catchment area appropriate for a particular piece of diagnostic equipment. The provisions of any proposed project were required to be consistent with the needs identified in the local health plan and meet the criteria established to justify the service being proposed.

The initial implementation of CON legislation had little impact on the availability of facilities, services, and equipment. This was due primarily to the fact that health planning agencies had virtually no authority to enforce decisions made on CON applications. Healthcare organizations could, and often did, choose to ignore the ruling of the planning agency, and many cases can be cited in which facilities were built, services initiated, or equipment purchased after the CON application was disapproved.

The health planning legislation enacted in the 1970s expanded the authority of health planning agencies and instituted disincentives that planning agencies could use to encourage compliance with CON rulings. One of these disincentives was the threat of withholding federal healthcare funds (e.g., Medicare reimbursement) from healthcare organizations that did not comply with CON rulings.

There has been considerable debate over the success of the CON process in controlling the supply of facilities, services, and equipment and over the ultimate contribution that this process has made to the quality of care and the cost of services. This is not to mention the controversy over the appropriateness of any type of formal controls on the activities of healthcare organizations. There is no consistent pattern with regard to the impact that CON legislation has on the states in which the process is in effect today. The process appears to have a significant effect on the healthcare systems in some states and limited impact on others. To a great extent this reflects variations in the form the CON programs take and in the manner in which they are implemented. After the elimination of federal funding for comprehensive health planning, the various states (and some local jurisdictions) adopted widely divergent guidelines for the CON process. Several states, in fact, eliminated the CON process altogether. Some of these, however, have since reinstituted some form of the CON review process. For most states, the process is under continual review, with periodic efforts initiated to change the process in one way or another.

Most states that retain the CON process attempt to regulate capital expenditures, equipment acquisition, and the establishment of new services, although some regulate only one or two of these areas. Virtually all states that regulate capital expenditures have some minimum dollar threshold before a CON application is required. In many states, all hospital capital projects must be approved, but comparable projects proposed by a physician group may not require approval. The picture is further complicated by the fact that states vary with regard to the components of the system that are regulated. In some states, any new clinical service must be approved, while in others only home health or long-term care services, for example, require a CON application.

(continued)

Box 2.1 (continued)

The preparation of a CON application is typically a complex process that requires expertise on a wide variety of subjects. The application must justify the need for the project based on the characteristics of the service area and existing practice patterns. The project must be demonstrated to be financially sound, and this often requires the involvement of expert business analysts. The project must meet all legal requirements (CON mandated or otherwise), and physical plant components must be demonstrated to meet the guidelines set by the CON planning agency. Proponents typically have to demonstrate that they have community support for the project and that established utilization patterns will not be unduly disrupted. The project must adhere to the state health plan (if one exists) and to any guidelines in place related to minimum thresholds for services (e.g., a minimum of 20,000 residents to support a catherization laboratory). Because of the complexity of the CON application process, experts in the areas of market research, financial analysis, health law, architecture and engineering, and clinical areas, along with the standard complement of administrative types, are required for the successful development of a CON application.

A substantial application fee typically is required for the filing of a CON application and this in itself is a controversial issue. Some have argued that the filing fee itself constitutes a restraint on the free operation of the market in that it limits access to the process to those healthcare organizations that are already well established. In many states, the filing fee is used primarily to fund the operation of the CON agency.

There is no consensus as to the value of the certificate-of-need process as a tool in guiding the development of healthcare delivery systems. There are certainly arguments for and against this method of attempting to control the establishment of health services. The process itself continues to evolve, and modified versions of the CON process have been put in place in various states. Despite the reservations of some observers, it is likely that the CON process in some form will become increasingly important as the health planning movement becomes revitalized as the twenty-first century unfolds.

Reference

American Health Planning Association. (2002). *National directory of health planning, policy and regulatory agencies*. Falls Church, VA: American Health Planning Association.

This "experiment" in health planning came to an end under the Reagan administration in the early 1980s. Despite some successes, comprehensive health planning had not created many political allies and essentially had few constituents. As a result, the demise of these programs represented the end of any formal federal planning initiatives. Today, the federal government provides some limited support for health planning through initiatives like Healthy People 2010 and agencies like the Health Resources and Services Administration.

Organization-Level Planning

Under the "expansionist model" that drove healthcare from the end of World War II to the 1980s, planning focused almost exclusively on facilities, capital expenditures, and operations. Organization-level planning, in fact, was very much operation oriented throughout the 1970s. Since the concern was with day-to-day activities, a short-range focus on budgets, facilities, and programs dominated organization-level planning. Hospitals were the provider organizations most actively involved in planning. They were inherently internally focused and unlikely to think in terms of external factors.

The 1970s became a period of "institutional planning" which, although incorporating more "modern" planning techniques, continued to focus on bricks-and-mortar issues. In the 1980s "operational planning" was emphasized, with a focus on day-to-day operations, budgets, facilities management, and certificate-of-need activities.

By the mid-1980s the external environment began to exert its influence, and the world began to change for healthcare providers. Hospitals for the first time were faced with competition, deregulation, reduced reimbursement, and decreased utilization. In short, hospitals and other healthcare organizations were forced to start thinking strategically. The shift from a product orientation to a service orientation occurred during this period, and healthcare organizations became market oriented and consumer driven. The wave of mergers and acquisitions that characterized the 1990s served to encourage organization-level planning on the one hand while making it an even greater challenge on the other.

By the 1990s the planning concept had been widely accepted by healthcare organizations, if not totally incorporated into their cultures. Prompted by the industry-wide paradigm shift from medical care to healthcare, healthcare organizations began moving away from the more traditional types of facilities, budgeting, and operations planning toward strategic, marketing, and business planning.

Current Status of Health Planning

Since the end of federally funded health planning initiatives in the early 1980s, virtually no health services planning has occurred at the national level. The planning apparatus, as limited as it was, suffered dismantlement under the Reagan administration. Today, there is no "home" in the federal structure for health planning. This is not to say that no planning-type activities occur; many do. However, these are not formally referred to as "planning" activities, and their effect is felt very indirectly.

Federal Level

The absence of any formal health planning activities on the part of the federal government understates the influence that the federal government maintains over the direction that the healthcare system takes. While not considered true planning, the federal government is involved in a number of activities that implicitly influence healthcare policy and practice. The major influence is probably exerted through the control of funding. The federal government accounts for a major portion of the nation's healthcare expenditures and nearly 50% of the expenditures on direct patient care. These funds are expended primarily through the operation of the Medicare and Medicaid programs. It has been suggested, in fact, that the introduction of Medicare has had a greater influence on practice patterns within the US healthcare system than any other single development.

A number of federal agencies are involved in programs that have functions that resemble planning. The U.S. Public Health Service (PHS) tracks the adequacy of primary care physicians and other clinicians and issues regular reports on health professional shortage areas. The PHS, in fact, is involved in programs such as the National Health Service Corps that seek to influence the distribution of primary care physicians into underserved areas. The Bureau of Health Professions, also within the Department of Health and Human Services, maintains databases on physicians and other medical personnel. Other agencies maintain inventories of health facilities and often evaluate the adequacy of such facilities for the communities they serve. The Health Resources and Services Administration (HRSA) is involved in *de facto* planning by virtue of determining the location of Federally Qualified Health Centers (FQHCs) and other health facilities through its grant-funding process. The Center for Medicare and Medicaid Services (CMS) also maintains databases on a wide range of facility types. Another agency tracks enrollment in health maintenance organizations. While none of these activities constitute planning in a true sense, the operation of these programs influences the allocation of resources and the development of health-related policies at the national level.

The most visible planning-type activity sponsored by the federal government is probably the Healthy People 2020 initiative sponsored by the Office of Disease Prevention and Health Promotion within the Department of Health and Human Services. Originally formulated in the late 1980s, the HP2020 program involves the identification of areas of concern in healthcare that could benefit from the policy-making influence of the federal government; goals and objectives have been developed for each category and benchmarks established. (See Box 2.2 for more detail on the Healthy People initiative.)

Box 2.2: Healthy People 2020
The Healthy People initiative sponsored by the federal government is perhaps the program that most closely resembles a national planning effort. The program is operated by the Office of Disease Prevention and Health Promotion within the U.S. Department of Health and Human Services. Inspired by a 1979 Surgeon General's report, the Healthy People initiative was established as a framework for improving the health status of the American population. While not a planning document in a technical sense, its intent is to encourage a second public health revolution that capitalizes on the significance of preventive health.

The Healthy People 2020 program was initiated following the 2010 program as a successor to the original Healthy People 2000 initiative established in 1990. Each program represents a comprehensive agenda for increasing years of healthy life, reducing disparities in health among different population groups, and improving access to preventive health services. For the federal government, the Healthy People 2020 provides a framework for measuring performance and serves as a strategic management tool. Success is measured by positive changes in health status, reduction in risk factors, and/or improved access to certain services.

In order to provide the foundation for the Healthy People initiative, extensive data collection activities were carried out related to 42 topic areas for the 2020 iteration. This effort involved the compilation of a great deal of information on these topics that can be used as a background for the establishment of program objectives. Continuous monitoring is subsequently undertaken in order to track the progress being made in reaching over 1300 Healthy People 2020 objectives.

For each of the 42 priority areas a series of objectives has been established. For the priority area of "Maternal, Infant and Child Health," for example, the objectives include the following:

MICH-1.3: Reduce the rate of all infant deaths (within 1 year)
MICH-3.1: Reduce the rate of deaths among children aged 1–4 years
MICH-5: Reduce the rate of maternal mortality
MICH-8.1: Reduce low birth weight (LBW)

Most of the objectives also spawn subobjectives that are even more specific. For example, the objective of reducing the infant mortality rate is accompanied by subobjectives that address the infant mortality rates for specific subpopulations (e.g., African Americans, Hispanics). Over time, greater emphasis has been placed on disparities in health status among various population groups. Since the inception of the Healthy People initiative, improved data collection has made more precise performance measurement possible.

While the Healthy People 2020 program provides a framework for planning, there is no formal implementation plan for reaching its objectives. Further, the program has no authority to mandate activities that would contribute to its

(continued)

Box 2.2 (continued)

stated objectives. Some indirect influence is exerted, however, through the selective channeling of federal research funds. Applicants for federal grant money, for example, must demonstrate that the projects being proposed are consistent with Healthy People 2020 objectives.

The priority areas for the Healthy People 2020 (HP2020) initiative are the following:

Access to health services[a]	HIV
Adolescent health	Immunization and infectious disease
Arthritis, osteoporosis, and chronic back	Injury and violence prevention
Blood disorders and blood safety[a]	Maternal, infant, and child health
Cancer	Lesbian, gay, bisexual, and transgender health[a]
Chronic kidney disease	Medical product safety
Dementias, including Alzheimer's disease[a]	Mental health and mental disorders
Diabetes	Nutrition and weight status
Disability and health	Occupational health
Early and middle childhood[a]	Older adults[a]
Educational and community-based programs	Oral health
Environmental health	Physical activity
Family planning	Preparedness[a]
Food safety	Public health infrastructure
Genomics[a]	Respiratory diseases
Global health[a]	Sexually transmitted diseases
Healthcare-associated infections[a]	Sleep health[a]
Health communication and health information technology	Social determinants of health[a]
Health-related quality of life and well-being[a]	Substance abuse
Hearing and other sensory or communication disorders	Tobacco use
Heart disease and stroke	Vision

[a]New for HP2020

Additional information on Healthy People 2020 can be obtained from the Office of Disease Prevention and Health Promotion in Washington, DC, or from the Healthy People website at www.healthypeople.gov.

Further, by allocating funds—almost always with strings attached—for facilities development and health professions training, the federal government has influenced the number and location of hospitals and the characteristics of the physician pool. By influencing the use of medical education funds, for example, the federal government has attempted to redistribute physician personnel from specialty care to primary care and to augment nursing education capacity. The funding of the nation's huge medical research industry has also been a major indirect contributor to the direction of the healthcare system. By setting funding priorities and allocating dollars accordingly, the federal government through the National Institutes of Health (NIH) has dictated what is to be considered important for research purposes. The fact that prevention still is given a backseat to treatment and cure, for example, reflects existing priorities for resource allocation.

Federal agencies also exert a planning-type influence through the regulatory powers held by the national government. These are felt in a variety of ways, from the operation of the Occupational Health and Safety Agency (OSHA) to the activities of the Food and Drug Administration (FDA) to the regulations promulgated by the Centers for Medicare and Medicaid Services (CMS).

Regional Level

Planning activities at the regional level have never been well developed, and limited venues exist today for introducing planning at that level. The only situations in which regional planning occurs in any sense are through the operation of regional authorities such as the Appalachian Regional Commission and the Mississippi Delta Regional Commission. While these are not healthcare initiatives per se, healthcare issues are often addressed. While such regional authorities may include funding for health-related activities, they generally have no authority for implementing healthcare initiatives.

State Level

Many states retained a health planning structure after the demise of federally funded planning in the 1980s. Some continue to develop state health plans, with the level of effort, the scope, and the implications of the planning varying widely from state to state. Few state planning agencies have any significant authority to implement plans, with monitoring and oversight being essentially the limit of their influence.

One of the primary functions inherent in comprehensive health planning was the operation of the certificate-of-need process. Under the traditional health planning framework, any healthcare organization seeking to add or change a service or facility was required to certify that a need existed. This certification process was based on certain standards that were in place and on the priorities established within the particular state's health plan. The intent was to encourage the orderly development of facilities, equipment, and services and, at the same time, limit duplication of services. As of 2001, 36 states and the District of Columbia continued to operate certificate-of-need programs, although at differing levels of intensity (American Health Planning Association 2002).

States exert some of the same indirect influences on the healthcare system that the federal government does. Healthcare is a major item in all state budgets, with the Medicaid program typically representing a major expenditure. Public health expenditures are also likely to be a significant budget item and the allocation of funds for direct patient care (e.g., for mental health services) may be substantial. The control of funding for the Medicaid program alone has no doubt done much to influence practice patterns.

State agencies are responsible for most of the licensing and regulation of health facilities and personnel. Hospitals, nursing homes, home health agencies, and many other facilities and programs must meet state requirements for licensure and abide by state-initiated regulations. All health professionals must maintain state-issued licenses in order to practice. While these are seldom considered planning activities, they exert an indirect influence on the practice patterns found within a state. Attempts by various state licensing agencies to exclude foreign-trained physicians from licensure, for example, represent an indirect planning activity related to healthcare personnel.

State agencies have considerable public health responsibilities, including the monitoring of environmental conditions and other threats to the health of the populace. While the operation of these programs does not constitute true planning, their presence does influence the approach taken to the management of numerous health issues. With the emergence of the population health movement (see Chap. 4), public health agencies are being required to think strategically and to develop at least some semblance of a strategic plan.

Local Level

At the local (city or county) level, the extent of planning activities varies widely. Most communities do not maintain formal health planning organizations today. However, in a few communities well-established planning authorities may exert inordinate influence. For the most part, planning activities at this level are voluntary on the part of the participants, and local planning agencies typically have limited funds and few regulatory powers.

Numerous national initiatives, particularly on the part of major foundations, have encouraged grassroots planning activities at the local level. The long-standing Local Initiative Funding Program (Robert Wood Johnson Foundation) and the Association for Community Health Improvement (ACHI) are two examples. The National Association of County and City Health Officials (NACCHO) also plays an active role in encouraging local health planning activities through its Turning Point Program. NACCHO has also been instrumental in the development of the Mobilizing for Action through Planning and Partnerships (MAPP). These organizations have provided seed money and technical support for the development of public/private consortia designed to establish a planning process, however, informal, at the community level.

Local health authorities formally established for the management of the public health system or some other "public" health function may, through their normal operations, constitute an indirect force for health planning. They influence which services are reserved for the public sector and thereby have an impact on private sector practice patterns. If, for example, the county hospital board establishes a neonatal intensive care unit in the public hospital, this may preclude the need for such services in the private sector.

Local health departments may be large and influential organizations, particularly in major cities. Examples include the Los Angeles health department with a \$32 billion budget, the New York health authority with its system of public hospitals, and the City of Chicago health department with 1600 employees. The policies and subsequent actions of such agencies no doubt have implications for the direction taken by the local healthcare system.

Renewed Interest in Planning

The 1990s witnessed renewed interest in community-wide health planning, and this revival has extended into the twenty-first century. After a decade-long absence, the scorned "p" word—planning—started reappearing in the healthcare literature during the mid-1990s. The topic of planning is becoming more frequently listed in professional association programs, and there is growing public discourse surrounding the issue of health planning.

A number of factors have no doubt contributed to this reemergence of interest. At a theoretical level, the paradigm shift from a medical care emphasis to a healthcare emphasis calls for a different approach to the management of health and illness, an approach that calls for systematic planning. At a more practical level, the recognition that the problems surrounding healthcare are not going to go away and the fact that many of these problems can be traced to a lack of planning are contributing to this revitalization. The attention drawn to community-based healthcare initiatives by the Clinton administration as it struggled with healthcare reform in the early 1990s probably was another contributing factor.

While full-scale planning activities are still uncommon, a number of planning-like activities should be noted. Attempts at developing community health information management systems (CHMIS) in a number of communities reflect the felt need to coordinate patient information. Other data generation and dissemination efforts further reflect this trend toward a more systematic approach to the management of the healthcare delivery system. The growing interest in "population-based" healthcare—on the part of both public and private sector healthcare organizations—further reflects this emerging planning orientation. Certain provisions of the Affordable Care Act encourage health planning efforts and even mandate periodic community health assessments for not-for-profit hospitals.

Regardless of the form that this new planning takes, it is undoubtedly going to be a lot different from the traditional approach embodied by the comprehensive health planning initiatives of the 1960s and 1970s. The healthcare world has changed dramatically, and the planning approach must be revised to reflect this. Unprecedented resources are available to put into the planning effort, and there appears to be an opportunity to establish a community-wide planning framework that can be successful in this new environment. (A detailed discussion of the future of health services planning is included in Chap. 14.)

Historically, there has been little relationship between planning at the community level and organization level. The two types of planning have involved different entities and have been triggered by different factors in the environment. Realistically, community-wide planning has never been as comprehensive as it theoretically should be, and significant fragmentation has always existed even in the face of aggressive community-wide planning. Until the 1980s organization-level planning was not concerned with the external environment, and no connection was seen between the internally oriented planning of the organization and the community-wide planning carried out by government agencies. The only interface typically occurred when a private sector healthcare organization had to pose its project proposal within the context of an existing health plan.

Today, there appears to be considerable convergence between the two types of planning. The reemerging community health planning movement appears to be adopting some of the techniques from organization-level planning, and proponents of the new community health planning are encouraging the participation of private sector providers. The impetus for some of these community health planning movements has come from business leaders, and the emergence of new planning initiatives that include both public and private entities is encouraging.

Healthcare organizations, on the other hand, have come to realize that planning in isolation is not truly planning. Many organizations are beginning to take a population-based approach that, by definition, causes them to include a much wider range of community entities in their planning activities. Examples of joint efforts to develop community health information systems and the appearance of public/private initiatives aimed at community health issues suggest that a certain level of convergence is occurring. In addition, providers with tax-exempt status are increasingly being pressured to coordinate their initiatives with community-wide initiatives that are underway. (These issues are discussed further in Chap. 13.)

Health Services Planning in Other Countries

One other perspective that is worthwhile pursing in our introductory discussion of health services planning is the comparative perspective. How does health planning in the United States fare in comparison to the health planning activities of other countries?

The United States is exceptional among comparable industrialized countries in its lack of health planning. Most European countries, along with Canada and Japan, have centralized healthcare systems characterized by strong planning components. In fact, most of these countries have a long history of government involvement in the planning of health services. Unlike the United States, private sector healthcare is severely limited or unknown in these societies.

Health planning in most industrialized countries is integrated into broader social and economic planning functions. Health is seldom seen as an independent issue but as one very much wrapped up with socioeconomic considerations. For these reasons, health planning in such societies tends to be very comprehensive in its approach. Top-down planning is the rule, with policies set in many cases at the upper administrative levels and passed down to the field.

Even among developing countries, there is growing emphasis on system-wide health planning. While many aspects of the US healthcare system are admired, the United States is unlikely to serve as a model for countries seeking to initiate health planning at the national level. Other countries must be looked to for examples of national planning efforts.

Little effort has been made to provide comparative data on health planning activities for various countries. Readers are left to examine health planning activities on a country-by-country basis.

Reference

American Health Planning Association. (2002). *National directory of health planning, policy and regulatory agencies* (9th ed.). Falls Church, VA: American Health Planning Association.

Further Reading

American Health Planning Association. Retrieved from http://www.ahpanet.org/
Association for Community Health Improvement. Retrieved from http://www.healthycommunities.org
Benjamin, A. E., & Downs, G. W. (1982). Evaluating the national health planning and resources development act: Learning from experience? *Journal of Health Politics and Law, 7*(3), 707–722.
Green, A. (2007). *An introduction to health planning in developing countries* (3rd ed.). London: Oxford.
Health policy and planning (periodical). London: Oxford University Press. Retrieved from https://academic.oup.com/heapol
Health Resources and Services Administration. Retrieved from www.hrsa.gov
Institute of Medicine. (2013). *U.S. health in international perspective: Shorter lives, poorer health.* Washington, DC: National Academy Press.
Landrum, L. B. (n.d.). Health planning is alive and well. Retrieved from http://www.ahpanet.org/policy.html
National Association of County and City Health Officials, Washington, DC. Retrieved from http://www.naccho.org
Robert Wood Johnson Foundation, Princeton, NJ. Retrieved from http://www.rwjf.org
Steen, J. W. (n.d.). Certificate of need: A review. Retrieved from http://www.ahpanet.org/articles.html
U.S. Department of Health and Human Services, Office of Disease Prevention and Health Promotion. *Healthy People 2010*. Retrieved from www.healthypeople.gov

Chapter 3
The Social and Health Systems Context for Health Services Planning

Any planning activity requires a complete understanding of the context in which planning is taking place. It is impossible to understand a healthcare system without an appreciation for the environment in which it exists. For effective planning to occur, planners must first fully understand the nature of the existing system for which they are planning, including the background on how the system evolved to the point it has.

By the same token, effective planning cannot occur without an in-depth comprehension of the population that the plan is meant to serve. The social, political, and economic characteristics of the target population must be thoroughly understood, along with the lifestyles, attitudes, and other traits that characterize that population.

While it is not possible to describe all of the social and health systems dimensions that are important for framing a health plan, the key issues are addressed in the sections that follow. This chapter also reviews the development of the US healthcare during the second half of the twentieth century within the context of the social, demographic, and healthcare developments that affected it.

The Sociocultural Context

The healthcare system of any society can only be understood within the sociocultural context of that society. Similarly, the approach to planning (indeed, even the fact that a planning initiative exists) reflects the structure and the value system of the particular society. No two healthcare delivery systems are exactly alike, with the differences primarily a function of the contexts within which they exist. Thus, the social structure of a society, along with its cultural values, serves to define the healthcare system. The form and function of the healthcare system reflect the form and function of the society in which it resides (Parsons 1951).

Every society has certain functions that must be performed if that society is to survive. These functions include reproduction of new society members, socialization of these new members, distribution of resources, maintenance of internal order, provision

© Springer Science+Business Media, LLC, part of Springer Nature 2021
R. K. Thomas, *Health Services Planning*,
https://doi.org/10.1007/978-1-0716-1076-3_3

for defense, accommodation of the supernatural, and, importantly for our purposes, providing for the health and well-being of its population. In every society, societal structures (referred to as "institutions") are established to meet these needs. Some form of family evolves to manage reproduction, some form of educational system to deal with socialization, some form of economic system to deal with the allocation of resources, and so forth. A service system of some type evolves to deal with the health and welfare of the population.

The form that a particular institution takes varies from society to society. A society's cultural history, its environment, and its relationship with other societies all contribute to the shaping of its various institutions. There are numerous forms that can be taken by the family, political institution, and economic institutions, with the particular form being uniquely tailored to the situation of that society. Similarly, there are a variety of forms the healthcare institution can assume.

Considering the types of health systems that exist among the world's societies, one might speak in terms of "traditional" healthcare systems (e.g., shamanism among American Indians), more complex traditional systems such as holistic Asian systems (e.g., Ayurvedic healthcare), capitalistic systems (e.g., the for-profit healthcare in the United States), socialized systems (e.g., the National Health Service in Great Britain), and communistic systems such as those that once existed in the what was then the Soviet Union and can be found today perhaps only in Cuba.

No one system of healthcare delivery is intrinsically better or worse than any other; each has evolved in response to particular social, cultural, and environmental considerations, and each is uniquely suited to its particular society. If the system is not suited to the society, it must transform itself in response to societal needs or disappear.

The importance of any institution varies from society to society. Historical and environmental factors, as well as the particular society's value system, influence the importance of the respective institutions. Traditional societies emphasize the family and religious institutions, while the economic and healthcare institutions may be poorly developed. Modern industrial societies tend to place more emphasis on the economic and educational institutions, while the family and religious institutions tend to be relatively neglected. In recent decades, the healthcare institution has become increasingly important in industrial societies as well. This has been particularly the case in the United States.

It is only in modern industrial society that healthcare has developed as a distinct institution. For most of human history, society's provision for the healthcare needs of the population has occurred within the framework of the family or the religious institution. Traditional societies lack the scientific underpinnings for the development of a formal healthcare system. An absence of emphasis on rationality and a dependence on the supernatural as an explanatory factor in the existence of health, illness, and death typically preclude the development of a distinct healthcare system. As societies have become more complex, healthcare systems have come increasingly distinct and separate from other institutions of society.

The Cultural Framework

The restructuring of US institutions during the twentieth century was accompanied by a cultural revolution resulting in extensive value reorientation within American society. The values associated with traditional societies that emphasized kinship, community, authority, and primary relationships became overshadowed by the values of modern industrialized societies, such as secularism, urbanism, and self-actualization.

The "modern" values that emerged within the United States after World War II supported the development of "Western" medicine. The values that emerged in the twentieth century still serve to color the nature of American society and place emphasis on economic success, educational achievement, and scientific and technological advancement. These values supported the ascendancy of healthcare as a dominant institution during the last half of that century.

Implicit throughout the evolution of American healthcare has been the importance of economic success, and the US system emerged as the only for-profit healthcare system in the world. Today, the profit motive remains strong as for-profit national chains have absorbed much of the nation's health services delivery capacity. The free enterprise aspect of healthcare is linked to other American values such as freedom of choice and individualism.

Other values became important as American culture evolved in the twentieth century. For example, change became recognized as a value in its own right. At the same time an activist orientation emerged that called for a proactive approach to all issues, including healthcare. The aggressive approach taken by Americans in the face of health problems reflects this activist orientation.

The conceptualization of "health" as a value in the US society represented a major development in the emergence of the healthcare institution. Prior to World War II health was not perceived as a distinct value but was vaguely tied in with other notions of well-being. Public opinion polls prior to WWII did not identify personal health as an issue for the US populace, nor was healthcare delivery considered a societal concern. By the 1960s, however, personal health had climbed to the top of the public opinion polls as an issue, and the adequate provision of health services became an important issue in the mind of the American public.

Once health became established as a value, it was a short step to establishing a formal healthcare system as the institutional means for achieving that value. An environment was created that encouraged the emergence of a powerful institution that supported many contemporary American values. Some of them, like the value placed on human life, were considered immutable. The emerging scientific, technological, and research communities contributed to the growth of the industry. Support from the economic, political, and educational institutions assured the ascendancy of this new institutional form.

Societal Trends

The twentieth century spawned a dependence on formal institutions of all types and this created a favorable environment for the emergence of healthcare. The political and educational systems, for example, came to be seen as responsible for functions performed informally in earlier times. Healthcare, however, provides possibly the best example of this emergent dependence on formal solutions, since it is an institution whose very development was a result of this transformation. Our great-grandparents would have considered formal healthcare as a last resort in the face of sickness and disability. Few of them ever entered a hospital, and not many more regularly utilized physicians. Today the healthcare system is seen as the first line of resistance, not only for clear-cut medical problems, but also for a broad range of psychological, social, interpersonal, and spiritual problems.

The transformation of American society in the twentieth century clearly affected the provision of healthcare, as the traditional managers of sickness and death—the family and the church—gave way to more formal responses to health problems. The health of the population became in part the responsibility of the economic, educational, and political systems and, eventually, of a fully developed and powerful healthcare system. Traditional, informal responses to health problems gave way to complex, institutional responses. "High-touch" home remedies could not compete in an environment that valued high-tech (and subsequently high status) responses to health problems.

Demographic Trends

Today, perhaps more than at any time in the past, demographic trends are shaping the demand for health services, both at the national and the local level. By looking at specific demographic attributes of the US population and their present and future trends, analysts can predict both the level and types of health services that will be utilized at various distant time periods. These demographic trends are important in that they contributed to the composition of the US population; this, in turn, influenced the morbidity profile of the population. The healthcare system that emerges should ultimately represent a response to the morbidity characteristics of the population. Indeed, the demographic transformation of the American population in the twentieth century might be considered a major, if not *the* major, determinant of the needs to be addressed by the healthcare system.

This is the case due to another transformation that demographic trends spawned. The changing demographic characteristics triggered the "epidemiologic transition" that took place in the United States in the second half of the twentieth century. As the mortality rate for the American population declined during the twentieth century and life expectancy increased, a significant change occurred in the morbidity and mortality profile of the population (Omran 1971).

Throughout recorded history, acute health conditions had constituted the major health threat and the leading causes of death. Communicable, infectious, and parasitic conditions, accidents, complications of childbirth, and other acute conditions were a constant companion to human beings. At the beginning of that century, the leading causes of death were conditions such as tuberculosis, influenza, and other communicable diseases.

During the second half of the twentieth century, the changing demographic profile led to a shift away from acute conditions to chronic conditions as the predominant health problem. Improving living conditions, better nutrition, and higher standards of living, accompanied by advances in medical science, reduced or eliminated the burden of disease from acute conditions. This void was filled, however, by the emergence of chronic conditions as the leading health problems and leading causes of death. The older population that resulted from these developments was now plagued by hypertension, arthritis, and diabetes, as well as numerous conditions that reflected the lifestyles that emerged within the American population in the second half of that century. (See Box 3.1 for additional detail on the epidemiologic transition.)

There are several important consequences for health and healthcare as a result of demographic change. As social factors have supplanted biological and genetic determinants of health and illness, patterns of morbidity for the US population have changed significantly. These "modern" causes of health problems have not only shifted the nature of the health conditions faced by the population but also contributed to the emergence of distinctive patterns of morbidity. While biologically gener-

Box 3.1: The Epidemiologic Transition

Perhaps the most significant trend affecting healthcare during the twentieth century was the shift from acute conditions as the dominant type of health problem to chronic conditions. Referred to as the "epidemiologic transition", this development has major implications for healthcare delivery and, indeed, for our perceptions of the very nature of health and illness. Acute conditions such as infectious, communicable diseases and injuries had been the leading health problems and causes of death throughout human history. Until well into the twentieth century in the United States, yellow fever, whooping cough, influenza, and tuberculosis were leading causes of death. Acute conditions such as these are characterized by rapid onset, rapid and predictable progression, and some ultimate disposition (i.e., either recovery or death). Further, most acute conditions can be attributed to some disease organism within the affected party's environment.

The predominance of acute conditions led scientists to develop the germ theory of disease causation. This in turn led to the development of the medical model approach to addressing health problems. The medical model assumes that the causes of virtually all conditions can be isolated in the form

(continued)

Box 3.1 (continued)

of microorganisms or otherwise reduced to physical or biochemical causes. If these etiological factors can be counteracted, then a cure can be achieved. This approach became the foundation of twentieth-century Western medicine and continues to be a dominant paradigm in healthcare today.

By the middle of the twentieth century, acute conditions began to be displaced by chronic conditions as the primary type of health problem. Chronic conditions tend to be gradual in their onset, of long or infinite duration, and often cumulative in their effect. Chronic conditions are less likely to be caused by factors external to the individual (although some causes are clearly exogenous) and are more likely to arise from within the victim and reflect social and psychological influences. Thus, chronic conditions are more frequently linked to lifestyle, environmental factors, and even the psychological state of the affected party.

Chronic conditions typically cannot be cured but only managed. The chronic conditions that have become increasingly common include arthritis, hypertension, and diabetes. Although sometimes resulting in death (although often indirectly), chronic conditions seldom contribute directly to mortality but are more likely to interfere with the affected party's quality of life and/or result in disability. Unlike acute conditions, chronic conditions can seldom be cured and become lifelong afflictions for those so affected.

Two important interdependent factors have contributed to the epidemiologic transition. The first is the impact of medical science on acute conditions. During the twentieth century the United States witnessed the eradication of most of the major killers from earlier times and a general reduction in the burden of disease on society. Once individuals were spared the premature deaths often caused by acute conditions, they were able to live long enough for chronic conditions to take their toll.

The second factor contributing to the epidemiologic transition was the better living conditions and higher socioeconomic status that came to characterize Americans during the twentieth century. A safer environment, better nutrition, and other factors contributed to a healthier and more long-lived population with Americans able to survive to much older ages on the average. While acute conditions are no respecter of age, they often have their greatest impact on the youngest age cohorts. Chronic conditions, on the other hand, are much more common among older populations. As the US population has continued to age, the older cohorts have grown in significance while the younger cohorts have declined. As older persons have come to account for a larger proportion of the population, chronic conditions have become more common.

(continued)

Box 3.1 (continued)

With chronic conditions dominating the morbidity profile, a growing mismatch has developed between the dominant approach of the healthcare system and the healthcare needs of the population. The medical model was developed to address acute conditions and is much less salient with regard to the management of chronic conditions. With more people living to old age, chronic health problems have become endemic within the US population. Although the healthcare delivery system is adapting to the epidemiologic transition, it still has a long way to go to successfully address the needs of a population characterized primarily by chronic conditions.

Reference

Omran, A. R. (1971). The epidemiologic transition: A theory of the epidemiology of population change. *Milbank Memorial Fund Quarterly, 49,* 515ff.

ated illnesses did not necessarily correlate with age, sex, race, or other demographic attributes, the diseases of civilization affect narrower, more specific segments of the population. Thus, contemporary patterns of morbidity are associated with variations in the demographic attributes of subpopulations. The emergence, persistence, and even augmentation of these disparities in health status among segments of the US population have become a growing concern for health professionals.

The changes observed in morbidity patterns during the second half of the twentieth century included the redistribution of disease within the population along demographic lines. Clear patterns of distribution resulted in the concentration of certain health problems among specific demographic subgroups. Diseases of civilization tend to follow patterns of distribution corresponding to race and ethnicity, income and education, and even sociocultural factors such as marital status, occupation, and religion. Thus, a distinctive disease configuration could be identified for most demographic subgroups. The morbidity profile for low-income African Americans, for instance, became much different from that of affluent white Americans; the health conditions of poor, white rural residents differed from those of upwardly mobile urban residents; and the health status of second- and third-generation immigrants diverged from that of newly arrived immigrants (Box 3.3). The patterns of morbidity distribution that have emerged are so significant that they are viewed not just as differences but as disparities. The latter term reflects the fact that members of some groups are increasingly affected by certain diseases. The social determinants of health have a disproportionate impact on certain subpopulations—the poor, minorities, immigrants, poorly educated, and other vulnerable populations. These disparities have contributed to the bifurcation of the population by health status: While one portion of the population maintains relatively high health status, the other portion of the population faces an inordinate share of chronic diseases and adverse health conditions. While these patterns of disease distribution by themselves are not inherently discriminatory, the fact that certain disadvantaged groups are characterized by higher rates of most contemporary conditions than other groups is noteworthy. As a result of persistent health disparities, it is now reasonable to expect that certain subgroups will suffer from differential morbidity and mortality rates. Once these disparities are established, they tend to be self-perpetuating.

A consequence of these developments has been the establishment of a demographic profile for most health conditions. Even though most chronic conditions in contemporary societies are widespread throughout the population, they are likely to be concentrated among certain groups, creating a unique disease-specific pattern. For example, although diabetes affects all demographic groups, higher rates of prevalence and mortality can be seen among certain subgroups than others. Similarly, heart disease as the leading cause of death is widespread throughout the population, but it has a greater impact on certain subpopulations. The populations most affected by these disparities are minorities, the poor, and the least educated.

This section cannot begin to address all of the demographic trends now underway nor all of the related issues addressed by health demographers. Therefore, it focuses on the key demographic trends and their likely implications for health services planning.

The Changing Age Structure

The first, and perhaps most important, demographic trend in the United States is the population's changing age distribution. The aging of America has obviously been one of the most publicized demographic trends in history. The implications of this trend for health services demand have been well documented, with age arguably the single most important predictor of the demand for health services.

The "internal" restructuring of the age distribution of the population has particular significance for the demand for health services. Population growth within the older age cohorts (age 55 and above), particularly among the oldest-old (age 85 and over), is faster than that in the younger cohorts. The total population increased by 10% between 2000 and 2010, while the population aged 85 and over increased by over 30%. The movement of the baby boomers out of the "middle ages" made the 45- to 65-year-age group the largest age cohort in the first decade of the twenty-first century. Several younger cohorts (i.e., those 25–34 years) have experienced a net loss of population. A continued "shortage" of younger working-age individuals will persist well into the twenty-first century (Cole 2019).

With the majority of baby boomers having transitioned into the senior category by 2020, the US population is exhibiting an age structure that is unprecedented. As of this writing, the population included as many people over 85 years as those under 5 years. The number of US citizens under 18 years of age has actually declined since 2010. With increased longevity and declining birth rates, this trend is expected to continue for the foreseeable future.

An automatic accompaniment to the aging of America has been the feminization of the population. The changing age distribution has important implications for the population's male/female ratio. Generally speaking, the older the population, the greater the "excess" of females. Except for the very youngest ages, females outnumber males in every age cohort. Among seniors, females outnumber males two to one, and, at the oldest ages, there may be four times as many women as men. This results in a relatively older age structure for women and, in 2010, the median age for women was 37.2 years compared to 35.8 years for men. Further, 43.5% of the female population was aged 55 or over, compared to 34.9% of the male population. In 2010, the "excess" of females over males in the US population amounted to nearly 6 million.

Racial and Ethnic Diversity

Another demographic trend exhibited by American society that began in the late twentieth century and has continued into the twenty-first century is its increasing racial and ethnic diversity. America has once again become a nation of immigrants, with the numbers of newcomers from foreign lands during the 1990s and 2000s equaling historic highs. Long-established ethnic and racial minorities are growing at faster rates than are native-born whites. As a result, the visibility of non-Hispanic whites in the US population is decreasing.

The cumulative effect of the trends of the past several years has been a diminishing of the relative size of the non-Hispanic white population and the growing significance of the black, Asian, and Hispanic components of the US population. The 2010 census revealed an America that was 72.4% white, 12.6% black, 4.8% Asian American and Pacific Islander, and less than 1% American Indian/Alaskan Native (based on reporting of a single race). The remainder fell into the "other" racial category or reported two or more races.

The figure for the white population includes most Hispanics and they accounted for 16.8% of the total population (not factoring in the undercount of Hispanics). Thus, non-Hispanic whites accounted for approximately 56% of the US population in 2010. This compares to 71% in 1980, 67% in 1990, and 62% in 2000. Since most of the population growth during the next two decades will be a function of immigration, the proportion of non-Hispanic whites within the population will continue to decline.

A great deal of variation in age exists among the racial and ethnic groups, a factor that allows demographers to make relatively accurate projections of the future racial and ethnic composition of the population. The Anglo (non-Hispanic white) population has by far the oldest age structure and the Hispanic population the youngest, with a difference of 17 years in median age in 2010 (44 versus 27 years). The median age for the black population is 32 years and for the Asian population 35 years. The differential in age distribution is expected to continue into the foreseeable future, as illustrated by the relative proportions of children recorded for the various racial and ethnic groups. A telling statistic is the fact that, in 2010, minorities accounted for half of the children under 5, years but for only 36% of the total population.

Given the fact that the US healthcare system has historically been geared to the needs of the mainstream white population, the trend toward greater racial and ethnic diversity cannot help but have major implications for the nature of the system. Any planning activities must take into consideration the changing characteristics of the population and the demands that these changes will make on the healthcare system.

Changing Household and Family Structure

Another demographic development characterizing the US society is its changing household and family structure. This trend is no surprise to demographers, although it has seldom been linked to health issues. For decades, the family has been undergoing change. First it was high divorce rates, then it was less people marrying (and those who did marrying at a later age), and then it was less people having children (and those that did have children having fewer of them and at a later age).

In 2010, the census reported that 56.6% of the US population over 15 was married, a very low figure by historical standards. Some 26.9% had never married, 11.9% were separated or divorced, and 6.3% were widowed. These figures for the non-married categories are all high by historical standards. Given that health status and health behavior differ considerably among the various marital statuses, the current and future array of statuses should be a concern for the health planner (U.S. Census Bureau 2011).

These changes in marital status have had major implications for the US household structure. It has meant that what is popularly considered the "typical" American family (with two parents and x number of children) has become a rarity, accounting for only 24% of the households in 2010. Today, married couple (without children) households have become the most common household form, but this type of household accounts for less than 28% of total households. "Nontraditional" households have become the norm, and an unprecedented proportion of households are one-person households.

As with marital status, the changing household structure has important implications for both health status and health behavior. The demands placed on the healthcare system by two-parent families, single-parent families, and elderly people living alone are quite different and require different responses. The continued diversification of US household types for the foreseeable future will require commensurate modifications in the healthcare delivery system.

Consumer Attitudes

Although patterns of consumer attitudes in the US society tend to be complex, it is clear that a new orientation has occurred with regard to healthcare. For the most part, today's consumer is much more knowledgeable about the healthcare system, much more open to innovative approaches, and much more intent on playing an active role in the diagnostic, therapeutic, and health maintenance processes.

The movement toward gaining control of one's health was spearheaded by the baby boom cohort that is now facing the chronic conditions associated with "old age." This population was responsible for the introduction of innovative healthcare arrangements such as health maintenance organizations, urgent care centers, and birthing centers. This is the group that was influential in limiting the discretion and control of physicians and hospitals. This cohort also provided the impetus for the rise of "alternative therapy" as a competitor for mainstream allopathic medicine.

The approach to healthcare favored by the baby boom population was more patient centered than the traditional approach and more likely to emphasize the nonmedical aspects of healthcare. In general, baby boomers were less trusting of professionals and institutions and control oriented to the point of stubbornness. This group was more self-reliant than previous post-generations and placed greater value on self-care and home care. It was both outcome oriented and cost sensitive. It is a generation that prided itself in getting results and extracting value for its expenditures. While this cohort is beginning to die off, its members influenced the reshaping of the healthcare landscape for several decades.

To a certain extent, the new attitudes toward healthcare exhibited by baby boomers reflected the rise of consumerism across many segments of society. *Consumers* (as opposed to *patients*) expect to receive adequate information, demand to participate in healthcare decisions that directly affect them, and expect the healthcare they receive to be of the highest possible quality. Consumers want to receive their healthcare close to their homes, with minimal interruption to their family life and work schedules. They also want to maximize the value that they receive for their healthcare expenditures.

The Transformation of the US Healthcare System

It is not appropriate to speak of a modern healthcare system in the United States until after World War II. Prior to that time, healthcare as an institution was poorly developed and accounted for a negligible proportion of societal resources. It remained an institutional nonentity until the period following World War II when it began a rapid rise to become a major US institution.

There are two aspects of any healthcare system to be considered: (1) the disease theory system and (2) the health services delivery system. The disease theory system involves the underlying philosophies and assumptions that support the system. It represents the explanatory framework that addresses the nature of sickness and disease and serves as the foundation for the health services delivery system. Just as scientific medicine rooted in germ theory provides the underpinning for modern American healthcare, a religious belief system based on the influence of the supernatural provided the disease theory system for many traditional healthcare systems.

The delivery system involves the actual provision of healthcare. This is the component with which the general public is most familiar. Unless some type of crisis or public debate develops, participants in the delivery system are not likely to give much consideration to the underlying disease theory system. Nevertheless, changes in the nature of the disease theory system will have major implications for the health services delivery system and the thrust of any health planning.

The development of the healthcare system following World War II can be divided into seven stages, roughly equating with the five decades of the last half of the twentieth century and the first two decades of the twenty-first. Each of these stages will be briefly discussed in turn.

The 1950s: The Emergence of "Modern" Medicine

As American society entered a new period of growth and prosperity following the end of World War II, the modern US healthcare system began to take shape. The economic growth of the period resulted in increased demand for a wide range of goods and services, including healthcare. "Health" was coming to be recognized as a value in its own right, and considerable resources were expended on a fledging healthcare system that had lain dormant during the war.

The 1950s witnessed the first significant involvement of the federal government in healthcare, as the Hill-Burton Act resulted in the construction of hundreds of hospitals to meet pent-up postwar demand. Health insurance was becoming common and, spurred by the influence of trade unions, healthcare benefits became a major issue at the bargaining table.

World War II had also served as a giant "laboratory" for pioneering a wide range of medical and surgical procedures. Trauma surgery was essentially unknown prior to the war, and trauma and burn treatment capabilities were now available to apply in a civilian context. New drug therapies were being introduced, and formal health services were coming to be seen as a solution for an increasing number of problems.

The 1960s: The Golden Age of American Medicine

During the 1960s the healthcare institution in the United States experienced unprecedented expansion in personnel and facilities. The hospital emerged as the center of the system, and the physician—much maligned in earlier decades—came to occupy the pivotal role in the treatment of disease. Physician salaries and the prestige associated with their positions grew exponentially (Starr 1982).

Private insurance became widespread, offered primarily through employer-sponsored plans. The Medicare and Medicaid programs were introduced and these initiatives expanded access to healthcare (at government expense) to the elderly and poor, respectively.

New therapeutic techniques were being developed, accompanied by growth in the variety of technologies and support personnel required. New conditions (e.g., alcoholism, hyperactivity) were identified as appropriate for medical treatment, causing an increasing proportion of the population to come under "medical management." Complete consumer trust existed in the healthcare system in general and in hospitals and physicians in particular.

Some murmurs of dissent were heard due to the lack of access for certain segments of the population. Even here, there was virtually no criticism of the disease theory system that underlay the delivery system. It was felt that the infrastructure was sound and that tinkering with the delivery system was all that was required.

The 1970s: Questioning the System

Entering the 1970s the healthcare system appeared to be continuing along a track of expansion and growth. New techniques continued to be introduced, and there appeared to be no limit to the application of biomedical technology. Even more new conditions were identified, and increasing numbers of citizens were brought under medical management financed through private insurance and government-subsidized plans. The hospital was entrenched as the focal point of the system, and the physician continued to control more than 80% of the expenditures on health services.

While many issues related to healthcare delivery were raised during the 1970s, the increasing cost of care garnered the most attention. Clearly, the United States had the world's most expensive healthcare system. The costs were high and they were increasing much faster than those in other sectors of the economy. While it was once assumed that resources for the provision of healthcare were infinite, it came to be realized that there was a limit on what could be spent to provide health services. Coupled with questions about access and effectiveness, the escalating cost of care was a basis for widespread alarm.

During this period the underlying foundation of the healthcare system was questioned for the first time. Earlier criticism had been directed at the operation of the system, and it had been assumed that the disease theory system was sound. Hence, a "Band-Aid" approach had been advocated rather than major surgery. As the 1970s ended, more and more voices were being raised concerning the underlying assumptions of the system.

The 1980s: The Great Transformation

The 1980s will no doubt be seen by historians as a watershed for the US healthcare. The numerous issues that had been emerging over the previous two decades came to a head as the 1980s began. By the end of the decade, American healthcare had become almost unrecognizable to veteran health professionals. Virtually every aspect of the system had undergone transformation, and a new paradigm began to emerge as the basis for the disease theory system (Strauss and Corbin 1988).

The escalating—and seemingly uncontrollable—costs associated with healthcare prompted the Medicare administration to introduce the prospective payment system. Other insurers soon followed suit with a variety of cost-containment methods. Employers, who were footing much of the bill for increasing healthcare costs, began to take a more active role in the management of their plans.

This transformation resulted in considerable shifts in both power and risk within the system. The power that resided in hospital administrators and physicians was blamed for much of the excess costs and inefficiency in the system. Third-party payors, employers, and consumers now attempted to share in this power. Large groups of purchasers emerged that began to negotiate for lower costs in exchange for their "wholesale" business. Insurers, who had historically borne most of the financial risk involved in the financing of health services, began shifting some of this risk to providers and consumers.

Developments outside of healthcare were also having significant influence. Chief among these was the changing nature of the American population. The acute conditions that had dominated the healthcare scene since the inception of modern medicine were being supplanted by the chronic conditions characteristic of an older population. The respiratory conditions, parasitic diseases, and playground injuries of earlier decades were being replaced in the physician's waiting room by arthritis, hypertension, and diabetes. The mismatch between the capabilities of the healthcare system, and the needs of the patients it was designed to serve became so severe that a new disease theory system began to emerge.

The 1990s: The Shifting Paradigm

Although change occurs unevenly throughout a system as complex as American healthcare, many are arguing that by the late 1990s a true paradigm shift was occurring. Simply put, this involved a shift from an emphasis on "medical care" to one on "healthcare." *Medical care* is narrowly defined in terms of the formal services provided by the healthcare system and refers primarily to those activities that are under the control of medical doctors. This concept focuses on the clinical or treatment aspects of care and excludes the nonmedical aspects. *Healthcare* refers to any function that might be directly or indirectly related to preserving, maintaining, and/or enhancing health status. This concept includes not only formal activities (such as visiting a health professional) but also such informal activities as preventive care (e.g., brushing teeth), exercise, proper diet, and other health maintenance activities.

After the 1970s the importance of the nonmedical aspects of care became increasingly appreciated. The growing awareness of the connection between health status and lifestyle and the realization that medical care is limited in its ability to control the disorders of modern society had prompted a move away from a strictly medical model of health and illness to one that incorporates more of a social and psychological perspective (Engel 1977).

Despite this changing orientation, an imbalance remained in the system with regard to the allocation of resources to its various components. Treatment still commanded the lion's share of the healthcare dollar, and most research was still focused on developing cures rather than preventive measures. The hospital remained the focal point of the system, and the physician continued to be its primary gatekeeper. Nevertheless, each of these underpinnings of medical care was substantially weakened during the 1980s, with a definitive shift toward a healthcare-oriented paradigm evident by the 1990s. (Box 3.2 discusses the implications of the shifting emphasis from medical care to healthcare.)

Box 3.2: From Medical Care to Healthcare

Most observers of the healthcare scene argue that the overarching development in healthcare of the late twentieth century was the paradigm shift from an emphasis on medical care to an emphasis on healthcare. Although the two terms are often used interchangeably, there are major differences characterizing the two concepts, differences that have major implications for health planning.

Medical care is narrowly defined in terms of the formal services provided by the healthcare system. It refers primarily to those functions of the system that are under the influence of medical doctors. This concept focuses on the clinical aspects of care—i.e., diagnosis and treatment—and excludes consideration of the nonmedical aspects of care. *Healthcare* is more broadly defined and refers to any activity that directly or indirectly contributes to preserving, maintaining, and/or enhancing health status. Healthcare includes not only formal health-seeking activities (e.g., visiting a health professional), but also involvement in oral hygiene, exercise, and healthy eating habits.

Throughout the twentieth century, the dominant paradigm in Western medical science was the medical model of disease. Built on the germ theory formulated late in the nineteenth century, the medical model provided an appropriate framework within which to address and respond to the acute health conditions prevalent well into the twentieth century. Since the 1970s, however, there has been a steady movement of activities and emphases away from medical care and toward healthcare. Despite the ever-increasing sophistication of medical technology, the importance of the nonmedical aspects of care had become increasingly appreciated. The growing awareness of the connection between health status and lifestyle and the realization that medical care is limited in its ability to cure the disorders of modern society had prompted a move away from a strictly medical model of health and illness to one that incorporates more of a social and psychological perspective.

A number of factors had contributed directly or indirectly to this shift in orientation. Clearly, the "epidemiologic transition," through which acute conditions have been displaced by chronic disorders, has played a major role. As acute conditions waned in importance and chronic and degenerative conditions came to be predominant, the medical model began to lose some of its salience. Once the cause of most health conditions ceased to be microorganisms within the environment and became aspects of lifestyle, a new model of health and illness was required. The chronic conditions that had come to

(continued)

Box 3.2 (continued)

account for the majority of health problems did not respond well to the treatment-and-cure approach of the medical model. Chronic conditions could not be cured but had to be "managed" over a lifetime, and this called for a quite different approach.

Independent of this trend was the growing dissatisfaction of patients with the operation of the healthcare system. Further, the runaway costs of the system had led observers of all persuasions to question the wisdom of pursuing the one-size-fits-all approach to solving health problems using traditional medical care.

The transition from medical care to healthcare has affected everything from the standard definitions of health and illness to the manner in which healthcare is delivered. Health status is now defined as a continuous process rather than in terms of a specific episode of care. The causes of ill health are now sought in the environment and the social context of the individual as often as they are sought under the microscope. The importance of the non-medical component of therapy has come to be recognized and fathers are now allowed to participate in childbirth, and families are encouraged to participate in the treatment of cancer patients. Perhaps the most significant indicator of the paradigm shift is the fact that the term "patient" itself is increasingly being replaced with terms like "client," "consumer," and even "customer."

At the close of the twentieth century, the healthcare institution continued to be beset by many problems. It was argued that the system was too expensive, that it failed to address contemporary health problems, that it was not contributing to the improved health status of the population, and that large segments of the population were excluded from mainstream medicine. The fact that "administrative costs" account for 23% of the US healthcare dollar (compared to less than 10% in socialized systems) suggests that there are considerable inefficiencies in the system. (For a review of the status of the US healthcare system at the end of the twentieth century, see Wilensky and Newhouse 1999.)

2000–2010: New Millennium Healthcare

As the twenty-first century dawned, the US healthcare appeared to be entering yet another phase, one that reflected both late-twentieth-century developments and newly emerging trends. The further entrenchment of the healthcare paradigm appeared to be occurring, as the medical model continued to lose its salience. This trend is driven in part by the resurgence of consumerism and the emergence of a consumer-choice market. At the same time, financial exigencies and consumer demand were encouraging more holistic, less intensive approaches to care.

The new millennium also witnessed continued disparities in healthcare, exacerbated by the growing number of uninsured individuals and a depressed economy that turned healthcare into a "luxury" for many Americans. Disparities existed in health status among various racial and ethnic groups and among those of differing socioeconomic status. Disparities existed in the use of health services and even in the types of treatment that were provided to individuals in different social categories.

Information technology became an increasingly important driving force. The new healthcare called for effective information management and data analysis. The demands of the Health Insurance Portability and Privacy Act (HIPAA) brought information technology issues to the forefront. This was accompanied by the rise of e-health, perhaps the most significant development in healthcare in several years. The use of the Internet in the distribution of health information, servicing of patients and plan enrollees, and the dissemination of healthcare products promised to significantly change relationships within the healthcare arena. (Box 3.3 discusses the link between immigration and health status).

Box 3.3: Immigration and Health Status

The health of immigrants and its implications for American society have long been discussed, commented on, and at times hotly contested. In the early part of the twentieth century, immigrants were portrayed as sickly, likely to transmit infectious diseases, and a burden to local governments. Research eventually showed that infectious diseases had less to do with immigration and more to do with the neighborhood conditions, where immigrants frequently resided in cramped, crowded tenements with unsafe drinking water and unsanitary sewage removal systems. More recently, another picture has emerged that depicts immigrants from some countries as healthier and hardier than US-born residents.

First-generation immigrants are by and large healthier than native-born Americans, although they are more likely to be affected by certain communicable and infectious diseases that are rare within the US population or have been previously eradicated. Subsequently, the health status of second- and third-generation immigrants tends to decline, as they adopt a health status profile similar to native-born Americans.

The terms "immigrant paradox" and "epidemiological paradox" are frequently used to refer to the fact that immigrants tend to have better health outcomes than the native born. This paradox is especially pertinent for immigrants who come to the United States with low levels of education and income. Yet the sources of this paradox are not well understood.

Social and cultural factors are offered as explanations for the immigrant health advantage, particularly in explaining why their health status may worsen over time. Immigrants may come to the United States with behaviors and values that lead to healthy diets and lifestyles, but over time, they and their children learn US norms and practices that may be less healthy in the long term, such as a steady diet of fast foods, heavy alcohol and substance consumption, and less involvement in family life.

(continued)

Box 3.3 (continued)

Smoking is a lifestyle factor that has a large effect on mortality rates. Immigrants in the United States have lower rates of smoking than the native-born of the same ethnicity or the general native-born population. New migrants to the United States also tend to have lower rates of smoking than do people in their countries of origin, but over time the risk of smoking increases as they stay in the United States.

Despite these promising and noteworthy findings, there is no single definitive explanation why immigrants generally have better health outcomes than the native-born, or why their health eventually declines over time and over generations. Past research on these topics tends to use different datasets, conceptual models, analytic samples, measures, and time periods. Most existing datasets that include large samples of immigrants do not include extensive information about health status and other social conditions prior to the migration experience. Moreover, existing datasets are unable to track immigrants to fully capture how health changes over time and what factors may contribute to these changes. There is evidence, however, that selection, return migration, and social and cultural factors contribute to some extent to the immigrant health advantage and the changes in health over time.

Source: National Academies of Sciences, Engineering, and Medicine. (2015). Health status and access to care. In *The integration of immigrants into American Society*. Washington, DC: The National Academies Press.

The 2010s: Emerging Paradigms

The second decade of the twenty-first century witnessed continued realignment and restructuring of the US healthcare system. Trends that had begun in previous decades, such as the merger of healthcare organizations, increased vertical integration, and acquisition of medical practices by hospitals and health systems, continued. From a marketing perspective, the emphasis on consumer engagement continued to grow, and the use of social media as a force for healthcare marketing gathered steam as healthcare consumers became increasingly Internet savvy.

The most significant development in healthcare since 2010 has been the introduction of the Affordable Care Act (ACA). The ACA made quality health insurance more accessible and affordable to tens of millions of Americans and put significant restrictions on the practices of health insurance companies. The establishment of a national health insurance exchange and the creation of levels of insurance coverage led to a surge in marketing activities. Traditional insurers now had access to millions of consumers who had once been beyond their reach. As a result, insurers needed to better understand the characteristics of a larger number of consumers, many of whom had not been previously insured, to price coverage appropriately and to determine the needs of new populations.

The ACA mandated that not-for-profit hospitals conduct community health needs assessments at least every 3 years. As part of this mandate, hospitals were required to assess the health status of the broader community (i.e., beyond their patient pool), identify community health needs, and develop ameliorative approaches to addressing health needs identified in the community. These functions were typically relegated to the planning department. An important related issue was the political and ideological controversy surrounding the introduction of the ACA—a fight that continues today. Box 3.4 describes key provisions of the Affordable Care Act.

Box 3.4: Key Provisions of the Affordable Care Act

The federal Patient Protection and Affordable Care Act (P.L. 111-148), signed March 23, 2010, as amended by the Healthcare and Education Reconciliation Act, signed March 31, 2010, is also referred to as the Affordable Care Act (ACA). The 900+ page act contains many provisions, with various effective dates. Other papers in this series address specific topics in more detail.

Key Federal Provisions

Provisions included in the ACA are intended to expand access to insurance, increase consumer protections, emphasize prevention and wellness, improve quality and system performance, expand the health workforce, and curb rising healthcare costs.

Expand Access to Insurance Coverage

The ACA aims to extend health insurance coverage to about 32 million uninsured Americans by expanding both private and public insurance. Key provisions do the following, effective Jan. 1, 2014, unless otherwise noted:

- Require employers to cover their workers, or pay penalties, with exceptions for small employers.
- Provide tax credits to certain small businesses that cover specified costs of health insurance for their employees, beginning in tax year 2010.
- Require individuals to have insurance, with some exceptions, such as financial hardship or religious belief.
- Require creation of state-based (or multistate) insurance exchanges to help individuals and small businesses purchase insurance. Federal subsidies will limit premium costs to 2% of income for those with incomes at 133% of federal poverty guidelines, rising to 9.5% of income for those who earn between 300% and 400% of the poverty guidelines.
- Expand Medicaid to cover people with incomes below 133% of federal poverty guidelines.
- Require creation of temporary high-risk pools for those who cannot purchase insurance on the private market due to preexisting health conditions, beginning July 1, 2010.

(continued)

Box 3.4 (continued)

- Require insurance plans to cover young adults on parents' policies, effective Sept. 23, 2010.
- Establish a national, voluntary long-term care insurance program for "community living assistance services and supports" (CLASS), with regulations to be issued by Oct. 1, 2012.
- Enact consumer protections to enable people to retain their insurance coverage (see next section).

Increase Consumer Insurance Protections

The ACA enacted several insurance reforms, effective in 2010, to accomplish the following:

- Prohibit lifetime monetary caps on insurance coverage and limit the use of annual caps.
- Prohibit insurance plans from excluding coverage for children with preexisting conditions.
- Prohibit insurance plans from cancelling (rescinding) coverage, except in cases of fraud.
- Establish state-based rate reviews for "unreasonable" insurance premium increases.
- Establish an office of health insurance consumer assistance or an ombudsman program.
- Establish the share of premiums dedicated to medical services (minimum medical loss ratios).

Additional insurance reforms were to become effective Jan. 1, 2014, including those to prohibit most insurance plans from excluding people for preexisting conditions, discriminating based on health status, and imposing annual monetary caps on coverage, and reforms to require guaranteed issue and renewal of policies, premium rating rules, nondiscrimination in benefits, and mental health and substance abuse parity.

Emphasize Prevention and Wellness

The ACA contains provisions intended to prevent illness, including the following highlights:

- Establishes a Prevention and Public Health Fund, to provide grants to states for prevention activities, such as disease screenings and immunizations, beginning in 2010.
- Creates the National Prevention, Health Promotion and Public Health Council to coordinate federal prevention efforts, including those to address tobacco use, physical inactivity, and poor nutrition.
- Requires insurance plans issued after March 23, 2010, to cover certain preventive care without cost-sharing, such as immunizations; preventive care for children; and specified screening for certain adults for conditions such as high blood pressure, high cholesterol, diabetes, and cancer.

Box 3.4 (continued)

- Increases the federal share of Medicaid payments by 1 percentage point for certain preventive services, for which states do not charge a copayment, effective Jan. 1, 2013.
- Increases Medicare payments for certain preventive services, effective Jan. 1, 2011.
- Establishes a federal home-visiting initiative to help states foster health and well-being for children and families who live in at-risk communities.
- Requires restaurant chains with 20 or more locations to label menus with calorie information and to provide other information, upon request, such as fat and sodium content.
- Requires Medicaid programs to cover tobacco cessation services for pregnant enrollees.
- Requires a federal public education campaign about oral health.

Improve Health Quality and System Performance
The ACA contains several provisions related to improving quality and system performance, including, but not limited to, the following:

- Comparative research to study the effectiveness of various medical treatments
- Demonstration projects to develop medical malpractice alternatives and reduce medical errors
- Demonstration projects to develop payment mechanisms to improve efficiency and results
- Investments in health information technology
- Improvements in care coordination between Medicare and Medicaid for patients who qualify for both
- Options for states to create "health homes" for Medicaid enrollees with multiple chronic conditions to improve care
- Data collection and reporting mechanisms to address health disparities among populations based on ethnicity, geographic location, gender, disability status, and language

Promote Health Workforce Development
The ACA addresses workforce issues through a number of provisions, including reforms in graduate medical education training; increases in health profession scholarship and loan programs; support for training programs for nurses; support for new primary care models, such as medical homes and team management of chronic diseases; increased funding for community health centers and the National Health Service Corps; and support for school-based health centers and nurse-managed health clinics.

(continued)

Box 3.4 (continued)

Curb Rising Health Costs

Key provisions of the ACA that intend to address rising health costs include providing more oversight of health insurance premiums and practices; emphasizing prevention, primary care, and effective treatments; reducing healthcare fraud and abuse; reducing uncompensated care to prevent a shift onto insurance premium costs; fostering comparison shopping in insurance exchanges to increase competition and price transparency; implementing Medicare payment reforms; and testing new delivery and payment system models in Medicaid and Medicare.

State Roles in Implementation

States play numerous roles and have various responsibilities under the ACA, ranging from implementing new health insurance requirements to expanding their Medicaid programs by Jan. 1, 2014. In some cases, states may implement provisions—or defer to the federal government to do so—such as establishing a temporary high-risk pool or creating and administering health benefit exchanges. Other briefs in the series provide additional details and highlight state roles and responsibilities.

Source: Reprinted with permission from National Conference of State Legislatures. (2019). *The affordable care act: A brief summary*. Retrieved from https://www.ncsl.org/research/health/the-affordable-care-act-brief-summary.aspx

Another development during this decade was the emergence of the pay-for-performance model of healthcare—a reimbursement arrangement with the potential to turn the healthcare system on its head. Providers historically were reimbursed on a fee-for-service basis for the treatment of individual patients. The emerging pay-for-performance model, however, emphasized quality over quantity, outcomes over processes, and group health improvement over clinical care for individual patients. This emphasis often involved a shift to some form of capitated payment, whereby providers are paid a specified amount "per head" for the management of a defined group of patients, and their rewards are based on their ability to improve the overall health status of that group rather than their success with any individual patient. As with the ACA, the pay-for-performance movement has meant that providers need to know much more about their patients and prospective patients to effectively manage their care.

One approach developed to address the pay-for-performance environment was the establishment of accountable care organizations (ACOs). ACOs typically involve the joint efforts of providers and insurers, which together take responsibility for the management of a defined group of patients to more effectively control their health status and ensure the appropriate use of health services. The Centers for Medicare & Medicaid Services has sponsored a number of initiatives to encourage the establishment of ACOs. Under an ACO system, providers share any cost savings that are identified, but they also face the threat of financial penalties if there is no demonstrated improvement in group health. The ACO model is still in the early stages of development, and only time will tell whether ACOs will become a mainstay of the healthcare system. The movement toward ACOs will require both providers and insurers to develop a better understanding of the needs of patients and other healthcare consumers.

Another major development of the decade—and one that promises to overshadow the rest—is the growing influence of the population health model. This model represents the culmination of several decades of efforts to address dysfunction in the US healthcare system and reflects changes in the makeup of the patient population, the nature and causes of disease, and, most importantly, the failure of the healthcare system to effectively address twenty-first-century health problems. Population health refers to an approach to determining health status that focuses on a defined population as a whole rather than on individual patients or consumers, and involves using innovative means to measure health status beyond traditional epidemiological metrics. Population health also refers to a method of advancing community health improvement that emphasizes upstream rather than downstream approaches—focusing on the social determinants of health status and deemphasizing the importance of clinical care for the improvement of health. (The population health model will be discussed in more detail in Chap. 4.)

These developments have implications for health planning and reinforce the importance of planning in the contemporary healthcare environment. There is a growing need to understand the characteristics of patients and consumers (primarily nonclinical), the attributes of groups of patients (including their lifestyles and motivations), and the social determinants of health status and to use that information to predict future health problems and health services demand. Among health professionals, planners are in the best position to perform these functions and may conceivably become as influential as clinicians in determining the future health status of target populations. Chapter 4 extends the discussion of twenty-first-century trends as it describes the developing environment for health services planning.

References

Cole, N. L. (2019). *Understanding major demographic shifts in the U.S.* Retrieved from https://www.thoughtco.com/demographic-shifts-of-age-and-race-in-the-us-3026679

Engel, G. (1977). The need for a new medical model: A challenge for biomedicine. *Science, 196,* 129–135.

Omran, A. R. (1971). The epidemiologic transition: A theory of the epidemiology of population change. *Milbank Memorial Fund Quarterly, 49,* 515ff.

Parsons, T. (1951). *The social system.* New York: Free Press.

Starr, P. C. (1982). *The social transformation of American medicine: The rise of a sovereign profession and the making of a vast industry.* New York: Basic Books.

Strauss, A., & Corbin, J. M. (1988). *Shaping a new healthcare system*. San Francisco, CA: Jossey-Bass.

United States Census Bureau. (2011). *American families and living arrangements*. Retrieved from www.census.gov/population, www.socdem/hh-fam/cps2010.html

Wilensky, G. R., & Newhouse, J. P. (1999). Medicine: What's right, what's wrong, what's next? *Health Affairs, 18*, 92–106.

Further Reading

Pol, L. G., & Thomas, R. K. (2012). *The demography of health and healthcare* (2nd ed.). New York: Plenum.

Chapter 4
The Changing Environment for Health Planning

Introduction

As the US population was evolving into its contemporary profile, the US healthcare system was undergoing a major transformation of its own, and these developments have had major implications for planning. Ostensibly, the goal of the US healthcare system is to manage illness and advance the health status of the population. It could be argued, however, that the system at some point became diverted from its primary goal as competition on the part of various vested interests influenced the course of American medicine. Some, in fact, would argue that the needs of the patient became subordinated to the needs of the system.

As for-profit insurers became dominant (and even not-for-profits took on similar characteristics) the aims of the system became perverted. Health insurers were less and less concerned about the needs of their plan members and increasingly concerned about the needs of their shareholders. The involvement of insurers ran up the cost of care and diverted resources away from patient care to administrative costs. The focus on profits over people led to a wide range of abuses that, due to the political influence of a now-powerful insurance industry, went unaddressed. This situation ultimately influenced the enactment of the 2010 Affordable Care Act with its provisions for addressing the worst of the abuses. However, to a great extent the damage had already been done. Health insurers were firmly entrenched as "middlemen" between the patient and the healthcare system. For better or worse, the ACA assured that this intercession would continue.

Another development during the last quarter of the twentieth century was the emergence of the pharmaceutical industry as a major force. Originally established as a community resource and supported by the federal government, a private pharmaceutical industry emerged to become a major player on the healthcare scene. Previous success in the creation of vaccines and lifesaving drugs gave the pharmaceutical industry unwarranted credibility. Drug therapy became the fastest growing component of healthcare delivery, and pharmaceutical companies came to be among the most profitable of American industries.

© Springer Science+Business Media, LLC, part of Springer Nature 2021
R. K. Thomas, *Health Services Planning*,
https://doi.org/10.1007/978-1-0716-1076-3_4

These developments did not occur in a vacuum but unfolded over a period of time within the context of a changing society. The convergence of a number of trends created a situation that is dynamic and unlike anything previously experienced by US society. A variety of developments inside and outside of healthcare have contributed to a reconsideration of a number of aspects of our healthcare system.

Americans increasingly turned to the healthcare institution in the late twentieth century—despite its obvious deficiencies—for a wide range of social, psychological, and even spiritual issues. Physicians came to be regarded as experts on virtually any human problem. This expansion of scope is evidenced by the fact that today less than half of the people in a primary care practitioner's waiting room suffer from a clear-cut medical problem. They are there because of emotional disorders, sexual dysfunction, social adjustment issues, nutritional problems, or some other nonclinical threat to their well-being. Despite the fact that physicians are generally not trained to deal with these conditions, the healthcare system is seen as an appropriate place to seek solutions to these and other nonmedical maladies.

These developments served to distract the system from its ultimate goal. The impact of care had become diluted while competing interests shifted the emphasis away from patient care. Importantly, these factors have led to the extreme misallocation of resources, as they became focused on specialty care rather than primary care, on high-tech diagnostic techniques, and on the most expensive but often least effective treatments.

It was within this context that planning emerged as a core function for various types of healthcare organizations in the twentieth century. Planners dutifully took up the cause of supporting the system that was emerging. While it was business as usual for most players in the healthcare space, significant changes were occurring behind the scenes, often unnoticed by key stakeholders. Planners were playing the game by the rules as written without realizing that the game was being changed as they carried out their mission.

An Evolving Environment

The expansion of the US population thanks to the baby boomers was accompanied by an expansion of the healthcare system as American medicine found its footing in the 1960s and 1970s. The "golden age" of American medicine witnessed an expansion of the healthcare institution in every conceivable manner. Lifesaving drugs supplemented the vaccines that had been introduced in earlier years, and the medical experience gained during World War II introduced advanced surgical techniques to the general public. The scope of medicine expanded dramatically as new procedures and new technologies allowed clinicians to treat an ever-expanding range of problems—problems that now extended beyond the traditional ills to conditions historically thought beyond the purview of medical doctors.

For two or three decades after the war there was a comfortable fit between the healthcare system and the needs of the population it served. The healthcare system practiced what could best be described as white middle-class medicine with increasingly standardized protocols for assuring a consistent quality of care. Health insurance had become widespread, and there was a cozy relationship between health service providers and the insurance industry. The health status of the population steadily improved, with much of the credit accorded to the healthcare system. Although public health measures were actually responsible for much of the improvement in health status, they were seldom accorded the same accolades as feats of "heroic" medicine.

While this one-size-fits-all healthcare system was effective in responding to the healthcare needs of the majority of the population, small but significant minority groups were excluded from the fruits of modern medicine. African Americans in particular were often excluded from the benefits of the system—either deliberately early on or *de facto* during later years. If people did not fit the mold of white middle-class patients, they were often labeled as "bad patients" and treated accordingly. This situation was not limited to minority group members but also included poor people who were often excluded from the system or shunted to inferior public services.

Changing Patient Characteristics

By the turn of the century, the characteristics of the US population had changed dramatically. Not only did these developments create a population with traits that were mostly unprecedented, but their unfolding had major consequences for the health services planning enterprise. Now in the twenty-first century we realize that patients are several years older on the average than a generation ago, and the children who were ubiquitous in medical offices 20 years earlier have become a dwindling population. The proportion of the population that is non-Hispanic white has shrunk considerably, and a majority of school-aged children are now from minority populations. While the greatest increase has been recorded for the Hispanic population, the proportion of citizens from all nonwhite racial and ethnic groups has increased dramatically bringing considerable diversity to the physician's waiting room. Women continue to outnumber men in our society (by more than 6 million) and in the doctor's office waiting room.

Importantly, the proportion of the population's adults who are married has declined dramatically since the baby boom generation. Not only are fewer people marrying but also those who do are having fewer children. Thus, fewer patients live in intact families or are even part of a family household. The healthcare system operates to a certain extent on the assumption that patients have support in the household to assist with healthcare needs.

As acute conditions waned in importance and chronic and degenerative conditions came to the forefront, patients were now presented with different health problems. Once the cause of most health conditions ceased to be environmental microorganisms and became aspects of lifestyle, a new model of health and illness was required. The chronic conditions that had come to account for most health problems did not respond well to the treatment-and-cure approach of traditional medicine and had to be managed over a lifetime.

This changing patient profile was also accompanied by the transformation of the "patient" into a "consumer." Consumers had different characteristics from patients. While "patient" implies a dependent, submissive status "consumer" connotes more proactive involvement in the therapeutic process. This newly minted consumer exhibited a different attitude, and was more knowledgeable about the healthcare system, more open to innovative approaches, and more intent on playing an active role in the diagnostic, therapeutic, and health maintenance processes. This resulted in a shift from patients as passive recipients of healthcare to consumers as active players in the management of their own health. These new attitudes were fostered by baby boomers and perpetuated by successive groups of Generation Xers and Millennials.

The fact that patients now had quite different characteristics than those in the past has important implications for the operation of the healthcare system and for planning functions. We realize today that children are different from adults, males are different from females, whites are different from nonwhites, the affluent are different from the poverty stricken, and so forth. This precludes the operation of the one-size-fits-all healthcare system of the past. This means that adult medicine (particularly older adult care) has become more important than pediatric care. Geriatric medicine has become a distinct specialty area, and there is increasing attention to long-term care, home healthcare, and end-of-life care. Much of the emphasis in female healthcare has shifted from obstetrics to gynecology, and "men's health" has emerged as a specialty area. Cultural competency has become a buzzword as the diversity characterizing the American population has encroached on the healthcare system.

The increased diversity of the patient pool has raised sensitivity with regard to the health disparities that exist. It has long been documented that members of racial and ethnic minority groups often suffer from inordinate health problems, lack of access to care, and inferior care when they do receive it. Pursuing "business as usual" without taking ethnic perspectives into consideration runs the risk of not only alienating a large segment of the patient population but also delivering ineffective care. The health disparities that have emerged due to a failure of the system to accommodate a diverse patient population underscore the need for a new model of care.

Changing Disease Etiology

The shift from a predominance of acute conditions to a predominance of chronic conditions was accompanied by a significant change with regard to disease causation. The major killers a century ago (and throughout human history) were almost invariably the result of a single factor. Today's major killers, on the other hand, reflect the interaction of a variety of factors, made possible by a long life that allows prolonged exposure to carcinogens and pollutants and the emergence of degenerative diseases. The contemporary approach to etiology argues for a more complex view of disease causation, one that takes into consideration the interdependence of various biological and nonbiological factors.

While the population was aging it was also experiencing a shift in its lifestyle characteristics. Perhaps no other societal trend had done as much to encourage a new paradigm as changes in the way Americans lived. "Lifestyle," simply put, refers to patterns of behavior or the way of life characterizing a population. (References are made to an individual's "lifestyle" but it is group patterns of living that are of interest to this analysis.) A lifestyle typically reflects the attitudes, values, and worldview of members of a particular group as well as the behavior patterns that reflect these characteristics. While individual lifestyles are sometimes considered voluntary, members of various groups tend to have their attitudes and behaviors shaped and ultimately constrained by group norms.

The diseases that have come to be dominant within the US population are increasingly referred to as "diseases of civilization," reflecting the notion that our "civilized" way of life is contributing to our health problems. These diseases appear to increase in frequency as countries become more industrialized and more people live to old age. Chronic conditions of this type are due to the combined effect of a lifetime of stress and wear and tear and the unhealthy lifestyles that have been simultaneously adopted. The list of diseases of civilization is long and includes Alzheimer's disease, athcrosclerosis, asthma, cancer, chronic liver disease and cirrhosis, chronic obstructive pulmonary disease, type 2 diabetes, heart disease, metabolic syndrome, Crohn's disease, nephritis, chronic renal failure, osteoporosis, stroke, depression, obesity, and sexually transmitted infections.

The growing importance of lifestyles as a determinant of health status is symptomatic of the extent to which the etiology of disease has changed. Throughout much of the twentieth century it could be argued that society members were "innocent bystanders" when it came to the source of disease. After all, biological pathogens in the environment were responsible for the bulk of the health problems. Exposure to communicable disease was haphazard with disease distribution within the population essentially random. With diseases of civilization on the other hand society members were doing the harm to themselves and could not blame environmental pathologies.

These developments all contributed to the evolving role of health planning. As we entered the twenty-first century, planners were forced to take an increasingly expansive view of their responsibilities. They were faced with a much more diverse audience with an ever-changing variety of needs, including many nontraditional patients who have different perspectives on health and healthcare and respond differently to the options offered by the healthcare system.

Adapting to a Changing Environment

At this point it might be worthwhile to review the distinction between medical care and healthcare. *Medical care* is narrowly defined in terms of the formal services provided by the healthcare system and refers primarily to those functions of the healthcare system that are under the influence of medical doctors. This concept focuses on the clinical or treatment aspects of care, and excludes the nonmedical aspects of healthcare. *Healthcare* refers to any function that might be directly or indirectly related to preserving, maintaining, and/or enhancing health status. This concept includes not only formal activities (such as visiting a health professional) but also such informal activities as preventive care (e.g., brushing teeth), exercise, proper diet, and so forth.

Since the 1970s there has been a steady movement of activities and emphasis away from medical care toward healthcare. Despite the ever-increasing sophistication of medical technology, the importance of the nonmedical aspects of care has become increasingly appreciated. The growing awareness of the connection between health status and lifestyle and the realization that medical care is limited in its ability to control the disorders of modern society have prompted a move away from a strictly medical model of health and illness to one that incorporates more of a social and psychological perspective (Engel 1977).

Despite this changing orientation, an imbalance remained in the system with regard to the allocation of resources to its various components. Treatment still commanded the lion's share of the healthcare dollar, and most research was still focused on developing cures rather than preventive measures. The hospital remained the focal point of the system, and the physician continued to be its primary gatekeeper. Nevertheless, each of these underpinnings of medical care was substantially weakened during the 1980s, with a definitive shift toward a healthcare orientation becoming evident during the 1990s. By the end of the century, references to medical care in the press—both public and professional—had become rarer, as references to "healthcare" came to dominate. As those financing care become more convinced of the value of "health" measures relative to "medical" measures, the need for a new model became more obvious.

With regard to the goal of community health improvement, the shift from medical care to healthcare did not represent much of an improvement over the medical model. This was primarily due to the fact that the emphasis remained on the individual patient. While recognizing that today's patients have different characteristics from yesterday's and, thus, should be treated differently, this approach still attempted to address health problems one patient at a time. While the emergence of this new paradigm was considered a positive sign by many observers (if not yet fully embraced by healthcare providers), the celebration was relatively short lived.

After a century of improving health status, the unthinkable appeared to be occurring: the health status of the US population was declining. As far back as the 1980s and 1990s some observers argued that there were signs that the trend toward continuously improving health was being compromised. There was scattered evidence at first with these isolated cases of declining health status seen as anomalies that were not reflective of the overall trend. However, early in the twenty-first century there was growing evidence for a reversal of century-long trends toward improved population health.

Many have argued, in fact, that our healthcare system is actually playing a role in our system's failure to improve the health of the population and may even be contributing to the deterioration of our health status. The system's sins of omission— e.g., its failure to provide access to care for a large segment of the population—have contributed to poor community health. Similarly, the system's sins of commission— e.g., misdiagnoses and hospital treatment errors—have further contributed to the declining health status of the US population. In fact, it has been established that the healthcare system is now the third leading cause of death after heart disease and cancer (Sipherd 2018).

The Role of Health Planning

The question has arisen as to whether or not planning—as limited as it might have been—has contributed to the lack of progress in improving community health. While planners have been active—knowingly or not—in promoting this new paradigm, they may have inadvertently contributed to its failure in achieving its primary goal. It could be argued, in fact, that planners have been guilty of encouraging over-utilization of healthcare resources. While it is hard to determine what the "right" amount of utilization is, the main concern has been generating more volume without much consideration of other factors. Thus, there are those who contend that as a population we are overtested and overtreated—efforts that not only may not contribute to improved patient care or community health status but may also actually do harm in the form of overly aggressive testing, incorrect diagnoses and/or unnecessary treatment which may in fact be life threatening. Box 4.1 discusses the relationship between the use of health services and health status.

Planners at the organizational level can also be accused of promoting more high-end and complex (read: expensive) services rather than more appropriate and less expensive treatments. With the pressure from healthcare administrators to generate as much revenue as possible and increasingly expensive biotechnology, no one wants expensive equipment to remain idle.

Despite the proven benefits of prevention and efforts to address health problems "upstream," the brunt of planning efforts has been directed toward the encouragement of treatment for existing conditions. Today, we realize that this reflects historical patterns of rewards for quantity rather than quality and an emphasis on payment based on volume.

It could also be argued that a broad-based approach to planning casts a wide net risk promoting the wrong services to the wrong consumers. There has still been a tendency to promote services to audiences that may not benefit from the services or may actually be harmed by them. This is a particular danger when it comes to marketing planning.

Finally, there is the criticism that has emerged as a result of the system's failure to improve community health: The planner's perception has been that the healthcare system (and usually *only* the healthcare system) was capable of addressing health issues and improving community health status. This perception reflects the lofty status that we have accorded our healthcare system and its ability to fight disease and prolong life. This notion is certainly not restricted to planners, and society wide we have been sold on the power of healthcare to achieve these goals. As will be demonstrated below, this faith in the healthcare system has been misplaced, calling for an approach to community health planning that truly includes the community. This applies not only to community-wide planning but to organization-level planning as well. Box 4.1 discusses the impact of more care on health status.

Box 4.1: Does More Care Mean Better Health?
Our system has labored under the delusion that more care means better health and that the health status of the population will be improved by providing greater access to health services. This approach has been applied at the individual patient level as well, where overtreatment was preferred to undertreatment. The potential harm from therapeutic "overkill" was considered preferable to the perceived danger of limiting diagnosis and treatment. Today, there are growing doubts about the benefits of incremental "doses" of care and some outright accusations that overdiagnosis and overtreatment are health threats in their own right.

In the United States, the healthcare system has exhibited a steady increase in the expenditure of resources on healthcare. This can be concluded based on various measures of resource allocation, with one of the most straightforward related to per capita expenditures. Per capita expenditures for health services almost doubled between 1990 and 2000 and then almost doubled again between 2000 and 2010. While there is evidence of a slowing in the increase in healthcare costs, an increase of 22% was recorded between 2010 and 2014.

An examination of the experience with Medicaid in the United States found that enrollment in the Medicaid program led to increased access to services and greater utilization of services. Compared with the uninsured adults, the Medicaid adults were 25% more likely to report that they were in good to excellent health (versus fair to poor health), 40% less likely to report that health declined in the last 6 months, and 10% more likely to screen negative for depression. In addition, access to Medicaid improved adults' mental health markedly. However, Medicaid's impact on physical health could not be conclusively verified. It is contended that multiple factors may mitigate the impact of coverage on clinical outcomes, including unmeasured barriers to access, missed diagnoses, inappropriate medication, patient noncompliance, and ineffectiveness of treatments (Paradise and Garfield 2013).

(continued)

Box 4.1 (continued)

A study conducted in Canada (Cooper 2016) found that lower income populations used healthcare services more than their counterparts who had higher levels of income and education. However, their clinical outcomes appeared to worsen over time, leading patients to record even more primary healthcare visits. Overall, patients' use of health services had little cumulative explanatory impact on the associations between mortality and socioeconomic status. The greater use of services by disadvantaged patients simply reflected their worse health status and did not make up for the effects of their lower socioeconomic status. A review of relationship between the amount of care and health status suggests that access to health services alone cannot eliminate historical health and social disparities (Alter et al. 2011).

It is possible to examine this relationship more globally by accessing the one consistent measure of health status available over time—self-reported health status. As noted above, per capita expenditures for healthcare have been steadily and dramatically increasing for a quarter of a century. If we examine self-reported health status for this same time period, it is difficult to claim improvement commensurate with the growth in expenditures. In fact, over the past decade and a half there appears to be no improvement and perhaps even some decline in self-reported health status for the population overall. According to the Behavioral Risk Factor Surveillance System (BRFSS), the proportion of the population reporting only poor or fair health increased from 8.9% in 2000 to 10.1% in 2010 and remained stable at a higher rate up through 2016. While one should not conclude too much about declining health status from these figures, it certainly cannot be claimed that the population's health status improved over this time period.

There is a growing contention that the health status of the US population is actually *declining* (Thomas 2016). Again, there is no way to definitively measure the level of health status but, based on an examination of a variety of factors, there is plenty of evidence that, at the very least, the long-standing trend toward improved health status has stagnated and, on some measures, has been reversed despite greater consumption of health services. This provides additional support for the lack of correlation between more care and improved health status.

Sources: Alter et al. (2011), Cooper (2016), and Thomas (2016).

Limitations to the Healthcare Paradigm

A major reason that the new paradigm was not effective in improving population health is that it continued to treat health conditions as problems. It has become increasingly clear that most health problems represent *symptoms* of some deeper issue rather than being the problems themselves. Members of populations who would be clearly considered "sick" by traditional standards often conceptualize health and illness differently from those making the assessment. The public may point to a different set of health problems from those conventionally identified by health professionals, with members of the public often classifying nonmedical problems as medical problems—citing poverty, lack of housing, lack of access to healthy food, and limited open space among others.

The "inconvenient truth" that emerges from these realizations is that our health-care system—really, any healthcare system—is not up to the task of improving community health in today's environment. This can be demonstrated in any number of ways. The emphasis remains on treatment and cure rather than prevention, maintenance, and enhancement. The focus on acute conditions still lingers despite the predominance of chronic conditions. When one considers the reasons that people present themselves for treatment we find a mismatch between the skills characterizing the practitioner and the problems brought by the patients. Perhaps less than half of patients present with a physical health problem, with large portions exhibiting emotional, psychological, or addiction issues; dietary or nutritional issues; or some other nonmedical problem.

At the same time, it has become increasingly clear that our society's health problems are being driven by factors that are outside the purview of the healthcare system. In reality, these forces—which are all apparent to health professionals by now—impact groups of people as much as individuals. Poverty does not affect individuals one at a time nor does a toxic environment. The extreme health disparities that have been observed are not a reflection of individual morbidity but of unfavorable health status at the group level.

The unescapable conclusion is that the approach taken by the US healthcare system that emphasizes treating one patient at a time is not an effective model in the face of today's health problems. While the shift from an emphasis on medical care to healthcare involved an improvement in the management of patients, that was also its Achilles heel: It still focused on individual patients albeit in a different manner. The real shift that needs to occur is toward a focus on populations not individuals.

Whether or not one agrees with this conclusion, the handwriting was already on the wall.

Under the provisions of the Affordable Care Act not-for-profit hospitals must demonstrate strategies and tactics that address the needs of the entire service area population and not just their patients. The current emphasis on better access to care, improved quality of care, and cost-effectiveness requires healthcare providers to acquire an in-depth understanding of not only their existing patients but also all healthcare consumers within their service areas. Reimbursement models that emphasize pay for performance further reinforce the notion that providers will be rewarded based on their impact on groups of patients or consumers and not on individual success stories. Providers with capitated patient populations will similarly be rewarded based on the health status of the entire panel rather than any individual outcomes.

The Emergence of the Population Health Paradigm

Because of the failure of late-twentieth-century healthcare to solve our healthcare problems, there is growing interest in the concept of "population health" among health professionals, policy analysts, and government agencies. As an approach that assesses health from a population rather than a patient perspective, it represents an opportunity for developing a better understanding of the health status of populations—whether they are patients or not—and an innovative approach to improving a population's health status. The concept is still evolving and the term "population health" has been used very inconsistently. Healthcare providers claim that they are using a population health approach to more efficiently manage their patients; consultants have rebranded themselves as population health experts to capitalize on this trend; and vendors claim to be able to support their clients' population health needs. Yet, it is clear that when one looks beneath the surface there is widespread misunderstanding of the concept at best and outright misuse of the term at worst.

Deprez and Thomas (2017) have recently attempted to address the confusion surrounding the concept of population health by developing a more useful definition. They view the definition as having two dimensions: noun and verb. As a noun, population health refers to the status of the population reflecting its health and wellbeing as measured by several population-based measures thought to be relevant. The emphasis is on broad measures of health, some of which might be considered as the sum of individual health status and others as attributes of the group as a whole.

> *Population health, n.*, An assessment of the health status of a population that uses aggregate data on non-medical as well as medical factors to measure the totality of health and wellbeing of that population.

As a verb, population health refers to an approach to improving health status that operates at the population level rather than at the individual (or patient) level. The approach focuses on social pathology rather than biological pathology and involves the "treatment" of conditions within the environment and policy realms in addition to the provision of clinical services to individual patients. While an underlying assumption is that a population health approach aims to improve health status by focusing on the healthcare needs and resources of *populations* not individuals, it does not rule out specific patient-based medical treatment but views healthcare as only one component of a health improvement initiative.

The application of the population health model can be explored at two different levels— a microlevel view that considers population health as it relates to the delivery of care and a macro-level view that considers population health from a societal perspective. At the microlevel one approach might be to identify individuals at high risk and intervene to reduce their risk. At the macro-level the approach might involve reducing the average risk level for the total population by initiatives or policies addressing the social determinants of health.

Intervening with individuals at high risk is generally the domain of clinical medicine, although public health authorities coordinate certain clinically implemented programs in order to achieve population health objectives. Some programs such as breast cancer screening and childhood vaccinations involve individual encounters but have population-level objectives. Ultimately, some initiatives targeting individuals at the microlevel will have macro-level implication while others will not.

Attributes of Population Health

There is little agreement as to the attributes of the population health model, just as there is no consensus with regard to the term's definition. However, the following attributes—each with implications for planning—are thought to characterize the population health approach.

Recognition of the Social Determinants of Health Problems

Social factors are powerful determinants of health status (and health services utilization). An emphasis on understanding the social determinants of health is critical to the population health model, and the importance of social pathology over biological pathology must be recognized. Depending on the source it could be argued that social determinants account for 40–60% of the variation in health status among subgroups of the population. If social factors are considered the root cause of observed health problems, any health improvement initiative should take these factors into consideration.

Focus on Populations (or Subpopulations) Rather than Individuals

Application of the population health model involves measuring the health status of the total population rather than simply assessing the clinical readings (e.g., reduction of A1C, blood pressure) for individual patients and combining them into an aggregate health status index. Since regulators, payers, and other evaluators will increasingly reward healthcare providers for their effectiveness in managing groups of patients, consumers, or plan members, the social context characterizing targeted populations will become increasingly important.

Shift in Focus Away from Patients to Consumers

Once the healthcare industry was introduced to planning in the 1960s, it was inevitable that "patients" would come to be seen as "consumers." The trend was already underway with baby boomers who wanted the benefits of quality care as patients coupled with the efficiency, convenience, and value that they had come to expect as consumers. This represented a significant conceptual leap for healthcare providers and one that foretold the future direction of the healthcare industry.

Geography as a Predictor of Health and Health Behavior

There is increasing recognition of the importance of the spatial dimension in the distribution of health and ill health. One of the most significant—and some would say disturbing—findings from decades of health services research is that the utilization of health services varies in terms of geography. Where one lives is a powerful determinant of the kind and amount of medical care received. Rates for various procedures may vary by as much as a factor of 10, reflecting among other things local practice patterns, insurance coverage, availability of services, and consumer lifestyles. Now, it has been determined that one's ZIP Code of residence is the best predictor of one's health status and, by extension, health behavior (Roeder 2014). (See Box 4.2 for a discussion of the role of geography in influencing health status.)

Box 4.2: Where You Live Should Not Determine How Healthy You Are
Where you live, learn, work, and play make a big difference in how healthy people are. According to the Robert Wood Johnson Foundation which is promoting a "culture of health," a range of factors, like education, employment, income, family and social support, community safety, and physical environment, impact the population's health. In many communities, healthy choices are easy choices for their residents. In these communities, there are plenty of gyms, safe places to jog, and community recreation centers with high-quality swimming pools and sports fields. Children play and exercise in well-maintained parks and have access to affordable nutritious foods.

But in many other American communities, there are obstacles to healthy living: parks and playgrounds are littered, broken, or unsafe. School meals are low in nutritional value, school vending machines sell junk food, and students do not get regular physical education classes. There are few places to get out and exercise—some communities do not even have sidewalks for walking. Access to fruit and vegetables is limited because there are no supermarkets. Dilapidated housing, crumbling schools, abandoned factories, and freeway noise and fumes cause illness and injury. The poor overall conditions cause

(continued)

Box 4.2 (continued)

higher levels of obesity and chronic disease, including diabetes, heart disease, and cancer, leading to higher healthcare costs. One major factor in the health of a community is whether or not they have a strong public health system.

Public health departments should help improve the health of communities, since they are responsible for finding ways to address the systemic reasons why some communities are healthier than others and for developing policies and programs to remove obstacles that get in the way of making healthy choices possible. There is increasing concern about the ability of public health to fulfill this function. Clearly, this is a matter that requires a population health approach but there are concerns that public health is not positioned to play a major role in implementing such an approach.

Health planners are often charged with identifying the location and characteristics of at-risk consumers, and under provisions of the Accountable Care Act hospitals are required to demonstrate an understanding of the connection between geography and health status. The ability to identify the health-related characteristics of residents of various areas will be an increasingly important skill for planners.

Health Status Measured at the Community Level

A community-based (participatory) understanding of what the critical health issues are is a prominent feature of population health. While some argue that community health status represents the sum total of the health status of the individuals within the community, a population health approach would posit the existence of a state of health that exists independent of the health of the individuals who make up the population. This would explain the fact that certain communities exhibit persistent health problems over time regardless of who resides in the community. Even personal lifestyles might be thought to reflect the influence of the social groups with which individuals are affiliated.

Acceptance of the Limited Role of Medical Care

It has become increasingly clear that while the cost of healthcare to consumers influences the amount of care consumed, there is no evidence that more care translates into better health. Indeed, a premise of the population health model is that health services make a limited contribution to the overall health status of the population. The US population consumes increasing amounts of healthcare resources per capita, yet our health status is not improving and may, in fact, be declining.

Changes in Health Behavior Are Not Ultimately Individual Actions

As noted above, health status and decisions made with regard to health behavior are not thought to be the result of individual volition but reflect the impact of the individual's social context, cultural milieu, and life circumstances. The population health model recognizes that improvement in personal health status needs to be addressed within the context of the social or community environment (i.e., the source of health problems) in a manner that leverages group pressure for health improvement.

Traditional Ways of Measuring Health Status May Not Be Appropriate

The ways in which health status has historically been measured depend on indicators that have relevance for health professionals. Not surprisingly these indicators represent a biomedical bias. Any assessment of health status should reflect the perspectives of the community rather than those imposed externally by health professionals. The problems identified through community input are not likely to correspond with those recognized by the healthcare establishment. Even the public health department's criteria for assessing health issues may differ from those held by the general public.

Improvements in Community Health Require Collective Impact

On the assumption that the healthcare system cannot improve the health of the population, the responsibility falls to the larger community. No one organization can have a significant impact on the health status of the community's population, especially in light of the variety of factors that are now known to influence health. Involvement by a wide range of community organizations—supported by but not led by the healthcare system—is necessary to create the collective impact that is required to "move the needle" when it comes to community health improvement. This includes involvement by representatives of the education, housing, economic development, criminal justice, and transportation sectors. Involvement on the part of government agencies related to policy making is also critical for the generation of the collective impact necessary to improve community health.

Identifying the Problems Not the Symptoms

As the impact of social factors on health status has become documented, the argument is increasingly being made that the health conditions exhibited by a population are not the *problems* per se but are *symptoms* of underlying problems. Thus, the morbidity levels exhibited by various populations are a reflection of the social determinants of health and illness that are, in effect, the true problems. The presence of

Economic Stability	Neighborhood and Physical Environment	Education	Food	Community and Social Context	Health Care System
Employment	Housing	Literacy	Hunger	Social integration	Health coverage
Income	Transportation	Language	Access to healthy options	Support systems	Provider availability
Expenses	Safety	Early childhood education		Community engagement	Provider linguistic and cultural competency
Debt	Parks	Vocational training		Discrimination	
Medical bills	Playgrounds				
Support	Walkability	Higher education			Quality of care

Health Outcomes
Mortality, Morbidity, Life Expectancy, Health Care Expenditures, Health Status, Functional Limitations

Fig. 4.1 Social determinants of health (source: Artiga and Hinton 2018)

disease can thus be seen as the manifestation of these underlying conditions. This perspective is supported by research that suggests that disadvantaged populations are likely to identify as "health problems" such factors as lack of food, inadequate housing, and unsafe streets.

Critics of the US healthcare system point out that we have been treating these symptoms while not addressing the true cause of the problems. Putting a Band-Aid on the wound is of limited usefulness if the underlying infection is not addressed, and an approach that addresses symptoms without affecting a true cure is clearly ineffective when it comes to improving population health. This explains the fact that there is no correlation between health resources expended and health status. Further, it is now acknowledged that better access to health insurance does not guarantee access to care and that access to care does not assure utilization of services. Finally, utilization of services does not necessarily foster better patient outcomes and by itself clearly does not contribute to improved population health. Figure 4.1 provides an overview of the social determinants of health.

Emerging Patterns of Morbidity

As social factors have supplanted biological and genetic determinants of health and illness, patterns of morbidity for the US population have been significantly affected. These "modern" causes of health problems have not only shifted the nature of the health conditions faced by the population, but also contributed to the emergence of distinctive patterns of morbidity. While biologically generated illnesses were no respecter of age, sex, race, or any other demographic attributes, "diseases of civilization" are relatively selective in their choice of "victim." Thus, contemporary patterns of morbidity are associated with variations in the demographic attributes of various subpopulations. Patterns of disease distribution follow racial and ethnic dimensions, income, and educational lines, and even correspond to sociocultural factors such as marital status, occupation, and religion.

This means a distinctive disease configuration can be identified for most demographic subgroups. The morbidity profile for low-income African Americans now looks a lot different from that of affluent white Americans, the health conditions of poor white rural residents look a lot different from those of upwardly mobile urban residents, and the health status of second- and third-generation immigrants looks a lot different from that of newly arrived immigrants.

The other consequence of these developments has been the establishment of a demographic profile for most health conditions. While most chronic conditions in contemporary societies are widespread throughout the population, they are likely to be concentrated more among certain groups than others, creating a unique disease-specific pattern. Thus, while diabetes affects all demographic groups in society, the disease exhibits higher rates of prevalence and mortality among certain subgroups than others. Similarly, heart disease as the leading cause of death is widespread throughout the population but has a greater impact on certain subpopulations.

The patterns of morbidity distribution that have emerged are of such a significance that they are not just viewed as *differences* but as *disparities*. The latter more negative term reflects the fact that members of some groups are increasingly affected by contemporary health problems. The social determinants of health have a disproportionate impact on certain subpopulations—the poor, minorities, immigrants, the poorly educated, and other "vulnerable" populations. This development has contributed to the bifurcation of the population in terms of health status, into a portion of the population that, while not totally free of chronic conditions, maintains relatively high health status and another portion of the population that faces an inordinate share of chronic problems and adverse health conditions.

While these patterns of disease distribution by themselves are not inherently discriminatory, the fact that certain disadvantaged groups are characterized by higher rates for most contemporary conditions than other groups is noteworthy. These disparities in turn lead to certain connotations that are transferred to the populations that are adversely affected. Because of persistent health disparities it is not unreasonable to now *expect* that certain subgroups suffer from differential morbidity and mortality rates. Once these disparities are established they tend to be self-perpetuating.

The Emergence of Population Health Management

A number of developments have encouraged healthcare providers to apply what they consider a population health approach at the microlevel to the delivery of care. To distinguish between the population health approach and the version that is applied within the context of healthcare delivery the term *population health management* is increasingly being used. If the emphasis is on serving clinical patients (even if considered as a group), managing service utilization, or controlling costs, this should be considered population health management as opposed to straight population health. Efforts at improving the individual experience of care, reducing the per capita cost of care, and improving the health of "captive" populations can all benefit from a population health approach. Many clinicians and medical managers, in fact, have begun to use the term population health management to describe "the iterative process of strategically and proactively managing clinical and financial opportunities to improve health outcomes and patient engagement, while also reducing costs" (Kindig 2015).

Alternatively, the Agency for Healthcare Research and Quality (AHRQ) uses the term "practice-based population health" to describe the application of population health principles to patient populations (Cusack et al. 2010). The AHRQ definition reads: "an approach to care that uses information on a group of patients within a primary care practice or group of practices to improve the care and clinical outcomes of patients within that practice."

While efforts geared toward improving the effectiveness of care (e.g., the Triple Aim movement) continue to emphasize (perhaps inappropriately) the care of individual patients, there are ways in which to apply population health principles to the healthcare delivery system. The major developments that have implications for planning are as follows:

Emphasis on Group Outcomes

There has been a major shift away from evaluating (and rewarding) providers for the successful management of individual patients. While the successful treatment of serious conditions is important, Medicare and other third-party payers are more concerned about how a clinic's 100 patients or a health plan's 1000 enrollees are faring—and not just in terms of a specific health issue but in terms of their overall health status. Thus, the significance of clinical outliers is minimized with those evaluating effectiveness or paying for services looking for across-the-board improvement rather than individual successes. Hospital executives' efforts at improving the overall health of a "managed" population, in fact, are increasingly being considered in their evaluations (Conn 2016).

Emphasis on Quality Rather than Quantity

There has been a shift away from rewarding providers based on the *number* of cases treated, diagnostic tests run, or procedures performed toward rewards for the *quality* of these services provided and their subsequent impact on the health of patient populations. "Quality" is notoriously hard to define and measure, but providers will increasingly be judged on this basis. Quality measures can be thought to provide a global indicator of the effectiveness of the care provided to a group of patients, plan members, or employees.

Moving Away From Disease Management

For nearly two decades, health plans and employers have attempted to control costs through the implementation of initiatives such as "disease management" and "patient management." The intent was to micromanage the care for a select number of high-cost patients. Diabetics has been a common target for such efforts with some programs going so far as to assign case managers to assure timely access to services and encourage patient adherence. Such programs have resulted in some limited financial benefits related to those patients but have failed to contribute to the overall health of the targeted population. Micromanaging a small number of patients has been found to have little impact on overall health, while focusing on at-risk populations, for example, has tended to yield better results. Ultimately, any initiative that attempts to improve population health of one patient at a time is not going to be effective in today's healthcare environment.

Emphasis on "Community Benefits"

There is growing concern that healthcare providers (often with tax-exempt status) are focusing on their existing patients to the detriment of the health of the community. There is pressure on not-for-profit hospitals in particular to generate "community benefits" beyond the services they provide to their patients. Indeed, the Patient Protection and Affordable Care Act of 2010 mandated that not-for-profit hospitals conduct a comprehensive community health needs assessment at least every 3 years. The legislation made it clear that the emphasis was on the extent to which these providers served the total community and not just their own patients. In fact, existing regulations require that a plan be developed for addressing any identified gaps in services within the community whether or not the provider is involved in the delivery of these services.

Emphasis on Nonclinical Factors

A major contribution of the population health "movement" has been the spotlight placed on nonclinical factors and their impact on health status and health behavior. It has become increasingly clear that the demographic, socioeconomic, and psychographic attributes of populations play an important role in the health problems they exhibit and the subsequent health behavior of their members. These nonclinical factors often override any impact of the healthcare delivery system. These attributes determine who gets sick and with what disease, the likelihood of seeking treatment and/or complying with doctor's orders, and what happens to them after they leave the doctor's office or hospital. Indeed, it is now realized that one's ZIP Code of residence is a prime predictor of health status (Roeder 2014) and that hospital readmissions are more a function of nonclinical factors than of anything that transpires in the healthcare system (Hu et al. 2014).

Emphasis on Patient/Plan Member/Employee Engagement

Much of the ineffectiveness that has been documented related to the delivery of care has been traced to the failure to engage patients, plan members, employees, and consumers in positive health behaviors. Social marketing efforts have been primarily geared to mass audiences, and interventions typically involve one-size-fits-all initiatives. A population health approach would involve the identification of subpopulations and their attributes, allowing for engagement efforts customized to the needs of targeted populations. Population health emphasizes the segmentation and profiling of defined populations in terms of their salient characteristics, thereby allowing for more informed intervention efforts. Box 4.3 lists some situations likely to be faced by health planners.

Box 4.3: What Do These Scenarios Have in Common?

The following scenarios might be thought of as illustrating issues increasingly common among healthcare organizations:

- A hospital is penalized for unacceptably high rate of readmissions within 28 days.
- A hospital realizes that its outcomes vary widely based on the demographic characteristics of its patients.
- A provider loses its capitated panel of patients from a managed care plan due to failure to meet health status benchmarks.
- An EAP provider loses money due to the high level of overutilization of some services and underutilization of other services.
- A behavioral health organization loses a contract with a state insurance plan due to its inability to effectively communicate with its covered lives.
- A Medicaid managed care organization loses money due to its inability to manage the utilization of its services by its enrollees.
- A hospital is reprimanded by the IRS for failure to take the needs of the service area population into consideration in the preparation of its CHNA.

(continued)

Box 4.3 (continued)

- A county government is faced with escalating healthcare costs due to excessive preventable admissions and inappropriate use of the emergency room at its public hospital.
- An accountable care organization (ACO) fails to quality for "shared savings" under its contract with CMS.

The factor that all of these entities have in common is the need to address the issues affecting a *population*, a need that cannot be addressed using traditional methods. These challenges cannot be met by providing clinical care to individual patients. And they cannot be met unless the entity has a much more in-depth (and more nuanced) understanding of the characteristics of the affected population.

The challenges facing these organizations range from cost containment, patient management, community health improvement, appropriate utilization, and member retention among others. Despite these disparate challenges all are faced with the need to adopt a population health approach, an approach that allows them to view the challenge in terms of groups of people—whether they be patients, consumers, plan members, employees, or others—who can be profiled in terms of their salient characteristics and be served, managed, assessed, or enhanced using methods that address the groups (and subgroups) in a wholesale manner.

Attributes of Population Health Management

Population health principles that can be applied to healthcare delivery and require the attention of planners include the following:

Segmenting and Profiling Populations and Subpopulations

Rather than focusing on the characteristics of individual patients, population health emphasizes the attributes of groups—whether they be patients, employees, plan members, or consumers. The need to develop an in-depth understanding of the characteristics of targeted populations has never been greater, and a first step is the identification of meaningful segments within any targeted population. Segmentation could be based on demographic or psychographic characteristics, levels of utilization, at-risk status, and a variety of other attributes. Once these segments have been identified they can be profiled in terms of their salient characteristics.

Implementing "Group Therapy"

While traditional clinical medicine is designed to manage one patient at a time, population health emphasizes the management of groups of patients (however the group may be defined). This may involve something as simple as group diabetes education management efforts or something as complex as developing an advanced treatment strategy for a defined set of patients. All plan members at risk of diabetes, for example, could be singled out for particular attention. Efforts to introduce interventions, educational programs, or marketing initiatives can take the characteristics of various population segments into consideration in a more targeted fashion.

Implementing Patient Education

One existing activity at most healthcare organizations that could be considered a candidate for population health management is health education. Social marketing is a well-established method for educating consumers, and various providers have attempted to implement patient education activities for groups of patients who exhibit similar characteristics. Patients, plan members, and employees may be at various stages in the process of health improvement and exhibit different levels of health literacy. Some may be only at the point of realizing they have health issues, some may be informed but unmotivated, and some may actively be involved in positive health behavior and require ongoing support. Marketers can play a role in tailoring educational programs to the needs of the respective segments and developing engagement plans that take these differences into consideration.

Accounting for Life Circumstances

Life circumstances can perhaps be thought of as the everyday manifestations of the social determinants of health. These are the factors such as health literacy, joblessness, food insecurity, housing insecurity, and unsafe neighborhoods that affect both the health status and health behavior of defined populations. We now realize that what has happened to a patient before they enter treatment and what happens to them after they leave treatment have more of an impact on their clinical outcomes than the actual clinical care provided. Forewarned is forearmed and providers who have prior knowledge of the characteristics for which they have responsibility should be able to provide better care.

Community Health Needs Assessment

Progressive healthcare organizations have historically conducted community health needs assessments of various types—typically for the own strategic planning purposes. Now—at least for certain hospitals—this is not an option as the Affordable Care Act requires not-for-profit hospitals to conduct a comprehensive community health needs assessment at least every 3 years. Even providers who have routinely conducted community health assessments are not likely to comply with newly enacted provisions of the Act. Tax-exempt hospitals must demonstrate an understanding of the healthcare needs of the total community (even those segments that it does not serve), identify gaps in services (even those that it does not provide), and formulate a plan for addressing the gaps that have been identified.

A key factor here is that the emphasis is on *consumers* and not just existing patients. Thus, a major hospital has to look beyond its walls into the community to identify issues that it must address even if they are not related to a service it provides. For example, hospital ABC does not provide behavioral health services but finds through the community assessment process that there is a serious gap between the needs of the community and the behavioral health services that are available. Theoretically, at least, this hospital must quantify these gaps, demonstrate to the federal government that it has a plan to address them, and be able to document through subsequent assessments its effectiveness in helping to close the identified gap. Box 4.4 presents an example of the use of a CHNA for population health management.

Box 4.4: Case Study: Using a Community Health Needs Assessment to Improve Patient Care

A major hospital system in medium-sized southern city conducted a comprehensive community health needs assessment in compliance with the Affordable Care Act. In conducting the assessment the analysts discovered a particular ZIP Code whose residents were responsible for a large proportion of the hospital's uncompensated care. Additional research was conducted to determine the nature of the issues surrounding the high use of healthcare resources by residents of this particular community.

The research uncovered a significant number of residents with comorbid chronic conditions who were frequent users of the hospital's emergency department and regularly admitted as inpatients. It was also found that these high utilizers were clustered in certain locations suggesting that the local environment had an impact on health status and that there was a culture of ill health that brought these patients together and led them to use similar health services.

(continued)

Box 4.4 (continued)

The research also found that there was a significant portion of the population at high risk for chronic conditions, particularly diabetes. The remainder of the population was only at moderate risk but given the illness-inducing attributes of the community there was concern over their future health status. Each of the three populations—high utilizers, high risk, and low risk—was profiled in terms of their demographic, socioeconomic, and psychographic characteristics. This information was used to inform the development of customized programs for each of these groups.

As a result of this exercise the hospital developed a three-tiered approach for addressing the health issues facing this community. For the 100 chronically ill high utilizers a case management program was established that involved the micromanagement of the care for each of these patients. Efforts were made to assure that they received timely treatment, adhered to their medical regimen, and to the extent possible maintained a healthy lifestyle. For the estimated 4000 at-risk residents, an intensive patient education effort was developed that targeted their areas of residence. Like the high utilizers, the at-risk populations also tended to cluster together. For the relatively healthy low-risk population a social marketing program was developed that provided general information on healthy lifestyles and prevention.

Although much of the impact of such programs is difficult to quantify, the case management efforts vis-à-vis the high utilizers paid significant dividends in terms of reduced emergency department utilization and inpatient admissions. Many of the 4000 at-risk patients who received screening and prevention materials actually entered treatment programs for chronic conditions, although it is difficult to determine how much impact the hospital initiative had in this regard. Follow-up surveys found that members of the general population (low-risk segment) had been exposed to health education materials and many had actually participated in health fairs located in areas with concentrations of high-risk residents.

Creating Financial Efficiencies and Maximizing Revenue

The financial welfare of healthcare providers is never far from the surface and, not surprisingly, efforts toward population health management often focus on introducing financial efficiencies and maximizing revenue. Measures of success are increasingly focusing on the extent to which providers or health plans are providing cost-effective services. Providers that hope to survive the current environment must be able to control costs and maximize revenue. CMS is increasingly offering financial incentives to Medicare providers who manage patients efficiently. To this end a number of vendors have developed methodologies (often under the label "population health") for assisting providers, health plans, and accountable care organizations in improving their financial performance. CMS has encouraged such activity through its "shared savings" initiative.

Barriers to Population Health Management

Healthcare providers are naturally drawn to population health management since it is a comfortable fit with activities with which they are familiar. Despite this growing affinity for this approach, there are a number of factors that present challenges to applying this methodology within the context of healthcare delivery.

Limited Appreciation of Population Health and Its Usefulness

Despite the growing interest in population health, many if not most healthcare providers have a limited understanding of what it involves. Few in fact appreciate the macro-level application of population health while more are beginning to appreciate its application to the delivery of care. When health professionals consider challenges related to the delivery of care, they most frequently consider such things as the efficient processing of patients, controlling utilization and maximizing revenue. These are pressing concerns for healthcare administrators, but the usefulness of population health management is not likely to be immediately obvious under the pressure of delivering care.

Lack of Appreciation for the Nonclinical Contributors to Health Status

To the extent that the population health approach can be applied to the delivery of care, a major benefit is its emphasis on the nonclinical aspects of care. Although few providers are unaware of the influence of poverty, inadequate housing, food insecurity, and domestic violence on the health of the population, acknowledging these factors does not necessarily create a connection to the practice of medicine or the delivery of care. Part of the failure to acknowledge the importance of social determinants is the notion that things that go on "out there"—i.e., outside the walls of the institution—are beyond the influence of healthcare providers. Although this is true to a great extent, it can be argued that better care could be provided if providers were armed in advance with information on the life circumstances of their patients and the potential importance of social determinants on their health status.

Lack of Incentives to Incorporate Population Health Management

Historically there has been pressure on healthcare providers to process as many patients as possible as efficiently as possible. In fact, the pressure to do so has only increased as managed care arrangements have become widespread and increasing numbers of physicians are working under quotas as employees. This is not an environment that encourages the thoughtful introduction of population health management, and existing financial incentives discourage many activities that would be promoted through population health. Not only do financial considerations influence consumer and patient behavior, but they also influence the practice patterns of physicians. If there are financial incentives encouraging physicians to see more patients, conduct more tests, or provide more services, physicians will respond rationally by increasing volume. Today, incentives are changing rapidly as the emphasis shifts to ensuring greater access, more effective outcomes, and lower costs, but these new incentives have to be incorporated into the system before many providers embark on radical restructuring.

Discontinuity with Other Types of Nonmedical Services

It has become increasingly clear that medical care alone cannot advance population health. A comprehensive range of services is required to supplement the benefits of clinical medicine. Given the extent to which nonclinical factors contribute to health status, the system must be able to link healthcare providers with the providers of services existing independent of medical care. Obvious possibilities that come to mind are dentists, eye care specialists, mental health counselors, and social workers.

There is a wide range of services thought to have an impact on clinical outcomes that are typically not considered by the system except for the occasional social worker or discharge planner. These include services related to housing, food security, personal safety, environmental threats, and range of social determinants discussed in previous chapters. The lack of interface between providers of clinical services and these "external" service providers and the absence of financial incentives to establish such interfaces represent clear barriers to the implementation of population health management.

Lack of Data to Support Population Health Management

While significant advances have been made in accessing and analyzing the voluminous amount of clinical data available to healthcare providers, gaps remain with regard to the data required for population health management. Most data focus on historical utilization patterns for existing patients and do not provide much assistance to clinicians and administrators seeking to apply population health management principles. There is a lack of actionable data to allow analysts to appreciate the factors that influence health status and clinical outcomes for their patients, plan members, or employees.

Providers have limited information, for example, on the life circumstances of their patients that are likely to affect their health status and their ability to benefit from treatment, information that is not likely to be obtained during history taking. As a case in point, a clinician is not likely to know the economic circumstances of a patient (although these are of immense importance) and may not even know what type of insurance coverage (if any) a patient has. Similarly, a clinician is not likely to know the living arrangements of the patient, although these are likely to affect one's ability to adhere to a medical regimen.

Lack of Tools for Population Health Management

There is no doubt that the amount of knowledge—and the expertise required of physicians—has increased exponentially in recent years. Today, it is impossible for the best informed physician to be knowledgeable concerning the range of factors that contribute to health status and health behavior. Further, within a population health framework they need access to information—particularly of a nonmedical nature— that would support their decision-making. Not only is the requisite data not available but also there are few tools available to the practitioner for applying population health management. To effectively apply this model, practitioners need a toolkit that allows them to input the available data and generate "red flags" that would allow them to anticipate health problems and challenges to care on the part of their patients. These same needs exist with regard to insurance plan members and employees.

Planning and Population Health

The changes taking place in healthcare as a result of the emerging population health model and other developments suggest a changing role for the healthcare planner. As the focus shifts from the individual consumer to *communities* of consumers, the knowledge and skills of marketers take on new significance. Effective health planners:

- Need to understand patient populations
- Need to understand consumer populations
- Need to understand utilization and financial management
- Must become involved in strategic planning at the organizational level
- Must adapt community health needs assessment methodologies to reflect the current environment
- Need to understand the social determinants of health (and be able to measure them)
- Need to be able to reconceptualize the notion of health status
- Need to adapt to an increasingly diverse patient population

Clearly, the evolving healthcare environment offers both challenges and opportunities for health planners. The challenges arise from the need to adjust to changing conditions that are creating situations that are unprecedented in the industry. This requires radical rethinking of the goals and objectives of the healthcare system and, by extension, the planning function. Opportunities arise not only within the context of these challenges but also through the emergence of an expanded vision of the role of planning and the increasing number of "pressure points" where planning skills might be brought into play. As with most changes that have impacted healthcare over the past decades, the changing environment offers the opportunity for planners to creatively leverage their skills to the benefit of their healthcare organizations and the health of the community.

References

Alter, D. A., Stukel, T., Chong, A., & Henry, D. (2011). Lesson from Canada's universal care: Socially disadvantaged patients use more health services, still have poorer health. *Health Affairs, 30*(2), 274–228.

Artiga, S., & Hinton, E.. (2018, May). Beyond healthcare: The role of social determinants in promoting health and health equity. San Francisco, CA: Kaiser Family Foundation. Retrieved from http://files.kff.org/attachment/issue-brief-beyond-health-care

Conn, J. (2016). Hospital execs earn bigger bonuses as value-based care takes hold. *Modern Healthcare*. Retrieved from https://www.modernhealthcare.com/article/20160806/MAGAZINE/308069982/hospital-execs-earn-bigger-bonuses-as-value-based-care-takes-hold

Cooper, R. (2016). *Poverty and the myths of welfare reform*. Baltimore, MD: John Hopkins University Press.

Cusack, C. M., Knudson, A. D., Kronstadt, J. L., Singer, R. F., & Brown, A. L. (2010, July). *Practice-based population health: information technology to support transformation to proactive primary care*. Rockville, MD: Agency for Healthcare Research and Quality Publication No. 10-0092-EF. Retrieved from https://pcmh.ahrq.gov/sites/default/files/attachments/Information%20Technology%20to%20Support%20Transformation%20to%20Proactive%20Primary%20Care.pdf

Deprez, R., & Thomas, R. (2017). Population health improvement: It's up to the community—Not the healthcare system. *Maine Policy Review, 25*(2), 44–52.

Engel, G. L. (1977). The need for a new medical model: A challenge for biomedicine. *Science, 196*(4286), 129–136.

Evans, R. G., Barer, M. L., & Marmor, T. R. (Eds.). (1994). *Why are some people healthy and others not? The determinants of health of populations*. New York: Aldine de Gruyter.

Hu, J., Gonsahn, M. D., & Nerenz, D. R. (2014). Hospital socioeconomic status and readmissions: Evidence from an urban teaching hospital. *Health Affairs, 33*(5), 778–785.

Kindig, D. (2015, April 6). What are we talking about when we talk about population health? *Health Affairs Blog*. Retrieved from http://healthaffairs.org/blog/2015/04/06/what-are-we-talking-about-when-we-talk-about-population-health/

Paradise, J., & Garfield, R.. (2013, August 2). *What is Medicaid's impact on access to care, health outcomes, and quality of care? Setting the record straight on the evidence*. San Francisco, CA: Kaiser Family Foundation. Retrieved from http://kff.org/report-section/what-is-medicaids-impact-on-access-to-care-health-outcomes-and-quality-of-care-setting-the-record-straight-on-the-evidence-issue-brief/

Roeder, A. (2014, August 4). *ZIP code better predictor of health than genetic code*. Boston, MA: Harvard T.H. Chan School of Public Health. Retrieved from www.hsph.harvard.edu/news/features/zip-code-better-predictor-of-health-than-genetic-code/

Saxena, A. (2015, October 29). *Improving medicine with predictive modeling*. Hospitals & Health Networks. Retrieved from www.hhnmag.com/articles/6662-improving-medicine-with-predictive-modeling

Sipherd, R. (2018, February 22). *The third leading cause of death in the US most doctors don't want you to know about*. CNBC. Retrieved from www.cnbc.com/2018/02/22/medical-errors-third-leading-cause-of-death-in-america.html

Thomas, R. K. (2016). *In sickness and in health: Disease and disability in contemporary America*. New York: Springer.

Further Reading

Bailey, J. (2014). *The end of healing*. Memphis, TN: The Healthy City.

Deprez, R., & Manchester, C. (2018). *Improving the health of the community through population health assessment, 27*(2), 51–59. Retrieved from https://Census.gov/data/tables/2011/demo/families/cps-201.html

Chapter 5
Health Services Demand and Utilization

Introduction

The demand for health services ultimately drives all healthcare planning activities. In fact, the demand for services is the *raison d'etre* for any healthcare organization. Most decisions on whether or not to offer a service will be predicated upon presumed levels of demand. Once a service is offered, virtually all decisions related to the continued provision of that service will reflect this factor. For this reason, health planners spend a great deal of their time and effort trying to determine current and future levels of demand for total health services or for the specific services offered by the organization involved in the planning process.

The issue of demand carries us back to the question of who (or what) are we planning for. In the case of community-wide planning, the demand for the widest range of services possible must be taken into consideration. For planning to be truly comprehensive, the demand for virtually every type of service must be determined, ranging from consumer education programs to chronic disease management to trauma care.

At the organization level, the focus is considerably narrower. The emphasis will be on the demand for the services currently offered by the organization or for services that are under consideration. If the organization is multipurpose like a hospital, the planner will need to consider a relatively wide range of services (although not as comprehensive as that considered by the community health planner). On the other hand, a local home health agency serving exclusively Medicare patients will be concerned with a fairly narrow range of services.

The factors influencing the level of demand for health services have become increasingly complex, and past utilization patterns are seldom predictive of future utilization. The significant demographic, socioeconomic, and psychographic transformation that the US population has been undergoing has served to "naturally" modify the level of demand. At the same time, managed care arrangements and other developments in healthcare "artificially" influence the level of demand for

© Springer Science+Business Media, LLC, part of Springer Nature 2021
R. K. Thomas, *Health Services Planning*,
https://doi.org/10.1007/978-1-0716-1076-3_5

health services. These developments have made the task of projecting demand for health services an increasingly challenging task at a time when the ability to do so is critical for the survival of most organizations.

A complicating factor for hospitals in particular is the fact that some service offerings may be mandatory whether or not there is a documented demand. In some cases, a major component such as emergency services may be required by law—even though there may be limited demand and/or the offering of the service involves a financial hardship on the hospital. In other cases, certain capabilities may be required by state licensure agencies or by a hospital accreditation agency, services that might not be offered otherwise. Finally, hospitals may feel obligated to offer certain services in order to be competitive with other healthcare providers. Ultimately, there is likely to be an imperfect match between the services offered by the hospital and those that are needed or wanted by the community.

Defining "Demand"

"Demand" is an imprecise concept as applied to health services and the term is often used interchangeably with other terms. In fact, there is technically no one definition of demand in common usage. The concept is sufficiently vague and is used in so many different ways that it is difficult to provide an operational definition.

Part of the confusion in terms of defining (and measuring) health services demand stems from a lack of agreement as to *who* the customer for health services is. Typically, the services demanded by the end user, usually the patient, are the primary consideration. However, other customer groups such as physicians, health plans, and employers may play a part in determining demand. For health plans, the customer may actually be the benefits manager for an employer-sponsored plan. For medical supply or equipment companies it may be retail distributors.

Perhaps the best way to approach the demand concept is by examining its component parts. From a planning perspective, demand can be conceptualized as the ultimate result of the combined effect of (1) healthcare needs, (2) healthcare wants, (3) recommended standards for healthcare, and (4) actual utilization patterns (Berkowitz et al. 1997).

Healthcare Needs

Healthcare needs can be defined in terms of the overall health status of a population or more specifically in terms of the number of conditions that require medical treatment found within that population. Theoretically, it is these needs that justify the existence of the facility. The health conditions included here are those that an objective evaluation—e.g., a physical examination—would uncover within the population. These might be thought of as the *absolute* needs that exist in "nature" without the influence of any other factors. All things being equal, the absolute level of need should not vary much from population to population. The epidemiologically based needs that a team of health professionals would identify in a "sweep" through a community could be considered to represent the "true" prevalence of illness within the population.

A population with certain characteristics can be expected to experience a specified level of various health conditions based on these characteristics. However, these absolute needs, at least in contemporary societies, do not translate directly into demand. In fact, the mismatch between these baseline needs and the ultimate utilization of services is substantial. There are many conditions that go untreated (indeed, even undiagnosed) for various reasons. There are many other conditions for which treatment is obtained that would not be identified among the absolute needs of the population. For example, no team of epidemiologists assessing the healthcare needs of a community is likely to identify the sagging facial skin as a health problem. Yet, tens of thousands of facelifts are performed in the United States every year by medical doctors. The existence of a clinically confirmed need, then, is not a prerequisite for the presence of demand for a service.

Healthcare Wants

Healthcare wants can be conceptualized as the wishes or desires for health services on the part of a population. Unlike needs, wants would not necessarily be uncovered by a sweep of public health investigators through the community. Wants are shaped less by the absolute needs of the population than by the variety of factors that influence the consumption of other goods and services. In fact, many health services that are consumed are considered medically unnecessary or elective. These reflect the operation of wants rather than needs. Examples of these services include tummy tucks and laser eye surgery for nearsightedness. The US healthcare system has adapted itself to the existence of wants as well as needs, and important components of the system cater to those desiring elective services.

The extent to which healthcare wants are a consideration in the planning process depends on the type of planning being performed. Community-wide planning ideally should emphasize the baseline needs of the population, although, realistically, the wants of the population must be taken into consideration if the approach is to be truly comprehensive. At the organizational level, the type of organization and the services it offers will dictate whether needs or wants are the main consideration. Certainly an AIDS clinic deals with basic needs, and there are few elective procedures relevant to the treatment of patients with AIDS. On the other hand, a plastic surgeon specializing in body sculpting is likely to focus on the want-driven demand generated by those motivated by vanity. At the same time, if this plastic surgeon also maintains a reconstructive surgery practice for trauma victims, both wants and needs may be a consideration in planning.

Recommended Standards for Healthcare

The third dimension involves recommended standards for the provision of healthcare. As healthcare professionals have become more attuned to prevention and health maintenance, the number of recommended procedures has increased. This component involves primarily diagnostic procedures or disease management procedures that are recommended for patients with certain symptoms or who are at risk for certain health problems.

The medical community has developed standards that call for diagnostic tests at a certain frequency, the performance of certain medical procedures at specified times, and the implementation of various treatment plans on the part of certain patients. A wide range of diagnostic procedures are now indicated for certain age groups and other population segments at risk of various health conditions. For example, an annual mammogram is recommended for all women over 50, regular prostate exams for all men over 40, and regular cholesterol exams for individuals at risk of certain conditions.

As Americans have become increasingly health conscious, a growing number of standards have been put into place. For example, a few years ago cholesterol tests were limited to patients actively under medical management. Today, cholesterol tests are recommended for everyone at specific intervals, along with pap smears and breast exams for women, prostate exams for men, and a growing number of other diagnostic and screening procedures.

Health Services Utilization

The fourth dimension of demand involves the actual utilization of health services. The utilization level is frequently used as a proxy measure for demand, in that utilization rates can be calculated for virtually any type of health service or product. More data are available related to health services utilization than for the other dimensions of demand, primarily because utilization data are routinely collected for administrative purposes whenever a health service is provided. Utilization rates indicate the level of activity within the healthcare system, as opposed to theoretical demand.

Because of the perceived relationship between demand and utilization, analysts may sometimes work backward from utilization levels and use them as a proxy for demand. However, utilization does not equal demand and, depending on the circumstances, the level of demand may exceed actual utilization or, conversely, utilization levels may exceed reasonable demand for services. For example, there may be less utilization than expected because of limited access to health services. On the other hand, some services may be overutilized for various reasons (e.g., insurance coverage, physician practice patterns) unrelated to the level of demand.

While the use of readily available utilization data may appear to be a no-brainer for estimating demand, this source of data is not without its drawbacks. The "reported cases" method for estimating utilization (and, hence, demand) is limited in the sense that reported cases are just that—only cases that have been reported to healthcare entities. Many individuals with clinically identifiable conditions were never diagnosed and, thus, have never become part of the morbidity record. Many others may have utilized health services but were not actually suffering from the condition for which treatment was sought. These caveats require that health planners use caution in using utilization data as a basis for estimating health services demand.

Factors Influencing Demand

The factors that combine to influence the level of demand today are multiple and their interactions are complex. Knowledge of the cultural background, lifestyle patterns, and financing arrangements of a population may be a better predictor of the type and level of services that will be utilized than knowledge of the actual level of morbidity characterizing that population. The section below describes some of the factors influencing the level of demand.

Population Characteristics

A variety of population characteristics influence the demand for health services. These can be assessed in terms of their effect on health status and health behavior. While a detailed discussion is not possible in this context, the correlation between population characteristics and health status and health behavior is summarized below. (See Pol and Thomas (2011) for a detailed review of the relationship between demographic characteristics and both health status and health behavior.)

At first blush one would think that the state of the population in terms of *biological factors* would play a significant role in health behavior. Although health problems may be thought of as essentially biological problems, the correlation between the morbidity profile of a population and its healthcare utilization is not nearly that direct. While biological characteristics may predispose the individual to various health problems, other factors may eventually determine the type and amount of health services utilized. Biological factors are comparable to the healthcare "needs" described above and may or may not translate into utilization.

Psychological factors correlated with health services demand include personality types and attitudinal traits, as well as the emotional responses evoked by health problems. Clearly, fear, vanity, and pride come into play in the use of health services. The relationship between these factors and health behavior can become exceedingly complex as can be seen in the case of the hypochondriac or in cases where fear pushes one person to seek treatment but prevents another from visiting the physician. In the contemporary US healthcare environment, fear, pride, and vanity play a large role in the demand for many elective procedures (e.g., cosmetic surgery, stomach resection). Because of the individualized nature of psychological traits, it is difficult to directly correlate them with health services utilization. In any case, there is limited useful data available on psychological characteristics available to planners.

Lifestyle and psychographic factors have important implications for healthcare wants, needs, and behavior. Over time, lifestyles have been accorded a growing role in the population's morbidity profile and its health behavior. The propensity to utilize health services may be more highly correlated with lifestyle characteristics than it is with other variables. A specific constellation of health behavior can be associated with each lifestyle category, making lifestyle an important predictor of health behavior. To a certain extent, lifestyles override, or at least refine, differences based on demographic traits.

A number of *demographic characteristics* influence utilization. *Age* is probably the single best predictor of health services utilization. Age is related not only to levels of service utilization but also to the type of services utilized and the circumstances under which they are received. This is true whether the indicator is for inpatient care, tests, and procedures performed, or virtually any other measure of utilization. Different conditions are associated with each age cohort, resulting in demands for differing types of services. The aging of the US population has been a major factor in the changing morbidity profile with an older population suffering from a growing range of chronic conditions.

The *sex* of the consumer is another factor influencing utilization rates. In the United States, females are more involved in the healthcare system than men and are heavier users of health services in general. They tend to visit physicians more often, take more prescription drugs, and, in general, use other facilities and personnel more often. Women are also more aware of the health services that are available and quicker to turn to health professionals when symptoms occur. Their role in influencing the health behavior of others is an important consideration.

Racial and ethnic characteristics influence the demand for health services, with the most clear-cut differences identified between African Americans and non-Hispanic whites. Certain Asian populations and many ethnic groups also display distinctive utilization patterns. While differences in utilization may be traced to differences in the types of health problems experienced by these populations, many of the differences reflect variations in lifestyle patterns and cultural preferences. Different perceptions of and expectations for the healthcare system are also likely to exist among various racial and ethnic populations. The increasing racial and ethnic diversity of the US population has had a significant impact on health behavior.

Marital status is related not only to levels of demand but also to the type of services utilized and the circumstances under which they are received. The marital statuses generally considered are married, never married ("single"), divorced, and widowed. Different levels of morbidity are associated with each marital status category, resulting in demands for differing levels and types of services. In addition, marital status is a main determinant of household structure, and this further influences health status and health behavior. These factors, along with the lifestyles associated with various marital statuses, probably have more impact on utilization than do actual differentials in morbidity.

The *income level* of a population is probably one of the best predictors of the utilization of health services. The distribution of health problems within the population is highly income specific. Income influences both involvement in informal health behaviors and use of formal health services. There is a correlation between income level and the amount of health services utilized, as well as with the types of services utilized and the circumstances under which they are received. This is true whether the indicator is for inpatient care, outpatient care, diagnostic tests, procedures performed, or virtually any other measure of utilization. Factors that are indirectly associated with income (e.g., access to health insurance) further influence both health status and health behavior.

The relationship between *educational level* and utilization resembles that for income. The distribution of health problems within the population is to a certain extent associated with educational status, and the educational level of the population is probably one of the better predictors of the demand for health services. Educational level influences the type of job (and thus income) of individuals as well as their level of health literacy. Education is related to both the type and level of health services utilization.

There is a relatively direct and positive relationship between *occupational and industrial characteristics* of a population and health services utilization. Various occupations are associated with different health risks and access to insurance among other factors. The type of occupation, as well as occupational status, has been correlated with the utilization of health services. Different levels of morbidity are associated with each occupational status category, resulting in a demand for different levels and types of services.

Associations between *religious affiliation and degree of religiosity* and health behavior are probably the most idiosyncratic of any of the demographically related associations. These relationships have been exposed to limited research so that clear patterns are difficult to discern. Further, in the United States, religious affiliation and participation tend to be associated with so many other variables that makes it difficult to isolate the influence of these variables per se. Nevertheless, there is evidence that health status, and the subsequent use of services, is correlated with measures of religiosity and this may be an important factor in some communities.

Technological Factors

The healthcare technology available to a society has a significant influence on the consumption of health services. The services that can be made available will be a function to a great extent of the technology to which the system has access. In the United States, the technological advances of the past few years have routinized many procedures considered impossible in the past and played a major role in changing the setting in which healthcare is provided. During the last two decades of the twentieth century, surgery was transformed from a predominantly inpatient activity to a predominantly outpatient endeavor.

Advances in technology usually lead to higher levels of utilization of the services that are supported by the new technology. Indeed, some operations like laser eye surgery could never have been performed without certain technological advances. Thus, the availability of certain types of technology on the part of a provider is a controlling factor with regard to the services that can be offered.

Technological advances have been responsible for major changes in the practice of medicine and, thus, in utilization patterns. These advances have contributed to the shift to less invasive procedures, facilitated the emergence of home health as a major source of care, and created a home testing "industry." In fact, the short recovery time now possible with less invasive surgical techniques has served to reduce the average length of hospital stay.

The impact of technology has been particularly felt in the area of diagnostic testing in recent years. The variety of tests that can be performed has increased dramatically, including the expanded use of home testing procedures. The amount of diagnostic testing performed by healthcare providers has come under criticism, and Box 5.1 discusses this issue of overtesting.

Box 5.1: Overtesting: Why More Is Not Better
More accurate and more frequent diagnostic tests have been credited with improving the healthcare system's ability to identify and subsequently treat a wide range of medical conditions. The apparent benefits accorded to extensive diagnostic testing have resulted in greater enthusiasm on the part of physicians for testing and established expectations on the part of patients.

Over the past several years some health professionals have raised questions over the necessity for the increased reliance on diagnostic testing on the part of physicians. They argue that extensive and often unwarranted testing adds unnecessary costs to healthcare delivery, results in numerous false positives, actually increases the risk of misdiagnosis, and in the worst cases results in unnecessary, and sometimes fatal, medical intervention. It has been argued that only 20% of medical procedures are evidence based and this issue may be greater for diagnostic testing.

Overtesting may be defined as the use of (1) non-recommended screening tests in asymptomatic patients or (2) more testing than necessary to diagnose patients with signs or symptoms. Given these concerns, what accounts for the growing reliance on diagnostic testing and the insistence of prospective testing on asymptomatic individuals? There are at least five reasons why clinicians overtest and each is discussed in turn.

(continued)

Box 5.1 (continued)

First, there is a belief among physicians that ordering many tests will help detect subclinical disease. When ordering unproven screening tests for asymptomatic patients without good reason, few consider the low yield, high cost per diagnosis made, and considerable toll of false positives. Anecdotal accounts of unexpected diagnoses discovered on "routine" testing help perpetuate overtesting. But even the best tests yield more false positives than true positives when the prevalence of what one is testing for is low. Abnormal results that later prove erroneous engender unnecessary anxiety and needless follow-up testing.

Second, tests are often ordered to practice "defensive medicine." Defensive medicine's role in overtesting is well established. Ninety-one percent of physicians surveyed recently reported ordering more tests or procedures than needed to protect themselves from malpractice suits. Yet overtesting has been cited as a major contributor to $55 billion annual malpractice "industry."

Third, a lack of knowledge or confidence often encourages overtesting. Where deficits exist in individual knowledge, it can feel more reassuring to order batteries of tests. Admittedly, it is difficult if not impossible for practicing physicians to keep up with the various developments in medical knowledge. Unfortunately, it has become common for physicians to try to bridge this gap through excessive testing.

Fourth, some unnecessary testing is due to patients' expectations. Many patients expect panels of tests at regular intervals. Physicians may worry that a patient's satisfaction depends upon ordering many tests, and, indeed, there are cases of patients who "doctor shop" until they obtain the tests they think they need. Ordering tests, like giving antibiotics for viral infections, is often easier than explaining reasons behind not doing so, but the choice is between good medicine and easy medicine. Indeed, the problem of misguided expectations often finds its roots in patients' prior experiences with physicians.

Finally, another insidious, yet remarkably common, contributor to overtesting is the profit motive. The odds of ordering common laboratory tests are up to eight times higher among physicians with financial stakes in an on-site laboratory, even after adjusting for patient and practice differences. Further, it has been pointed out that primary care physicians are often unable to make a profit on office visits; they have to rely on income from diagnostic tests to make up this difference. This is not even considering the fact that once a major piece of biomedical equipment is purchased, the pressure is on to utilize it as much as possible.

Overtesting clearly has a variety of causes but a factor that might underlie many of these is a function of the training received by physicians. Overtesting is often learned in training, either during an era when "more is better" had no evidence to refute it or from a mentor who trained in such an era. Preoperative testing serves as a prime example of the roles defensive medicine and lack of

(continued)

Box 5.1 (continued)

knowledge play in overtesting. Primary care physicians often receive surgeons' requests for panels of laboratory tests preceding minor outpatient procedures, as well as chest radiographs and electrocardiograms that do not appear to take into account the type of surgery, patient's age, or history. While some training programs have begun placing increased emphasis on the importance of judicious testing, their impact on entrenched practices will be a long time in coming.

The increasing interest in population health may force healthcare providers to reassess their reliance on diagnostic tests. With the emphasis on efficiency, patient safety, and outcomes being promoted through this new paradigm, the possibility of a reconsideration of rampart testing becomes more likely.

Reference

Greenberg, J. (2014). Over-testing: Why more is not better. *The American Journal of Medicine*. Retrieved from https://www.amjmed.com/article/ S0002-9343(13)00967-4/pdf

Structural Factors

One final consideration in the examination of demand involves the *structural factors* that encourage or discourage the use of health services. Chief among these are the financial arrangements that exist for paying for care. One indicator of the likely level of demand is the type and extent of health insurance coverage for individuals and families, with the availability of insurance identified as one of the best predictors of the demand for services. When Medicare, for example, introduces reimbursement for a previously uncovered procedure, there is typically a surge in the performance of that procedure. Conversely, when insurers increase the burden of copayments and/or higher deductibles to their insured members, the use of health services often declines in response. When reimbursement for a service is improved, the use of those services tends to increase; the opposite is likely to occur when reimbursement is decreased.

Changing reimbursement arrangements also exerts an influence on practice patterns. Hospitals face restrictions on the services they can provide when health plans are trying to control claims, with changing reimbursement patterns and regulatory pressures forcing physicians to change their practice patterns as well. It has been suggested, in fact, that the reimbursement changes under the Medicare program over the past 25 years have done more to influence the practice patterns of US healthcare providers than the combined effect of technological developments during the same time period.

The second structural consideration has to do with the availability of services in the form of facilities and personnel. Until recent cost-containment measures were instituted, it was apparent that the level of health services utilization was to a great extent a function of the facilities and health professionals available. It was remarkable to observe that, if a community built a new hospital or recruited additional physicians, it suddenly found the demand for hospital care and physician services escalating. On the other hand, situations can be observed in which the demand for services is not being met because of a lack of facilities or personnel. In others an oversupply of facilities and/or personnel may result in the overutilization of health services—i.e., at a level that exceeds reasonable demand.

To the extent that a maldistribution of health facilities and personnel persists in the United States, there are going to be chronic problems with regard to access. Even in urban areas with ample community resources, some of the resources may not be truly accessible to all segments of the population. Until access can be factored out as a variable, it will continue to influence the level of health services utilization.

Research over the past two decades has revealed a surprising variation in the patterns of practice of physicians and, to a lesser extent, hospitals. Far from being an exact science, medicine involves frequent value judgments on the part of physicians and other practitioners. While there are individual differences among physicians within the same market area in terms of the volume and types of services provided to similar patients, there are even more striking variations from market to market (Center for Evaluative Clinical Sciences 1999). Local practice patterns significantly influence the level of service utilization, creating differences of several magnitudes between market areas in some instances. (See Box 5.2 for a description of the Dartmouth Atlas of Healthcare that illustrates variations in practice patterns across the nation.)

Box 5.2: The Dartmouth Atlas of Healthcare
The analysis of healthcare service areas has been hampered historically by a lack of data on realistically defined medical catchment areas. The development of accurate boundaries for market areas often required extensive primary research and, if a large number of markets were involved, this process could be extremely tedious and time consuming. In addition, health planners often did not have access to the data necessary for delineating appropriate service area boundaries.

For more than 20 years Dartmouth University Medical School with funding from the Robert Wood Johnson Foundation has compiled and monitored trends in health services utilization and associated factors. The project uses Medicare data to provide comprehensive information and analysis about national, regional, and local markets, as well as individual hospitals and their affiliated physicians. These reports and the research upon which they are based have helped policy makers, the media, healthcare analysts, and others improve their understanding of the efficiency and effectiveness of the US healthcare system. This valuable data forms the foundation for many of the ongoing efforts to improve health and health systems across America.

(continued)

Box 5.2 (continued)

The researchers have established a publicly available source of data providing researchers, payers, regulator, and innovators with metrics quantifying the temporal and regional patterns of healthcare spending and utilization. The website allows users to download complete data sets of selected variables spanning decades.

Researchers at the Center for Evaluative Clinical Sciences at Dartmouth use Medicare utilization data to divide the United States into clearly identifiable hospital service areas (HSAS) that are subsequently grouped into regional hospital referral areas (HRRs). The most recent data are available for 2016 with the reporting time period depending on the type of data being accessed. Their website provides access to all Atlas reports and publications, as well as interactive tools to allow visitors to view specific regions and perform their own comparisons and analyses.

The results of this project were initially made available in *The Dartmouth Atlas of Healthcare in the United States* but all reports and data are now available online at www.atlasdata.dartmouth.edu. The initial publication was the first widely available reference to detail and compare the dramatic differences in healthcare resources, utilization, and expenditures at the national, regional, and local hospital market levels across the nation. Regional supplements have been produced along with state-specific products for a few states. Reports on categorical diseases (e.g., cardiology) are being produced.

Unlike traditional approaches to service area delineation that follow political boundaries, the Dartmouth study examined sub-county referral patterns in order to establish more realistic service areas. The Dartmouth Atlas offers many revealing insights into the state of our healthcare delivery system, particularly the large variations found from community to community in the utilization rate for health services. The authors have concluded that, indeed, geography is destiny when it comes to the use of health services.

The Atlas allows the analyst to focus on a carefully defined hospital service area and access a wide variety of statistics specific to that service area. Or the analyst may wish to compare a variety of service areas in different parts of the country on the basis of certain characteristics. Information is available at the service area level on hospital resources, expenditures, utilization, and outcomes. Data are also available on Medicare expenditures, distribution of physicians, and performance rates for common procedures. Published reports based on atlas data can be found at https://www.dartmouthatlas.org/research-articles/.

Reference

The Dartmouth Institute. (2019). *Understanding geographic variations in healthcare*. Retrieved from https://www.dartmouthatlas.org/

The Elasticity of Health Services Demand

The recorded level of health services utilization reflects a combination of the needs, wants, and recommended standards of the population, as well as the impact of the structural factors noted above. While each category of "demand" represents a different type of challenge for health services planners, the real challenge is to be able to determine what combination of these factors is relevant for a particular situation. The determination of demand is clearly a multifaceted process that involves a number of different dimensions. While it may be appropriate, depending on the situation, to use either need, want, and recommended standards or utilization as a proxy for demand, ultimately some type of blended concept must be developed that more precisely specifies effective demand.

A surprising fact to many is that the demand for most health services is relatively elastic. Although economists once considered medical care to be the one service for which demand was truly inelastic, this is not a contemporary perspective. Conventional wisdom stated that, if an individual were sick, the individual would consume health services, *and*, if an individual received health services, he/she must be sick. This assumption only applies, however, to rare life-threatening situations for which treatment will almost invariably be received regardless of any other characteristics of the patient or the healthcare system. For every episode requiring lifesaving efforts, there are thousands of healthcare consumption situations, many involving individuals who are not technically sick. Further, as lifestyles and social determinants have come to influence health status and health behavior more dominantly, the potential for elasticity has increased.

Examples of the elasticity of sickness can be found in wartime when military physicians at induction centers adopt a quite different standard of what constitutes disability than in peacetime ... or in the old Soviet factory system where absenteeism was routinely granted for health reasons when the quotas were being met but no illness was recognized when the factory was not meeting its quota. US society today, in fact, reflects this notion of elasticity in that a larger proportion of the population is under medical management than at any time in the past. However, it could be argued that the population as a whole is healthier than it has ever been. In this situation, there is a relatively low level of illness but a relatively high level of sickness. In fact, it has even been argued that the truly ill get the least medical care while those who are healthiest receive the most.

Measuring Health Services Utilization

The indicators that are commonly used to measure health services utilization are discussed in the sections that follow. Each of the key utilization indicators is discussed in turn, although the various aspects of these indicators cannot be discussed in detail in the limited space available here and not all possible indicators are included. (See Box 5.3 for an overview of coding systems employed to measure utilization.)

Box 5.3: Coding Systems in Healthcare

The health services planner is likely to be overwhelmed by the variety of coding schemes that are utilized in the US healthcare system. Unfortunately, a number of different systems are in use, and it is impossible to understand the functioning of the system without a working knowledge of the manner in which conditions and procedures are classified and recorded. The classification systems briefly described below are commonly used; however, more information than can be provided here will ultimately be required to gain an understanding of these various systems.

International Classification of Diseases

The most widely recognized and used disease classification system is the *International Classification of Diseases*, now in its tenth edition (abbreviated ICD-10). The ICD system is the official classification scheme developed by the World Health Organization (WHO) within the United Nations. In the United States a version of the ICD system is used that reflects the modifications necessary in keeping with current medical practice in American hospitals. The ICD-9 version was replaced in the United States by ICD-10 in 2015.

The ICD system is designed for the classification of morbidity and mortality information and for the indexing of diseases and procedures that occur within hospital settings and certain other healthcare settings. The present classification system includes two components: diagnoses and procedures. Two different sets of codes are assigned to the respective components and the codes are detailed enough that very fine distinctions can be made among different diagnoses and procedures. (A different system is used for recording procedures in physicians' offices and other outpatient settings.)

Originally, the ICD system was designed to facilitate communication concerning diseases worldwide, to provide a basis for statistical record-keeping and epidemiological studies, and to facilitate research into the quality of healthcare. However, additional functions have evolved in which the system is used as a coding scheme for facilitating payment for health services, evaluating utilization patterns, and studying the appropriateness of healthcare costs. While the epidemiologist may find this system invaluable for studying the distribution and spread of disease, its primary use within the US healthcare system has come to be related to financial management (i.e., as a coding system for patient billing).

The diagnosis component of ICD-10 comprises 22 disease and injury categories and 2 supplementary classifications. In each category, major specific conditions are listed in detail. The expanded number of characters of the ICD-10 diagnosis codes provides greater specificity to identify disease etiology, anatomic site, and severity.

ICD-10 Code Structure:

Characters 1–3—Category

(continued)

Box 5.3 (continued)
Characters 4–6—Etiology, anatomic site, severity, or other clinical detail
Character 7—Extension

The following example shows the more detailed information gained through the added characters.

S52: Fracture of forearm

S52.5: Fracture of lower end of radius

S52.52: Torus fracture of lower end of radius

S52.521: Torus fracture of lower end of right radius

S52.521A: Torus fracture of lower end of right radius, initial encounter for closed fracture

In the above example, S52 is the category. The fourth and fifth characters of "5" and "2" provide additional clinical detail and anatomic site. The sixth character in this example indicates laterality, i.e., right radius. The seventh character, "A," is an extension that provides additional information, which means "initial encounter" in this example.

The supplementary classifications are a concession to the fact that many nonmedical factors are involved in the onset of disease, responses to disease, and use of services. These additional categories attempt to identify causes of disease or injury states that are external to the biophysical system.

Procedure categories were introduced for the first time with the ICD-9 version. The procedure component is divided into major categories keyed to specific body systems (e.g., nervous system, digestive system), and one involves diagnostic procedures and residual therapeutic procedures. A two-digit scheme is used, with a code being carried out to two decimal places when necessary to provide more detail. The system was designed to accommodate usage to both hospital and ambulatory care settings.

Much like the disease-coding scheme, the procedure classification system is heavily used for financial management and determination of patterns of utilization, although it retains its uses for epidemiological studies.

Current Procedural Terminology
While the ICD classification system focuses on procedures performed under the auspices of a hospital or clinic, the *Current Procedural Terminology* (CPT) system relates exclusively to procedures and services performed by physicians. Physician-provided procedures and services are divided into five categories: medicine, anesthesiology, surgery, radiology, and pathology and laboratory services. In its fourth edition (CPT-4), this system identifies each procedure and service with a five-digit code number. This method attempts to facilitate accurate, specific, and uniform coding for physician offices.

(continued)

Box 5.3 (continued)

Examples of coded procedures include surgical operations, office visits, and X-ray readings. The most accurate descriptor is determined from the CPT guidebook by the provider, and that code is assigned. In addition to the identifying code, the five-digit number allows for modifiers to be appended. Modifiers may indicate situations in which an adjunctive service was performed. The manual also contains some useful information on accepted definitions for levels of care and extensiveness of consultation. Some 7000 variations of procedures and services are catalogued.

Another set of codes has been developed to supplement the CPT codes. The Common Procedure Coding System (HCPCS) was developed by the Healthcare Financing Administration before its name was changed to Centers for Medicare and Medicaid Services. HCPCS involves a listing of services provided by physicians and other providers that are not covered under the CPT coding scheme. These include certain physician services along with nonphysician services such as ambulance, physical therapy, and durable medical equipment.

Diagnosis-Related Groups

Spiraling healthcare costs during the 1980s launched an era of cost containment. Efforts aimed at slowing healthcare expenditures have been initiated primarily by the federal government in response to the financial demands placed on the Medicare program, the Medicaid program, and other federally supported healthcare initiatives. The most significant step in this regard was the introduction of prospective payment as the basis for reimbursement for health services rendered under the Medicare program. Hospitals, physicians, and certain other providers of healthcare are informed at the beginning of the financial accounting period about the amount that the federal government will pay for inpatient services for a particular category of patient.

The prospective payment system (PPS) limits the amount of reimbursement for services provided to each category of patient based on rates determined by the Centers for Medicare and Medicaid Services (CMS), the federal agency that administers the Medicare program.

The basis for prospective payment is the *diagnosis-related group* (DRG). Using the patient's primary diagnosis as the starting point, CMS has developed a mechanism for grouping all hospital patients into over 500 DRGs. The idea is to link payment to the consumption of resources, with the assumption that a patient's diagnosis should be the best predictor of resource utilization. The primary diagnosis is modified by such factors as other coexisting diagnoses, the presence of complications, the patient's age, and the usual length of hospital stay in order to derive the 500+ diagnostic categories.

For many purposes—e.g., general reporting, statistical analysis, and planning—DRGs represent too fine a distinction among conditions. For these purposes, DRGs have been grouped into 23 major diagnostic categories (MDCs). These MDCs are based primarily on the different body systems.

(continued)

Box 5.3 (continued)

DRGs are categorized as either medical DRGs or surgical DRGs. In the calculation of reimbursement for services, each DRG is given a weight. The weight is the major factor in a complicated formula for determining the rate of reimbursement for each hospital participating in the Medicare program.

Although introduced for use in federal healthcare programs, the DRG system was quickly adopted by other health plans as a basis for reimbursement. This system has become the standard classification system in use for hospitalized patients in the United States and has been adopted by other countries around the world.

Ambulatory Payment Classification

As the prospective payment system based on DRGs was being implemented to control the cost of inpatient care for Medicare, much of the medical treatment was being shifted to an outpatient or ambulatory setting. Any cost savings realized by the Medicare program on the inpatient side were being eroded by growing expenditures for ambulatory services. This situation prompted the development of a system similar to DRGs for the outpatient environment referred to as *ambulatory payment classification* (APC).

As with DRGs, APCs focus on the facility component of healthcare costs and not on physician charges. The intent of CMS is to contain outpatient facility costs, introduce some controls over outpatient services utilization, and create a prospective system that works similar to DRGs. The basis for the fee is the patient visit rather than the entire episode as in the case of DRGs. An APC-specific diagnosis code has been developed and CPT codes continue to be used to classify procedures and ancillary services. Introduced in August of 2000, APC codes are now being widely used in outpatient facilities.

Diagnostic and Statistical Manual

The definitive reference for the classification of mental disorders is the Diagnostic and Statistical Manual of Mental Disorders (DSM), which is currently in its fifth edition (DSM-5). Published by the American Psychiatric Association, the DSM remains the last word on mental illness classification despite long-standing criticism of its scheme. Its 18 major categories of mental illness and more than 450 identified mental conditions are considered exhaustive. The DSM is derived in part from the ICD. Like the ICD, it is structured around five-digit codes. The fourth digit indicates the variety of the disorder under discussion, and the fifth digit refers to any special consideration related to the case. Unlike the other classification systems discussed, the DSM contains detailed descriptions of the disorders categorized therein and thus serves as a useful reference.

References

Abraham, M., Ahlman, J. T., Connelly, J. L., et al. (2010). *Current procedural terminology*. Chicago, IL: American Medical Association.

(continued)

Box 5.3 (continued)

American Psychiatric Association. (2013). *Diagnostic and statistical manual of mental disorders* (5th ed.). Arlington, VA: American Psychiatric Publishing.

Center for Medicare and Medicaid Services. (2011). *CMS adopts policy and payment changes for outpatient care in hospitals and ambulatory surgery centers.* Retrieved from https://www.cms.gov/newsroom/press-releases/cms-adopts-policy-and-payment-changes-outpatient-care-hospitals-and-ambulatory-surgical-centers

World Health Organization. (2016). *International statistical classification of diseases and related health problems* (10th ed.). Geneva: World Health Organization.

Hospital admissions is one of the most frequently used indicators of health services utilization, since the hospital represents the focal point for treatment in the system. The terms "admissions" and "discharges" are used to refer to episodes of inpatient hospital utilization. The hospital admission rate serves as a proxy for a variety of other indicators, since hospital admissions are correlated with tests conducted, surgeries performed, and allocation of other resources. Since hospital care is both labor and capital intensive, one admission carries a great deal of weight in terms of significance in overall healthcare expenditures. Admissions may be measured for the entire community or the particular facility or be decomposed into components of utilization. This could involve the calculation of admission rates by clinical specialty, demographic attribute, geographic origin, payor category, and so on.

Patient days refers to the number of hospital days generated by a particular population. The total number of patient days is calculated and converted to a rate (i.e., the number of patient days per 1000 residents) and is calculated in terms of the number of patient days generated per 1000 residents. This indicator refines hospital admissions as an indicator by reflecting the total utilization of resources, since measuring patient days serves to adjust for variations in length of stay for various conditions. Like admission rates, patient days may be calculated by diagnosis, type of hospital, patient origin, and payer category. The long-term trend has involved a steady decline in patient days, and changes in reimbursement procedures have made the patient day more of a standard unit for the measurement of resource utilization than the actual hospital admission.

Another indicator used to measure hospitalization is the *average length of stay*. This is typically reported in terms of the average number of days that patients remain in the facility during a specified time period. This metric is also based on the patient day indicator and involves dividing the total patient days generated for a time period (usually a year) and then dividing the total by, in this case, 365 days. This indicator provides a good measure of resource utilization as well. In fact, Medicare and many healthcare plans reimburse hospitals on a per diem rate.

There are several *other facility indicators* that might also be mentioned. While not all of them carry the significance of hospital admissions, each is important in its own way. Utilization rates may be calculated for nursing homes, hospital emergency rooms, hospital outpatient departments, freestanding emergency centers, freestanding minor medical centers, freestanding surgery centers, and freestanding diagnostic centers, among others.

Perhaps one of the most useful indicators of health services utilization is the volume of physician encounters. This is typically measured in terms of *physician office visits* although telephone contact and physician visits to hospitalized patients are sometimes considered. Since the physician is the "gatekeeper" for most types of health services, and since virtually everyone uses a physician's services at some time, physician utilization is a more direct measure of utilization levels than hospital admissions. Physician utilization rates are often broken down by specialty, since the level of utilization for different specialties varies dramatically.

There are *other types of personnel* for whom utilization rates might be calculated. Most of these, like physicians and dentists, are independent practitioners who practice without the supervision of other medical personnel. Examples include optometrists, podiatrists, chiropractors, nurse practitioners, and physician's assistants, as well as various mental health counselors and therapists. Other healthcare personnel, who generally cannot operate independently, but for whom utilization rates might be calculated, include home health nurses and various technical personnel. Physical therapists and speech therapists are other categories of healthcare personnel for whom utilization rates might be developed if, for example, the analyst was involved in planning for rehabilitation services.

As the importance of home healthcare has grown in recent years, the volume of *home healthcare visits* has taken on more importance. The range of services provided has been expanded and a much broader segment of the patient population is considered appropriate for home care. Home-care utilization is typically measured in terms of visits by various types of personnel. Thus, a population might be considered to have a certain number of home nurse visits or home physical therapist visits as indicators of utilization. Alternatively, the number of residences (i.e., the rate per 1000) receiving home care might be calculated.

Another indicator of the use of health services that is sometimes used is the level of *drug utilization*. Although patient care providers typically have limited use for information on drug utilization, analysts representing other entities such as pharmaceutical companies do. These analyses typically focus on the consumption of prescription drugs, since these (rather than over-the-counter medicine) are thought to more closely reflect actual utilization of the formal healthcare system. While the level of drug prescribing can be determined from physician and pharmacist records, rates of consumption for nonprescription drugs must be determined more indirectly.

Rates of prescription drug utilization are typically calculated in two different ways. First, the number of prescriptions *written* by physicians and other clinicians is tracked, and this can be converted to the number of prescriptions within a given year per 1000 population. Alternatively, the average number of prescriptions written annually per person may be calculated. Second, the number of prescriptions *filled* might be determined and the average number and rate per 1000 residents are calculated. The former information is obtained from surveys of consumers or physician offices and the latter from pharmacy records. There is inevitably a discrepancy between the number of prescriptions written and the number filled. The question of the ultimate disposition of prescribed drugs also arises as some drugs are never consumed and others may be diverted for inappropriate and even illegal purposes.

The indicators of utilization considered the most salient will depend on the level of planning that is taking place and the type of plan. In the case of community-wide planning, the planner will probably be interested in most of the indicators discussed above, due to the comprehensive nature of this type of planning. At the organization level, the type of utilization indicators of interest depends on the nature of the organization and the type of plan that is being implemented.

Changing Patient Characteristics

The demographic trends that played out over the last quarter of the twentieth century dramatically reshaped the patient population in the United States, with major consequences for healthcare marketing. By the second decade of the twenty-first century, seniors accounted for nearly one-third of patients, and the children who had been ubiquitous in physicians' offices 20 years earlier were declining as a proportion of the patient population. The proportion of the US population that is non-Hispanic white has shrunk considerably, and a majority of school-aged children are now from minority populations. While the greatest increase has been recorded for the Hispanic population, the proportion of citizens from all nonwhite racial and ethnic groups has increased dramatically, bringing considerable diversity to physician waiting rooms. Women continue to outnumber men (by more than 6 million), meaning that the majority of patients are female.

Importantly, the proportion of adults who are married has declined dramatically since the baby boom generation. Not only are fewer people marrying, but also those who do are having fewer children. Thus, fewer patients live in traditional nuclear families or are even part of a family household. Nevertheless, the healthcare system still operates on the assumption that people live in families—and are covered by family health insurance plans—and that patients have household support to assist with their healthcare needs.

Since health services planning is a prospective endeavor, it is important to be able to predict future characteristics of a population. This is a relatively easy exercise for some attributes but more challenging for others. Either way, planners must be able to project the characteristics of patients into the future in order to effectively plan for anticipated changes in the demand for services.

Estimating the Demand for Health Services

Knowledge about the current level of demand for health services, however measured, is important for the planning process. Even more important, however, is the anticipated future level of demand characterizing the population under study. A variety of techniques have been developed for projecting future demand, and three of these are discussed below.

Traditional Utilization Projections

The simplest and most straightforward approach to projecting the utilization of health services involves straight-line projections that extend historical trends. For example, it was common in the past to review several years' experience with hospital admissions and then extrapolate this trend into the future. This approach was very intuitive in that, if the trend had been upward, it continued to rise. On the other hand, if a downward trend had been recorded, the assumption was that historical patterns would persist in the future.

Few market analysts would utilize this approach in today's healthcare environment. Developments external to the healthcare arena have such an impact on the demand for services and ultimate patterns of utilization that extrapolating from the past to the future is not practical, with the past no longer being a guide to the future. This situation has forced a much more sophisticated approach to the projection of utilization.

Population-Based Models

The most powerful factor in terms of predicting health services utilization is the size of the population. A change in the number of people served tends to have the greatest impact in terms of changes in utilization expected in the future. Because of the importance of population size and because population projections are likely to be both readily available and fairly reliable, population-based projections have become the most common predictive technique used in forecasting health services use.

The easiest approach is simply to multiply the projected population by known utilization rates. Thus, population-based models involve two components: (1) appropriate population estimates and projections and (2) accurate utilization rates. Population estimates and projections are available from a variety of sources and for various levels of geography.

While some benefit can be derived from basing demand estimates on the total population, the analysis typically examines utilization in terms of age and sex. Changes in age distribution occur frequently and these changes can have a major effect on utilization. Utilization patterns for males and females vary significantly, and these must be taken into consideration. The easiest way to express the effect of age is to employ sex- and age-specific use rates. As more data have become available, the population may also be examined in terms of race, income, insurance, or some other attribute.

Utilization rates may be expressed in terms of hospital admissions or physician visits per 1000 residents per year, patient days per 1000 residents per year, live births per 1000 females aged 15–44 per year, and so forth. These rates can be adjusted to account for regional differences when appropriate. The utilization rates of interest can be applied to different age/sex categories and adjusted for other attributes to the extent they are available.

While population-based demand projection models in all of their permutations offer an intuitively appealing approach to the issue, there are limitations to their usefulness. On the one hand, the mobility of the population in contemporary America introduces an element of uncertainty into the projection process. The cohort effect certainly plays a role in determining differential utilization patterns, and it is no longer safe to contend, for example, that the utilization patterns of 65-year-olds today will be the same as for 65-year-olds 20 years ago. Thus, applying an age-specific rate to today's elderly that is based on past experience may be risky.

Utilization rates themselves are given to change. All things being equal in terms of population characteristics, there are numerous factors that influence utilization rates. Many of these have already been discussed including availability of services, financing arrangements, and level of managed care penetration. Who could have predicted, for example, the decline in hospital admissions that resulted from the introduction of the Medicare prospective payment system and the emergence of managed care? A technically sound methodology would combine the impact of both (1) changes in population composition and (2) changes in the prevalence rates associated with various subgroups within the population. The influence of developments of this type makes the prediction of future levels of utilization a challenge. Box 5.4 describes the use of predictive analytics in projecting health status and health behavior.

Box 5.4: Using Predictive Modeling for Health Services Planning
Health planning requires access to data on a population's health conditions and its service utilization. This information is often not available and, even if available, may not be accessible in a timely fashion. Effective planning requires estimates of current health conditions and utilization as well as projections for both of these categories of data. Predictive modeling can be utilized to provide the data necessary for developing estimates and projections of the health conditions affecting a population and the volume and type of health services utilized. Metrics are generated for disease incidence and prevalence as well as for anticipated utilization of outpatient and inpatient services. While these data are computer generated, they can provide important benchmarks and planning metrics for defined populations to assist the work of healthcare providers, health plans, employers, and other interested parties. These predictive models can be interfaced with population health assessments and adapted to a wide range of healthcare initiatives.

The principal inputs for the typical predictive model are (1) National Center for Health Statistics (NCHS) rates for incidence/prevalence of disease and health services utilization and (2) the population count for a specified population by age and sex in 5-year intervals. Population counts may be keyed to a geographical area (including custom geographies) or any defined popula-

---

(continued)

Box 5.4 (continued)

tion and NCHS survey data provided through several recurring studies are utilized for this model. Predictive modeling is applicable to most defined populations of patients, health plan members, employees, and consumers. The delineation of a population may be in terms of a geographic area or another appropriate basis for segmentation (e.g., age, household income, educational attainment, Mosaic lifestyle group).

These population health assessment methods can be applied to a wide variety of planning requirements. An application may be as simple as estimating the number of diabetes cases in a given ZIP Code or as complex as a complete set of disease prevalence and service utilization estimates for a comprehensive community health needs assessment (CHNA). Illustrations of the range of healthcare applications for the assessment process include:

- Profiling a health service area, defined geography, or target population
- Selecting a site for a clinic, urgent care center, or other facility
- Performing feasibility studies for a clinic or other health facility
- Determining the requirements for specific resources in a geographic area in terms of services, personnel, facilities, and equipment
- Developing a strategic plan, business plan, or marketing plan for a healthcare organization
- Determining the combination of physician specialists required to serve a defined population
- Developing resource allocation and network development plans for health insurers and ACOs
- Determining over- or underutilization of health services for a defined patient population

Predictive modeling does not require access to personal health data but can interface estimates and projections with actual data to develop a more comprehensive view of a population's morbidity patterns and likely health services utilization.

Econometric Models

Econometric models include a variety of different techniques for projecting future phenomena in complex situations. In their simplest form, econometric models represent a type of time series analysis. In effect, they attempt to statistically improve on the projection model discussed above that extrapolates past trends into the future.

Econometric models use equations that project utilization as a function of the interplay of various independent variables. With a complex phenomenon like the utilization of health services, it makes sense to generate forecasts based on multiple factors rather than a single one. The more the factors employed in predicting future utilization, it is argued, the greater the probability of accurately predicting trends.

Econometric prediction addresses such factors in a series of mathematical expressions. The equation that is ultimately used is the one that best "fits the curve" in terms of historic demand, and can, thus, be extrapolated into the future. For this complex form of econometrics to work, of course, projections are needed for numerous independent variables in the equation.

Many analysts have attempted to apply econometric models to the prediction of health services demand. In today's environment, however, econometric models have limited utility because of the unpredictability and instability characterizing the patient population and developments in the delivery and financing of health services.

References

Berkowitz, E. N., Pol, L. G., & Thomas, R. K. (1997). *Healthcare market research*. Burr Ridge, IL: Irwin Professional Publishing.
Center for Evaluative Clinical Sciences. (1999). *The Dartmouth atlas of healthcare*. Hanover, NH: Center for Evaluative Clinical Sciences.
Pol, L. G., & Thomas, R. K. (2011). *The demography of health and healthcare*. New York: Plenum.

Further Reading

Babalol, O. (2017). Consumers and their demand for healthcare. *Journal of Health and Medical Economics, 3*, 6. Retrieved from http://health-medical-economics.imedpub.com/consumers-and-their-demand-for-healthcare.php?aid=21061
Bouwens, J., & Krueger, D. L. (2019). Embracing change: The healthcare industry focuses on new growth drivers and leadership requirements. Retrieved from https://www.russellreynolds.com/insights/thought-leadership/embracing-change-the-healthcare-industry-focuses-on-new-growth-drivers-and-leadership-requirements
Morder Intelligence. (2019). Cosmetic surgery and services market: Growth, trends, and forecast (2019–2024). Retrieved from https://www.mordorintelligence.com/industry-reports/cosmetic-surgery-and-services-market

Chapter 6
The Planning Process

Introduction

Health planning involves a series of steps that move the process from the first organizational meeting to a finalized plan (and beyond). Although the planning process has become increasingly standardized, there is no *one* process that fits all situations. While the variations that exist share common traits, each takes a slightly different approach. The process for community-wide planning is somewhat different from that for organization-level planning, and each type of organizational plan calls for variations in the planning process.

Despite these differences, all planning processes include certain components, and the sections that follow offer a "generic" outline of this process. The extent to which this process varies for different levels of planning and different types of plans will be noted in the discussion.

The Planning Model

The model diagrammed in Fig. 6.1 presents a general framework for the planning process. It applies to virtually any type of planning and is charming in its simplicity. There are two types of factors that influence the current status of the community's health system or the healthcare organization: internal factors and external factors. Combined, these determine the current situation of the community or the organization. Once the desired situation has been specified, the difference between the existing situation and the desired situation (the "planning gap") can be determined. Once identified, the planning gap becomes the target for subsequent planning activities. Although the discussion that follows suggests a much more complicated process, ultimately health services planning comes down to the ability to identify gaps and address them (Fig. 6.1).

© Springer Science+Business Media, LLC, part of Springer Nature 2021   115
R. K. Thomas, *Health Services Planning*,
https://doi.org/10.1007/978-1-0716-1076-3_6

Fig. 6.1 The Planning Process

Steps in the Planning Process

Planning for Planning

A great deal of preparation is involved in the planning process; thus "planning for planning" consumes much of the early effort. The first step in any planning process involves identifying the mandate under which the planners are to operate. The planning process may be initiated, for example, in response to a felt need within the community, a health problem that is not being adequately addressed, or a crisis faced by the organization. It may also be driven by some political motivation or some immediate financial consideration. The "why" of the planning process is likely to color all subsequent activities and should be addressed early in the process.

Much of the early planning activity is organizational in nature. It involves identifying the key stakeholders, decision makers, and resource persons that must be taken into consideration. At the community level, identifying these players and soliciting participation is as much of a political process as it is a technical process. While there is no foolproof combination of team members that assures success, certain categories of participants must be included whether the planning is taking place at the community level or the organization level. These include representatives of the various stakeholders, key decision makers, opinion leaders, and representatives of various substantive areas. It is important that the planning process be inclusive, involving people who have significant influence in the community (for example, elected officials), as well as the people who are most likely to be affected by the plan (such as residents of low-income neighborhoods).

In order to plan for the total community, participants should include representatives of both private sector providers and public health agencies, both physical medicine and mental health interests, and representatives of acute, chronic, and long-term care services. To be truly community based, representatives of "marginal" clinical groups such as chiropractors, podiatrists, psychologists, and alternative therapists should be included.

At the organization level, the selection of key participants is equally important and likely to be "political" to a certain extent. In fact, it is much easier for one inappropriately chosen participant to torpedo the planning effort with an organization that it is at the community level due to the more "public" nature of the latter. The selection of participants is particularly ticklish within an organization, in that the process may have negative outcomes for some of those chosen to participate.

At the organization level, the internal participants in the planning process should be drawn from a wide range of functional areas. To the extent it exists, the planning department should drive this process in partnership with the organization's leadership. The staff of the marketing department should play a key role and, if there is a research department, the efforts of the two should be combined. Depending on the issues, finance, human resources, and other key departments, including clinical departments, may play a role. Moreover, it is hard to imagine an efficient planning process being carried out today without the full cooperation of the information technology department.

The planning process itself needs to be outlined at this stage. The format for the process, the objectives of the process (not the plan at this point), and such practical issues as the frequency of planning team meetings should be considered. Importantly, the purpose of these meetings—e.g., work sessions, progress reporting, and decision-making—must be determined.

Stating Assumptions

One of the critical steps at the outset (and actually at any juncture in the planning process) is the stating of assumptions. "Assumptions" are the understandings that drive the planning process, and, if they are not specified early in the process, planning team members may find themselves well down the road holding conflicting notions of what the process is really about. Assumptions might be made concerning the macro-environment (e.g., community economic conditions), the regulatory environment (e.g., current CON regulations), or the microenvironment (e.g., shifts in market shares   among competitors). Assumptions can also relate to demographic trends, reimbursement practices, internal resource availability, and any number of other aspects of the health-care system.

From a community-wide planning perspective, an assumption might be made, on the one hand, that any plan that disturbs existing practice patterns will not be accept-able. Obviously, such an assumption places serious constraints on the process. On the other hand, an assumption may be made that, for this planning initiative, "nothing is sacred," thereby giving the planners, theoretically at least, a free hand to consider any options. These assumptions might be thought of as the "facts of life" with which the planners are going to have to live.

Assumptions should be made by organization-level planners about the market that is being considered. These would include assumptions related to the nature of the market (and its population), the political climate, the position of other providers, and so forth. At the organization level, assumptions might also be made concerning the internal environment. These may relate to financial status, personnel capabilities, existing contracts, and the like. For example, the assumption that virtually no finan-cial resources are available internally for plan implementation is an important con-straining factor.

Assumptions should be stated with regard to the scope of the planning process. While it is hoped that the process at the community level will be comprehensive, this cannot be assumed. There may be reasons that certain aspects of the system are not taken into consideration in this process. For example, it has not made sense in the past to include local military facilities in the planning process, since they involve distinct services that cater to a discrete population, with neither services nor popula-tion overlapping with the community. The scope of the process is clearly an area of potential controversy, and assumptions regarding the scope should be agreed upon as early in the process as possible.

Some assumptions can—and should—be stated at the outset of the planning pro-cess. Others will be developed as information is collected and more in-depth knowl-edge is gained concerning the community, its healthcare needs, and its resources. The same will be true in the planning process for an organization. Although assump-tions will undoubtedly be refined as the planning process continues, it is important to begin with at least general assumptions identified.

Reviewing the Mission

In any planning initiative, the mission(s) of the entities involved should be considered. If no planning process is currently in place at the community level, a mission statement should be developed early in the process. If a planning process is already established, the mission driving that process needs to be revisited. In those rare cases in which a single agency is charged with the development of the community-wide plan, the mission statement of that agency should be reviewed. The mission established for community-wide planning will inevitably be broad and idealistic and should guide the goal-setting process.

At the organization level, the mission statement of the organization should be examined early in the planning process. Even if a mission statement is in place, it is easy to lose sight of the organization's mission, particularly in the day-to-day operation of a healthcare organization. It is important to reach consensus on the mission, since the thrust of subsequent planning will be guided by the mission statement. In a rapidly changing environment, it may be found that the activities of the organization may no longer match its mission statement, and the nature of the organization's current activities may call for a revised mission statement. Until some level of consensus on mission is reached, it is not likely that much effective planning will take place within the organization.

Initial Information Gathering

No planning process should ever begin "cold." A lack of knowledge displayed in the first organizational meeting is likely to forever sour any possible progress. As much before-the-fact knowledge as possible should be obtained from any available source. For community-wide planners, this may involve a "literature review" of materials that have been prepared on the local healthcare system. Newspaper articles that describe various aspects of the system may be available, and many communities produce health-related publications. Increasingly, community report cards are being developed by various organizations, and this information may help inform organizations for planning purposes. Some of these, like policy and procedure manuals, may have been developed for internal use. Others, like marketing material, are for public consumption. Publicly held companies and organizations that are tax exempt must both file reports on their status. The document review should include any previous plans that have been developed and any research projects or consultant studies that have been conducted. While these reports are likely to have limitations, they can provide at least a partial view of certain aspects of the planning target.

This review should be accompanied by interviews with knowledgeable individuals within the community, both inside and outside the medical establishment. For community-wide planning, the scope should be as wide as possible. There are always going to be varying "versions" of the healthcare story, with the assessment of the system changing with one's perspective. At a minimum, one should be familiar with the perspectives of the key institutional players, major decision makers and opinion leaders, and political influentials. Importantly, the perspective of community residents should be incorporated at an early stage.

This initial information gathering process should also reveal something about the history of the current system. While planning is futuristic in its outlook, its future is likely to be inextricably intertwined with its past. Current relationships take the form they do because of historical developments, and past experiences and relationships will color any future developments. Past relationships—both positive and negative—are likely to have implications for the future.

Leveraging initial information is equally valid at the organization level. The organization's "life history" will be instructive in developing a plan for its future. The corporate culture will exert a strong influence on the planning process, and this culture typically can only be understood in the light of its historical development. For this reason, a historical review of the organization is an essential component of most internal audits.

During initial information gathering, the major issues that are driving the process should be identified. While these issues will be continuously clarified, the initial identification of issues provides a starting point for further research. While the issues at the community level are likely to be much broader than those for the organization, they have the same effect in terms of the planning process. They may or may not be the issues that are ultimately addressed, but the fact that someone considers them to be issues must be taken into account.

This background research should identify the decision-making process for the community healthcare system, at least to the extent it can be isolated. How are decisions made with regard to the expenditure of public healthcare funds? What healthcare organizations are influential politically? Who has the grassroots support of the community?

At the organization level, the identification of decision makers is even more important. The ultimate success of the planning process will have as much to do with internal relationships as it does with external factors. Initial information gathering should determine who plays what roles and how the relative clout of the respective parties is likely to impact the planning process. A lack of buy-in from key decision makers is a "death sentence" for any plan.

As part of this process, any potential barriers to the planning initiative should be identified. Certain barriers are likely to become obvious during this early stage of inquiry, and individuals or organizations that are clearly resistant to the planning process are likely to surface. Any immutable patterns of behavior on the part of members of the medical community should be identified. While some barriers can be surmounted, others might not be. These understandings become a part of the assumptions that drive the process.

The Project Plan

Early in the process of planning for planning, a project plan should be developed. The project plan systematically depicts the various steps in the planning process and specifies the sequence that they should follow. The project plan also indicates the relationships that exist between the various tasks and, importantly, the extent to which the completion of some tasks is a prerequisite for the accomplishment of others.

Project planning tools like Gantt charts help create a framework within which planners can work. Project management tools such as the program evaluation review technique (PERT) and the critical path method (CPM) offer useful aids for estimating the resources needed for the project and clarifying the planning and control process. PERT involves dividing the total research project into its smallest component activities, determining the sequence in which these activities must be performed, attaching a time estimate for each activity, and presenting them in the form of a flowchart that allows a visual inspection of the overall process. The time estimates allow planners to determine the critical path through the chart. These tools can be readily accessed today using computer software packages. (See Fig. 6.2 for a simplified depiction of a Gantt chart.)

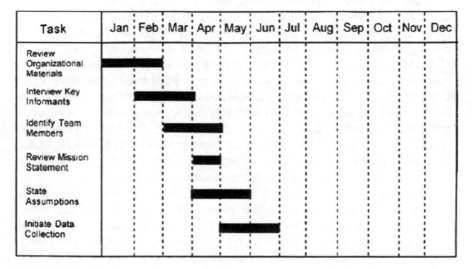

Fig. 6.2 Sample Gantt chart

Environmental Assessment

The first step in the formal data collection process involves an environmental assessment (sometimes referred to as an "environmental scan"), regardless of whether the planner focuses on a community or an organization (sometimes referred to as an "environmental scan"). This assessment typically begins at the macro-level of analysis. This would ordinarily involve analysis at the national level, although, for some organizations with multinational operations, it could take place at the international level. The macro-level analysis should be followed by analysis at the regional level if appropriate. The environmental assessment at the state level is particularly important, given the role that states play in the regulation of healthcare. Finally, the assessment should address the microlevel or the local environment. Ultimately, most healthcare organizations operate locally, and the local environment should be carefully analyzed within the context of national and state developments. The topics to be covered are identified below, with more detail provided in Chaps. 7 and 8.

As a starting point for the environmental assessment, broad *societal trends* should be analyzed and their implications for the local environment considered. Among those to be considered are demographic trends, economic developments, lifestyle trends, and even shifts in attitudes. The same type of analysis should be applied to *healthcare industry trends* to identify any developments that are likely to affect the community or the organization. These could include trends in reimbursement (discussed below), changing organizational structures within the delivery system, and introduction of new treatment modalities.

Regulatory, political, and legal developments should be reviewed for their implications for the community or the organization. At the federal and state levels, a number of regulatory functions exist, while states have primary responsibility for licensing health facilities and personnel. The potential impact of regulatory, political, and legal developments at all levels of government should be considered.

Developments in the area of *technology* can exert a major influence on the course of the healthcare system. Technology here is considered in the broadest possible light, covering medical and surgical treatment modalities, pharmaceuticals, biomedical equipment, and information management. Many observers have been surprised at the impact of the Internet on healthcare, and the emergence of social media is having significant implications for healthcare organizations. Other technology trends that are likely to impact the system or the organization should be identified.

Reimbursement arrangements related to the provision of care are a major factor in determining the nature of a healthcare system. The reimbursement practices of Medicare have a substantial impact on practice patterns, and the influence of managed care on the healthcare system cannot be ignored. Anticipated changes in reimbursement are the single most important consideration in some planning contexts.

This review of the social, political, economic, and technological trends affecting the environment provides a starting point for subsequent background research and a context within which additional knowledge can be framed. These trends should be initially analyzed at the macro-level and subsequently "stepped down" to the geographic level appropriate for the community of organization in question. Box 6.1 describes some of the additional data needed to support the environmental assessment.

Box 6.1: The Importance of Non-health-Related Data

Although the healthcare industry generates massive amounts of data, it is often not accessible to those who need it. Unlike other industries there is little effort (and even ability) to collect data nationwide and establish central repositories for use by participating organizations. Even if such a repository existed, it would be of limited use to the majority of providers who serve local or regional populations. While such a resource would be useful to policy makers, health economists, and others who are interested in a global perspective on the system, it would not be very useful to most parties interested in adopting a population health approach.

Hospitals and other providers of health services do, however, generate extensive amounts of internal data. The operation of such complex organizations invariably generates massive amounts of data on operations, utilization, clinical activities, finances, human resources, and other aspects of the operation. This type of information has generally been internal in nature and was restricted to the activities that take place within the walls of the organization (even if it tries to operate, for example, as a "hospital without walls"). This glut of data has often given healthcare organizations the sense that they had all of the data they needed.

Most healthcare organizations today recognize that internal data is only one side of the data coin. Increasingly, healthcare provides are seeking to acquire "market data" that provides insights into the world outside the organization's walls. Indeed, it is not possible to establish benchmarks, calculate market shares, or develop business plans among other activities without access to external market data. It has become well established within the industry that internal data in isolation is not very useful except for tracking internal activities.

Aggressive healthcare organizations have historically developed strategic plans or at least business plans to guide their decision-making. This process required the acquisition of extensive external data for purposes of generating market intelligence. This typically involves information on the configuration of the organization's market area, a detailed profile of the population within that target area, projections of future health problems and future demand for services, forecasts of insurance coverage, and even competitive analyses. While the market intelligence generated to support the development of these plans was extensive, it tended to be collected on a one-off basis with typically little continuous monitoring between episodes of business or strategic planning.

There is increasing pressure at least on not-for-profit hospitals to expand their external data collection to include more in-depth analyses, a broader range of data topics, and more frequent data collection. Provisions within the 2010 Patient Safety and Affordable Care act (ACA) require that hospitals that are tax exempt must complete pursuant to their not-for-profit status a comprehensive community health needs assessment (CHNA) at least every 3 years in order to maintain their not-for-profit status.

(continued)

Box 6.1 (continued)

Not only does this provision require that extensive external market data be collected, but it also demands that the hospital go beyond the traditional types of data and collect information on the entire community and not just its patient population. The fact that a provider must be accountable not just for the health and well-being of its patients but also for the health status of the entire community it serves is a radical idea. Provisions of the ACA call for not only assessing the health status of the total population but also identifying unmet needs within that population even if those needs are unrelated to services that are typically provided by that hospital. For example, a hospital that does not routinely provide behavioral health services but finds that there are serious unmet needs in that regard must, according to IRS regulations, develop a plan for addressing those unmet needs. Further, at the time of the next CHNA the hospital theoretically at least must document what it has done to address this *community* need.

Clearly, this is a major plank in the population health platform with hospitals now expected to place as much emphasis on consumers in general as they do on their own patients. Further, the hospital will not be allowed to rely exclusively on its own data but must demonstrate that it has accessed resources in the community beyond its own walls. The ACA specifically mandates that the local health department be involved in the CHNA along with other health-related organizations. It further specifies that any organizations inside of and outside of healthcare be consulted to the extent it can provide insights into the needs of the general population. Extracting information from organizations outside of the system and even organizations outside of healthcare further supports the need for a population health approach.

This leads us to a more radical phenomenon related to data collection: the emphasis on non-health-related data. As will be discussed in more detail in a subsequent chapter, data must be collected on a wide range of topics that historically have not been linked to the health of the population. The recognition of the social determinants of health status has opened the door to the acquisition of data on a wide range of topics historically ignored by healthcare organizations. While most analyses include data on the demographic and socioeconomic characteristics of the service area population, additional information is now required on the lifestyles of consumers, their social context and cultural milieu, and the life circumstances that have implications for health status and health behavior. In keeping with the population health approach, this information is not collected for individuals per se but for groups within the population. So, it is not so important to know that John Doe has certain characteristics but that 100 John Does in ZIP Code 99999 have those characteristics in common.

Even more radical is the notion that data must be collected on topics previously thought to have no implications for health status. Attributes like income, educational level, and employment status for the target population would continue to be collected, but also data on the social and physical environment,

(continued)

> **Box 6.1** (continued)
> availability of affordable and adequate housing, employment options and job training opportunities, access to affordable and healthy food, access to green spaces and recreational activities, access to transportation, and exposure to crime and violence. The significance of this type of information has been highlighted as it has become increasingly obvious that no level of medical care can overcome poverty, environmental threats, malnutrition, and health implications of a stressful environment.

Baseline Data Collection

The environmental assessment provides the backdrop for the collection of baseline data on the community or the organization. This process identifies the who, what, when, where, and how of the community and its healthcare system or, in the case of organization-level planning, the current position of the organization vis-à-vis the market. These data provide the basis for any future comparisons and are the yardstick by which the success of the planning process will be measured.

In compiling baseline data for planning purposes, certain steps in the process should be followed. Whether the situation is being analyzed in terms of demographic characteristics, health status, or health resource availability, the same sequence should be followed. For every component analyzed, the planner should identify, inventory or quantify, profile, and assess. These steps are discussed in turn:

Identify. The first step always involves the identification of the factors on which data are to be collected. For example, the demographic traits, health status indicators, and categories of resources that are to be studied should be specified. The factors that should be identified are determined by the characteristics of the community and/or the organization.

Inventory/Quantify. Once the relevant factors have been identified, they must be inventoried. An "inventory" of demographic characteristics, for example, can involve a range of population characteristics. Similarly, an inventory of health status characteristics could involve the quantification of various indicators. An inventory of services or facilities may involve a count of relevant units with appropriate annotation.

Profile. Once the inventories are complete and the various measures have been quantified, it is possible to profile the community or the organization in terms of the relevant variables. This profile represents a composite "snapshot" of the community as it currently is constituted or the current status of the organization. No judgment is made at this point, but a state-of-the-community or state-of-the-organization picture is generated.

Assess. The final step in the process involves an assessment of the conditions that have been identified. Once the community has been profiled in terms of demographic characteristics, for example, it is possible to interpret this information within the context of the planning process. Once the profile of the organization has been established in terms of utilization rates, for example, it is possible to give meaning to these statistics. Questions such as the following can then be addressed. What are the implications of continued population redistribution for health services demands? What are the implications of the continued aging of the population? How does the overall health status of the community compare to that of other communities? Is the physician-to-population ratio favorable or unfavorable? What does the decrease in cardiology volume mean? The answers to these and similar questions will provide a starting point for subsequent planning activities.

Profiling the Community or Market

With community-wide planning, the delineation of the "community" will usually be obvious. It will typically coincide with the geographic unit that comes under the jurisdiction of the government entity that is involved in planning. Thus, if the state of Mississippi is initiating a community-wide planning process, the state would be considered the "community." If the Jackson County planning authority is sponsoring the initiative, Jackson County is likely to constitute the "community."

There may be situations in which the boundaries of the community are not clearly defined. For example, a regional planning authority may be established to address the needs of an area that cuts across state lines and involves a number of counties. Or a hospital service area may bisect a county or cross-state lines. The delineation of the boundaries of the "community" in this case requires a different approach. Techniques developed for determining the service area for a specific healthcare organization might be used in these cases. (These techniques are discussed in Chap. 8.)

As part of this community profiling process, the regional setting should be taken into consideration, since different regions of the country have their own cultural patterns. Variations observed in clinical practice patterns can often be attributed to differing community cultures. Thus, the *community type* should be a consideration when collecting baseline data. Whether the dominant community type within the planning area is urban, suburban, or rural will have important implications for both health status and health behavior. The community assessment process should also consider local *environmental factors* to the extent that they impact health status.

In the case of organization-level planning, the service area might be conceptualized as its "market," and the market for the organization may coincide with the service area for community planning purposes. On the other hand, the market area boundaries for an organization may extend beyond the jurisdiction of the planning agency or, in other cases, may be more restrictive than the area covered in community planning. Or the market for the organization may not be tied to geography but represent a subgroup of the total community, as in the case of a cosmetic surgery practice that caters only to older, upscale individuals who can afford this vanity service.

Profiling the Organization

At the organization level, the collection of baseline data begins with the organization itself. Healthcare organizations routinely generate a large amount of data as a by-product of their normal operations. Many types of data can typically be extracted from internal records, including patient characteristics, utilization trends, and sources of revenue.

These data may be acquired through the performance of an *internal audit*. The internal audit typically involves a number of components. An audit examines the organization's *structure*, its *processes*, its *customers*, and its *resources*. The components included and the emphases placed on them will depend on the nature of the planning engagement.

This process will include the identification of the separate units within the organization to be subsequently described and assessed. A hospital, for example, will have a number of departments that must be considered. A specialty group practice may include both diagnostic and therapeutic components or feature a number of service lines to be considered. The current status of each organizational component should be reviewed, along with past trends and expected future developments.

The following list illustrates aspects of the organization that might be addressed by means of an internal audit:

- Services and products offered
- Nature, number, and characteristics of customers
- Utilization patterns for services and products
- Revenue generated by service and product
- Staffing levels and personnel characteristics
- Internal management processes
- Financial characteristics
- Pricing structure
- Marketing arrangements
- Locations of service outlets
- Referral relationships
- Customer satisfaction

At the end of this process, the planner should be able to answer the questions raised above: Who are we? What are we doing to whom? Where are we doing it? How are we doing it? And, ultimately, how well are we doing it? (These issues are addressed in more detail in Chaps. 7 and 8.)

Profiling the Population

The characteristics of the population residing in the community or the market area must be determined through an *external audit* that expands on the environmental assessment. Many of the same types of data will be collected for both the community and organization planning levels. The main categories of data that should be collected on the community's population include demographic data, sociocultural data, psychographic or lifestyle data, and data on insurance coverage and consumer attitudes.

In assessing the health status of a population, community-wide planners frequently make use of some type of health status index that serves to quantify the needs of the community and its subcommunities. The current health status of the community will be an important determinant of the level of demand for health services and serves as the baseline against which the effectiveness of planning will be measured. The emphasis, of course, will be on those dimensions that are relevant to the needs of the community or the organization.

For community-wide planning the approach to defining and measuring health status is being reconsidered. There is concern that the conceptualization of health status on the part of health professionals does not allow for a "true" measure of health status. An approach that applies epidemiological measures from the top down is increasingly thought to be misleading. Mortality rates in particular are thought to be of limited usefulness in assessing community health status. Increasing emphasis is being placed on measures of morbidity to the extent that they are available, and there is growing interest in the role of social determinants in the health status of communities. Attempts are underway to redefine health status in more meaningful terms that reflect the perspective of community residents rather than health professionals. The emphasis on social determinants also provides an opportunity to assess health status prospectively rather than depending on a snapshot of the current situation.

Planners are also concerned with the patterns of health behavior that characterize a population. Health behavior can be defined as any action aimed at restoring, preserving, and/or enhancing health status. Formal medical behavior is defined in terms of such indicators of utilization as physician visits, hospital admissions, and emergency room visits. Health behavior also includes informal actions on the part of individuals that are designed to prevent health problems and maintain, enhance, or promote health. Historically, the emphasis in the analysis of health behavior has been on the formal services provided by healthcare practitioners.

While community health planners will be interested in the broad range of health behavior, healthcare organizations will focus on those indicators of health behavior that are most relevant for their operations. Hospitals, for example, are likely to require information on almost all of the indicators described throughout this book.

Organizations offering more limited services will focus on specific indicators of utilization in their analyses.

The information developed through the external audit provides the basis for estimating the demand for health services characterizing the population. It is this need for services that must be compared to the community resources described below in order to determine the planning gap.

Community Resources Inventory

The other side of the coin from the needs assessment is the resource inventory. The healthcare resources available to the community must be identified and ultimately matched to the identified needs. These resources include health facilities and equipment, healthcare programs and services, health personnel, financing options, and existing networks and relationships at a minimum.

The list of factors to be considered in the community-wide planning process may appear overwhelming, but this is the level of comprehensiveness that is required in order to develop an adequate picture of the community under study. All of these components are important in one way or another, and almost any one of them could have a substantial impact on the system.

At the organization level, the resource inventory will inevitably be much more focused than that for community-wide planning. The emphasis will be on those facilities, programs, personnel, and other resources that are relevant to the organization in question. Ultimately, the resources that are inventoried will reflect the type of organization, the nature of its services, and the type of planning being conducted.

In recent years the notion of community "health assets" has come to be recognized. Generally, when an inventory of healthcare resources is implemented the focus is on manifestations of the formal healthcare system, the facilities, personnel, and programs that are commonly identified. The argument has been made that these resources may or may not be considered *assets* in the eyes of community members. A clinic that only accepts insured patients or a hospital that discourages Medicaid patients would not be considered much of an asset to community residents. For this reason, contemporary health asset assessment processes cast a wider net to include resources that may not be recognized by health professionals but are considered assets to the community. Research in various communities has identified as health assets churches, community development corporations, funeral homes, and even barber and beauty shops. This situation, then, requires that those performing an environmental assessment be cognizant of the fact that there may be resources not readily recognized by an outside assessor.

Assessing Health Status and Healthcare Resources

It is essential that once the community's needs and resources have been identified and inventoried they be evaluated. A number of approaches can be utilized in this regard, although all ultimately involve some type of comparative analysis. The assessment of an indicator of health status, for example, could involve a comparison with that same indicator at a previous point in time, a comparison with the indicator for a comparable community, a comparison with the state or national average, or a comparison with some standard that has been established. In fact, an indicator should probably be assessed from all of these perspectives.

At this point, various analytical techniques might be utilized, such as a gap analysis or SWOT analysis. These techniques are useful in determining the state of the community or the state of the organization prior to proceeding with the planning process. These analytical techniques are discussed in more detail in subsequent chapters.

Summarizing the Preliminary Analysis

Enough information should now be available to present a summary statement of the analysis up to this point. This may involve a state-of-the-community report for community-wide planning or a state-of-the-organization report for organization-level planning. This report should include a comprehensive description of the community or organizational environment, a status report on the internal situation (in the case of an organization), and a report describing the overall status of the community or market area.

This information should provide the basis for conducting a SWOT analysis at this point. A *SWOT analysis* examines the strengths, weaknesses, opportunities, and threats related to markets, organizations, or products. The SWOT analysis has become a common technique for assessing the position of a healthcare organization in its market. This technique examines the organization, its environment, and the ways the organization and environment interact. The planning team, along with any other key influential, should review the material and draw conclusions with regard to the strengths, weaknesses, opportunities, and threats relative to the community or the organization.

The status report thus should include the strengths, weaknesses, opportunities, and threats identified during the analysis. It should also include an "issues statement" based on the results of the analysis to this point. The issues statement will help clarify the process and narrow the focus of the planning team. This is also a point at which the mission statement and the original assumptions should be revisited.

This report presents an opportunity to frankly describe the state of the community's health system or the state of the organization and serves as the launching point for subsequent plan development. This is a critical point in the planning process, in that it presents the baseline data against which any progress will be measured. It also assures that everyone involved in the process is on the same page and agrees with the stated assumptions and the understandings generated by the process up to this point.

Considering Strategies

This is a point at which the choice of strategy might be considered (although some planners would place this step later in the process). While strategies are typically associated with organization-level planning, they should not be ignored when community-level planning is being conducted. The strategy refers to the generalized approach that is to be taken in response to the challenges identified to this point.

With community-level planning, this may mean choosing between a public health approach, a free market approach, an educational model of development, or a public/private consortium approach, to name a few. The emergence of the population health model described in Chap. 4 provides another option. Any one of these could be thought of as a strategy and serve as the framework for subsequent planning.

Any strategy developed for community-wide planning should meet several criteria. It should provide overall direction for the initiative, fit the available resources, minimize resistance, reach the appropriate targeted groups, and, ultimately, advance the vision of the community or the organization. Chapter 9 on strategic planning offers additional input on this issue.

At the organization level, the choice of strategy is critical. The strategy sets the tone for subsequent planning activities and, in effect, sets the parameters within which the planners must operate. Examples of strategies that might be adopted by organization-level planners include a market dominance strategy, a niche strategy, a flanking strategy, or a coalition strategy, to name a few. (Specific strategies are discussed in more detail in Chap. 8.)

The research undertaken to this point should have generated enough information on the environment and the issues to be addressed to allow for at least a general strategy to be formulated. While the precise strategic approach to be taken may not be specified at this point, at least the options can be narrowed. This will serve to focus subsequent planning activities by eliminating strategies that are considered unproductive. Under a community-wide planning scenario, for example, it may be determined that changing the lifestyle patterns of the population represents a more realistic path to reaching planning objectives does facilities construction, for example.

Clearly, the planning approach will be quite different if facility regulation is the focus. Similarly, if a hospital determines, based on available data, that it cannot compete head on with the major player in the market area, its adoption of a "second fiddle" or "flanking" strategy will channel planning in a different direction than if a more confrontational approach was chosen.

Inventing the Future

The final consideration at this juncture is the development of a scenario that depicts where the community or organization would like to be at some specified point in the future. Time horizons of 5, 10, and 15 years might be considered. A scenario should be developed that describes the range of services that are envisioned, the patterns of referral and utilization, the health status of the community, and so forth for specified points in the future. At the organization level, the scenario should describe the organization as envisioned in terms of future characteristics such as size, personnel composition, service complement, position in the market, stance relative to competitors, volume of services, locations, payor mix, and any other characteristic that is considered important.

The desired future position represents the target that the planning process is intended to achieve. Of course, the visionary should be tempered by the feasible and the ideal by the practical. One approach, in fact, might be to develop a best case/worst case/probable case set of scenarios. This allows for a range of outcomes that can be assessed in terms of their level of acceptability.

Developing the Plan

The effort up to this point provides the foundation for actual plan development. If the initial work is properly carried out, the planning process should flow smoothly, at least from a technical perspective.

Setting the Goal(s)

Goals are generalized statements about an ideal state that will serve as the target for future development. They specify the desired form of the community healthcare system or, alternatively, the future characteristics of the organization and generalized accomplishments that the organization would like to achieve. As in other planning activities, the goal should meet certain criteria before it is accepted, including compatibility with the organization's mission statement. Goals establish the tone for the rest of the planning process, since all subsequent components are derived from them.

The goal or goals that are established should reflect the information that was provided in the summary report based on initial information gathering. Goals may be stated before the planning exercise begins with the understanding that they may be modified once more information is available. Preferably, though, goal setting should be driven by information generated through the assessment process.

Goals tend to be idealistic, and this is particularly true in the community-wide planning context. At the community level, the goal may call for "establishing an effective and efficient delivery system that serves the needs of the entire community." At the organization level, on the other hand, the goal will be more specific to the mission of the organization and may, for example, call for "positioning ABC orthopedic group as the premier sports medicine provider in the region."

The number of goals to be established depends on the complexity and size of the organization, the nature of the issues at hand, and the type of planning being undertaken. If the focus is narrow, a single goal may be appropriate. On the other hand, the complexity of many healthcare organizations mandates the establishment of multiple goals. Goals ultimately may be established specific to particular issues or units within the organization. In that case, efforts must be made to coordinate planning and assure that competing or conflicting goals are not established.

Specifying Objectives

Objectives refer to the specific targets to be reached in support of goal attainment. To many, these represent the "tactics" that support the plan's strategies. Objectives should be developed in response to the major opportunities or problems identified and should represent potential solutions (or at least part of the solution) for these issues.

While goals are general statements, objectives should be very specific and stated in clear and concise terms. Any concepts referenced in an objective must be operationalizable and measurable. Objectives must also be time bound, with clear deadlines established for their accomplishment. Finally, they must be amenable to evaluation. This characteristic is particularly critical since the success of the process will be measured by the extent to which objectives have been met. It may take years before the achievement of a goal can be determined, so objectives provide the basis for short-term evaluation of progress toward a goal. This is a critical point in the planning process since the baseline traits to be used for evaluation must be measurable.

Objectives are stated in such terms as follows: The rate of teen pregnancy in the community will be reduced from 15% to 10% by the end of 2025 (in support of the goal of improving the reproductive health of the community). Or the hospital's orthopedic practice will recruit a sports medicine specialist within the next 12 months (in support of the stated goal of expanding the organization's orthopedic product lines).

Several objectives may be specified for each goal. Four or five would not be uncommon, although many more than that become unwieldy (especially if more than one goal is being considered). Multiple objectives are common since it is likely that action will be required on a number of different fronts in order to attain a specified goal. The objectives should be reviewed by all appropriate parties and possibly by some party outside the organization such as experts on the local healthcare system.

It may be useful to organize planning team members into working committees for each specific objective. These work groups should deal with the various substantive issues that must be addressed (e.g., reproductive health, chronic disease). This approach serves to coordinate and focus efforts so the work group will have the greatest possible impact. At the community level, appropriate "support" organizations should be brought in to assist with plan implementation and to provide exposure to "best practices" related to their areas of expertise.

Any barriers to accomplishing the stated objectives of the system or the organization should be identified and assessed. The extent to which these barriers can be overcome must be determined. A specialty practice, for example, may have felt that its market share could be greatly enhanced by assigning half of its physicians to a different hospital. However, upon further reflection, it was determined that its primary competitor who was entrenched at the other facility would create such a furor that any advantage would be compromised. In the case of insurmountable barriers, an objective may simply have to be eliminated.

Prioritizing Objectives

The planning process typically generates a number of equally important objectives. In many cases it may not be feasible to pursue all of the objectives that have been identified. Even if staff, money, and other resources are not an issue, it may not be possible to address all of them within a reasonable time frame or to pursue all objectives simultaneously. As a result, the prioritization of objectives becomes an important step in the process.

There is no one foolproof procedure for prioritizing objectives and the approach to prioritization is likely to vary with the situation. Whatever approach is used, consensus should be developed on the prioritization process before it is time to implement it.

There are a number of questions that might be asked to help determine the order of priority for the pursuit of objectives. While these probably relate more directly to organization-level planning than to community-wide planning, most of them can be adapted to either situation. Representative queries include the following:

- What are the most urgent issues, issues that will bring about dire consequences if they are not resolved?
- What are the pivotal issues, issues that contribute most directly to the mission and goal?
- Which objectives must be addressed as a prerequisite for achieving other objectives?
- What objectives will provide the greatest return for the planning "investment"?
- Which objectives can be achieved quicker, easier, and less expensively than others?
- Which objectives will result in the most visible or most tangible results?
- Which objectives will have the most lasting impact and/or can maintain themselves over time?

- Are objectives with short-term benefits more important than those with long-term benefits?
- Which objectives face the least barriers?
- What is the level of risk characterizing the options and to what extent is risk an issue?
- Which objectives will involve multiple benefits if they are achieved?
- Which objectives are critical to filling important gaps in services or addressing organizational weaknesses?
- To what extent is there likely to be a negative response to the achieving of an objective?

The challenge is to identify on the front end the criteria that are most important. It may even be necessary to utilize different sets of criteria within one planning initiative due to the nature of the project. The application of these priorities is likely to result in the elimination of some objectives that may not be workable, although they may have seemed like a good idea when they were first proposed.

One other consideration at this point is the possibility of unanticipated consequences resulting from the meeting of any of the objectives. Although it may appear tedious, it is important to specify the likely consequences of carrying out each objective. This should involve a determination of both intended and unintended consequences. Too often the positive aspects of the situation are examined in isolation from the negative consequences that result from the pursuit of the objective. For example, a well-intended plan by a hospital to establish a network of urgent care centers may have the unintended consequence of alienating community physicians practicing in the targeted neighborhoods.

Specifying Actions

The next step in the planning process is a critical one, in that this is where the planning team specifies the actions to be carried out. For each of the objectives that have been identified (and have survived the various "cuts"), a set of actions must be specified. This process essentially breaks down the procedure for meeting objectives into manageable steps. It is one thing to indicate what actions should be taken, and it is another to specify *how* they are to be carried out. For this reason, an implementation plan must be developed that lays out the required tasks.

A number of action steps are likely to be required for each objective. Just as several objectives must be met in order to attain a single goal, numerous actions must be performed to achieve an objective. These actions take a wide range of forms, from the most mundane of support activities to highly complex tasks. Many of these actions imply a certain sequence and this is a point at which the original project plan might be further refined to specify the sequencing of the action steps. Box 6.2 describes the use of a strategy map in plan development.

Box 6.2: Strategy Maps for Health Planning
In order to aid health planning efforts, Insightformation has developed the concept of strategy maps. Strategy maps are generated as an ongoing flexible framework that separates objectives—the building blocks of the strategy map—from the measures, targets, and actions that are also part of the strategy management system. Objectives describe specific changes, but do not specify how those changes will be measured. Rather than trying to quantify each of the multitude of actions that go into the strategy, the measures within population health strategy maps are used to monitor progress toward achieving the strategic objectives, allowing for a simpler, more powerful management system.

Given how long it takes to build consensus and to implement changes that significantly improve population health outcomes, a well-designed strategy must be articulated in a way that will not need to change every year. If the strategy consists primarily of short-term actions, then the strategy will likely need to be re-created annually, wasting time and disrupting efforts to create bigger, more durable changes.

Community health strategy maps are often organized into three layers (called "perspectives") with a general cause-and-effect logic flowing from bottom to top:

- Outcomes
- Strategies
- Asset and capacity development

Each of these layers contains a series of objectives. The objectives in the outcomes perspective might include "reduce obesity" or "minimize diabetes prevalence." The objectives in the strategies perspective might include "school gardening initiative" or "improve infrastructure for biking and walking." The strategy map should focus on changes that the community will be working to achieve, not just current actions or ongoing operations.

The order in which the elements of a strategy management system are created is very important. It is best to build consensus on the framework of objectives (the strategy map) before wrestling with the details of measures, targets, and actions. Establishing a consensus on the objectives makes it easier to reach agreement on the subsequent steps that organizations will take to measure and implement the strategy. These steps can be delegated to different groups after objectives are in place. An example of a strategy map is presented below.
Source: Reprinted with permission from Insightformation.com

Implementing the Plan

Planning is ultimately only an exercise, albeit a meaningful one. The payoff comes in the implementation of the plan. The planning process creates a road map which the community or the organization must use to get where it wants to go. It is at the implementation stage, however, that the process often breaks down. The oft-repeated maxim that "the last plan is still sitting on the shelf" generally reflects a failure in implementation rather than any flaw in the plan itself.

The transition from planning to implementation is difficult under the best of circumstances. It involves a hand-off from the planning team to the management team. Implementation must occur at several different levels and within different sectors of the community or divisions of the organization. For this reason, the implementation of the plan requires a level of coordination that few organizations and certainly few communities have in place.

To a certain extent, planning is talk, but implementation is action. Very little about the system or the organization has to be changed during the planning process (although some change inevitably occurs as a by-product). However, the implementation plan is likely to require significant change within the community or the organization. These changes are likely to affect management processes, information systems, and corporate culture, in addition to more mundane work routines.

Implementation is particularly a challenge for planners at the community level. There may not be an organization in place to take charge of the implementation process. Implementation may require a coalition of various community organizations, with no one organization capable of managing implementation (even if all others agreed that they should do it). Further, there is likely to be no organization in a position to coordinate the various parties, both public and private, that must be included in the process.

Within an organization, the ability to assign responsibility for plan implementation certainly exists, although there will always be difficulties in carving out staff time from existing responsibilities. This challenge is made greater for working managers, unless the activities generated by the plan already fall under the responsibilities of the manager. Few clinicians, for example, would agree that organizational planning is part of their job description, but often they are the only ones in a position to guide implementation. Ultimately, engaging the appropriate parties in the process is one of the greatest challenges for the planning team. For this reason, total buy-in from top administrators must be assured from day 1 since it is likely to require pressure from "upstairs" to assure compliance.

Steps in Implementation

In order to approach plan implementation systematically, the planning team should develop both a detailed project plan and an implementation matrix. An implementation matrix can be developed using a spreadsheet and should lay out who is to do what and when they are to do it. The matrix should list every action called for by the plan, breaking each action down into tasks, if appropriate. For each action or task the responsible party should be identified, along with any secondary parties that should be involved in this activity. The matrix should indicate resource requirements (in terms of staff time, money, and other requirements). The start and end

Zoom: Nurture Early Childhood Brain Development

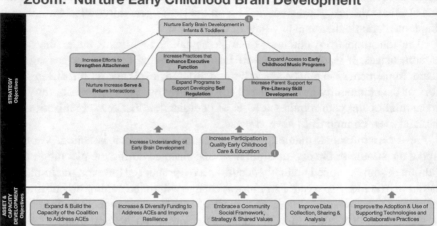

Fig. 6.3 Implementation matrix (source: reprinted with permission from Insightformation.com)

dates for this activity should be identified. Any prerequisites for accomplishing this task should be identified at the outset and factored into the project plan. Finally, benchmarks should be established that allow the planning team to determine when the activity has been completed. (Figure 6.3 presents an example of an implementation matrix.)

The nature of the progress indicators used will be determined by the type of plan. In many cases, *operational* benchmarks will be important. These may relate to utilization levels, facility development, or staffing changes, as well as others. *Clinical* standards may be established in many cases as well. These may focus on outcomes such as a reduction in the hospital mortality rate or improvement in surgical outcomes. *Financial* benchmarks are likely to be included in many plans. The success of planning activities will often be measured in terms of such factors as revenue, profit, or return on investment.

Requirements for Implementation

The resource requirements from the implementation matrix should be combined to determine total project requirements. This will determine the extent to which the project will require *operating funds* and *capital investment*, including any *facilities and equipment* requirements. In addition, the *human resource* requirements should be determined, and *information system* requirements specified. Any changes in *governance or management* will need to be outlined, along with anticipated *marketing* needs.

The prerequisites for plan implementation noted above ultimately must involve the budgetary process. In fact, the failure of many planning initiatives can be attributed to the inability to translate plans into budgets. This represents a challenge for any organization and the shorter the time frame, the greater the challenge. The budgetary process might be considered antithetical to the strategic planning process in that it reflects a refinement of current budgetary requirements rather than a proactive consideration of future organizational needs. For this reason, the planning process must include those parties in the organization who are likely to influence the budgetary process.

The extent of the requirements may have to be addressed in relation to available funds and any other fiscal constraints. The fact that financial resources will almost always be limited means that adjustments may be required in the implementation plan. This may mean that activities may have to be delayed, modified, or eliminated altogether. This is one of the reasons that objectives should be prioritized during the formulation of the plan.

Means of Implementation

Implementation of the plan at the community level will involve a wide variety of community organizations, and this creates an inevitable management challenge for community-wide health planning efforts. In some cases, it may be possible to use the authority vested in the planning entity to enforce changes through regulatory efforts. In most cases, however, the changes must be voluntary so the process focuses more on education, persuasion, and coordination than on control. At the organization level, the means used to implement the plan will transcend various departments and units out of necessity.

The implementation process is likely to employ both direct means and indirect means. The direct means of implementation have been addressed to a certain extent through the development of the implementation matrix and the identification of resource requirements. *Budgeting activities* that provide for the allocation of resources are typically utilized to directly facilitate the plan. Direct methods may also include changes in *policies and procedures* to allow various activities to occur. In the case of community-wide planning, direct means may involve the enactment of regulations that affect the actions of healthcare organizations. Ultimately, the organization-level plan may require changes in the *organizational structure* and/or *management processes*. The extent to which these direct means of implementation are utilized depend, of course, on the type of organization and the type of plan.

Indirect means of plan implementation might also be utilized. These are indirect in the sense that they support plan implementation rather than being directly involved in task performance. At the organization level these methods might include making changes in *physical facilities* that allow certain activities to occur. Various forms of *communication* might be utilized to support implementation. Certain *sym-*

bolic actions might be taken that provide psychological support for the operationalization of the plan.

Perhaps the most extensive of the indirect means deals with the community mindset or the *corporate culture* of the organization. At the community level, the emphasis may be on creating an environment that encourages healthy lifestyles and
behavior patterns. Interventions intended to encourage healthy behaviors are likely
to be unsuccessful if implemented in an environment that does not support healthy
lifestyles. In many cases, the corporate culture of the organization will have to be
modified in order for plan implementation to be successful at the organization level.
If a planning mindset does not already exist, this will have to be incorporated into the
culture. If the culture emphasizes strict organizational divisions, a new way of thinking may have to be introduced in order to implement the plan across divisional lines.

"Products" Generated by the Planning Process

The most tangible "product" derived from the planning process is the planning document that is generated. This is where the process is "put to paper" and is the document that summarizes the background information, lays out the vision developed
through the process, and describes how this vision will be attained. This document
should also include an implementation plan that will specify the steps that must be
followed to turn the plan into action.

The process should also generate a database of information on the community
and/or the organization that can be utilized to support future planning activities and
ancillary projects. In fact, it would be an unusual plan that did not generate ideas for
heretofore unconsidered projects. In some cases, the plan may be long forgotten, but
its legacy of a comprehensive database on the community or the organization may
live on. For this reason, the creation of such a resource should be an explicit objective
of any planning process. A database can be updated, expanded, and otherwise developed over time to support not only this project but also future efforts of various types.

Less tangible products include a new perspective on the nature of the system or
the organization, the identification of available resources (perhaps heretofore
unknown), a new understanding of the players in the community or within the organization, a newfound appreciation of the public's perspective, and so forth.

An even more important intangible product is the establishment of a process for
planning that, hopefully, will persist after the end of the discrete project. Remember,
"the plan is nothing, but planning is everything." If a planning mindset has been
inculcated, the process will take on a life of its own. Planning should become established as an inherent part of the operation and rather than an episodic event. This
mindset should be developed to the point that decision makers stop and think about
"the plan" before they make any important decision.

The Evaluation Plan

The notion of evaluating the planning project should be top of mind on the first day of the process, and the means for evaluation should be built into the process itself. Evaluation is necessary to determine the success of the process. This is important to those involved in the process, as well as to any parties that may be assessing the value of the planning initiative. For example, grant makers and funders will usually want to know how many people were reached and served by the initiative, as well as whether the initiative had the community-level impact it intended to have. Community groups may want to use evaluation results to guide them in decisions about their programs, and where they are putting their efforts. Researchers will most likely be interested in proving whether any improvements in community health were definitively caused by your programs or initiatives.

Evaluation techniques focus on two primary types of analysis: process (or formative) analysis and outcome (or summative) analysis. The former evaluates systems, procedures, communication processes, and other factors that contribute to the efficient operation of a program. Outcome evaluation focuses more on end results or what is ultimately accomplished. Process evaluation essentially measures efficiency, while outcome evaluation measures effectiveness (Adams and Schvaneveldt 1991). In addition, there is growing interest in *impact* evaluation, particularly at the community level. The primary question for impact evaluation is this: What long-term impact has occurred as a result of the achievement of stated goals?

Process evaluation and outcome evaluation may overlap in various stages of the analysis. For example, it is not enough to report that regular planning meetings are being held. The process evaluation should measure the extent to which the meetings are achieving the results that they are intended to. Both types of evaluation have a role to play in the project. Using the project plan as a guide, the process can be monitored and regular progress reports presented.

Evaluation should involve ongoing monitoring of the planning process, including benchmarks and/or milestones for assessment along the way. This will require the clarification of the objectives and goals of the initiative. Once the questions to be answered through evaluation have been identified, the next step is to decide which methods will best address those questions. Some of the methods to be utilized include a monitoring and feedback system; member surveys about the initiative; goal attainment report; behavioral surveys; interviews with key participants; and, for community-wide planning, community-level indicators of impact.

Although evaluation techniques are often praised for their bottom-line objectivity, they are also useful in healthcare where it is not possible to place a dollar value on everything. Thus, cost-effectiveness analysis may take into consideration the intangible aspects of the service delivery process in its evaluation. Hence, strict cost/benefit analyses are likely to be less suitable for use in healthcare than in most other industries.

Data collection and benchmarking are extremely important to understand progress and community improvement, and documenting the process of community or organizational change is an ongoing task that should occur on a regular basis. Community-wide planners should submit updates to the public and organization-level planners to the key parties involved in the organization.

As noted earlier, it is unlikely that a health plan will be completed without being modified in one way or another. This type of "on-the-fly" revision is inevitable in a rapidly changing environment. At the end of the planning period, it is important to reassess the healthcare environment for community-wide planning and the internal characteristics of the organization for organization-level planning. Questions should be raised such as the following: What developments have subsequently occurred that will affect the plan or the implementation of its provisions? What actions have been taken supportive of the plan that were not anticipated? Have there been new developments that affect resource requirements? Have subsequent actions on the part of competitors affected the "strategic balance"?

Ideally, each component of the planning process should be revisited with these concerns in mind. The assumptions should be reviewed along with the mission statement. The baseline data should be updated to account for the time lapse since the planning process was initiated. The emphasis here will, of course, depend on the type of plan.

The strategy chosen should be reviewed to determine if it is still the best approach in view of possible changes in the environment. For example, has the collaborative strategy selected failed due to unanticipated competition on the part of "collaborators"? The goals and objectives should be revisited to assure that they are still appropriate in the light of any changes in either the internal or the external environment.

Realistically, the planning process is likely to require a substantial shift in mindset for most healthcare organizations. For continuous revision and replanning to occur, the organization must truly become a "planning organization." This level of commitment will require that planning become an inherent part of the culture. If this can be accomplished, the above activities should easily follow.

Reference

Adams, G. R., & Schvaneveldt, J. D. (1991). *Understanding research methods*. New York: Longman.

Roeder, A. (2014). "ZIP Code Better Predictor of Health Than Genetic Code." Retrieved from www.hsph.harvard.edu/news/features/zip-code-better-predictor-of-health-than-genetic-code/.

Further Reading

Association for Community Health Improvement. *Planning initiative supported by the American Hospital Association*. Retrieved from www.achi.com

American Health Planning Association. *Health planning tools*. Retrieved from www.ahpanet.org

Insightformation. *Health planning tools*. Retrieved from www.insightformation.com

National Association of County and City Health Officials. *Tools for community health planning*. Retrieved from www.nacho.org

Public Health Foundation. *Web-based planning guides*. Retrieved from www.phf.org

Chapter 7
The New Community Assessment Process

Introduction

The community assessment component is a critical part of the community-wide planning process. Without this assessment as a foundation for the planning process, any planning would be "shooting in the dark." Not only would planners lack a general understanding of the environment, but also the uniqueness of the community could not be appreciated.

This chapter presents a general framework for conducting a community assessment. It lays out the steps involved in performing the assessment preparatory to carrying out the planning process. The outline presented is relatively generic, and the planner should realize that this framework may need to be adapted to the situation of the particular community.

The first step in the community assessment process involves the development of a general picture of the community and its healthcare system. This process will include a review of pertinent background materials and interviews with key participants in the community inside and outside of healthcare. The intent is to develop enough background on the community to thoughtfully craft the remainder of the plan.

The "literature review" should include any materials that have been prepared on the local healthcare system. Newspaper articles may have been published that describe various aspects of the system, and many communities produce health-related publications. This review of print materials should include any previous plans that have been developed and any research projects or consultant studies that have been conducted. University researchers are likely to have conducted studies on the local healthcare system, and government agencies often compile reports on various aspects of the system. Health facilities may have submitted certificate-of-need applications or other reports to governmental agencies, and these are often a matter of public record.

© Springer Science+Business Media, LLC, part of Springer Nature 2021
R. K. Thomas, *Health Services Planning*,
https://doi.org/10.1007/978-1-0716-1076-3_7

A second component of this stage of information gathering involves interviews with knowledgeable individuals within the community, both inside and out of the medical establishment. Those interviewed should include anyone currently involved in any planning activities in the community, representatives of the major private sector healthcare organizations, public health leaders, and representatives of the physician community. With the increasing interest in the social determinants of health, it is important that representatives of other sectors (e.g., education, housing, criminal justice) be included. Major decision makers, opinion leaders, and political influentials should also be included.

While the intent is to develop a general picture of the community healthcare system, this process represents an opportunity to identify any major issues from the perspective of those interviewed. The issues that are driving the planning process should especially be identified, since these may provide focus for subsequent assessment activities. This process should also identify some key informants who might serve as useful resources later in the planning process.

The background research should also identify the decision-making process for the community's healthcare system, at least to the extent that it can be isolated. How are decisions made with regard to the expenditure of public healthcare funds? What healthcare organizations are politically influential? Who has the grassroots support of the community? What government agencies are involved? What type of public-private interface exists?

Any potential barriers to the planning initiative should be identified as part of this process. Individuals or organizations that are clearly resistant to the planning process should be identified at this point. Immutable patterns of behavior that must be considered should also be identified. These understandings with regard to barriers become a part of the assumptions that drive the process.

The Origin and Nature of CHNAs

Distinguishing between individual needs and the wider needs of the community is important in the planning and provision of local health services, and this realization has led to the development of community health needs assessments (CHNAs). If community needs are ignored then there is a danger of a top-down approach to providing health services, which relies too heavily on what "outside experts" perceive to be the needs of the population rather than what they actually are.

As originally conceived, CHNAs have the following attributes (Wright et al. 1998):

- Health needs assessment is the systematic approach to ensuring that the health service uses its resources to improve the health of the population in the most efficient way.
- The CHNA involves epidemiological, qualitative, and comparative methods to describe health problems of a population; identify inequalities in health and access to services; and determine priorities for the most effective use of resources.

- Health needs to be assessed are those that can benefit from healthcare or from wider social and environmental changes.
- Successful health needs assessments require a practical understanding of what is involved, the time and resources necessary to undertake assessments, and sufficient integration of the results into planning and commissioning of local services.

In the nineteenth century the first medical officers for health were responsible for assessing the needs of their local populations. More recently, relative health needs were assessed on the basis of standardized mortality ratios and socioeconomic deprivation for different populations, with the notion of more efficient planning for distribution of health service resources. Health needs assessment has thus come to mean an objective and valid method for assessing needs in support of an evidence-based approach to planning health services.

Although health needs assessments have traditionally been undertaken by public health professionals looking at their local population, these local health needs should be paramount to all health professionals. Indeed, the Affordable Care Act requires that all not-for-profit hospitals conduct a community health needs assessment at least every 3 years. Hospitals and primary care teams should both aim to develop services to match the needs of their local populations. Combining population needs assessment with personal knowledge of patients' needs may help to meet this goal.

Over the past 30 years, expenditures on healthcare have risen much faster than the cost increases reported in other sectors, and healthcare is now one of the largest sectors in the US economy. Medical advances and demographic changes will continue to put upward pressure on costs. At the same time the resources available for healthcare are limited. Many people have inequitable access to adequate healthcare, and many governments are unable to provide adequate services. In addition, there is a large variation in the availability and use of healthcare by geographic area and point of service. Availability is often inversely related to the need of the population served.

Today, the assessment of health needs is not simply a process of listening to patients or relying on personal experience. It is a systematic method of identifying unmet health and healthcare needs of a population and making changes to meet these unmet needs. It involves an epidemiological and qualitative approach to determining priorities which incorporates both clinical and consumer perspectives. This approach must balance clinical, ethical, and economic considerations of need—that is, what should be done, what can be done, and what can be afforded.

Health needs assessment should not just be a method of measuring ill health, as this assumes that something can be done to tackle it. Incorporating the concept of a capacity to benefit introduces the importance of effectiveness of health interventions and attempts to make explicit what benefits are being pursued. Economists argue that the capacity to benefit is always going to be greater than available resources and that health needs assessment should also incorporate questions of priority setting. This suggests that needs assessments may become distractions from the difficult decisions of resource rationing.

Ultimately, health needs assessment provides the opportunity for:

- Describing the patterns of disease in the local population and the differences from district, regional, or national disease patterns
- Learning more about the needs and priorities of patients and the local population
- Highlighting the areas of unmet need and providing a clear set of objectives to work toward in meeting these needs
- Deciding rationally how to use resources to improve the local population's health in the most effective and efficient way
- Influencing policy, interagency collaboration, or research and development priorities

Importantly, health needs assessment also provides a method of monitoring and promoting equity in the provision and use of health services and addressing inequalities in health.

Environmental Assessment

Once a basic understanding of the community and its healthcare system has been established, a number of other data collection activities can be initiated. The first step in the formal data collection process involves an environmental assessment or "scan." "Environment" here is viewed in the broadest of terms, encompassing any aspect of society at any level that could be construed to have implications for community planning activities. The assessment should begin at the national level and be carried down to the level at which the planning is occurring. Thus, the analysis should include the national level, the regional level (if appropriate), the state level, and ultimately the level of the community under study.

Societal Trends

Broad societal trends should be analyzed and their implications for the local environment considered. These societal trends should include demographic trends, economic considerations, lifestyle trends, and even shifts in attitudes. Examples of pertinent trends abound. For example, the most significant demographic trend characterizing the US society is the overall aging of the population, coupled with the replacement of the large baby boom population as it ages with Millennials and Gen Xers. This national trend has major implications for the delivery of care nationally, and there are few local communities that will not be affected by age-related demographic trends. Another example of a society-wide demographic trend with implications for healthcare is the growing racial and ethnic diversity characterizing the US society. This development may ultimately come to be more important than societal aging.

Broad economic trends are also a consideration, since a community's economic circumstances influence both health status and health behavior. Periods of economic prosperity have different implications for healthcare than periods of recession or economic downturn. Similarly, a state of full employment affects healthcare differently from a situation of high unemployment. These economic conditions have implications for health status, health behavior, and ability of the population to pay for healthcare.

Changing national lifestyles are another trend with implications for healthcare. A current example involves the health and fitness consciousness characterizing much of the American population. The fitness "craze" that began in the 1980s has created an unprecedented demand for health clubs, health food, athletic goods, and sports medicine. At the same time, much of the population continues to practice poor health habits, habits that have serious implications for the nation's morbidity profile.

Trends in consumer attitudes are another area of inquiry, and even changes in these attitudes at the national level may have implications for local communities. A case in point involves home healthcare. Until the 1980s the general public considered home care a less-than-desirable alternative to hospital care. However, over the past decade or so home care has come to be seen by many as the setting of choice wherever possible, and third-party payers have come to recognize the financial benefits of avoiding nursing home care.

Health Industry Trends

Developments in the healthcare industry should be examined to identify any trends at the national and state levels that are likely to affect the local community. These could include trends in financial arrangements (discussed below), changing organizational structures within the delivery system, or introduction of new treatment modalities. The trend away from inpatient care in favor of outpatient care continues to be a major factor in the healthcare arena. Recent examples of other industry trends include the rapid growth of cosmetic surgery and the current interest in rehabilitation.

Another recent industry trend with implications for the provision of healthcare is the emergence of large national for-profit chains that have exerted a tremendous influence on the healthcare system. Recent years have also seen the emergence of employers and employer coalitions as key players in the healthcare environment. The current emphasis by Medicare on pay-for-performance reimbursement is another example of national trends with implications for planning. Box 7.1 describes the pay-for-performance movement in healthcare.

Box 7.1: Pay-for-Performance Reimbursement

In an effort to control the cost of healthcare while assuring the highest quality of care, pay-for-performance approaches to reimbursement are being tried. "Pay-for-performance" is an umbrella term for initiatives aimed at improving the quality, efficiency, and overall value of healthcare. These arrangements provide financial incentives to hospitals, physicians, and other healthcare providers to carry out such improvements and achieve optimal outcomes for patients. Pay-for-performance has become popular among policy makers and private and public payers, including Medicare and Medicaid. The Affordable Care Act expands the use of pay-for-performance approaches in Medicare in particular and encourages experimentation to identify strategies that introduce greater efficiency and effectiveness..

The predominant fee-for-service system under which providers have historically been paid has led to increased costs by rewarding providers for the volume and complexity of services they provide. Since it has been established that a higher intensity of services does not necessarily result in higher quality care and can even be harmful, third-party payers are pushing back against the traditional fee-for-service arrangement.

By the early 2000s, the deficiencies in the quality of US healthcare had become glaring, and pay-for-performance emerged as a way for payers to focus on quality while at the same time reducing costs. The typical pay-for-performance program provides a bonus to healthcare providers if they meet or exceed agreed-upon quality or performance measures and/or demonstrate year-to-year decreases in the rate of avoidable hospital readmissions.

Pay-for-performance programs can also impose financial penalties on providers that fail to achieve specified goals or cost savings. For example, Medicare no longer pays hospitals to treat patients who acquire certain preventable conditions during their hospital stay, such as pressure sores or urinary tract infections associated with the use of catheters.

The quality measures used in pay-for-performance generally fall into the four categories as described below:

- Process measures (e.g., provision of evidence-based services)
- Outcome measures (e.g., improvement in patient test results)
- Patient experience (e.g., patient satisfaction with service)
- Structure measures (e.g., availability of appropriate equipment)

In the public sector, the Centers for Medicare and Medicaid Services (CMS) has established a value-based purchasing program to provide incentives for physicians and providers to improve the quality and efficiency of care. CMS has also been involved in a number of pay-for-performance demonstration projects testing a variety of approaches among different categories of providers. In the private sector, a number of pay-for-performance programs are in operation.

(continued)

Box 7.1 (continued)
Reference
James, J. (2012). Pay-for-performance. *Health Affairs Health Policy Brief.*
https://doi.org/10.1377/hpb20121011.90233

Regulatory, Political, and Legal Developments

To a great extent what happens inside the healthcare industry is influenced by developments outside of healthcare. At the federal and state levels, a number of regulatory functions exist and, with the stroke of a pen, the healthcare environment can be dramatically altered. Federal regulations governing the operation of the Medicare and Medicaid programs are an important case in point. On the other hand, states have primary responsibility for licensing health facilities and personnel. Almost overnight, state agencies could enact provisions that dramatically alter the playing field. Examples abound in which a state agency has placed a moratorium on nursing home construction or home health licensures or an agency has determined that nurse practitioners should be allowed to write prescriptions. While these may involve narrow bureaucratic directives, such decisions can have a life-or-death effect on many healthcare organizations.

The political environment clearly has both direct and indirect implications for the operation of the healthcare system. Even though no legislation was enacted as a result of the Clinton administration health reform initiative in the early 1990s, the environment that was created as a result of the national debate encouraged many healthcare organizations to position themselves in anticipation of possible reform initiatives. The handling of the certificate-of-need process for a new health facility by a state agency—indeed, whether there is a C-O-N process at all—reflects the political environment of the state.

Legal activities at the national, state, and local levels also have implications for the local healthcare system. There are numerous examples of recent legislation at the national level that have influenced physician referral patterns, the length of stay for women undergoing childbirth, and the ability of patients to sue health maintenance organizations. Even more legal issues are dealt with at the state level and could have important implications for the local healthcare system.

Technology Developments

Developments in the area of technology can exert a major influence on the course of the healthcare system. The history of healthcare has, to a great extent, been a history of technological developments. While few major technological breakthroughs have occurred in recent years, a variety of refinements in available technology have influenced the course of the healthcare system. The introduction of new drugs has changed the manner in which behavioral health problems are addressed, refinements in biomedical equipment have made home care more feasible for a range of conditions, and microsurgical techniques have contributed to the shift of care from the inpatient to the outpatient setting.

The next major technological development is likely to be in the area of information management. Efforts on the part of communities to develop community health information management systems (CHIMS) for sharing patient data are indicative of the trend toward more sophisticated information management.

Reimbursement Trends

A strong argument could be made that the financing arrangements available for the provision of care are the major factor in determining the nature of a healthcare system. Most of the major watersheds in the history of US healthcare can, in fact, be traced to financing-related events. Notable among these are the introduction of health insurance, the enactment of the Medicare and Medicaid programs, and the introduction of the prospective payment system during the 1980s. In more recent years, the emergence of innovative financing arrangements involving health maintenance organizations, preferred provider organizations, and other entities has changed the healthcare landscape. Various reimbursement trends are now driving the future direction of the healthcare system.

Financing issues may be impacted by all levels of government as well as by private sector third-party payors. Specific examples of the impact of changing regulations are found in the areas of ambulatory care and physician reimbursement. Changes in reimbursement that encouraged the use of outpatient services rather than inpatient services have had a tremendous effect on the operation of the healthcare system. Changes in the procedure through which Medicare reimburses primary care physicians relative to specialists have had a number of implications for medical practitioners.

Local financing issues may be as important as trends in national programs. The safety net that serves the medically indigent is likely to be locally funded. A reduction in funding for the public hospital or the community's charity clinics may have an immediate and disturbing effect on care for the medically indigent. Changes in a state's Medicaid program could have equally devastating effects on the availability of care for the affected populations.

Baseline Data Collection

The environmental assessment establishes the backdrop against which further analysis takes place. The next step in the data collection process involves developing baseline data on the community. These baseline data provide the foundation for the planning process, the basis for any future comparisons, and the yardstick by which the success of the planning process will be measured. This process identifies the who, what, when, where, and how of the community and its healthcare system.

Profiling the Community

In most cases, the delineation of the "community" will be obvious, in that it is the geographic unit that comes under the jurisdiction of the government entity that is involved in planning. There may be situations, however, when the boundaries of the community are not clearly defined. For example, a regional planning authority may be established to address the needs of an area that cuts across state lines and involves a number of counties. The delineation of the boundaries of the "community" in this case requires a different approach. Techniques developed for determining the service area for a specific healthcare organization might be used in these cases. (These techniques are discussed in Chap. 8.)

As part of this community profiling process, the regional setting should be taken into consideration. Different regions of the country have their own cultural patterns, and these seem to have persisted despite the rapid "massification" of the US society. Different regions report varying levels of prevalence for certain health problems, and the variation in utilization of health services is now well documented (Center for Evaluative Clinical Sciences 1999). At the very least, regional variations must be considered when health services demand is being estimated or projected for a particular community.

The *community type* should also be a consideration when collecting baseline data. Whether the dominant community type within the planning area is urban, suburban, or rural will have important implications for both health status and health behavior. Not only will the circumstances surrounding the health of the population be different for different community types, but the challenge of planning for different community types exists.

The community assessment process should consider local *environmental factors* to the extent that they impact health status. There is growing evidence that aspects of our environment account for as much as 20% of the difference in health status. High levels of environmental pollutants, the presence of toxic waste dumps, and issues related to drinking water all have implications for the health status of the population under study.

In profiling the community, the temporal dimension is an important issue. Whether determining the needs of the population or the resources available to meet these needs, three time horizons must be taken into consideration. The current inventory of needs and resources (the present) is a starting point. However, it is also important to develop a sense of the historical trends (the past) that are affecting the community. Is the population growing or declining? Are the characteristics of the population different today than they were 5 years ago? Is the trend toward closing of hospitals or adding more beds?

The most important time frame, however, is the future, since planning by definition is futuristic. In fact, one of the factors contributing to the failure of past planning efforts has been the tendency to plan for today's or, worse, for yesterday's issues. A plan should address tomorrow's issues and, to this end, the process should identify to the extent possible the future characteristics of the population, its future health service needs, and likely future developments with regard to resources.

Profiling the Population

The population of the community must be profiled along a number of dimensions. This is a point in the process that the planning audit (see Chap. 6) can be utilized, with the common categories of data utilized in the profiling process described below.

Demographic Data

Demographic data serve as the foundation for most health planning activities. Not only are demographic data important for profiling the community, but they serve as the basis for the calculation of a number of statistics relevant to the planning analysis. While an understanding of the demographic composition of the target population is important in its own right, this information is also essential for identifying the prevalence of health conditions and determining utilization patterns within the community.

From a health planning perspective, it is useful to categorize demographic variables into *biosocial* variables and *sociocultural* variables. Biosocial characteristics are clearly distinguished as demographic variables by their link to biological traits. The demographic variables included in this category are *age*, *sex*, and *race*. (*Ethnicity* is sometimes included because of its close relationship to race.)

Age is probably the best single predictor of the utilization of health services. Age is related to not only levels of service utilization but also the type of services utilized and the circumstances under which they are received.

The *sex* of the consumer is another factor influencing utilization rates in the US society. Females are more active than males in terms of health behavior and are heavier users of the healthcare system. They tend to visit physicians more often, take more prescription drugs, and, in general, use other facilities and personnel more often.

The *population pyramid* is a useful way of simultaneously depicting the age and sex structure of a population graphically. A population pyramid involves a presentation of the age-sex distribution of a population by means of a bar graph where each bar represents one age-sex group. Female age cohorts comprise one side of each bar and males the other and the ages are typically presented in 5- or 10-year intervals. The "shape" of the pyramid discloses a great deal of information about the population in question and this information can be converted into estimates of the demand for health services. (Figure 7.1 presents an example of a population pyramid.)

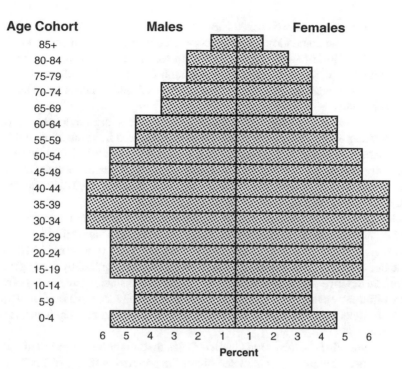

Fig. 7.1 Population pyramid

Racial and ethnic characteristics influence the demand for health services, and, as a result of recent trends, this aspect of population composition is becoming increasingly important for health planners. Detailed information on the racial and ethnic characteristics of the population should be compiled, including qualitative data on attitudes and preferences. While differences in utilization may be traced to differences in the types of health problems experienced by these populations, many of the distinctions reflect variations in lifestyle patterns and cultural preferences. Because the public sector plays an important role in addressing the healthcare needs of minority populations, data on race and ethnicity are critical.

Sociocultural traits are important in profiling the population because of their correlation with health status and health behavior. The sociocultural variables reflect one's position in the social structure and the variables discussed below include marital status and related attributes, education, income, occupation/industry, and other sociocultural factors. Additional information on insurance coverage, psychographic categories, and community attitudes is included.

Marital status, household structure, and, to a degree, *living arrangements* are all of interest to health planners. Marital status refers to one's current legal status with regard to marriage. Household structure refers to involvement in the physical household—i.e., where one actually lives. Living arrangements refer to the relationship between those sharing a household—i.e., roommates, married with children, and unmarried relatives. For community health planners, marital status and household structure may have implications for the types of health problems that exist and the patterns of health services utilization.

Education is an important factor to consider during planning, since the educational level of the population is closely correlated with both health status and health behavior. This information is often important for the development of services that are compatible with the level of sophistication of the target audience. Certainly, from a social marketing perspective, the level of education needs to be taken into consideration.

Income and related variables, such as poverty status, are obviously critical for any planning at the community level. Income, measured in terms of annual household income or per capita income, is an important predictor of both the level of morbidity within the community and likely patterns of health services utilization. The overall level of community affluence will influence both the healthcare "wants" of the population and the level of resources available.

Occupation and *industry* are important variables in profiling a community. Not only do individuals in different occupations and industries have differing consumer behavior habits, but also the occupational or industrial mix of an area is an excellent indicator of the mix of healthcare services and products required by the target population. Distinctive patterns of healthy and unhealthy behavior have been correlated with different occupations and industries. Further, the occupational structure is likely to determine the extent to which employer-sponsored health insurance is available.

There are other sociocultural characteristics that might be important in different communities. Religion is a characteristic of the population that is difficult to measure and has, in fact, played a limited role in community-wide planning. However, there are occasions when knowledge of a community's religious preferences may be appropriate for health services planning, especially if there are strong ties to church-affiliated health facilities in the community under study. The language spoken by the community population or subpopulations may also be a factor influencing healthcare communications and efficient delivery of services.

The *insurance coverage* characterizing a community's population is an increasingly important topic for consideration by planners. While the community's "payer mix" may be more relevant to specific healthcare providers, the means of financing healthcare is not an unimportant issue for community health planners. It could be argued, in fact, that the utilization patterns within the community are to a great extent a reflection of the payer mix.

In analyzing the community's ability to pay for healthcare, the proportion of residents covered under various forms of insurance is an important consideration. Commercial (or private) insurance has typically included both group and individual coverage. This category has historically included the not-for-profit Blue Cross/Blue Shield plans and, increasingly today, managed care plans.

Other major payer categories include those covered under the federally sponsored Medicare and Medicaid programs. Medicare coverage is primarily for the elderly, but it does include a growing proportion of disabled enrollees. Medicaid coverage reflects the participation of the medically indigent in the joint federal-state Medicaid program. In some communities, many Medicare enrollees may also be enrolled in Medicaid.

There are miscellaneous categories of government coverage that should be considered, although their size is usually negligible. These would include other federal programs for categorical conditions, state programs for specific diseases, and coverage under military-related programs such as the CHAMPUS program.

A residual category that remains after the other payer categories have been identified is generally referred to as the "self-pay" category. This involves a wide range of population segments that typically have little in common except for a lack of insurance coverage. This includes uninsurable individuals who, due to past medical histories, cannot obtain insurance. It includes the working poor who do not qualify for Medicaid yet do not have access to or cannot afford private insurance. This category also includes the homeless whose lifestyles mitigate against any type of permanent situation and the independently wealthy who prefer to pay out of pocket for healthcare should it be necessary.

The self-pay category is small in relative terms, but the growth in the number of uninsured individuals has served to swell its ranks. Estimates in 2000 placed the number of uninsured Americans over 40 million (or more than 15% of the population), although the introduction of the ACA addressed much of this. Periods of high unemployment within the US workforce also have an impact on the extent of health insurance coverage.

In community health planning, much of the emphasis is placed on the Medicaid and self-pay categories. These are populations that tend to be the most vulnerable in the face of health problems and are the most likely to place demands on the public health system. While the numbers of nonpaying patients are small in the overall scheme of things, the burden of dealing with indigent patients can be considerable in communities where they constitute a significant portion of the population.

Psychographic Data

It has become increasingly common to profile consumers in terms of their *psychographic characteristics* and assign them to lifestyle clusters. Psychographics refers to the values, attitudes, and lifestyles that characterize a defined population segment. Lifestyle segmentation systems have been developed by a variety of vendors have increasingly come into use in healthcare. The approach involves dividing the population up into a large number of segments (usually 50–60) that can then be profiled in terms of various characteristics including health status and health behavior. Psychographic factors are particularly important in examining attitudes toward one's health and the likelihood of involvement in healthy or unhealthy behaviors.

Psychographic analysis can help determine the likely health priorities and behavior of a population subgroup. This is important because groups that are similar demographically may be different in terms of their lifestyle-influenced health behavior. For example, one category of elderly healthcare consumers may prefer general practitioners for their primary care needs, while another category prefers physicians trained in internal medicine. While psychographic characteristics are considered more important for organization-level planning, knowledge of the psychographic clusters characterizing a community provides a useful perspective for community health planning.

The *attitudes* characterizing the population being planned for is another dimension that must be considered. "Attitudes" may encompass perceptions, preferences, and expectations. The attitudes displayed by consumers in the community are likely to play a significant role in the direction the planning process takes, influence what is actually accomplished through the process, and, in fact, determine whether the process is carried out at all. In the community-wide context, planning initiatives are likely to rely heavily on health education programs and preventive actions that depend on appropriate consumer attitudes for their success.

The community's attitudes, for example, may reflect a pro-physician or pro-hospital stance. In other cases, there may be strong positive or negative perceptions (whether based on fact or not) with regard to various institutions or providers. There may be preferences for certain types of practitioners or methods of treatment over others. Some communities may be very traditional in their attitudes toward healthcare, while others may be quick to embrace alternative treatment modalities.

Another important consideration is the *cultural preferences* of the target population. These cultural preferences (often reflected in lifestyles) may not be directly related to health behavior although many are. Social group preferences for marital status or family size may affect the health status of the population. More directly, dietary habits, exercise patterns, and patterns of unhealthy behavior (e.g., smoking and alcohol use) affect the health status of the population and ultimately the demand for health services. To the extent that healthy or unhealthy behavior is encouraged by the individual's cultural context, this is an important consideration for planners.

Noteworthy examples abound with states like Louisiana and Nevada cited for cultural preferences that could be detrimental to health status, while Utah is cited as a state whose cultural preferences promote good health and longer life. The fact that Wisconsin and Puerto Rico forfeited federal highway construction dollars in the past rather than raising the legal age for alcohol consumption reflects the prevailing cultural preferences in those locales.

Identifying Health Characteristics

A number of dimensions must be considered in examining the health characteristics of the population. This involves the collection of data on the variety of health indicators used to determine its health status and, in turn, estimate the population's healthcare needs. This information should be supplemented with data on health behavior, including existing utilization patterns and informal health practices. The following categories of data should be considered in developing a health profile.

Fertility Characteristics

Fertility characteristics refer to the attributes and processes related to reproduction and childbirth. Fertility behavior should be considered by the planning analyst because of its effect on population size, growth, and composition. Fertility patterns exert a major influence on both current and future patterns of health services utilization. The most direct link involves the healthcare needs of mothers and children prior to, during, and after birth, with each phase involving unique service and facility needs. Other requirements emerge when all stages of the reproductive process are considered. For example, healthcare providers and clinic facilities are major sources of contraception-related services. Disorders related to the male and female reproductive systems place additional demands on healthcare providers, and infertility treatment is a growing component of the healthcare system.

In community-wide planning, many of the health-related issues can be linked to the level of "problem" pregnancies within the community's population. Trends in infant mortality, low-birth-weight babies, births to adolescents, and births to unwed mothers all have implications for the healthcare needs of the community.

Morbidity Characteristics

Morbidity, or the level of sickness and disability within a population, is a major concern for health planners. Morbidity analysis involves identifying both the static and dynamic aspects of sickness, as well as how those patterns affect mortality. Several measures have been developed and adopted that are commonly used in morbidity analysis. Although little success has been made in establishing an overall measure of morbidity for individuals or populations, indicators for specific conditions are frequently used. These indicators include incidence and prevalence statistics for specific conditions, symptom checklists, and various measures of disability. "Reportable" conditions are of particular interest to public health officials, since they relate to conditions that have the potential to spread to epidemic proportions.

Some health conditions are monitored through reports from health facilities, sample surveys, and ongoing panel studies. Federal health agencies conduct periodic surveys of hospital inpatients and ambulatory patients in clinics and other outpatient settings. In addition, databases have been established for the systematic compilation of data on inpatient utilization and, to a lesser extent, outpatient utilization. These data collection efforts allow for the identification of cases for a wide variety of conditions and the monitoring of the level of these conditions over time.

Another group of morbidity measures is referred to as disability measures. Like other aspects of morbidity, disability is difficult to measure within a population. While it would appear simple to enumerate the blind, deaf, crippled, or otherwise handicapped, the situation is actually quite complex. Many individuals who are legally or technically considered disabled function normally, thereby blurring the lines between those who are disabled and those who are not.

Beyond the standard morbidity data collected, there are a number of categories of data that might be considered. Health planners have come to recognize that some important metrics have been neglected, especially since some of these metrics reflect the concerns of community residents. Feedback from community members, in fact, is likely to present a much different picture of health issues than that from health professionals. Neglected metrics include data related to obesity, behavioral health/substance abuse, oral health, and domestic violence to mention a few.

Quantifying Morbidity Data

Assuming that adequate data are available, various measures of morbidity can be calculated. Two of the most useful measures are incidence and prevalence rates. An incidence rate refers to the number of new cases of a disease or condition reported over a certain time period expressed as the number per 1000, 10,000, or 100,000 people at risk. A prevalence rate refers to the total number of persons with the disease or condition in question at a specific point in time expressed as the number per 1000, 10,000, or 100,000 people at risk.

The prevalence rate always exceeds the incidence rate, since the former is a component of the latter. The only time the two rates are comparable is when the condition under study is acute and of very short duration. For example, the incidence rate would almost equal the prevalence rate at the height of a 24-hour virus epidemic, since victims recover almost as quickly as they are infected.

Incidence and prevalence rates are both important for profiling the target population. If the analyst knows, for example, that the incidence rate for a certain medical condition is 17 per 1000 population aged 65 years and over (and it is assumed that the incidence rate for that procedure will remain constant for the next 5 years), then the number of cases can be projected 5 years into the future if the size of the population of persons aged 65 and over for the service area in question is known. The incidence rate is simply multiplied by the projected population to determine the expected number of cases. The prevalence rate can be used in much the same way when the condition is a chronic one. This is precisely how many hospitals and other healthcare providers forecast the demand for their services.

Mortality Characteristics

Mortality refers to the process of population attrition through death. Mortality analysis includes the study of those who die as well as the health conditions that contribute to their deaths. Mortality studies investigate the who, how, why, and when issues related to dying.

The most basic way to measure mortality is simply to count the number of deaths. Compiling death counts over a period of years has helped identify trends with regard to increases or decreases in mortality. Further, deaths can be cross-classified by the medical, social, and economic characteristics of the deceased. Two of the most useful of these characteristics to planners are the cause of death and the age at which death occurred.

The simplest measure used in mortality analysis is the crude death rate (CDR). This rate expresses the number of deaths as a rate per 1000 population. The fact that not all of the population is at the same risk of death, however, limits its usefulness. As a result, age-adjusted death rates (ASDRs) are often generated.

It may also be useful to decompose the CDR into cause-specific components and to calculate the percentage of total deaths attributable to each cause. These figures, which are derived by dividing the number of deaths from one cause by the total number of deaths, represent the proportion of population dying of a specific cause. A cause-specific mortality rate may provide some perspective on the morbidity characteristics of a population in the absence of more direct morbidity statistics.

Although mortality remains an important health status indicator for health planners, its usefulness is somewhat limited in contemporary society. Relatively few deaths occur each year and these tend to be clustered among the elderly who are dying from conditions associated with aging. Further, the chronic conditions that have become predominant in the US society are typically not directly associated with mortality. Individuals suffering from chronic conditions (e.g., hypertension) are likely to die from some other, more proximate cause (e.g., heart failure). Therefore, the designated cause of death may not be an accurate indicator of the health status of the deceased. For these reasons, mortality patterns are less useful for profiling the health status of the population than morbidity data.

Social Determinants of Health

There is growing recognition of the contribution of social factors to the level of ill health within a population and to the health disparities that exist between various groups within society. This realization has been a major factor in the emergence of the population health movement. As biological pathogens and genetics have waned as etiological factors, social factors have come to the fore. While we could claim to be "victims" of pathogens or genetics, we cannot claim to be blameless when it comes to contemporary causes of ill health.

As individuals and as a society we are, in fact, responsible for most of the health problems that currently affect us. As individuals we affect our own health through the lifestyles we pursue. These lifestyles are "social" to the extent that they are mediated through the groups of which we are members. We all face pressure to conform to the lifestyle characteristics of the groups with which we are affiliated often without being aware of their influence.

As a society we have encouraged unhealthy lifestyles through the promotion (and even the subsidization) of unhealthy—but profitable—food choices. We have also allowed an unacceptable level of environmental degradation. Environmental pollutants contribute to the high rate of cancer and air pollution to the surging rate of chronic obstructive pulmonary disease. We have contaminated our soil and water with lead and other chemicals with the recent lead poisoning tragedy in Flint, Michigan, representing the tip of the iceberg. We have tolerated an unacceptable level of housing deterioration, with a large segment of the population forced to live in unsafe and unhealthy housing.

At a deeper level we have allowed if not outright fostered the emergence of a level of socioeconomic inequality perhaps never experienced by the US population. As more and more financial resources are concentrated among the wealthiest in society, lower- and working-class populations have access to fewer resources. This translates into unhealthy lifestyles and a lack of access to health services, thereby creating a perpetual cycle of financial distress and ill health.

As the impact of social factors on health status has become documented, the argument is increasingly being made that the health conditions exhibited by a population are not the *problems* per se but are *symptoms* of underlying problems. Thus, the morbidity levels exhibited by various populations are a reflection of the social determinants of health and illness that are, in effect, the true problems. The presence of disease can thus be seen as the manifestation of these underlying conditions. This perspective is supported by research that suggests that disadvantaged populations are likely to identify as "health problems" such factors as lack of food, inadequate housing, and unsafe streets.

This observation is further reinforced by virtue of the low priority that is placed on health by certain subgroups—not because they do not desire to be healthy but because other more pressing concerns take priority. Research by the federal government finds that people living in poverty face a level of basic expenses for necessities that exceeds their available income (U.S. Department of Health and Human Services 2015). While limited information is available on the priorities of the poor in the United States, international research (World Bank 2001) has found that the urban poor worldwide are most concerned about lack of jobs, unsanitary environments, food meeting basic needs, food insecurity, and lack of education. Health and healthcare are subordinated to other problems. This pattern was reinforced by a study of low-income residents of Washington, DC (Danis et al. 2011) in which respondents were questioned with regard to the factors that would contribute to improved health status. The researchers found that the interventions ultimately prioritized by the greatest percentage of individuals were health insurance (95%), housing vouchers (82%), dental care (82%), job training (72%), adult education (63%), counseling (68%), healthy behavior incentives (68%), and job placement (67%). Medical care was not considered a major contributor to health status, with respondents focusing on social factors as much as personal health when amelioration was discussed.

Critics of the US healthcare system point out that we have been treating these symptoms while not addressing the true cause of the problems. Putting a Band-Aid on the wound is of limited usefulness if the underlying infection is not addressed, and an approach that addresses symptoms without affecting a true cure is clearly ineffective when it comes to improving population health. This explains the fact that there is no correlation between health resources expended and health status. Thus, we now acknowledge that better access to health insurance does not guarantee access to care. Access to care does not assure utilization of services. Utilization of services does not necessarily foster better patient outcomes and clearly does not contribute to improved population health. Our system has labored under the delusion that more care means better health and that the health status of the population will be improved by providing greater access to health services.

It is hard to ignore the fallacy of this perspective. Providers are well aware of the high rate of recidivism despite the best efforts of the medical community. Patients return for care repeatedly because their symptoms were treated but not the underlying disease. Research on hospital readmissions has found, for example, that readmission has little to do with the care that was received but almost everything to do with the conditions associated with the patient prior to admission and after discharge from medical care (Hu et al. 2014).

Improvement in population health will require attention to the root causes of ill health within the population. Over 20 years ago healthcare analysts initially posited the social determinants of health and illness (Evans et al. 1994). The emergent approach was described as a "common focus on trying to understand the determinants of health of populations." Foreseeing the breadth of the population health approach, this work brought together research findings from epidemiology, biomedical science, psychology, sociology, economics, political science, and history. While, as seen below, our understanding of the social determinants of health and illness has been significantly advanced since then, we still have a lot to learn about the connection between social conditions and health status.

The first step in this process is to identify the factors that immediately influence the health status of the population in question and, beyond that, to identify the underlying social determinants that have a significant if less direct impact on health status. Both levels of influence are discussed below along with the factors that contribute to the health disparities identified within the population.

Intermediate Causes

While there are deep-seated social conditions that influence a population's health status, there are some intermediate or proximate influences that might be considered first. Factors like poverty, limited education, lack of job opportunities, and similar factors may ultimately be blamed for variations in health status, but these factors are typically not routine daily considerations. There are other more mundane circumstances that reflect these underlying determinants that have a more immediate impact.

These conditions might be described as "life circumstances" to distinguish them from more deep-seated social determinants. Life circumstances include the conditions of everyday living that constrain people's activities and influence their behavior. These might include household structure (e.g., living alone or in overcrowded conditions), housing adequacy, neighborhood safety, access to resources, and other factors that provide a context for understanding both health status and health behavior. Box 7.2 describes life circumstances and their implications.

Box 7.2: Life Circumstances and Health

There is growing concern among healthcare providers, third-party payers, and policy makers over the poor outcomes that are being generated by our health-care system. Even with access to the world's most advanced technology and best trained specialists, disappointing outcomes are often recorded. Further, there are significant disparities in the outcomes for different groups with simi-lar conditions. Members of different racial groups, for example, with similar health conditions, the same level of acuity, and the same treatment in the same health facilities, may record different outcomes (Hopper 2011). Findings of this type suggest that there are factors other than the quality of medical treat-ment that contribute to differential outcomes.

Increasingly, characteristics attributable to patients before and after medi-cal treatment are being analyzed for their effect on clinical outcomes. The "life circumstances" of patients and consumers are increasingly being seen as important drivers of health status, health behavior, and healthcare outcomes. While there is no consensus with regard to what should be considered as life circumstances at this time, it is clear that certain attributes and conditions affect individual patients and consumers as well as families and social groups. Conditions identified by Peek (2014) include unemployment, lack of job opportunities, substandard housing, absence of health insurance, and low edu-cational attainment. In addition, ethnic group membership, language profi-ciency, and even religious affiliation can represent aspects of life circumstances. These attributes are frequently incorporated into assessments of health dis-parities within communities and can become deep-rooted attributes that pro-vide an ongoing negative backdrop for the lives of affected patients and consumers (Ellaway 2014).

Additional life circumstance attributes likely to affect households include family stability, housing security (as opposed to housing quality), safety of the living environment and surrounding community, quality of the physical environment, and access to affordable healthy food (Pace 2014). Other spe-cific factors include access to transportation, personal assistance and support resources, and information that informs individual health and well-being.

Collectively, life circumstances factors can offer insights into the varia-tions in observed health status and health outcomes. An early study noting the effect of life circumstances on the risk of death was completed by Fox et al. (1985), and more recent work linking life circumstances with mortality was completed by The Scottish Public Health Observatory (2014). In actuality, life circumstances may represent more important targets for remedial actions than the delivery of additional health services (Pedersen et al. 2011). Clearly, the impact of the delivery of clinical services is limited by the circumstances that affected the patient prior to and after the receipt of these services. Given the impact that life circumstances appear to have, it could be argued that putting a clinic on every corner would not improve health status if important life cir-cumstance issues are not addressed.

(continued)

Box 7.2 (continued)

Increasingly, an understanding of the social and environmental factors affecting individuals and groups of patients, employees, and consumers is required in order to (1) identify the context in which the patient or consumer functions and (2) anticipate the impact of the context on the therapeutic process. While the healthcare system can do little by itself to change the contextual life circumstances of patients and consumers within its service area, early and accurate intelligence on these risk factors can contribute to more effective operation of the healthcare system.

References

Ellaway, A. (2014). The impact of the local social and physical environment on wellbeing. In E. Burton & R. Cooper (Eds.), *Wellbeing and the environment* (Vol. 2). Oxford: Wiley-Blackwell.

Fox, A. J., Goldblatt, P. O., & Jones, D. R. (1985). Social class mortality differentials: Artefact, selection or life circumstances. *Journal of Epidemiology and Community Health, 39*, 1–8.

Hopper, K. (2011). *Disparities in cardiac rehab*. Unpublished presentation. Retrieved from http://www.aacvpr.org/Portals/0/events_edu/annual-meeting11/2011%20Online%20Syllabus%20PPT/BO31Hopper.pdf

Pace, K. (2014, January 24). *Get to root causes: Address poor health outcomes through a health equity lens*. Michigan University Extension. Retrieved from http://msue.anr.msu.edu/news/get_to_root_causes_address_poor_health_outcomesthrougha_health_equity_lens

Pedersen, P. V., Gronbaek, M., & Curtis, T. (2011). Associations between deprived life circumstances, wellbeing and self-rated health in a socially marginalized population. *The European Journal of Public Health, 22*(5), 647–652.

Peek, M. (2014). Poverty's association with poor health outcomes and health disparities. *Health Affairs*. Retrieved from http://healthaffairs.org/blog/2014/10/30/povertys-association-with-poor-health-outcomes-and-health-disparities/

Scottish Public Health Observatory. (2014). *Community well-being: Key points*. Retrieved from http://www.scotpho.org.uk/life-circumstances/community-wellbeing/key-points

Some of these intermediate factors could be encapsulated under the heading of "lifestyle" since this term covers a range of attitudes, preferences, and behaviors that may be thought to contribute to one's health status and, ultimately, to the health status of groups within the population. Some aspects of lifestyle have been heavily scrutinized and clearly linked to health status. Factors such as dietary habits, participation in exercise, sleep adequacy, and avoidance of harmful substances are clearly linked to variations in health status. While these might be considered aspects of personal lifestyles they are still very much influenced by the groups in which they participate. It could be argued that some participate in these behaviors out of necessity (e.g., food deserts, lack of green space) and that issue is discussed below. At the same time members of certain subpopulations are likely to exhibit these characteristics even if they did have access to healthy foods and exercise facilities.

The use and abuse of tobacco, alcohol, and drugs (legal and illegal) are clearly aspects of the lifestyles of certain subpopulations. Even to the extent that members of these groups are aware of the dangers of substance abuse, they are encouraged by their peers to participate in these unhealthy activities. The same may be said for risk-taking behaviors and risky sexual activities. Despite the known risks, there are nevertheless social pressures to participate in such behaviors. Even wearing automobile seatbelts may be discouraged as "not cool" by members of some subpopulations. Box 7.3 discusses the use of lifestyle segmentation to study the impact of lifestyles on health status and health behavior.

Box 7.3: Case Study: Using Lifestyle Analysis to Predict the Use of Behavioral Health Services

During the last quarter of the twentieth century, behavioral health services emerged as an important sector of the US healthcare system. This umbrella term covered many conditions, including psychiatric problems, emotional disturbances, substance abuse, hyperactivity in children, and other conditions considered treatable by mental health professionals. Behavioral health services were considered to be in a different category from the treatment of physical illness, and a separate industry was developed for the management of behavioral health problems. Many health plans carved out behavioral health services, and, eventually, national managed care plans specializing in such services emerged.

By the late 1990s, the primary purchasers of behavioral health services— that is, major employers—were facing growing financial pressure because of increasing healthcare costs. Behavioral health services were particularly problematic because of the open-ended nature of many behavioral health conditions. At the same time, however, regulations that mandated parity between physical health coverage and behavioral health coverage were being enacted. Employers who wanted to offer behavioral health coverage to their employees were faced with a major cost-containment challenge.

ABC Health Services was a major player in the behavioral health arena, reporting an enrollment of more than three million members in its managed care plans. ABC was faced with the same issue other behavioral health plans had to address: customers who could not distinguish between plans and were shopping for the lowest price. As a result, ABC was losing clients to other, sometimes less efficacious plans that quoted lower prices.

In response to this situation, ABC developed an innovative approach to the market using lifestyle segmentation analysis. On the basis of records maintained on enrollees who participated in its behavioral health plans, ABC

(continued)

Box 7.3 (continued)

believed that the likelihood of using behavioral health services could be linked to certain lifestyle categories among employees. ABC also thought that the type and intensity of services used could be correlated with lifestyle cluster.

ABC subsequently profiled existing clients in terms of its MOSAIC lifestyle clusters (see Box 7.2). It found that approximately a dozen lifestyle clusters (of the 60 MOSAIC clusters at that time) were associated with a high propensity to use behavioral health services. Another ten lifestyle clusters were almost never associated with the use of these services. The remaining clusters did not appear to correlate with use or nonuse.

The cluster populated by middle-class suburban families tended to be characterized by high utilization levels, whereas the cluster populated by low-income rural families was characterized by low utilization levels. Furthermore, the older, affluent suburban household cluster had a high propensity for using alcohol-abuse services but not drug-abuse services. On the other hand, the single, affluent, urban, high-rise cluster had a high propensity to use drug-abuse services but not alcohol treatment services. Some clusters were characterized by episodic use of services (e.g., in response to some stressful events), while members of other clusters were characterized by recurrent use of services, indicating deeper problems.

ABC was able to use this information in marketing its behavioral health plan to existing customers and prospective clients. ABC representatives offered to profile the employees of existing customers, for example, to determine the extent to which the package of services offered by ABC was meeting their employees' needs. Profiling not only allowed ABC to more efficiently serve the existing client population but also helped the organization to predict future use of behavioral health services. The service mix could be subsequently adjusted to serve existing enrollees more efficiently and more cost effectively.

To attract prospective clients, ABC distinguished itself from other behavioral health plans by determining a configuration of needs for the target group of employees. By serving in a consultative role, ABC demonstrated greater expertise than its competitors in managing behavioral health clients. Further, ABC could offer a package of services tailored to the needs of its clients, rather than the one-size-fits-all plan offered by other firms. By developing an in-depth knowledge of the target population using lifestyle segmentation analysis, ABC was able to provide more effective services at competitive prices while raising the satisfaction level of employers and employees.

While the examples above refer to activities reflecting the volition of the actors, many aspects of lifestyle are imposed upon society members who have no ability to resist. While poverty may be viewed from a broad perspective to the extent that it affects a wide spectrum of life conditions, as an intermediate contributor it takes the form of the inability to afford food (or at least healthy food), to afford adequate housing, or to pay the utility bill—much less the ability to afford a fitness center membership fee.

At a secondary level the lack of financial resources creates a multiplier effect in that the dearth of resources means that there is no money for the childcare necessary to allow the individual to go to work or to school or for the transportation necessary to travel to work or school or to a job training program. The lack of money for food noted above also carries over to the work or school setting where it has been demonstrated that hungry or malnourished children and adults cannot perform school work or job activities effectively (Hickson et al. n.d.; Brown et al. 2007).

The lack of financial resources has implications for health behavior. Aside from its impact on access to healthy foods and exercise options, there is no money for basic prevention items such as soap and toothpaste. Importantly, there is no money available to purchase health insurance or to pay for health services when the need arises. As a result, members of certain populations are unable to participate in preventive activities or to access necessary health services. Even if basic care could be obtained from a free clinic or hospital emergency room, the ability to purchase necessary drugs may be limited. Thus, a financial exigency becomes transformed into an aspect of lifestyle.

Lifestyles also affect health behavior in several direct and indirect ways. A clear example relates to food preferences. Youth and many adults adopt a "fast-food lifestyle" and seldom eat any other type of food. To do so would risk ridicule from their peers. Healthy foods once promoted by certain subcultures (e.g., the greens and vegetables associated with African-American culture) are eschewed in favor of inexpensive but unhealthy processed foods. The churches patronized by members of certain subcultures are notorious for their unhealthy church supper fare. Mexican immigrants may give up corn-based food products for more "American" wheat-based products with negative consequences for their health (Giuntella 2012). Lifestyle attributes such as these have come to be seen as predictors of health behavior and, to a certain extent, health status.

One implication for people living under these circumstances is the low priority placed on personal health. In actuality, most of the US population displays a cavalier attitude toward their health despite the much-ballyhooed fitness movement. These problems are particularly acute among specific subpopulations. While we are frequently exposed to health promotional materials, the mere distribution of information on healthy lifestyles appears to have little impact. In fact, research (Beck 2016) has found that less than 3% of Americans exhibit what would be considered a healthy lifestyle (i.e., appropriate diet and exercise, avoidance of unhealthy activities).

Large segments of the population have been found to have little interest in health and wellness. A study (Thomas 2009) of an established African-American community in a southern city found that the residents were divided into three groups in terms of their interest in health and wellness (as determined through a consumer database): (1) little interest; (2) almost no interest; and (3) no interest whatsoever. It is absurd, of course, to suppose that the residents would not like to be healthy but, as a practical matter, they had other issues to deal with that were much more pressing at least in their minds.

One factor affecting certain subpopulations is lack of employment. Unemployment is another proximate contributor to poor health status and, aside from the obvious financial exigencies caused by unemployment, the impact of this on health status has been well documented. Research has shown that unemployed people are more likely to have poor health habits, characterized by excess drinking, smoking, lack of exercise, and a sedentary lifestyle. The fear of unemployment has been linked to increased cholesterol levels. Studies from around the world have found that people who had been unemployed in prior years had higher mortality rates than people never unemployed, with men much more likely to be affected. Further, unemployment increased long-term mortality when other risk factors are controlled for.

Unemployment is associated with a range of increased health problems (Strully 2009). For individuals with no prior health problems, being fired or laid off increased the risk of fair or poor health by 83% in this study. Previous unemployment was linked to a significant increase in acute myocardial infarction. The longer more frequently people are unemployed, the greater the cumulative risk. Research in Sweden (Voss et al. 2004) indicated that the higher death rates of previously unemployed individuals (followed over a 24-year period) were related to higher rates of suicide, accidents, cancer, and cardiovascular disease. The fact that these health risks continue for 24 years suggests that unemployment is a potentially dangerous life event. Indeed, the risks associated with unemployment may be of the same magnitude—or greater—as smoking, diabetes, and hypertension. Unemployment also serves as an additional source of stress for subpopulations that are already living under stressful conditions. Box 7.4 describes a methodology for assessing the impact projects are likely to have on health.

Box 7.4: The Health Impact Assessment
An approach that is being increasingly utilized to address the impact of external forces on the health status of a population is the health impact assessment (HIA). Governments and businesses are being encouraged to consider the consequences for health, and for health disparities, of proposed policies in transportation, housing, education, taxes, land use, and so forth. For example, a city council might replace an abandoned warehouse with a public park or offer tax incentives for supermarkets to locate in a "food desert" neighborhood. Health impact assessments have been commissioned to study the potential health consequences of policies concerning such diverse topics as minimum wage laws and freeway widening. Health impact assessments can help communities, decision makers, and practitioners make choices that improve population health through community design.

HIA is a process that helps evaluate the potential health effects of a plan, project, or policy before it is built or implemented. HIA brings potential positive and negative public health impacts and considerations to the decision-making process for plans, projects, and policies that fall outside traditional public health arenas, such as transportation and land use. The steps involved in conducting an HIA are as follows:

Screening. During screening, practitioners (who may include staff from health departments, foundations, private organizations, or others with training in HIA methodology) briefly describe potential connections between the pro-

(continued)

Box 7.4 (continued)

posed policy, program, plan, or project and the health of affected communities and individuals. If the proposed undertaking is likely to have significant health impacts—either positive or negative—and an HIA would provide additional information for the decision-making process, proceeding with the HIA process is recommended.

Scoping. This step identifies primary health outcomes of interest, affected and vulnerable populations, and issues identified by stakeholders. Practitioners also outline the research methodology, including data sources and analysis plans. Scoping determines the nature of community involvement and the depth of the assessment.

Assessment. This stage follows through on plans set during scoping and compiles relevant data and information for analysis. Data may be qualitative or quantitative and from a broad range of fields. Analyses should also incorporate stakeholder perspectives. Throughout the process, practitioners must be clear about the limitations of available data and findings.

Recommendations. HIA does not prescribe a decision. Rather, it presents actions to maximize health benefits and minimize harm, especially to vulnerable groups, for the decision alternatives. Recommendations specify the parties or stakeholders that should be responsible for implementation.

Reporting. The HIA report describes in detail the first four steps, including the proposed policy, plan, or program; stakeholders and their involvement; data sources and analysis; findings; recommendations; and a plan for monitoring and evaluation. The report must be clear and easily accessible to all stakeholders. For maximum utility, the report format and timeline should align with economic, political, and social considerations and decision points.

Monitoring and evaluation. The HIA process, impact of the HIA recommendations, and health outcomes after implementation should be evaluated. This stage is especially important given that HIA is a new and rapidly developing field. HIA is usually voluntary, though several local and state laws support the examination of health impacts in decision-making and a few explicitly require the use of HIA.

The health impact assessment is a useful tool to assess how a proposed decision will affect the health of a population and whether vulnerable populations are more likely to be impacted (or whether the health impacts are distributed evenly within the population). Since the goal of the HIA is to generate recommendations during the decision-making process that will protect health and reduce health inequities, the Centers for Disease Control and Prevention considers it as a promising tool for supporting community health improvement.

Health Behavior

Health behavior can be defined as any action aimed at restoring, preserving, and/or enhancing health status. Both formal activities such as physician visits, hospital admissions, and prescription drug consumption and informal actions on the part of individuals such as diet, exercise, and risk-taking should be considered. A number of indicators are used to quantify health behavior and the most common ones are described below.

Hospital admissions is one of the most frequently used indicators of health behavior. The terms "admissions" and "discharges" are used to refer to episodes of inpatient hospital utilization. The hospital admission/discharge rate is generally stated in terms of the number of admissions or discharges per 1000 population. For example, the hospital admission rate for the United States in 2016 of 104 admissions per 1000 population might be expressed in terms of 10 out of every 100 residents (or 10.4%) being hospitalized during that year.

The hospital admission rate serves as a proxy for a variety of other indicators, since hospital admissions are correlated with tests conducted, surgeries performed, and related services and products. For more specificity, admission rates may be broken down by patient category. For example, hospital admission rates by age group, place of residence, or diagnostic category might be calculated. In fact, the planner is more likely to be interested in diagnosis-specific rates than in overall rates.

Patient days refers to the number of hospital days generated by a particular population and is calculated in terms of the number of patient days generated per 1000 residents. This indicator refines hospital admissions to reflect the utilization of resources, since measuring patient days serves to adjust for variations in length of stay. Changes in reimbursement procedures, in fact, have made the patient day more of a standard unit for measuring resource utilization than the admission episode. Two hospitals with comparable admission levels may generate quite different numbers of patient days because of differences in their patient mix. Like admission rates, patient days may be calculated in terms of diagnosis, type of hospital, patient origin, and payer category.

Another indicator related to hospitalization is the *average length of stay*. This is typically reported in terms of the average number of days that patients remain in the facility. For example, the average length of stay (ALOS) at a general hospital in the 2014 was around 4.5 days. On the other hand, the ALOS for a maternity hospital might be around 2 days and for a psychiatric facility around 45 days. This indicator provides a good measure of resource utilization. In fact, many healthcare plans reimburse hospitals on a per diem rate.

There are several other facility indicators that might also be mentioned. While none of these has the significance of hospital admissions, each is important in its own way. Utilization rates may be calculated for nursing homes, hospital emergency rooms, hospital outpatient departments, freestanding emergency centers, mental health centers, urgent care centers, freestanding surgery centers, and freestanding diagnostic centers.

Perhaps one of the most useful indicators of health services use is the level of physician utilization as measured by *physician office visits*. The physician is the "gatekeeper" for most other types of medical care, and physician use is a more direct measure of utilization levels than hospital admissions, since virtually everyone uses a physician's services at some time.

Analysts usually calculate physician utilization in terms of annual visits per 1000 population. For example, a community of 30,000 might be expected to generate 120,000 physician visits per year, given the fact that residents average three physician office visits annually. Since physician utilization varies by specialty, rates for physician visits may be figured separately for the various specialties. Primary care physicians are likely to be visited more often than specialists. In community-wide planning, access to physician services is almost always an issue, making quality data on physician supply and demand critical.

There are other types of personnel for whom utilization rates might be calculated. Most of these, like physicians and dentists, are independent practitioners who practice without the supervision of other medical personnel. Examples include optometrists, podiatrists, chiropractors, and increasingly nurse practitioners and physician's assistants, as well as various mental health counselors and therapists. Physical therapists and speech therapists are other categories of healthcare personnel for whom utilization rates might be developed if, for example, the analyst were involved in planning for rehabilitation services. Utilization rates might be calculated in terms of visits per 1000 population, the average number of visits per person annually, or the proportion of the population using the particular type of therapist.

As the importance of home healthcare has grown in recent years, the volume of *home healthcare visits* has taken on more importance. Home-care utilization is typically measured in terms of visits by various types of personnel. Thus, a population might be considered to have a certain number of home nurse visits or home physical therapist visits as indicators of utilization. Alternatively, the proportion of residents (i.e., the rate per 1000) receiving home care might be calculated.

Community Resources Inventory

Once the healthcare needs and utilization patterns have been determined, the available community resources should be identified. "Resources" are viewed in the broadest sense here, ranging from facilities to personnel to sources of funding for healthcare. The focus here is on facilities involved in the direct provision of care. Although they may be important for some purposes, this discussion does not deal with "retail" establishments (e.g., pharmacies, opticians), rental services (e.g., durable medical equipment), or support services (e.g., laboratories, blood banks). The most important types of community resources are described below.

Facilities

A major component of resource identification involves the inventory of the facilities available for meeting the healthcare needs of the population. For community-wide planning, the broadest possible definition of "facility" is utilized. These include all types of facilities devoted to the treatment of physical or mental illnesses. The following are representative of the types of facilities that must be inventoried:

Hospitals

The central role of the hospital in the provision of care warrants a careful inventory of the area's inpatient facilities. This includes not only general hospitals but also any specialty hospitals that might serve the population. Some categories of hospitals may ultimately be eliminated from the analysis (such as military hospitals or others that serve small, selected populations), but all should initially be included. The number of available hospital beds should be determined, with careful attention paid to operational versus licensed beds.

Area hospitals should be profiled in terms of admissions, occupancy rates, specialty areas, and any other relevant characteristics. Market share should be calculated to the extent possible, trends in these indicators should be identified, and, of course, the physical location of hospitals and other facilities with regard to population concentrations needs to be considered. Any identifiable trends in the characteristics of local health facilities should be noted.

Clinics

The number of clinics providing health services should be determined, particularly since this is the setting in which most clinical encounters occur. ("Clinic" here refers to any freestanding outpatient facility that dispenses medical care.) The key category, of course, is the physician-based clinic, and these clinics should be inventoried in terms of size, specialty, and any other relevant characteristics. Most of these will be private practices, but community-based clinics (such as federally qualified health centers) should be included as well and counted toward the overall resource base. Other types of clinics (nonphysician) that should be considered include mental health centers and other behavioral health practices, dental clinics, eye care clinics, chiropractic clinics, and podiatric clinics. Urgent care centers should be included as well.

Nursing Homes

The other major institutional facility besides hospitals is nursing homes, and nursing home access has become a growing issue as the number of elderly Americans has increased. The number of nursing homes should be determined, along with the number of beds, occupancy rates, and categories of clients served. The type of reimbursement accepted is also an important consideration with regard to nursing home access.

Residential Treatment Facilities

Another form of institutional care involves residential treatment centers. Typically reserved for behavioral health and substance-abuse patients, residential treatment centers represent "inpatient" facilities in the sense that their clients remain overnight at the facility. They do not typically have the around-the-clock intensive clinical support that a hospital would provide. The types of clients that these facilities cater to is an important consideration in the inventory, as well as the type of reimbursement that is accepted.

Home Health Agencies/Hospices

Home health agencies have come to play a major role in the delivery of health services, particularly as the emphasis has shifted from inpatient care to outpatient care. These are technically not facilities in that they actually provide the care in the client's home. The range of services provided in a home setting has steadily grown and, in communities that suffer a shortage of physicians, home health agencies may represent an important source of care. The inventory should identify home health agencies in terms of the services they provide and the type of reimbursement they accept. They should also be identified in terms of organizational structure, such as freestanding/independent agency, affiliate of a national chain, and hospital-based program.

Hospices typically do not involve physical facilities but constitute a program of care that is implemented in the patient's home (although some hospice services may be provided in a hospital or another setting). Although hospice services will not be a major factor in the overall operation of the delivery system, they are necessary to assure a comprehensive range of services.

Mental Health Centers

Mental health services (increasingly referred to as behavioral health services) have often been overlooked in inventories of healthcare facilities due to the bias toward physical medicine. However, a growing proportion of the US population receives some type of mental health services and the demand is expected to grow as lifestyle- and stress-related conditions proliferate. Mental health centers should be identified in terms of their volumes, the types of clients they serve, and their sources of reimbursement.

Diagnostic Centers

As a result of the effort to move care out of the inpatient setting, a number of freestanding facility types have emerged, including outpatient diagnostic centers. These may be multipurpose diagnostic centers or they may focus on a particular diagnostic category such as radiology. The number and types of freestanding diagnostic centers should be determined as well as their organizational affiliation.

Surgery Centers

Freestanding outpatient surgery centers have been another product of the shift from inpatient to outpatient care. As various specialties have shifted their surgical load from the inpatient setting to the outpatient setting, outpatient surgery centers have been the primary beneficiaries. As with other facilities, the type of patients, volume of services, reimbursement arrangements, and organizational affiliation should be determined as part of the inventory.

Urgent Care Centers

Urgent care centers (called by a variety of names) have become increasingly common sources of basic health services. Initially developed as an alternative to emergency room care and as an option for off-hours care, urgent care centers have become a mainstay for segments of the population that do not have a regular source of care. They are, however, designed for one-time episodic care and technically do not serve as true primary care centers. The number of centers, their volumes, and their acceptable reimbursement should be determined, along with their organizational affiliation.

Programs and Services

A distinction is often made between "programs" and "services," with the former typically referring to a multipurpose operation that integrates a number of functions. The latter typically refers to a specific treatment modality that might be offered in a stand-alone fashion or as part of a program. Thus, an agency that provides personal assistants for the home might be considered to offer a service, while a home health agency that offers a full range of nursing services, rehabilitation services, and home infusion, in addition to personal assistance aides, would be considered to have a program.

To a great extent, the services available parallel the facilities that are available. Similar institutions, however, may offer quite different services and these distinctions must be identified. Services are often divided into the categories of inpatient and outpatient (or ambulatory) services. Inpatient services are typically provided by hospitals, but nursing homes, residential treatment centers, and some other institutional settings may be considered to provide inpatient services. Outpatient services (i.e., care not involving an overnight stay) may be provided by these same facilities, but are more likely to be offered by clinics, physician offices, and other freestanding facilities.

Other services that might be considered are emergency medical services, home health and hospice services, long-term care, and various community-based services. In addition, alternative therapy services should increasingly be considered as a category to be inventoried.

The identification of programs and services separate from health facilities and personnel is perhaps more important than it seems on the surface. This is primarily because services define the facility more than the facility defines the services in many cases. Further, healthcare consumers and referral agents are more likely to be seeking a particular service and may not care what type of facility provides it. For example, someone seeking treatment for an eating disorder will be searching for that type of service and it probably does not matter whether it is located at a hospital, a residential facility, or an outpatient facility. It would be rare for a consumer to select a hospital and *then* determine if it had the required service. (The exception would be cases where one's insurance restricted the use of facilities.)

Equipment

An inventory of the biomedical equipment available to the community should be included in the baseline data collection process. The availability (or lack thereof) of various types of equipment may become a major issue in the planning process. In fact, much of the planning effort should involve determining the appropriate complement of equipment to serve the population of the planning area. This inventory should take into consideration the type of equipment available, the level of utilization, the age and condition of the equipment, the ownership arrangements, and the types of reimbursement accepted.

In situations where critical equipment is lacking (e.g., a community without a magnetic resonance imaging machine), the unmet needs of the population in this regard must be considered. On the other hand, there are situations in which there is a surplus of certain types of equipment. This duplication of effort may result in unnecessary costs, underutilization of expensive equipment, and other situations detrimental to the system. Concerns over possible bioterrorism activities has raised awareness concerning the need for specialized equipment for use in the event of a nuclear, chemical, or biological attack.

Another important equipment category involves information technology. Any number of health initiatives at both the community and organization level have failed in recent years due to deficiencies in the information infrastructure. Healthcare continues to lag behind other industries in the adoption of contemporary information management technology, and many of the inefficiencies in the operation of the healthcare system can be attributed to this situation. An inventory and assessment of the information management technology available among the community's healthcare organizations are critical for effective community-wide planning. At the organization level, it is difficult to imagine the effective operation of any healthcare organization in the future, much less the initiation of planning initiatives, in the absence of an adequate information management infrastructure.

Personnel

It could be argued that the availability of clinical personnel within a community is the most important indicator of resource adequacy. The treatment capabilities available to the population are more a reflection of the personnel available than the facilities available. Personnel should be identified in terms of type, number, characteristics, and distribution.

Physicians

The physician remains the pivotal player in the healthcare system, despite the shifts in control that have occurred in recent years. For this reason, as precise an inventory of physician resources as possible should be carried out. Physicians should be inventoried as a group and in terms of their distribution by specialty. To the extent possible, other characteristics should be identified as part of the profile. These include subspecialty areas, ages, type of practice (e.g., office based, hospital), level of effort, hospital affiliation, and so forth. It is becoming increasingly important to determine the health plans with which a physician is affiliated (although that is probably more of an issue in private sector planning than for community-wide planning).

Developing an accurate inventory of the physician pool is one of the more challenging tasks in the community assessment process. There are no standard directories of physicians, and available sources such as the local medical society roster are typically far from complete and current. Recent trends involving frequent changes in group affiliation, opening of secondary and tertiary offices, and increasing physician employment have made the determination of physician full-time equivalents even more challenging. If there is a medical school in the community, many physicians may be splitting their time between patient care, teaching, and research. While medical residents at these institutions may represent a resource, it is difficult to know how to count them in terms of their effort.

A basic distinction that should be made in this inventory is between primary care physicians and specialty physicians. In general, the two categories of physicians perform separate functions within the medical community. The primary care physician is responsible for basic services and, as such, family practitioners, obstetricians, pediatricians, and general internists are considered the backbone of the system. Increasingly, they serve as the "gatekeepers" who channel patients into the system.

Community health planners are particularly interested in the adequacy of primary care services. An inherent component of any community health plan is the assurance that basic services are provided for. For this reason, community-wide plans always include standards for the level of primary care. The adequacy of the physician pool can be determined by applying such standards. The most common measure utilized is the physician-to-population ratio. For primary care, this approach has been formalized by the Healthcare Resources and Services Administration (HRSA) which publishes an annual report on areas that are underserved in terms of primary care.

Nursing Personnel

Nurses have historically served as the backbone of the healthcare delivery system while constituting the largest category of health personnel. While the number of nurses practicing in a community may be more a function of demand than supply, the existing nurse staffing patterns provide an important perspective on the delivery system. Increasingly, nurse practitioners, nurse clinicians, and other highly trained nursing personnel are practicing independently. In fact, such personnel, usually practicing under a physician's supervision, may provide the bulk of the primary care in certain underserved areas.

As of this writing, the United States is in the midst of an unprecedented nurse shortage. The average age of active nurses is increasing rapidly, and replacements are not being trained at a rate fast enough to replace those that are leaving the field. Today, in fact, there are several hundred thousand nursing vacancies nationwide. While an inventory of nursing resources may not have been a priority for community-wide planners in the past, it is a major consideration in today's environment. Even among planners at the organization level, the availability of nurses within the community often becomes an issue.

Other Independent Practitioners

Several categories of independent practitioners should be inventoried as part of this process. These include dentists, pharmacists, optometrists, chiropractors, and podiatrists. These practitioners typically occupy specific niches within the delivery system, usually supplementing but sometimes competing with the services of physicians. In fact, in an era of managed care, it has become common to substitute "lower" level services from optometrists, chiropractors, and podiatrists for the more expensive physician services of ophthalmologists, neurosurgeons, and orthopedic surgeons.

Mental Health Personnel

Mental health personnel are frequently overlooked when community assessments are conducted. Their position at the fringes of mainstream healthcare has historically prevented them from being effectively inventoried in such projects. The community assessment should identify and inventory the variety of practitioners that provide psychological, behavioral health, and psychiatric services to the community. These practitioners are likely to be especially important when the needs of the community's vulnerable populations are considered. The increasing prevalence of behavioral health problems should draw them more into the mainstream of health services delivery.

Alternative Therapy Providers

A new category of practitioners that now requires inclusion is the variety of alternative therapy providers that practice in the community. Until recently, such practitioners were considered outside the mainstream of conventional medical care. Today, however, it is realized that consumers spend a surprising amount of their healthcare dollar on alternative therapies (e.g., $30 billion in 2016). Alternative therapists are used both as adjuncts to conventional care and as substitutes. Thus, the community's complement of acupuncturists, herbalists, homeopaths, nutritional therapists, and so on should be identified along with the more conventional practitioners. This is especially the case in communities with large ethnic populations that are likely to maintain certain forms of traditional medical practices.

Networks and Relationships

A thorough inventory of community health services should include a review of existing networks and relationships within the delivery system. This aspect of the research is particularly challenging, since no "directories" of relationships are likely to exist for the community. Some of these relationships may be formal and totally overt; others may take the form of "gentlemen's agreements" and not be widely appreciated by the general public. In an era of managed care and negotiated contracts for health services, the existence of networks and relationships has taken on added importance. The significance of such situations cannot be overestimated and it could be argued that the presence or absence of certain relationships has been the main barrier to effective health services planning in many communities.

The assessment of community facilities should consider the relationships that exist among various organizations. Health systems with multiple facilities in the community should be identified, as well as facilities that are affiliated with or owned by facilities or health systems outside the community. The extent to which hospitals have diversified into other areas such as home health and hospice, urgent care centers, or fitness centers, for example, needs to be determined.

A similar process should be utilized with personnel to determine the relationships that exist. In most communities, provider networks have been established by hospitals, health plans, or some other entity. By virtue of participating in certain networks, health personnel may be restricted in terms of the hospitals and other facilities that they can use or the health insurance plans they can accept.

In some communities, business coalitions have been established by major employers to negotiate directly with healthcare providers and/or insurance plans. These relationships may involve exclusive contracts between major purchasers of care and local health systems that must be taken into consideration during the planning process.

An important aspect of this analysis involves referral relationships. "Referral patterns" is used broadly here to include actions that channel consumers toward the use of a service or the purchase of a product. It is increasingly important, for example, for hospitals to know which physicians are admitting patients (and who is referring to their admitters), for specialists to know what primary care physicians are referring patients to them, and for urgent care centers to know how their patients found out about them.

Referral patterns in the community-wide planning context are probably most important in relation to public health services and community clinics. The planner needs to develop a clear understanding of the processes by which consumers come to access publicly supported services and the extent to which the safety net protects the medically indigent.

Community Health Assets

As noted in the previous chapter community "health assets" have come to be increasingly recognized. Generally, when an inventory of healthcare resources is implemented the focus is on components of the formal healthcare system—the facilities, personnel, and programs that are commonly identified. The argument has been made that these resources may or may not be considered *assets* in the eyes of community members. A clinic that only accepts insured patients or a hospital that discourages Medicaid patients would not be considered much of an asset to community residents. For this reason, contemporary health asset assessment processes cast a wider net to include resources that may not be recognized by health professionals but are considered assets to the community. Research in various communities has identified as health assets churches, community development corporations, funeral homes, and even barber and beauty shops. This situation, then, requires that those performing an environmental assessment be cognizant of the fact that there may be resources not readily recognized by an outside assessor.

Sources of Funding

An understanding of the manner in which health services are funded within the community represents an important aspect of the analysis. The payer mix discussed earlier is clearly a starting point for determining how the community pays for healthcare and, ultimately, the population's relative ability to pay for services. The extent to which health services reimbursement relies on government funding in the form of Medicare and Medicaid is important. The level of commitment of funds for public health and charity services is also an important consideration. Any unique sources of funding, such as state programs for categorical disease treatment, should be identified. The sources of funding for mental health services also should be determined, since these typically are reimbursed under a different system than physical health services.

The approach to planning is likely to be quite different for communities with a high proportion of commercial insurance, a large Medicare population, or considerable numbers of Medicaid and uninsured patients. Indeed, the payer mix of the population must of necessity be topmost in the minds of planners at the organization level.

Assessing Health Status and Healthcare Resources

Once the community's needs and resources have been identified and inventoried, they must be evaluated. A number of approaches can be utilized in this regard, although all ultimately involve some type of comparative analysis. The assessment of an indicator of health status, for example, could involve a comparison with that same indicator at some previous point in time, with the indicator for a comparable community, or with the national average, or with some standard that has been established. In fact, an indicator should probably be assessed from all of these perspectives. Thus, if the indicator in question is infant mortality, the current infant mortality rate would be compared with historical rates (and hopefully a trend established), with the rates reported for a comparable community or a meaningful average (e.g., that for the state or the nation), and with established standards (e.g., the target infant mortality rate specified in the Healthy People 2020 program).

The number of factors that can be used to assess the healthcare system is almost limitless and too numerous to be listed. They can reflect demographic characteristics (e.g., dependency ratio, sex ratio), socioeconomic characteristics (e.g., poverty level, employment status), health status (e.g., premature births, preventable deaths), health behavior patterns (e.g., immunization level, prenatal care participation), health services utilization (e.g., mammography rate, physician visit rate), ability to pay for health services (e.g., uninsured population, Medicaid enrollment), facilities and personnel supply (e.g., physician-to-patient ratio, bed-to-population ratio), and so forth. As noted below, many of these factors can be utilized to create a community-wide health status index.

Health Status Indices

Efforts to scientifically measure health status go back to the 1960s when there was growing concern over the persistence of poverty (and its counterpart: poor health). Since there was no one indicator of health status available a lot of work focused on the development of a health status index.

The development of a health status index is often carried out in the course of a community assessment. The objective of the index is to provide a single number that can be viewed as an indicator of the health status of the community in question. This is done by combining data related to a number of relevant characteristics to create an index. The categories of data from which variables may be drawn include demographics, vital statistics, utilization measures, personnel levels, and various incidence and prevalence measures. This activity primarily involved mortality rates along with certain "proxies" for health status (e.g., poverty). These indices often include "process" measures (such as access to care, hospital admissions) and later more contemporary metrics (like obesity and physical activity) were added.

Outcome measures are so called because they ostensibly reflect the extent to which the healthcare system is effective. Outcome measures include such indicators as death rates, infant death rates, life expectancy, and potential years of life lost. Of these measures, the infant mortality rate is probably the most useful as a component of a health status index, since it represents far more than just the rate at which infant deaths occur; it speaks volumes about living conditions, nutritional levels, domestic violence, and a number of other dimensions of socioeconomic and health status.

Utilization measures are also used as components of a health status index. This includes indicators such as the hospital admission rate, rate of emergency room visits, physician visit rate, and so forth. These measures tend to be among the more controversial, since it could be argued alternately that these are positive or negative indicators.

Resource availability entails another important set of indictors. These include the ratio of hospital beds to the population, the ratio of physicians to the population, and other measures of resources. The rationale for the use of such indicators is that the level of resource availability should be correlated with higher health status. Although this, too, is controversial, such indicators are frequently employed in index construction.

Measures of functional state constitute an additional category of health status indicators. These include a range of measures such as days of work lost, days of school lost, bed-restricted days, activity-restricted days, and so forth. The use of these measures reflects the notion that individuals who are limited in their functional abilities reflect poor health status (regardless of the source of the limitation).

While this index by itself might not mean much, it can be used to compare subcommunities within the population to each other, to the community average, or to some other "standard." It can also be utilized to monitor changes in the community's health status over time or to compare the community to some national average or to an established standard of some type.

Various organizations have identified indicators that they think are important in the development of a health status index. Among these are the National Committee for Quality Assurance, the Institute of Medicine, and the Health Resources and Services Administration within the U.S. Department of Health and Human Services.

No one was particularly happy with the health status indices that were developed, particularly those health professionals who emphasized the importance of quality-of-life measures. To them, whether you lived or died was not the critical issues; it was one's state of well-being while they were alive. By the 1980s community health needs assessment (CHNA) methodologies had been introduced that attempted a comprehensive assessment of the health status of a community (however defined). Analysts attempting to conduct CHNAs were typically frustrated by a lack of a meaningful measure of health status and were reduced to developing a laundry list of metrics in an effort to include every possible indicator. Even so, the emphasis remained on traditional epidemiological data. We are at the point in the development of CHNAs where a new approach is required that implicitly involves the use of a more meaningful measure of health status.

There are several issues that have been noted with regard to these efforts at developing a health status index. First, the traditional approach to health status measurement assumes that health problems can be resolved by the healthcare system … and goes on to consider health status in that light. One of the key takeaways from recent thinking is that the healthcare system cannot be counted on to improve community health.

Second, the traditional health status index emphasizes the health of individuals and not populations. This leads to a situation where health status is considered the sum of individual health statuses and where the onus is on the individual to make the changes necessary to improve community health status.

Third, measures of health status originate from the perspective of epidemiologists rather than the perspective of members of the communities being assessed (in other words, from top down rather than bottom up). Members of the population in question are likely to have much different perspectives as to what constitutes good or bad health than analysts applying working within an epidemiological framework. Interview have been conducted with consumers for decades and it is likely that no man-on-the-street ever named "heart disease death rate" as the primary health problem. Nor did they name any number of other epidemiological measures as health problems.

As health professionals shifted their emphasis from narrowly defined "medical care" to a more broadly defined "healthcare" they failed to update the notion of health status. Today, with our newfound interest in the social determinants of health these probably would be considered determinants of health there is revived interest in a meaningful measure of health status.

The incorporation of the social determinants of health in health status measurement represents a qualitative change in approach. Traditional health status indicators have been relatively static and essentially presented a "snapshot" of a community's health status at a point in time. The inclusion of social determinants introduces a prospective dimension to the process of assessing health status by allowing planners to project likely health conditions in the future based on the current influence of these determinants. Thus, knowing that a community is designated as a "food desert" provides insights into likely future health problems such as obesity, malnutrition, and low-birth-weight babies.

Summarizing the Community Assessment

A number of different techniques can be utilized to assess the system at this point. Some would apply to selected aspects of the analysis, such as demographic analysis. Others, such as a gap analysis, would allow for a more comprehensive assessment of the needs/resources situation. Some of the most important techniques are discussed in Chap. 11.

The community assessment process should produce a document that summarizes the characteristics of the community and the issues relevant to health planning. The summary should describe the demographic and socioeconomic characteristics of the community and anticipated trends in these characteristics. It should summarize the community's health status and indicate any particular issues in this regard. The summary will describe the prevailing healthcare practices of the community including patterns of referral and utilization. It should also include an inventory of available health services and an assessment of their characteristics.

A critical determination in any planning process is the extent to which existing resources address the needs of the population. The findings in this regard will inform the remainder of the planning process. Identifying mismatches, maldistributions, and shortages or surpluses in healthcare resources provides the basis for much of the planning activity that follows. The ultimate objective is to identify unmet healthcare needs within the community and address them through the planning process.

The overall condition of the community should be described, with special attention to the gap between needs and services. These unmet health needs, along with other identified issues, will provide the basis for the subsequent planning activities that take place. This "state of the community" document provides the starting point from which all future conditions are measured.

While those developing plans for organizations have historically not focused on the community assessment process, some consideration of the broader community is becoming increasingly common. Not only does the community assessment provide a context for any planning initiatives that the organization may undertake, but also some level of community assessment is a prerequisite for implementing the population-based planning initiatives that an increasing number of healthcare organizations are pursuing.

References

Beck, J. (2016). Less than 3 percent of Americans live a 'healthy lifestyle'. *The Atlantic*. Retrieved from https://www.theatlantic.com/health/archive/2016/03/less-than-3-percent-of-americans-live-a-healthy-lifestyle/475065/

Brown, J., Shepard, D., Martin, T., & Orwat, J. (2007). *The economic cost of domestic hunger: Estimated annual burden to the United States*. Retrieved from http://www.sodexofoundation.org/hunger_us/newsroom/studies/hungerstudies/costofhunger.asp

Center for Evaluative Clinical Sciences. (1999). *The Dartmouth atlas of healthcare*. Hanover, NH: Center for Evaluative Clinical Sciences.

Danis, M., Kotwani, N., Garrett, J., et al. (2011). Priorities of low-income urban residents for interventions to address the socio-economic determinants of health. *Journal of Healthcare for the Poor and Underserved, 21*(4), 1318–1339.

Ellaway, A. (2014). The impact of the local social and physical environment on wellbeing. In E. Burton & R. Cooper (Eds.), *Wellbeing and the environment* (Vol. 2). Oxford: Wiley-Blackwell.

Evans, R. G., Barer, M. L., & Marmor, T. R. (Eds.). (1994). *Why are some people healthy and others not? The determinants of health of populations*. New York: Aldine.

Fox, A. J., Goldblatt, P. O., & Jones, D. R. (1985). Social class mortality differentials: Artefact, selection or life circumstances. *Journal of Epidemiology and Community Health, 39*, 1–8.

Giuntella, O. (2012). *Why does the health of immigrants deteriorate?* Retrieved from https://www.dartmouth.edu/~neudc2012/docs/paper_232.pdf

Hickson, M., Ettinger de Cuba, S., Weiss, I., Donofrio, G., & Cook, J. (n.d.). *Too hungry to learn: Food insecurity and school readiness*. Retrieved from http://www.childrenshealthwatch.org/wp-content/uploads/toohungrytolearn_report.pdf

Hu, J., Gonsahn, M. D., & Nerenz, D. R. (2014). Hospital socioeconomic status and readmissions: evidence from an urban teaching hospital. *Health Affairs, 33*(5), 778–785.

Hopper, K. (2011). *Disparities in cardiac rehab.* Unpublished presentation. Retrieved from http://www.aacvpr.org/Portals/0/events_edu/annualmeeting11/2011%20Online%20Syllabus%20PPT/BO31Hopper.pdf

Pace, K. (2014, January 24). *Get to root causes: Address poor health outcomes through a health equity lens.* Michigan University Extension. Retrieved from http://msue.anr.msu.edu/news/get_to_root_causes_address_poor_health_outcomesthrougha_health_equity_lens

Pedersen, P. V., Gronbaek, M., & Curtis, T. (2011). Associations between deprived life circumstances, wellbeing and self-rated health in a socially marginalized population. *The European Journal of Public Health, 22*(5), 647–652.

Peek, M. (2014). Poverty's association with poor health outcomes and health disparities. *Health Affairs.* Retrieved from http://healthaffairs.org/blog/2014/10/30/povertys-association-with-poor-health-outcomes-and-health-disparities/

Scottish Public Health Observatory (2014). Community well-being: Key points. Retrieved from http://www.scotpho.org.uk/life-circumstances/community-wellbeing/key-points

Strully, K. W. (2009). Job loss and health in the U.S. labor market. *Demography, 46*(2), 221–246.

Thomas, R. K. (2009). *Orange mound community assessment.* Memphis, TN: Health and Performances Resources.

U.S. Department of Health and Human Services (2015). Financial condition and health-care burdens of people in deep poverty. Retrieved from https://aspe.hhs.gov/basic-report/financial-condition-and-health-care-burdens-people-deep-poverty

Voss, M., Nylen, L., Floderus, B., et al. (2004). Unemployment and early cause-specific mortality: A study based on the Swedish twin registry. *American Journal of Public Health, 94*(12), 2155–2161.

World Bank (2001). *Attacking poverty: Opportunity, empowerment and security.* Retrieved from http://siteresources.worldbank.org/INTPOVERTY/Resources/WDR/overview.pdf

Wright, J., Williams, R., & Wilkinson, J. R. (1998). Development and importance of health needs assessment. *British Medical Journal, 316*(7140), 1310–1313.

Further Reading

Association of State and Territorial Health Officials. (2019). *Community health needs assessments.* Retrieved from https://www.astho.org/Programs/Access/Community-Health-Needs-Assessments/

HealthIT Analytics. (2017). *What are the top common social determinants of health?* Retrieved from https://patientengagementhit.com/news/what-are-the-top-common-social-determinants-of-health

Chapter 8
The Planning Audit

Introduction

All planning activities require an understanding of the entity being planned for and the environment in which that entity operates. This information is generally acquired through what is referred to as a "planning audit." The planning audit can take a variety of forms and typically includes an internal audit and an external audit. The nature of the audit will differ depending on the type of planning that is being undertaken. The audit for a strategic planning project will be different from that for a marketing plan. On the other hand, strategic planning and marketing planning emphasize the external audit over the internal audit, while financial planning, human resource planning, and facilities planning may emphasize the internal audit.

As was the case with the community assessment described previously, there is no one way to conduct a planning audit. Thus, this chapter does not attempt to present a definitive model for conducting a planning audit but a generic version that can be applied to virtually all situations with modifications for the particular setting.

Stating Assumptions

Here, as elsewhere, an important task involves the stating of assumptions. Assumptions should be stated at the outset of the project and may be modified or expanded as information is collected on the organization, the market, and the competitive situation. Assumptions can relate to many aspects of the process and to specific components. In fact, assumptions might be stated about the process itself indicating, for example, which issues can and cannot be considered in the planning initiative.

© Springer Science+Business Media, LLC, part of Springer Nature 2021   187
R. K. Thomas, *Health Services Planning*,
https://doi.org/10.1007/978-1-0716-1076-3_8

During the process of stating assumptions, the mission of the organization should be reviewed. If no mission statement is currently in place, one should be developed, since the mission statement serves as the organizing principle for the planning process. Although the mission statement may ultimately be revised during the course of the process, it provides a starting point for planning.

Preparing for the Planning Audit

The planning audit takes place after the initial information-gathering effort has been carried out. The analysts should have reviewed copies of any previously developed plans, research reports, or consultant studies as a starting point for more formal data collection. Interviews with knowledgeable individuals within the organization will have already been conducted. In many cases, key informants outside the organization may have been interviewed as well.

These initial information-gathering activities should have familiarized the planner with the key institutional players, major decision makers, and opinion leaders within the organization. This process should have also uncovered the major issues from the perspective of the respondents. While these issues are likely to be refined during the planning audit, they serve as "talking points" to get the process started.

As part of this process, any barriers that might impede the planning audit should be identified. These barriers may include individuals who are likely to be resistant to the process, sensitive data that the analysts may not have access to, or deficiencies in information management systems that may present challenges for the audit. This information helps form the assumptions that will inform the planning audit.

As part of preparations for the planning audit, the planner should develop a project plan for this component of the planning research. This plan will specify the activities that will be carried out as part of the planning audit. It will identify individuals and departments within the organization (and, to a lesser extent, without) who must be involved in the audit. It will also specify the types of information that will be required for each activity and lay out the sequence of events that must be followed in order to complete the audit.

An important final step in the preparation process involves alerting those in the organization that a planning audit is going to be undertaken and disclosing what that is going to involve. While the audit will involve a systematic and objective process of data collection and analysis, many within the organization might consider it as a quest for their "dirty laundry." For this reason, it is important that everyone involved is aware of the nature of the audit and that the threat represented by this process is minimized with regard to those within the organization.

Planning Audit Data Collection

The planning audit involves two major categories of data: internal data and external data. Knowledge of the internal characteristics of the organization is critical for the planning process and a great deal of effort is likely to be exerted developing a detailed understanding of its internal operations. (This type of analysis is rare in community-wide planning, since multiple organizations are involved in that process.) Data on the external environment is equally critical for the planning process, particularly if strategic planning, marketing planning, or business planning is being undertaken. For more introspective planning exercises (e.g., financial planning, facilities planning), the external environment must still be taken into consideration.

This section describes some of the types of internal and external data that are important in the planning audit. Additional information is provided on the sources of such data in Chap. 13.

The Internal Audit

All healthcare organizations have immediate access to a "gold mine" of information—their own internal records. Healthcare organizations routinely generate a large amount of data as a by-product of their normal operations. The types of data that can typically be extracted from internal records include, among others, patient characteristics, utilization trends, and sources of revenue.

These data may be acquired through the performance of an *internal audit*. The internal audit can be broken down into a number of functional areas for discussion purposes. An audit examines the organization's *structure*, its *processes*, its *customers*, and its *resources*. The structural analysis involves an examination of the "organization of the organization," identifying which personnel are responsible for which functions and, in the case of a hospital or physician group, profiling the medical staff or group partners.

This analysis of the organization's processes investigates the flow of customers through the system and the accompanying flow of information. It identifies and evaluates the lines of communication, from the decision-making process at the top to the transfer of operational minutiae at the bottom of the organization. The process analysis also involves a review of financial trends, including the price-setting process. The components included and the attention accorded to different aspects of the operation will depend on the nature of the planning engagement. (The internal audit on information sources is also discussed in Chap. 13.)

The following categories of information are typically included in the internal audit.

Management Processes

The internal audit should examine the management processes that are in place, since these impact so many of the other dimensions of the organization. The audit should review the organizational structure, examine the policies and procedures that are in place, and assess to the extent possible the level of efficiency and productivity characterizing the organization. The decision-making process needs to be understood and the readiness of management to participate in the planning process determined. The buy-in of management, of course, is essential for a successful planning initiative.

Information Technology

One of the first components of the internal operation that is likely to be considered is the organization's information technology. In the first place, the information management capabilities of the organization are going to influence the amount and quality of the data that can be generated for the planning analysis. More important, however, is the fact that information systems provide the foundation for performing most other functions within the organization. The efficient processing of customers, effective billing and collections, and tracking of marketing activities are just some of the uses for information technology.

While many healthcare organizations in the past have gotten by without adequate information management capabilities, that is not possible today. The demands for data are growing every day, and organizations that cannot respond will be at a competitive disadvantage. Further, incentives (both positive and negative) have been put into place to encourage the adoption of information technology on the part of healthcare providers. Detailed information must be available, for example, to negotiate managed care contracts or partnership arrangements. In fact, group purchasers are not likely to contract with providers that do not have the level of information management that the managed care plan demands.

Services/Products

An early step in the internal analysis is typically the identification of the services and products offered by the organization. In some cases, the "product" may be obvious; in others it may not be. An organization offering a single service or product may be easily profiled, but this situation seldom exists in healthcare. Most healthcare organizations provide a range of services and/or products, but they are not likely to have thought of them as unique marketing offerings. This step typically requires more effort in healthcare than in other industries, since scant attention is likely to have been devoted to specifying the nature of the services and products offered by the organization. Each service and product should be profiled not only in terms of the defining characteristics of the product or service, but also in terms of packaging, presentation, and any other factor that might influence the ability to market it.

Customer Characteristics

The customer analysis should identify and profile *all* of the organization's customers. These may be very specific (as in the case of a medical supply company whose only customers are blood banks) or very diffuse (as in the case of a general hospital that has multiple customer groups). For healthcare providers, patients are typically the customer group that receives the most attention. A basic profile of existing patients includes demographic and socioeconomic characteristics, case mix (e.g., diagnosis, procedures), payer mix, and place of residence. With this information, one can evaluate the "quality" of the current patient population, determine which segments are more "desirable," and identify the categories of patients one would like to target.

Utilization Patterns

An analysis of the level of utilization of the organization's services and products is a critical component of the internal analysis. Current levels of utilization in terms of admissions, office visits, procedures performed, or products sold provide the starting point for understanding the operation of the organization. The utilization measures emphasized in the audit will depend on the nature of the organization and the type of planning process.

Planners may categorize utilization in terms of a number of dimensions including clinical category (e.g., cardiology, orthopedics), patient characteristics (e.g., age, sex), payer category (e.g., Medicare, private insurance), and geographic origin of the patients in terms of their home ZIP Code or county.

Utilization analyses not only provide a "snapshot" of the organization's current status, but are also particularly important for tracking organizational performance. Thus, the analysis must examine past trends in utilization and include projections of future utilization patterns. Changes in utilization over time provide information on the changing status of the organization in relation to the market.

Financial Data

Information on the organization's financial status has become a critical component of the planning audit. Financial information has direct implications for product and service development, promotional activities, and competitive analyses. The relative financial performance of members of the medical staff may contribute directly to strategic marketing initiatives, and the mix of profitable and unprofitable services and products will affect the organization's bottom line. As managed care negotiations have become a more common aspect of organizational life, financial information has become increasingly important.

The internal audit should consider sources of income and the manner in which income is expended, especially since the organization's likely future payer mix will be a major predictor of its profitability. Billing and collection processes should be reviewed and an understanding of compensation arrangements developed.

Staffing and Other Resources

Staffing data represent a valuable information resource for virtually every health-care organization. Personnel databases may provide information on the residential location of the organization's staff, the match between those treating patients and the patients' characteristics, an inventory of skills and experience available, and opportunities for the marketing of services to the organization's employees. For hospital planning, internal databases are likely to contain extensive information on the characteristics of the medical staff.

The planner requires this information to evaluate the strength of various specialty areas, identify gaps in the medical staff or other personnel, anticipate future specialty shortfalls (e.g., an aging staff), and develop marketing programs that focus on particular specialty areas. For physician groups, especially larger ones, internal information on physician characteristics, their activity patterns, and their productivity levels provides important knowledge for assessing the group's position within the current healthcare "space" and determining how well it is positioned for the future demands of the market.

Referral Patterns

In an era of increasing competition, the identification of the various sources of customers becomes critical. It is particularly important to identify referral sources and track their activity. Hospitals need to know which physicians are admitting patients (and who is referring to their admitters), specialists need to know what primary care physicians are sending them patients, and urgent care centers need to know how their patients found out about them.

The term "referral pattern" is used broadly here to include any source of information that might lead to the use of a service or the purchase of a product. Healthcare organizations may collect information on referral at the time of patient intake or this information may be a routine part of the paperwork for some organizations. Many organizations do not systematically collect this information and be forced to perform primary research to determine where their customers are coming from.

Other methods of determining referral sources may also be used, particularly patient origin studies. A specialty group with a multicounty service area may find, for example, that certain counties are underrepresented in terms of referred patients and others are overrepresented. This would suggest that referral relationships are weak in some areas and strong in others.

Pricing Structure

The pricing structure for a product or service has become increasingly important for planning purposes. Not only is price a basis for differentiation between providers but also the pricing structure for a service may constitute a marketing device in its own right. The internal audit should determine how prices are set and review the existing price structure in the context of industry averages.

For many healthcare organizations, the internal audit will include a fee structure analysis. This analysis reviews the charges being levied by the organization and identifies fees that are too high or too low based on some objective external standard.

Marketing Activities

All marketing activities that the organization has in progress should be identified. Although this may appear to be an external concern, the internal structure for promoting the organization's services and/or products is as important as external marketing efforts. In addition, the status of internal marketing should be reviewed. This involves the manner in which customers are processed, the way staff interacts with the customer, and internal procedures for tracking customer activity. All marketing resources currently deployed should be identified.

The External Audit

The external audit is comparable to the environmental assessment (or environmental scan) performed in community-wide planning. The external audit is particularly important in organization-level planning because of the emphasis placed on the characteristics of the market in many types of plans. Thus, the analysis should begin at the national level and be addressed at the regional level if appropriate. The assessment should clearly be extended to the state level and ultimately brought down to the level of the market area in which the organization operates.

Societal Trends

As was the case with the community assessment, broad societal trends should be analyzed and their implications for the local environment considered. These include trends in demographics, economic conditions, lifestyles, and attitudes. The types of trends that are emphasized will depend on the nature of the organization and the type of planning that is to be conducted. Most analyses will include a review of broad demographic trends as a means of setting the context for planning.

Broad economic trends are also a consideration, even for an organization operating in a local market. The state of the economy has implications for the demand for

health services and the ability of consumers to pay for care. A state of full employment involves different implications for healthcare than does a situation with high
unemployment, particularly with regard to insurance coverage. National healthcare
chains are particularly susceptible to shifts in the national economy.

Trends in lifestyles may be very pertinent for certain healthcare organizations.
Developments like the emergence of the two-income household, the increase in
childlessness, and the fitness movement may have implications for a wide variety of
organizations. The growing interest in alternative therapies and other trends will
continue to reshape healthcare going into the twenty-first century.

Changes in consumer attitudes at the national level may have implications for
local market areas. The emergence of the baby boomers as a major force in society
was accompanied by a significant change in consumer attitudes. Baby boomers
exhibited different attitudes from previous generations and this "new consumer"
affected all aspects of healthcare. These new attitudes made possible the success of
urgent care centers, freestanding diagnostic centers, health maintenance organizations, and many other innovations in healthcare.

Health Industry Trends

Trends in the health industry itself should be analyzed to identify developments that
are likely to affect the local market area. These could include trends in reimbursement, changing organizational structures within the delivery system, and introduction of new treatment modalities. Current examples include changing attitudes
toward prevention and rise of alternative therapies. The emergence of new concepts
such as post-acute care, assisted living facilities, and long-term acute care facilities
may have an impact on organizations in the local market. Other industry trends
include the continued influence of large national for-profit chains and the emergence of employers and employer coalitions as key players in the healthcare
environment.

Regulatory, Political, and Legal Developments

The regulatory environment exerts a significant influence over healthcare organizations. At every level of government, regulatory functions exist that have important
implications for provider organizations. Federal regulations governing the operation
of the Medicare and Medicaid programs are an important case in point. At the same
time, states have primary responsibility for licensing health facilities and personnel.
State agencies may exert inordinate influence over the provision of care. A seemingly innocuous new regulation could easily prove to be a boon or a bane for various
healthcare organizations.

The political environment clearly has both direct and indirect implications for
the operation of the health system. Presidential mandates or congressional directives could have an impact that trickles down to the local market. At the state

level, the certificate-of-need process may have a significant impact on the ability of healthcare organizations to expand their operations or add new facilities, equipment, or services.

Legislative activities at the national, state, and local levels also have implications for the local healthcare system. Examples abound of recent legislation at the national level that influenced physician referral patterns, the length of stay for women undergoing childbirth, and the ability of patients to sue health maintenance organizations. State legislative activities may have even more impact at the local market level. The actions of city and county governing bodies may have implications for local healthcare organizations, with those in the public sector most likely to be affected by these actions.

Technology Developments

Developments in the area of technology have major implications for health services providers and ultimately influence the demand for various health services. Advances in medical and surgical treatment modalities, pharmaceuticals, biomedical equipment, and information management all affect certain healthcare organizations. The introduction of new drugs has changed the manner in which behavioral health problems are addressed, refinements in biomedical equipment have made home care more feasible for a wide range of conditions, and microsurgical techniques have contributed to the shift of care from the inpatient to the outpatient setting.

Reimbursement Trends

The type of reimbursement available for the provision of care has come to be a major consideration for healthcare organizations. The reimbursement picture is complicated by the variety of payers that potentially fund any healthcare provider. A provider's patient mix is likely to represent a variety of payers, and many patients may have their care reimbursed by more than one payer. The emergence of managed care with its special reimbursement arrangements has further complicated the picture. For this reason, healthcare providers have had to increase their claims management capabilities.

Healthcare providers are faced with having to carefully control their solicitation of customers in order to avoid attracting nonpaying customers and slow-pay or low-pay third-party payers. The reimbursement arrangements involved in managed care have become a major factor driving business decision-making in healthcare.

Financing issues may be introduced by agencies at all levels of government as well as by private sector third-party payers. Changes in reimbursement under federal insurance programs such as Medicare and Medicaid play an important role in altering practice patterns, and new vendors have emerged to provide consultation on these changing reimbursement patterns. Similarly, the services that private insurers do or do not cover can have major implications for healthcare organizations.

With the growing interest in pay-for-performance on the part of third-party payers, financial analysis merits additional attention. "Pay-for-performance" is an umbrella term for initiatives aimed at improving the quality, efficiency, and overall value of healthcare. These arrangements provide financial incentives to hospitals, physicians, and other healthcare providers to carry out such improvements and achieve optimal outcomes for patients. Pay-for-performance has become popular among policy makers and private and public payers, including Medicare and Medicaid. The Affordable Care Act expands the use of pay-for-performance approaches in Medicare in particular and encourages experimentation to identify designs and programs that are most effective.

Social Determinants of Health

Social determinants of health (SDoH) were introduced in the last chapter, and it is at this point in the environment assessment that their role needs to be considered. While a wide range of social determinants is likely to affect every community, distinct patterns are likely to be found from community to community. Housing stability (and homelessness) are likely to be found in most communities but their level of severity is likely to differ. Food deserts may be more common in some communities along with others. The extent and nature of environmental pollution are likely to vary between communities and also other aspects of the social and physical environment.

Health planners have not historically taken SDoH into consideration in a direct sense, although some may have viewed some of them as proxies for health issues. Today, however, the role of SDoHs cannot be ignored and the ability to affect the state of community health will require careful considerations of the social determinants.

Community Health Assets

One other consideration, also introduced in the previous chapter, is the availability of community health assets. While community health assessments have typically inventoried health system facilities, personnel, and programs, these assessments have tended to ignore community health assets. Some of these are neglected because they are considered informal health resources as opposed to the formal resources (e.g., hospitals, clinics) that planners are used to enumerating or because they are not recognized as assets.

Community residents may, on the one hand, not consider certain components of the healthcare system true assets while, on the other hand, recognizing other assets in the community as contributors to good health. Thus, churches, funeral homes, beauty parlors, and various community organizations to name a few might be recognized as forces for promoting health, forces that may not be recognized by the health professionals carrying out the assessment.

Specifying the Market Area

An important step in planning at the organization level involves the identification and profiling of the market area. This is particularly the case when such activities as strategic planning, marketing planning, and business planning are involved. The more the process involves the external environment, the more important the market area analysis is.

The market area in the organization plan is comparable to the service area in the community-wide plan. A "market" can be defined in a variety of ways. The definition utilized depends on the purpose of the analysis, the product or service being considered, the competitive environment, and even the type of organization conducting the research. Five different ways of conceptualizing a market are discussed below.

Geographically based definitions of the market are probably the most commonly used approach to specifying markets on the part of health planners. Most planning research, in fact, focuses on a census tract, ZIP Code, or county (or a group of any of these units) as the basis for analysis. The market area is typically delineated in terms of the boundaries of the geographical units chosen for analysis. (See Box 8.1 for a discussion of geographic units utilized in market research.)

In actuality, few markets (for healthcare or anything else) neatly follow political, statistical, or administrative boundaries. In fact, markets virtually always change faster than their formal boundaries, so there will invariably be some slippage between geographically based market area boundaries and the actual market area. Nevertheless, market areas are often "gerrymandered" to conform to geographic boundaries that represent a reasonable approximation of the service area under study. The primary reason for this, of course, is the fact that the available data are usually organized on the basis of existing geographic units.

The market may be defined at any geographic level by a healthcare organization. While providers tend to serve local markets, the emergence of national healthcare chains has clearly affected this situation. Certainly, national pharmaceutical and medical supply companies serve national and even international markets. Many national organizations conduct their planning on a regional basis. Since health plans are regulated by the various states, they are likely to develop plans at the state level.

Second, a market may be defined in terms of a *population segment* or some other component of the population. Planners often define the "market for product x" in terms of demographics, psychographics, or some other characteristic. Examples of markets defined in this manner are women of childbearing age or a psychographically defined segment such as "yuppies."

Markets conceptualized in terms of population segments can be exceedingly broad or quite narrow. If older Americans are considered the market, this obviously cuts a broad swath through the US population. Thus, the market for an AARP-sponsored health plan is likely to be broad and diffuse. On the other hand, if the senior population that requires nursing home care is depicted as the market, this is obviously a much narrower segment of the population. Similarly, the study could involve the market for a broad range of services (e.g., comprehensive inpatient services) or for a narrowly defined individual service (e.g., outpatient eating disorder treatment).

Another type of market may be viewed from the perspective of the service itself—i.e., a market defined by *consumer demand*. For example, healthcare organizations may seek to identify geographic areas where there are large concentrations of potential patients for a particular service. In this instance, markets are defined in terms of their healthcare needs. Examples of markets defined in this manner are the population in need of geriatric services or the one in need of behavioral health services. A hospital may consider virtually the entire population within its defined service area as part of its "market," while a home health agency may envision a narrowly defined subsegment of the population as its potential market.

Fourth, markets may be defined in terms of the healthcare *opportunities* adjudged to exist in a given area. A given location could be viewed with interest because there is a shortage of providers or a lack of facilities. An area that is characterized by a lack of competition obviously offers an opportunity for some organization. In other cases, the numbers of providers may be adequate, but the fragmentation of providers may offer an opportunity for an organization that can appropriately "package" its services. This approach might be thought of in terms of addressing the *effective* market.

Additional opportunities may be offered by areas that are characterized by a high level of "unmet" healthcare needs. These would include areas (or populations) that appear to need a certain level or type of services but, for whatever reason, are not receiving them. For example, a given population, according to a demand model, should receive a certain number of mammograms per year based on its size and composition. If the number of mammograms being performed annually is significantly lower, this may indicate an unmet need. (Note that many unmet needs exist in populations with limited resources; depending on the type of organization performing the research, these populations may or may not be appropriate candidates for targeting.)

Similarly, opportunities may exist in areas where a "gap analysis" indicates a shortfall in services or a mismatch between needs and services. The number of physicians or hospital beds that a given population should support can usually be determined utilizing various predictive models. If the number of physicians and/or hospital beds located in the area falls below the "expected" number, there may be opportunities in that market.

There is yet a fifth way to define a market, although in this case the term "market without walls" might be appropriate. Increasingly, certain markets are no longer defined in terms of geographic units or population segments. For example, the markets for contact lenses, health food supplements, and certain home testing products have become less dependent on location, since they may be purchased by mail order or through television or Internet shopping services. In addition, the advent of telemedicine allows a specialist in one location to receive electronically transmitted test results for a patient in a different location. The introduction of online pharmacies and even online physician diagnostic capabilities has contributed to a rethinking of what constitutes a market.

While markets are typically thought of in terms of the end user, markets may also be framed in terms of health professionals of one type or another. Physicians as a group constitute a market for many products and services, and the marketing efforts of pharmaceutical companies with regard to physicians are legendary. Hospital chief information officers may constitute the market for information technology vendors, while physician practice managers may represent the market for many products and services.

Perhaps the most important basis for market delineation is in terms of disease characteristics. Many organizations are "categorical" in their approach in that they only serve certain clinically defined categories of patients. When organizations view a market area in this manner, they do not actually "see" the total population but focus on a particular segment. This segment may be characterized by those affected by arthritis or diabetes, those requiring psychotropic drugs, or those undergoing organ transplantation. The market may also cut across demographic, psychographic, and payer groups. Thus, considerable planning research focuses on identifying the market in terms of disease categories.

Delineating Geographically Defined Market Areas

Effective planning requires an in-depth understanding of a healthcare organization's market area. The nature of the organization and the type of planning both contribute to its delineation. The first step typically involves the determination of the current market area for the organization for which the planning is being performed. The organization may be a hospital, a physician practice, or any other type of healthcare organization. There are a number of methods that can be used to specify the market area, and the method will vary with the type of service involved. For many services, it may be important to identify the primary, secondary, and even tertiary market areas.

The planner must first decide on the unit of geography to be used for the analysis. The choice of the geographic level depends on the amount of detail required and the type of market served. For a hospital or specialty group that serves multiple counties, the county is likely to be an appropriate unit for analysis. On the other hand, if the market is restricted to a particular county, it will probably be necessary to approach the analysis at the ZIP Code or even the census tract level. Thus, the market area for a neighborhood clinic or for a solo family practitioner is likely to be less extensive than a county and should thus be defined in terms of a smaller unit of geography.

One method for delineating a market area involves determining the source of origin for the organization's patients and, if appropriate, plotting the residences of recent patients on a map. The distribution of these patients should indicate the general market area for the organization, with the geographic area (e.g., ZIP Code, county) from which the majority of its admissions are drawn constituting the organization's market area.

A complex organization like a hospital may exhibit multiple market areas. The market area for general hospital services may be different, and much smaller, than that for more specialized offerings. Therefore, multiple market areas may exist for organizations that provide multiple services. The delineation of market areas should also account for patients who do not come from their residences, but from other facilities such as nursing homes or industrial sites (Pol and Thomas 2001).

Alternatively, market penetration rather than volume could be utilized to define the service area. It might be determined, for example, that the organization maintained high market penetration as measured by market share within selected ZIP Codes. All ZIP Codes in which the organization maintained a market share of 25% or more might be identified as the market area. It may turn out that these ZIP Codes do not necessarily correspond with the ZIP Codes identified in terms of patient volume. The planner must make a decision here as to which basis of market area delineation best suits the purposes of the project.

A third method for market area delineation involves establishing the maximum distance or driving time that consumers are willing to travel for a given health service. Computer software is available to perform this task, though in rapidly changing areas driving times can be significantly altered over a relatively short period of time. In general, this "drive time" method involves identifying the location of the service or facility and allowing the software to establish boundaries using the distance and travel time data specified. This represents a very pragmatic means of defining market area boundaries.

In some planning projects, the task may involve the delineation of a market area for a service or services not yet offered. Delineating these boundaries is much more difficult and usually requires multiple techniques. Initially, the residential distribution of patients using similar services should be plotted. If another organization is offering the same or similar services, then its market area boundaries should also be estimated. Distance/driving time data must be evaluated as well. However, a more subjective approach may be required because the service in question is new to the area. Data on the same service offered in a different market area may be available through professional networks. These data could help to establish time/distance parameters. Surveys of potential consumers of these services (e.g., physicians and patients) may also provide valuable information.

Once delineated, market area boundaries must be continuously monitored for change. Traffic patterns and driving times change, and market area boundaries may be significantly altered over a short period of time. Changes in tastes and preferences for services either on the part of physicians (e.g., increased interest in home infusion therapy) or patients (e.g., increased demand for outpatient services) must also be monitored to determine their effect on market area boundaries, as should the entrance or exit of competing organizations.

There may be situations, incidentally, in which the existing market area is not in keeping with the objectives of the organization. It may be that the composition of the identified market area is changing, as reflected in the characteristics of resident consumers. Or the organization's clientele may have moved away from the facility, as in the case of an inner-city hospital whose patients have moved to the suburbs but continue to patronize the facility. The question to ask becomes this: Is this the appropriate market area to use as a framework for planning?

The planner must decide at some point on the geographic unit for analysis. The important question involves the level of detail required, and this is going to vary with the situation. If the market area contains multiple counties, the county may serve as a satisfactory unit of analysis. On the other hand, if the market is restricted to a particular county, it would probably be necessary to approach the analysis at the ZIP Code or even the census tract level. (The various options for geographic levels are presented in Box 8.1.)

Box 8.1: Units of Geography for Health Services Planning

Virtually all health planning activities are linked to a particular geographic area. Planning agencies typically have a specific geographic area over which they have authority. Private sector healthcare organizations typically plan for "markets" that are delineated based on geography. Even when the target audience is a population segment rather than a geographic unit, this audience will ultimately be linked in one way or another to geography.

For our purposes, the geographic units used in health services planning can be divided into three major categories: political/administrative units, statistical units, and a residual category of units that do not fit into either of these categories. Each category is described below.

Political/Administrative Units

Political or administrative divisions are the most commonly used geographic units for planning purposes. This is partly due to the fact that many organizations involved in community planning have jurisdictions that coincide with political boundaries such as cities, counties, or states. Further, it is convenient for private sector organizations to use standard political or administrative units to establish their boundaries. Political units also are useful in spatial analysis since many statistics are compiled for political units. The following political and/or administrative units are frequently used by planners.

Nation

The nation (in this case, the United States) is defined by national boundaries. Although a few national chains may be interested in data at the national level, most healthcare organizations focus on lower levels of geography. However, national averages (e.g., mortality rates) are often important as a "standard" to which other levels of geography might be compared.

State

The major subnational political unit is the state, with data collected for 50 states, the District of Columbia, and several US territories. Because the individual states have responsibility for a broad range of administrative functions, many useful types of data are compiled at the state level. In fact, state agencies are a major source of health-related data. However, each state complies data independently of other jurisdictions, resulting in uneven data reporting from state to state.

(continued)

Box 8.1 (continued)

Counties

The county (or, in some areas, townships or parishes) represents the primary unit of local government. The nation is divided into over 3100 county units (including some cities that are politically designated as counties). The county is a critical unit for health services planning, since many healthcare organizations view their home county as their primary service area. Further, states typically report most of their statistics at the county level and the county health department is likely to be a major source of planning data. Even healthcare organizations with regional markets are likely to consider the county as the building block for data collection.

Cities

Cites are officially incorporated urban areas delineated by boundaries that may or may not coincide with other political boundaries. Although cities typically are contained within a particular county, many city boundaries extend across county lines. Because cities are incorporated in keeping with the laws of the particular state, there is little standardization with regard to boundary delineation. For this reason, cities do not make very useful units for planning analyses. In many cases, however, city governments are involved in data collection activities that may be useful to health services planners.

Congressional Districts

Congressional districts are established locally and approved by the federal government. These districts are typically delineated by means of political compromise and do not correspond well with any other geographic units. Limited amounts of data are collected at the congressional district level, and the boundaries tend to change over time, making these units not particularly suited for use in health services planning.

State Legislative Districts

State legislative districts have similar characteristics to congressional districts. They are drawn up by the states based primarily on political compromise. Very little data are collected for these political units and their boundaries are subject to frequent change. For these reasons, they are not very useful as units for health services planning.

School Districts

School districts are established for the administration of the local educational system. Although theoretically reflecting the distribution of school-aged children within the population, other factors may play a role in determining the configuration of school districts within a community. While school districts may be sources of data useful in developing population projections, few statistics are generated for this unit of geography.

Statistical Units

Statistical boundaries are established for a variety of purposes, but they are primarily created to allow various agencies of government to aggregate data in a useful and consistent manner. The guidelines for establishing most statis-

(continued)

Box 8.1 (continued)

tical units are promulgated by the federal government. The most important statistical units for planning purposes are discussed below.

Regions

Regions are established for statistical purposes by the federal government by combining states into logical groupings. Four regions have been established by grouping states based on geographic proximity and economic and social homogeneity. Health statistics are sometimes reported at the regional level by federal health agencies. (The term "regional" is also used informally to refer to a group of counties or states delineated for some other purpose than data compilation.)

Divisions

For statistical purposes, the federal government divides the nation's four regions into nine divisions. Each division includes several states, providing a finer breakdown of the nation's geography. Divisions are seldom used as a basis for health services planning.

Metropolitan Statistical Areas

Metropolitan statistical areas (MSAs) are delineated by the federal government as a means of standardizing the boundaries of cities and urban areas. Since each state has different criteria for the incorporation of cities, the MSA concept provides a mechanism for creating comparable statistical areas. An MSA includes a central city, a central county, and any contiguous counties that could logically be included within the urbanized area. An increasing amount of data is available on MSAs, and this unit is often used to designate a healthcare service area.

Urbanized Areas

An urbanized area as defined by the Census Bureau includes the entire densely settled area in and around each large city, regardless of whether or not the area is within the corporate limits. Although limited amounts of data are available for urbanized areas, knowledge about urbanized areas is important in developing a full understanding of the population distribution within a metropolitan area.

Census Tracts

Census tracts are small statistical subdivisions of a county established by the Census Bureau for data collection purposes. In theory, census tracts contain relatively homogeneous populations ranging in size from 1500 to 8000. For many purposes, the census tract is the ideal unit for health services planning. It is large enough to be a meaningful geographic unit and small enough to contribute to a fine-grained view of larger areas. The Census Bureau collects extensive data at the census tract level through the decennial census and annually through the American Community Survey. Much of the emphasis in community-wide planning is on the census tract level of geography.

(continued)

Box 8.1 (continued)

Census Block Groups

Census tracts are subdivided into census block groups that include approximately 1000 residents. A tract is composed of a number of block groups, each containing several blocks. This provides an even finer picture of a community at the tract level, although fewer data elements are likely to be compiled at the block group level.

Census Blocks

Census block groups are subdivided into census blocks, the smallest unit of census geography. The term "block" comes from the fact that the typical block is bounded on four sides by streets, although some other visible feature (e.g., railroad track, stream) or nonvisible feature (e.g., city limits) may serve as a boundary. Census blocks tend to be the most homogeneous of any unit of census geography, with the average block housing approximately 30 persons. Only a limited amount of data is available for census blocks.

Block Numbering Areas

In areas that were not divided into census tracts, the Census Bureau historically divided territory into block numbering areas (BNAs). These tended to be rural areas in which BNAs served the same purpose as census tracts. However, with the 2000 census, the two systems were combined and block numbering groups were phased out. BNAs remain useful when retrospective data collection is necessary.

ZIP Code Tabulation Areas

ZIP Code Tabulation Areas (ZCTAs) were introduced by the U.S. Census Bureau for tabulating summary statistics from the 2000 census. This geographic unit as developed to overcome the difficulties in precisely defining the land area covered by each ZIP Code used by the U.S. Postal Service (see below). Defining the extent of an area is necessary in order to accurately tabulate census data for that area. ZCTAs are generalized area representations of U.S. Postal Service ZIP Code service areas and are built by aggregating the Census 2000 blocks, whose addresses use a given ZIP Code, into a ZCTA which gets that ZIP Code assigned as its ZCTA code. They represent the majority USPS five-digit ZIP Codes found in a given area. For those areas where it is difficult to determine the prevailing five-digit ZIP Code, the higher level three-digit ZIP Code is used for the ZCTA code. The Bureau's intent was to create ZIP Code-like areas that would maintain more stability from census to census.

Other Geographic Units

A number of other geographic units are used in health services planning, particularly by private sector healthcare organizations. These units are often more suited to business development activities than are political or statistical units. However, the "custom" geographies that are delineated for planning purposes may take these units into consideration.

(continued)

Box 8.1 (continued)

ZIP Code

Unlike the geographic units previously discussed, ZIP Codes do not constitute formal government entities. ZIP Codes tend to be much larger than census tracts, sometimes including tens of thousands of residents. Their boundaries are set by the U.S. Postal Service and are subject to change as population shifts occur and/ or the needs of the postal service dictate. This lack of stability often means that ZIP Codes have limited value for historical analyses or for tracking phenomena over a long period of time. Further, ZIP Codes seldom coincide with census tracts or other political or statistical boundaries, making the synthesis of data for various geographies extremely difficult.

Nevertheless, the ZIP Code is a useful unit for defining the market areas of smaller physician practices, smaller hospitals, and even specialty niches for larger health systems. Commercial vendors compile a great deal of information at the ZIP Code level. Perhaps more importantly, healthcare organizations typically maintain ZIP Codes for virtually every consumer they come in contact with, making this an accessible geographic identifier linked to every customer record.

Markets

"Market" is a generic term for the target area or population identified by a healthcare organization. From a geographic perspective, it refers to the area that is included within the sphere of influence (however measured) of the healthcare organization. Frequently, the market area is constituted from individual ZIP Codes or counties, thereby creating a custom geographic unit. In other cases, the market may conveniently coincide with an existing political boundary (e.g., a county).

Areas of Dominant Influence

Taken from media advertising, the area of dominant influence (ADI) refers to that geographic territory (typically a group of counties) over which a form of media (e.g., television, newspaper) maintains predominance. This concept has been adapted for healthcare and could be thought of as the "effective" market for a particular healthcare organization.

In establishing "target" market areas for specific goods and services, there are certain established rules that should be applied. Targeted markets must be amenable to being ranked, they must be realistic in size, the targeted customers must be reachable, and the targeted customers must have some minimum level of response potential. Assuming that the market is of adequate size, another consideration is that the potential number of cases is the actual geographic distribution of prospective customers within the service area. The importance of customer distribution varies with the type of service and the characteristics of the population. Some services are supported by a local population and others by a more far-flung population. On the other hand, some populations are much more mobile than others or are otherwise more or less sensitive to travel times and/or distances.

Since the level of need within the target population may not correspond with the level of interest, it is important to determine the extent to which the population really *wants* the service. This is a point in the process where primary research may be required. Although it may be possible to conduct a psychographic analysis of the market area and, from that, develop an idea of the level of interest in a particular service, many situations will demand a survey of some type. Ideally, no new program or service should be introduced without a consumer survey, and the newer the service or the more unfamiliar the market being entered, the greater the need. Many new programs have failed because the actual level of interest of the target population was much less in reality than it was on paper.

The delineation of a market area often requires the calculation of an organization's overall market share or its share based on specific services or products. This could involve a hospital's share of the total area admissions, an orthopedic surgeon's share of all hip replacements, or a health plan's share of total health plan enrollment. Market shares can be calculated by dividing the organization's number of cases (e.g., admissions, office visits, procedures performed) by the total number of cases for the identified market area.

The organization's internal records of procedures, discharges, or diagnoses, for example, serve as the numerators for market share calculations. Denominators are derived in one of the two ways. First, in some markets, the denominator data are available as the result of public-sponsored record collection activities. For example, hospital discharge data are often collected by state health departments and aggregated at geographic levels such as the county. A simple calculation divides the number of discharges from hospital x in county y by the total number of discharges in county y.

The second way to gather data for rate denominators is to estimate the number of procedures and discharges using population and incidence information. The number of diabetes cases in market area z can be estimated by multiplying national or regional incidence rates by population data specific to age or other enumerated factors known to differentiate the probability of being diagnosed with diabetes. The reason for estimating the incidence is that in many instances there is no market-specific count of procedures, discharges, or diagnoses that can serve as the market share denominator.

It is not unusual to divide the market area into a primary market area, a secondary market area, and, often, even a tertiary market area. The techniques utilized above to specify the market area can be refined to create these sub-markets. For example, it might be determined that the geographic area from which the "closest" 50% of patients originate will be considered the primary market area and the area from which the next 25% of patients originate will be the secondary market area. All other locations that contribute patients are considered part of the tertiary market area. Varying planning or marketing approaches might be developed for the respective sub-markets.

Profiling the Population

Once the market area has been demarcated, the population of the identified area must be profiled. This process follows much the same steps as that for the community assessment but is more bound by geography. The factors taken into consideration in profiling the population for organization-level planning are likely to be much more focused than for community-wide planning.

In profiling the community, the temporal component is very important. Whether determining the needs of the target market or identifying competing services, three time horizons must be taken into consideration. Obviously, the current inventory of needs and resources is a starting point. However, it is also important to develop a sense of the historical trends that are affecting the community. Is the population growing or declining? Are the characteristics of the population different today than they were 5 years ago? Are the numbers of competitors increasing?

The most important time frame, of course, is the future, whether this means 2, 5, or 10 years. A plan should identify the future characteristics of the population, the future health service needs of that population, and any likely future developments with regard to competitive forces.

As with the community assessment process, the regional setting should be taken into consideration. Different regions of the country have their own cultural patterns, and these seem to have persisted despite the rapid change that has swept the US society. Different regions report varying levels of prevalence for various health problems, and the variation in utilization of health services is now well documented (Center for Evaluative Clinical Sciences 1999). Regional variations should be considered when health services demand is being estimated or projected for a particular market area. National healthcare organizations must take regional variations in practice patterns into consideration in their planning activities.

The type of community is also a consideration when collecting baseline data on the market. Whether the dominant community type within the market area is urban, suburban, or rural will have important implications for both health status and health behavior. Consumer attitudes are also likely to be different for the various community types, and the existence of sub-markets within the market area may be a complicating factor in the planning process.

Since the process followed for the external audit is similar to that for the community assessment described in the previous chapter, the details will be summarized here. The first type of data typically compiled is demographic data, including biosocial and sociocultural traits. At a minimum, the analyst would examine the population in terms of age, sex, race/ethnicity, marital status/family structure, income, and education.

In the process, the situation with regard to insurance coverage is typically assessed. The emphasis on insurance coverage will vary depending on the nature of the organization. The "payer mix" of a market area (and for the organization being planned for) is perhaps more directly significant to specific healthcare providers whose financial viability is a function of their payer mix. While many providers attempt to limit the number of self-pay patients they serve, there is a multibillion dollar market for elective services that are not typically covered by insurance plans. The vanity market involving facelifts, tummy tucks, and other cosmetic procedures is strictly driven by "uninsured" patients. Another example is the alternative therapy "industry" that has emerged to challenge mainstream medicine, built almost entirely on out-of-pocket payments.

The demographic analysis is often accompanied by an assessment of the psychographic characteristics of the market area population. Information on the lifestyle categories of the target audience can be used to determine the likely health priorities and behavior of a population subgroup. *Consumer attitude* are another dimension of the population that is typically considered at this point. The attitudes displayed by consumers in a market area are likely to have considerable influence on the demand for almost all types of health services. At the organization level, the attitudes of a wide variety of constituents besides direct consumers must be taken into consideration.

Identifying Health Characteristics

The health status of the market area population can be examined along a number of dimensions. Indicators of morbidity and mortality are of direct importance to health services planners, and indirect indicators such as fertility patterns also should be considered. These were discussed in some detail in the previous chapter, so they will only be summarized here.

Fertility characteristics refer to the attributes and processes related to reproduction and childbirth, and the importance of these characteristics varies depending on the type of organization and the type of plan. The number of births as well as the characteristics of those births, along with the attributes of the mothers and fathers of the children, form the basis for fertility analysis.

Historical patterns of fertility are a major influence on current patterns of health services demand. A wide range of service and product needs revolve around childbearing. Childbearing also triggers the need for such down-the-road services as pediatrics and contraception-related services. The demand for treatment of the male and female reproductive systems and the heightened interest in infertility treatment are by-products of management of the reproductive process.

The level of *morbidity* within a population is a major concern for health services planners. Incidence and prevalence rates can both serve a useful planning purpose and both may be employed as part of a planning analysis, depending on the nature of the project. This category includes disability indicators along with measures of morbidity in terms of disease prevalence. To the extent possible, planners need to project rates of incidence and prevalence into the future in order to plan for coming developments.

The study of *mortality* examines the relationship between death and the size, composition, and distribution of the population of the market area. Organization-level planners typically have less interest in mortality analysis than those involved in community-wide planning, since the latter are more concerned with the overall health status of the community. Nevertheless, mortality data is always examined to determine what it can tell us about the health status of the community.

Specifying Health Behavior

Health behavior, as noted earlier, involves any action aimed at restoring, preserving, and/or enhancing health status. This includes both the formal utilization of health services and informal actions on the part of individuals that are designed to prevent health problems and maintain, enhance, or promote health. Organization-level planners are likely to have a much more focused interest in health behavior than do community health planners. As at the community level, the analyst will examine health behavior in terms of both formal and informal actions, focusing on those indicators most relevant to the organization in question.

In terms of formal activities, the potential indicators include *hospital admissions, patient days, average length of stay, utilization of other facilities besides hospitals, physician office visits, visits to nonphysician practitioners, and drug utilization.* Among the indicators that have become important more recently are the utilization of freestanding medical facilities and various types of alternative therapies.

The Competitive Analysis

Most external audits involve some type of competitive analysis. The planning research should determine not only the position of the organization within the market but also its position relative to its competitors. In the absence of competitive data, it is difficult to gauge one's status in the market and even more difficult to measure change over time. In addition, many types of planning depend on the competitive analysis to establish the framework for developing strategies.

An important first step is a determination of the nature of the competition. Certainly, the competitive environment in healthcare has become cloudier as a variety of new forms of healthcare organizations have emerged. In simpler times, hospitals knew that other hospitals were their competition, cardiologists knew that other cardiologists were their competition, and so forth. Today, the environment has changed, and competition can take a number of forms. In the case of hospitals, many types of organizations besides hospitals have begun competing with their services. These are not always "outside" interests, in fact, since their own medical staffs may set up competing operations. The boundaries of specialty practice have become blurred as aggressive specialists seek to expand their range of services. The purveyors of alternative therapies have emerged to challenge mainstream physicians on many fronts.

The degree of detail involved in the competitive analysis depends on the nature of the organization and the type of planning that is being initiated. Ideally, the research process should develop the same body of knowledge on competitors as on the organization itself. Admittedly, complete access to internal records of competitors is not likely to be available, but much information will be public records or from internal documents that can be obtained. Depending on the nature of the competitor, information will be needed on services and products, pricing, volume or utilization, and staffing. In the case of a hospital a medical staff profile is needed as well). It will also be important to identify the locations of competitors' facilities.

Much of this information may be available from public sources, but it depends on the type of organization as well as reporting requirements in a state agency where it operates. Many healthcare organizations are required to file reports with the state on their operations. They may also be required to submit applications for various licenses or certificates. Certificate-of-need applications may be required for healthcare organizations adding facilities or services. Publicly held corporations must file a variety of reports that can be accessed and many privately held healthcare organizations publish annual reports. Recipients of Medicare reimbursement must file cost reports with the Center for Medicare and Medicaid Services. These types of reports are generally accessible to the public.

Certain information may be difficult to obtain. It would be helpful, for example, to know something about the financial status of competitors, their business plans, the contracts they have obtained, or the relationships they are developing within the community. Information of this type is not as readily available, but may be gleaned from interviews with key informants in the community.

In addition to this quantitative data, there is a qualitative aspect that should not be ignored. It might be important, for example, to determine the status of competing physicians with regard to their practices. While on the surface it might appear that there are a significant number of competing general surgeons in the community, closer inspection may indicate that one is practicing part-time due to some impairment, another is reducing his/her patient load as he/she transitions into retirement, and another is dissatisfied with his/her group affiliation and is considering moving out of town to practice. This type of qualitative information may require unorthodox research techniques but it can usually be obtained.

Patients and former employees of competitors are sometimes useful sources of market intelligence. Patients of competitors may be found among the organization's current customers or they may be uncovered through a random survey of the community. More aggressive analysts might even attempt "exit interviews" with patients leaving the competitor's facility. Competitors' patients may be a useful source of information on referral patterns, community perceptions and preferences, and customer satisfaction levels. Heightened concerns over the confidentiality of patient records demand the careful handling of any sensitive data.

Former employees of competitors provide a perspective of a different type. They have been inside the organization and will be familiar with its internal operation.

They may be able to provide a qualitative dimension that may offer insights into the strengths and weaknesses of a competitor. While it would be inappropriate to violate any confidentiality agreements, former employees typically freely offer valuable information if given the opportunity.

Finally, other practitioners, especially those involved in some type of referral relationship, are likely to be useful sources of information. Physician practices might start with their referring physicians as a source of information. From them it may be possible to determine their referral patterns and the reasons for choosing the specialists for referral that they use. It may also be possible to obtain a comparative perspective from these informants. Perhaps even more important is the information that can be obtained from those with whom there is no referral relationship. The reasons for existing referral patterns and any perceived deficiencies with the organization may be identified from these sources.

Market Area Perceptions and Attitudes

Another dimension that is particularly important in organizational planning is the perceptions and attitudes of the population of the market area. The population here is defined in the broadest sense to include any group whose opinion of the organization may have an impact on its success. The most important of these groups is the organization's customers. While this constituent group is easily recognized in most industries, the nature of the customer is complicated in healthcare. The patients of a specialty physician practice, for example, may be considered the customer; on the other hand, that practice is entirely dependent on referrals from other physicians, thereby placing referring physicians in a customer category.

In addition to the organization's customers, the groups from which it might be worthwhile to obtain information during the planning process could include the general public, the medical community, competitors, referral agents, local employers and business coalitions, health plan representatives, legislators and other policy setters, and organization's own employees. Depending on the nature of the organization and the type of planning initiative, the perspectives of some or all of these groups could be critical.

Summarizing the Planning Audit

The planning audit should produce a document that summarizes the internal characteristics of the organization and its position within its market area. The summary should describe the demographic and sociocultural characteristics of the market and report anticipated trends in these characteristics. It should describe trends in the market for the organization's services and review the competitive situation. The perceptions of various groups should be described and the organization's strengths and weaknesses outlined.

The summary should describe the opportunities that exist in the market and the steps necessary to take advantage of them. These opportunities should be tempered by the threats to the organization that exist in the environment. This "state-of-the-organization" document provides the starting point from which all future planning will ensue. (Chapter 12 presents techniques for developing an assessment of the market area.) Box 8.2 describes a "state-of-the-organization" report.

Box 8.2: The State-of-the-Organization Report

Once the data have been collected and interpreted, it is usually worthwhile to present a state-of-the-organization report. The report should provide enough information to prepare decision makers for the recommendations that will be forthcoming. The nature of the report will depend upon the issues that have been raised earlier, focusing on those of relevance to the organization.

The state-of-the-organization report should include the following sections summarizing the data collection up to this point:

- Overall societal/healthcare/service trends
- Market area delineation
- Market area population profile
- Market area population health characteristics
- Current position of the organization/product
- Customer profile
- Competitive situation
- Other likely future developments affecting the organization

This status report should include the strengths, weaknesses, opportunities, and threats identified during the analysis. It should include an "issues statement" based on the results of the analysis to this point. The mission statement and the original assumptions should also be revisited at this juncture.

This is typically a session that involves a certain amount of soul searching. The analysis is likely to generate some surprising findings, and challenges some of the assumptions held by administrators and clinicians. Thus, the presentation should provide a dose of reality if needed and indicate likely future developments with relevance for the organization. The presentation should be backed up with factual data, since disbelief and skepticism are likely to be expressed.

The state-of-the-organization report represents an opportunity to frankly describe the state of the organization. This allows all parties to "get on the same page" and to develop consensus with regard to the assumptions. This is the launching point for subsequent plan development.

References

Center for Evaluative Clinical Sciences. (1999). *The Dartmouth healthcare atlas*. Hanover, NH: Center for Evaluative Clinical Sciences.

Pol, L. G., & Thomas, R. K. (2001). *The demography of health and healthcare*. Burr Ridge, IL: Irwin Professional Publishing.

Further Reading

U.S. Census Bureau. Retrieved from www.census.gov

Chapter 9
Strategic Planning

Introduction

Strategic planning is a well-established activity in most industries, and, to many, it has become synonymous with corporate planning. Strategic planning has come to be seen as a prerequisite for any business activity, and in many ways it represents the epitome of contemporary business planning. Today, most healthcare organizations develop strategic plans, although some smaller organizations may not see the need or have the ability to implement the process. Strategic planning is *a formal, ongoing process for developing goals and implementing actions for positioning the organization in the market while matching available resources with market opportunities.*

This definition implies that planning is a "process" that involves both the development and the implementation of a systematic plan. This process focuses on "positioning," indicating the important relationship between the organization and its environment. It also recognizes the importance of matching available resources to opportunities, as this is the ultimate goal of any planning exercise.

The Functions of Strategic Planning

In today's healthcare environment the importance of strategic planning cannot be overemphasized. The notion of planning as a framework for decision-making applies to strategic planning more so than to any other type of planning. Rational choices in healthcare require a context that sets out objectives to be met, as well as agreed-upon criteria for decision-making.

The strategic plan serves as a mechanism for adapting to an ever-changing environment. The emphasis that it places on "positioning" vis-à-vis the market sets it apart from most other types of planning. Indeed, the nature of strategic planning

© Springer Science+Business Media, LLC, part of Springer Nature 2021
R. K. Thomas, *Health Services Planning*,
https://doi.org/10.1007/978-1-0716-1076-3_9

equips it to adapt to the moving target that the healthcare arena has become. Ultimately, a strategically oriented organization is one whose actions are aligned with the realities of the environment.

The strategic plan should provide an edge for the organization, making it better informed and better organized than its competitors. If the challenge is to "get there first" in healthcare today, the strategic plan should provide an advantage in this regard. If one cannot be first for some reason, the objective should be to be the best. This objective, too, is supported by the strategic plan.

The strategic plan should be the basis for resource allocation, particularly when scarce resources are being dispensed. Inherent in the definition is the matching of internal resources with opportunities within the market. If outside capital is required, few sources of capital will make major commitments in the absence of a strategic plan. Any joint venture partners or strategic development partners are going to inquire about "the plan" early in the discussions.

The strategic plan should also provide the basis for relationship development in an environment that is increasingly being driven by networks of providers, integrated delivery systems, and referral relationships. The plan should address the appropriateness of existing linkages and identify potential additional relationships.

Most importantly, the strategic plan should be a call to action. Indeed, many healthcare organizations have spun their wheels for years waiting for a clear direction to present itself. The strategic plan should, as the name implies, embody the organization's strategy. More than that, it should convey the vision of the organization and lay out the future scenario envisioned by the organization. Figure 9.1 presents an overview of the strategic planning process.

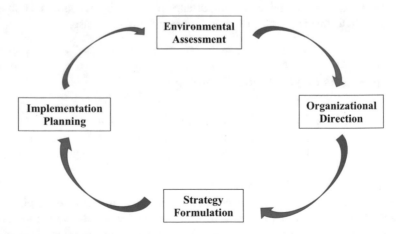

Fig. 9.1 Strategic planning model

The Nature of Strategic Planning

Strategic planning has a number of attributes that set it apart from other types of planning and illustrate its unique characteristics. Strategic planning is *lateral* in that it cuts across the various divisions of an organization. As such it requires coordination across organizational lines and demands more open cooperation across structure and function than other types of planning. Coordination is critical for both the development and implementation of the plan.

Strategic planning is *relative* in its orientation. Conceptually, strategic planning only exists as it relates to the external environment and other players in that environment. In a traditionally product-oriented industry, the relationship with the external environment is limited. In a service-oriented industry, like healthcare has become, the external environment is the *raison d'être* for strategic planning. Thus, the internal focus characteristic of traditional types of planning should be deemphasized. After all, the real issues are "out there" in the environment.

Strategic planning is *long term* in its orientation (or at least longer term than traditional forms of planning). Theoretically, strategic planning should include long-term goals, intermediate-term strategies, and short-term tactics. Five- or ten-year time horizons should typically be posited supported by more time-limited milestones.

Strategic planning should be *creative* in its orientation. This represents a major distinction between strategic planning and other types of planning. Creativity in budget planning or facilities planning may not be seen as a virtue. With strategic planning, however, creativity is *de rigueur* if the plan is to address the issues posed by the environment. The strategic planning orientation demands that conventional wisdom be left at the door of the conference room. This means no more "business as usual" and no more introspection. Strategic planning demands "thinking outside the box." For this reason, it is important to establish a vision and work backward from that, rather than starting with the present state of the organization and attempting to tweak it.

The strategic mindset also discourages a tactical focus. A short-term approach to planning is not appropriate in a context where longer range strategies are demanded. Tactics are more often than not reactive. The question should *not* be: "How do we counter a move by one of our competitors?" Strategic planning should be proactive in its approach. It should not be distracted by current circumstances but should focus on likely developments within the environment 5 years or more in the future.

Since strategic planning is about *positioning*, the vision of the strategic plan should reflect how the organization sees itself positioned within the environment 5 or 10 years into the future. This is the scenario from which the intermediate steps should be derived.

Strategic planning deals with the *business side* of the organization. The only other type of plan that is more focused on the business aspects is the business plan itself, and this should be a subcomponent or spin-off from the strategic plan. The objectives that are specified in the strategic plan are likely to be business objectives.

   Strategic planning is typically not a component of community-wide planning, although it would be inappropriate to contend that it should be totally excluded from planning at the community level. In fact, there is growing conviction that the goals of public sector organizations operating within the context of the community-wide plan cannot be reached without following strategic planning principles. This realization has prompted an unprecedented interest in strategic management among public sector healthcare entities.

The Strategic Planning Process

Planning for Planning

The first step in the strategic planning process involves planning for planning. This often starts with the following question: Why are we doing planning? It should be realized that strategic planning is virtually never done because it is the right thing to do. It is almost always prompted by a problem or perceived problem related to the organization. Further, the perceived problem is often not the real issue but, upon investigation, is found to be symptomatic of other issues. Thus, the approach that will be followed is more often a function of the desires and interests of those initiating the plan.

   Much of the early activity in the strategic planning process is organizational in nature. It involves identifying the key stakeholders, decision makers, and resource persons that must be taken into consideration in the process. This is the first step in developing an understanding of the organization and serves to generate the list of key informants to be utilized later in the data collection process.

   This phase also involves establishing a planning team that will guide the process. The nature of this team will vary from situation to situation, but its establishment is clearly a prerequisite for moving forward. Much of planning for planning involves determining who will participate in the process and, more importantly, who is to lead it. While there is no foolproof combination of team members that assures success, certain categories of participants must be involved. These include representatives of the various stakeholders, key decision makers, opinion leaders, and representatives of all constituent groups. The team should also include those representing various substantive areas within the organization. While it is not unusual to employ an outside consultant to assist in the development of the plan, the plan must ultimately be a product of the organization's staff. Therefore, it is imperative that the right personnel be engaged from the initiation of the project.

   It is clearly important to develop planning competence within the organization as well. This is an important first step in the development of a strategic mindset and, in most organizations, this represents a significant challenge. Inculcating a strategic mindset does not happen overnight, and it takes education and reeducation before it becomes established. For this reason, outside resources may be relied upon heavily during the organization's initial efforts at strategic planning.

The question often arises at this point as to who should do the planning. If this question relates to the internal resources, that must be decided by the organization. If the question refers to internal staff versus outside experts, it is a different matter. There are options with regard to the internal versus external resource debate. (See Box 9.1 for a discussion of internal versus external resources for planning.)

Box 9.1: Choosing Between Internal and External Resources

Few healthcare organizations have the internal resources readily available to develop a strategic plan. Even those organizations that are fortunate enough to have an established planning or research department are likely to have to marshal additional resources for the major undertaking of formulating a comprehensive strategic plan. When this issue comes up, a question is typically raised with regard to the use of internal versus external resources. That is, should the process rely primarily on staff and resources that exist within the organization or should much or most of the planning activities be outsourced to a consultant?

There are clearly advantages and disadvantages to each of these approaches. There is a natural tendency on the part of administrators to prefer to use existing resources to the extent possible, although this preference may not be shared by the staff that are already stretched thin by other responsibilities. Several arguments could be made for the use of internal resources. Obviously, staff is already in place and they are familiar with the territory. Existing staff members are aware of the history of the organization and know how it operates. They are aware of existing personnel and other resources and in a position to access and/or mobilize them. Given the desire to keep information on the organization "close to the vest" (and concerns over the confidentiality of clinical data), an argument could be made for keeping the data "in the family" lest it fall into the wrong hands. The argument is further made that the cost of the planning can be minimized by using people who are already on the payroll, an issue that will be revisited below.

One argument that is not always made but should be for the use of internal resources relates to the transition from planning to implementation. Developing a strategic plan is one thing; implementing it is another. When it is time to transition from planning to implementation, the process often breaks down. Emphasizing internal staff in plan development allows for a smoother transition toward operationalization of the plan. Even if different departments pick up the implementation process, they will be interfaced in one way or another with those involved in planning, allowing for a reasonable level of continuity. This is not likely to be the case with an outside consultant who coordinates the planning process but is long gone when the time for implementation arrives.

Many of the arguments for the use of internal resources for the planning process can also be viewed as disadvantages. In the typical setting, all personnel (including dedicated planning staff) will already have a full plate of

(continued)

Box 9.1 (continued)

responsibilities to which all of their time is committed. Carving out additional time for a major planning initiative is a logistical challenge and is likely to be accompanied by a considerable amount of negativity on the part of the staff.

The fact that existing staff already know a lot about the organization and its operation can be viewed as a drawback to the planning process. Being "too close to the problem" has its dangers, and existing staff are likely to have biases concerning certain departments and activities as well as preconceived notions about the direction the organization should take. Strategic planning calls for thinking "outside the box" and invariably results in a restructuring of the organization's operations and staffing. Individuals who serve to gain or lose from these developments may not be the best ones to be determining the course of the organization. The need for complete objectivity can make the use of internal resources problematic. Indeed, concerns of staff over the outcome of planning or the disclosure of certain information may make cooperation from various parties within the organization difficult to achieve.

The use of external resources also has several advantages. Outside consultants are likely to display a level of expertise not available within the organization. Even organizations with existing planning departments are not likely to have the capabilities of a consultant that specializes in plan development. The outside consultant is likely to have national experience and thus a perspective that internal staff are not likely to have. He will have been exposed to any number of strategic planning initiatives and have a broad understanding of both process and strategy. The consultant may have access to data sources, analytical techniques, and other resources that may not be available to internal staff.

The outside consultant can be expected to offer a degree of objectivity that may not be possible with internal resources. He is likely to come into the situation without any preconceived notions and be open to options that would never occur to internal staff or, if they did, be rejected out of hand. The outside consultant has no vested interest in the outcome of the plan and does not have to worry about pleasing a boss and not stepping on toes. Analyses can be carried out and decisions made without fear of future negative consequences for the consultant.

The ability of outside consultants to obtain complete and accurate information from the organization's staff is often debated. On the one hand, there may be suspicion on the part of staff with regard to the planning process and the intentions of the consultant. There may be fears that the information provided will be used to the detriment of the one providing it at some point. There may also be a concern over the provision of sensitive information (including clinical data) to an outsider who may, in fact, work for a competitor at some point in the future. Many employees are skeptical about the motives of the consultants and may, sometimes based on past experience, consider the process a waste of their time.

(continued)

Box 9.1 (continued)

On the other hand, outsiders can typically elicit information from staff that they would never disclose to their supervisor or coworkers. Their experience with other, similar situations may allow them to ask the right questions and more insightfully analyze the responses. Further, employees may welcome the opportunity to voice their complaints or put forth suggestions for which no previous opportunity for expression existed.

An outside consultant cannot be expected to be as familiar with the health-care environment in which the organization operates as its staff are likely to be. In healthcare, there are often deep-seated relationships and patterns of interaction in the community that may not be obvious. There are also aspects of the community that cannot be understood in the short time period during which the consultant is on the job. Factors that may be obvious to local health professionals may be totally missed by an outside consultant facing a daunting amount of information for analysis.

The fact that the outside consultant is not likely to be around once the plan is completed is an issue for concern. Given that the process often breaks down at the point that the process passes from planning staff to management, the consultant's absence as implementation commences can be a serious drawback. A few consultants advertise their willingness to assist with the implementation process but, in the typical case, the consultant will move on to another planning engagement when implementation begins.

The issue of cost is often a pivotal factor in the decision to use internal versus external resources. There is a belief that the use of existing staff is likely to be more effective than an outside consultant since they are already on the payroll. Indeed, they are being paid a lot less per hour than an outside consultant would charge. Further, it may be felt that adequate data are available from internal resources that do not have to be purchased to support the planning process.

This perspective represents an unrealistic view of the situation for most organizations. In healthcare in particular, managers seldom only manage but are also involved in "line" activities. Diverting their time and attention from clinical, technical, or administrative duties means that those responsibilities are not fulfilled or, more likely, they will be carried out by less capable parties or by "agency" staff that carry a significant cost premium. Further, the cost and effort involved in mobilizing the necessary staff is likely to be significant. The need to initiate data collection activities incurs additional costs; starting from scratch to perform primary research, for example, is much more expensive than utilizing the existing processes of an outside consultant. Ultimately, reliance on internal resources is a very expensive proposition when direct and indirect costs are considered, and there is the likelihood that it will not even yield the desired results.

Outside consultants are not inexpensive, and there is a tendency to evaluate their cost in relation to staff salaries. However, the consultant's hourly fee does not just cover an hour's labor, but it also pays for the expertise that the

(continued)

Box 9.1 (continued)

consultant brings to the project. It is difficult to place a price on insights that may never have surfaced without the input of the consultant. Given the significance of the strategic plan for the organization, it is hard to justify shutting off potentially critical options in order to save a few dollars. In the case of the consultant, they will not be fully compensated until they deliver the product; internal resources continue to be paid whether they produce a plan or not.

Ultimately, the choice between internal and external resources should not be an either/or decision. Indeed, the strategic direction must emanate from the organization's staff regardless of the level of outside involvement. For this reason, as well as others, both internal and external resources are utilized in appropriate proportion in successful planning projects. Existing staff have a lot to contribute, and data resources are likely to be available within the organization. On the other hand, outside consultants have the perspective and the technical skills to build on the knowledge of existing staff and the available internal resources. This approach capitalizes on the advantages offered by internal staff and external resources.

Stating Assumptions

One of the critical steps at the outset (and actually at any juncture in the planning process) is the stating of assumptions. Assumptions might be made considering the players involved in the local healthcare arena or about certain healthcare "facts of life." Assumptions also should be stated with regard to the nature of the market (and its population), the political climate, the position of other providers, and other factors that might affect the planning process.

Some assumptions can—and should—be stated at the outset of the planning process. Others will be developed as information is collected and more in-depth knowledge is gained concerning the market, its healthcare needs, and available services. Although assumptions will undoubtedly be refined as the planning process continues, it is important to begin with general assumptions. For example, "Managed care will continue to exert a major influence on the local market" or "We're number four in market share and there is no way we will ever be number one."

Initial Information Gathering

The data collection process begins with the gathering of general background information on the organization. This will include a review of any available organizational materials, such as publications produced by the organization (including annual reports), press releases, and marketing materials. It may even be appropriate to review the "vitae" of management and key clinical and technical personnel. Other potential sources of information include reports filed with regulatory agencies, business plans that have been presented to funding sources, grant applications, and certificate-of-need applications. Certain internal documents, such as executive committee minutes, planning retreat summaries, and evaluation studies, may also be useful.

It is also important to review any previous planning studies or consultant reports that have been developed for the organization. These documents may provide valuable background information on the organization, supply baseline data that can be used for comparison purposes, and provide an analytical framework that can be readily updated. These documents provide the basis, along with other information gleaned, for organizing the more formal aspects of the analysis.

Initial information gathering should include interviews with knowledgeable individuals within the organization. These should include a reasonable sampling of individuals within the organization who represent different functional areas, vested interests, and perspectives. For large organizations, these interviews may be restricted to key administrators and medical staff and perhaps one or more individuals with a handle on institutional history. Within a smaller organization such as a physician's practice, it may be possible to conduct initial interviews with medical staff, administrative staff, and perhaps other key individuals during initial information gathering.

What should the planner expect to learn from these materials and the initial interviews? The *major issues* should be identified, remembering that these may not be the same issues that prompted the planning initiative. The list of issues at this point may be relatively long and unrefined. Narrowing down the list to the most relevant issues will be part of the planning process.

The *organizational structure* should be identified. This means not only the stated structure but also the actual structure in terms of the manner in which the organization functions. This involves a review of the division of labor, the chain of command, and the internal communications channels.

The *key players* in the organization should be identified through this process and, when appropriate, any influentials external to the organization as well. The number of key players will vary depending on the size and complexity of the organization. Some key players are obvious, such as those in formal positions of authority. Division or department heads are also likely to be identified as key informants. Other critical participants may be those who are positioned to have access to critical information. These might include planning or marketing professionals, information systems professionals, the director of the medical records department, and the managed care liaison, for example.

Another category of key informant to consider would include those knowledgeable by virtue of their unique relationship within the organization. These might include a long-term personnel director or individuals who have worked at various levels and/or for different departments within the organization. Others may be important due to their role (often unrecognized formally) as opinion leaders. Some employees may, by virtue of contacts, personality, knowledge, or other traits, be considered influencers. In some hospitals, for example, a union representative may have an influence far beyond his/her formal title within the organization.

This stage of the process should also identify the *key constituents* of the organization. Who, in effect, must the organization report to? If it is a tightly held private organization, there may be few outside the organization that matter. On the other hand, if it is a private, not-for-profit entity, there are likely to be board members, regulators, and others to whom the organization must be accountable. If it is a publicly held company, the board of directors and its shareholders represent constituents of some importance as well. Other constituents to consider include patient groups, referring physicians, employee benefits managers, insurance plan representatives, and politicians. These must be identified during the initial stages of the analysis so this information can inform subsequent research.

Much of what is gleaned during initial information gathering could be considered to reflect the "corporate culture" of the organization. This term refers to the character of the organization's internal environment. There is now ample documentation of the manner in which the corporate culture affects the operation of an organization and, importantly, determines the extent to which the environment is amenable to the planning process. The culture of the organization will influence both the planning process and the implementation of the plan.

This initial information gathering should also identify any potential barriers to planning. What are the organizational considerations that may impede planning? Will communication issues prevent cooperation? What individuals or positions are likely to be resistant to the planning process? The planner is not likely to have the complete answers to these questions at this point, but an appreciation of potential roadblocks should emerge as background information accumulates.

The planner should now be in a position to begin to think in terms of the assumptions that will drive the planning process. It is possible at this point to make assumptions concerning the support of various parties, the organization's structure, the corporate culture, the quality of communication, the decision-making process, and so on. These assumptions help set the parameters for the planning process.

Profiling the Organization

This initial information gathering should lead to a sense of what the organization is and what business it is in. This will involve examining the existing mission statement and goals of the organization. If these are not stated, the assumed mission and goals should be identified. One of the real turning points for any healthcare organization is the point when it comes to grips with what business it is in. Hospitals who continued to think they were in the hospital business rather than the healthcare business found themselves at a competitive disadvantage with hospitals that realized they had a broader mission.

To this end, a couple of important questions must be addressed during the early stages of research. The first of these is: What is our product or products? This appears to be an easy question, but only few healthcare organizations can readily answer. This is partly because they have never thought in those terms, but also because it is not an easy question. Unless the organization's sole business is selling a healthcare "widget," the products and services offered are likely to be complex and not easily classified. What product does the specialty practice provide, for example? Health? Disease elimination? Prolonged life? Improved quality of life? Or looked at differently, is the product the individual procedure or diagnostic technique that is performed, or is it the holistic program of healthcare being offered? Regardless of the complexity involved, specifying the organization's products and services is an important step in developing a strategic mindset.

The second question is: Who are our customers? This issue is no less complex unless, again, the organization provides a very specific product to a very specific customer base. The more multipurpose an organization, the broader the range of customers it will have. For a hospital, it could be argued that the list of customers includes patients who receive services; family members and other decision makers who influence patient behavior; staff physicians; referring physicians; major employers and business coalitions; and insurance companies and managed care plans. In many cases, other providers of care may be customers; this is especially true with the emergence of networks of providers and integrated delivery systems. The list does not stop here, particularly if the hospital is tax exempt as a result of its not-for-profit status. In this case, other "customers" could include consumer advocacy groups, policy makers, legislators, regulators, and press. As with the product issue, the question of customers is complex. Clarification of the nature of one's customers is an important precursor to the development of a strategic mindset.

Prior to moving forward with additional research, it is usually worthwhile to present the planner's initial impressions to key decision makers. This provides an opportunity for all parties to get "on the same page" and to clear up any serious differences of perspective that may have developed. There are cases in which the findings from this initial stage of information gathering have resulted in a decision to not follow through with the planning process. There has also been the occasional courageous consultant who has pointed out that, unless certain changes were implemented in the behavior or perceptions of top management, it would be futile to implement the planning process.

Every planning initiative, of course, requires the development of a project plan to guide the process. This is particularly important with strategic planning due to the frequent need to cross departmental lines and coordinate the activities of units that may not be used to working together. (Project planning is discussed in Chap. 6.)

Baseline Data Collection

Assuming that there is consensus on moving forward with the planning process, data collection can now begin in earnest. Although the primary focus of strategic planning is the external environment, the process begins with a thorough self-analysis.

The Internal Audit

The "internal audit" as described in Chap. 7 has perhaps its most thorough application within the context of strategic planning. The intent of the internal audit is to determine who does what within the organization, when and where they do it, how they do it, and even why and how well they do it. It is amazing how many times it is discovered that the reason for an activity is never questioned until an outside consultant points out that the activity and staff members ask each other: "Why do we do that?"

The internal audit will involve additional interviews focused on specific aspects of the organization and its operation. It may require that questionnaires be administered to all or many of the staff. It will require access to a wide range of internal data describing operations, policies and procedures, staffing, finances, physical plant, information systems, and any other relevant aspect of the organization and its operation. The internal audit may even require the use of primary research methods to obtain certain information.

The planner quickly learns that there are at least four views of just about every aspect of the organization's activities. The first involves the written policies and procedures governing the process under study. The second involves the manager's version of what transpires. The third involves the employees' description of what happens. The fourth and final version reflects what actually does happen based on an objective assessment of the situation. While it is important that the actual process be identified, the other three versions are no less important to the planning process. Policies and procedures, as well as the perceptions of both management and staff, have implications for the direction the planning initiative takes.

The internal audit covers a wide variety of organizational features and can be incredibly detailed and thorough. The following list illustrates the aspects of the organization that might be addressed by means of an internal audit:

- Existing services and products
- Nature, number, and characteristics of customers
- Utilization patterns for services
- Sales volumes for products
- Staffing levels and personnel characteristics
- Internal management processes
- Financial status
- Fee/pricing structure
- Billing and collections practices
- Marketing arrangements
- Locations of service outlets
- Referral relationships
- Customer satisfaction

The internal audit for a strategic plan will typically involve some type of operational analysis. This is likely to include at a minimum analyses of patient flow, paper flow, and information flow. The operational analysis may also examine staffing patterns, physical space considerations, and productivity. This type of analysis can be highly technical and may require the use of outside resources.

The External Audit

The external audit in the strategic planning process begins with the same steps described in earlier chapters for assessing the organization's environment. The process starts with an analysis of the macro-environment and progresses through the various levels down to the microenvironment. Broad social trends are reviewed and developments within the economy are analyzed for their implications for healthcare. Health industry trends are reviewed, with attention paid to developments in the regulatory and reimbursement arenas.

The scope of the external audit will be determined by the nature of the organization and the issues being considered. For a major hospital or a health system many aspects of the healthcare environment will be important. For more specialized organizations, it may be possible to focus on those aspects of the external environment that have implications for that particular segment of the industry.

For most healthcare organizations, the analysis is carried down to the local market level. However, if the organization carrying out the planning is national in scope, the level of analysis may be different. Even so, most healthcare providers operate in a local environment. The "climate" of the community related to the range of issues addressed in the environmental assessment must be considered.

Defining the Market

The "market" for the organization can be defined in a number of different ways. The definition utilized depends on the purpose of the analysis, the product or service being considered, the competitive environment, and even the type of organization conducting the planning. Markets may be defined based on geography, demographics, consumer demand, disease prevalence, and so forth. The various bases for defining the market are discussed in detail in Chap. 6.

Profiling the Market Area Population

In the typical strategic planning initiative, a profile of the market area population is the first task. The type of information required on the market area population varies with the nature of the project. The first type of data typically compiled is demographic data, including biosocial and sociocultural traits. At a minimum, the analyst would examine the population in terms of age, sex, race/ethnicity, marital status/family structure, income, and education. In the process, the situation with regard to insurance coverage is typically assessed.

The demographic analysis is often accompanied by an assessment of the psychographic characteristics of the market area population. Information on the lifestyle categories of the target audience can be used to determine the likely health priorities and behavior of a population subgroup. *Consumer attitudes* is another dimension of the population that is typically considered at this point. The attitudes displayed by consumers in a market area are likely to have considerable influence on the demand for almost all types of health services. At the organization level, the attitudes of a wide variety of constituents besides direct consumers must be taken into consideration.

Identifying Health Characteristics

The health characteristics of the population will be identified following the steps outlined in Chaps. 6 and 7. The emphasis, of course, will be on those dimensions that are relevant to the needs of the organization.

Fertility characteristics refer to the attributes and processes related to reproduction and childbirth, and the importance of these characteristics varies depending on the type of organization and the type of plan. The number of births as well as the characteristics of those births, along with the attributes of the mothers and fathers of the children, form the basis for fertility analysis.

Historical patterns of fertility are a major influence on current patterns of health services demand. A wide range of service and product needs revolve around childbearing. Childbearing also triggers the need for such down-the-road services as pediatrics and contraception-related services. The demand for treatment of the male and female reproductive systems and the heightened interest in infertility treatment are by-products of the reproductive process.

The level of *morbidity* within a population is a major concern for health services planners. Incidence and prevalence rates can both serve a useful planning purpose and both may be employed as part of a planning analysis, depending on the nature of the project. This category includes disability indicators along with measures of morbidity in terms of disease prevalence. To the extent possible, planners need to project rates of incidence and prevalence into the future in order to plan for coming developments.

The study of *mortality* examines the relationship between death and the size, composition, and distribution of the population of the market area. Organization-level planners typically have less interest in mortality analysis than those involved in community-wide planning, since the latter are more concerned with the overall health status of the community. Nevertheless, mortality data is always examined to determine what it can tell us about the health status of the community.

The emphasis in most strategic planning initiatives will be on the morbidity profile of the population. The incidence and prevalence of various health conditions will drive much of the planning activity. For most organizations, the demand for health services derived from this level of need is what determines the market. Planners are likely to be interested in both the level of morbidity and the utilization patterns that it produces. As in other planning contexts, it is important to develop projections for these indicators of health status to assure that the plan is addressing future considerations rather than current ones.

The importance of an accurate assessment of health status cannot be overlooked. There is growing concern that traditional approaches to health status assessment are not appropriate for the contemporary environment. The long-standing emphasis on epidemiological data has historically provided an assessment from the perspective of health professionals, and some now contend that this can be misleading. The emerging approach to health status assessment involves more emphasis on the perspective of members of the population being assessed on the grounds that what they consider to be health problems is more relevant than those identified through a top-down approach. At the very least, any efforts to assess the health status of a population for which planning is occurring should involve a "triangulation" process whereby issues are examined from all relevant perspectives before an assessment is made.

Health Behavior

Health behavior can be defined as any action aimed at restoring, preserving, and/or enhancing health status. It involves such formal activities as physician visits, hospital admissions, and drug prescriptions, as well as informal actions on the part of individuals that are designed to prevent health problems and maintain, enhance, or promote health. An understanding of the population's health behavior should supplement the information previously developed on the market area's need for health services and, in some cases, utilization data represent the best source of this knowledge.

Obviously, healthcare organizations will focus on those indicators of health behavior that are most relevant for their operations. Hospitals are likely to require information on almost all of the indicators described throughout this book. Other organizations of more limited scope are likely to focus on specific indicators of utilization in their analyses.

The strategic plan is likely to require more detail on health behavior than other types of planning. The following types of health behavior may be considered, depending on the type of planning being carried out:

- Inpatient admissions:

  - Hospital admissions
  - Nursing home admissions
  - Residential treatment center admissions
  - Mental health facility admissions

- Outpatient visits:

  - Hospital outpatient visits
  - Hospital emergency room visits
  - Physician office visits
  - Other clinician office visits
  - Urgent care visits
  - Diagnostic center visits
  - Surgicenter visits
  - Mental health center visits

- Other service utilization:

  - Home health visits
  - Physical therapy treatments
  - Alternative therapy treatments

- Procedures performed:

  - Diagnostic
  - Therapeutic

- Prescriptions written

Many strategic planning initiatives require information on the informal aspects of health behavior as well. It may be important to determine the extent to which the market area population practices self-care, is involved in healthy lifestyle behavior, or emphasizes preventive behavior.

Competitive Analysis

The resource identification process characteristic of other types of planning takes the form of a competitive analysis in the strategic planning process. While there may be some reasons for identifying the full range of available health services within the market area, the focus will typically be on the organizations and/or services that are likely to be in competition with the entity doing the planning.

Options to consider for the competitive analysis are presented below, remembering that only selected ones may be relevant in a particular situation.

- Healthcare facilities:

  - Hospitals
  - Nursing homes
  - Physician offices
  - Community clinics
  - Nonphysician clinical offices
  - Residential treatment centers
  - Assisted living facilities (and other senior residential units)
  - Mental health facilities
  - Home health agencies/hospices
  - Urgent care centers
  - Freestanding diagnostic centers
  - Freestanding surgery centers
  - Specialty treatment centers (e.g., pain management)

- Healthcare equipment:

  - Biomedical equipment
  - Durable medical equipment
  - Information technology
  - Emergency services equipment

- Health personnel:

  - Physicians
  - Nurses
  - Nurse clinicians, physician assistants, and other physician extenders
  - Dentists
  - Optometrists
  - Podiatrists
  - Chiropractors
  - Mental health professionals
  - Rehabilitation therapists (e.g., physical therapists, speech therapists)
  - Clinical support personnel (e.g., radiology technologists)
  - Administrative support personnel (e.g., medical records technicians)
  - Alternative therapists

- Programs and services:

  - Inpatient programs/services
  - Hospital outpatient programs/services
  - Emergency services
  - Ambulatory care programs/services
  - Long-term care services

- – Community-based services
- – Home health services

- Funding sources:

  - – Commercial insurance (including managed care)
  - – Medicare (including Medicare HMOs)
  - – Medicaid
  - – Other federally funded programs (e.g., Veterans Administration)
  - – State funding sources (e.g., mental health services)
  - – Local funding sources (e.g., public hospital subsidy)

- Community health assets:

  - – Faith-based organizations
  - – Community development corporations
  - – Community associations
  - – Barber/beauty shops

- Networks and relationships:

  - – Formal hospital alliances
  - – Integrated delivery systems
  - – Provider networks
  - – Chain-operated facilities (e.g., hospitals, nursing homes)
  - – Contractual relationships
  - – Business coalitions for health

The final category, networks and relationships, has become increasingly important in the contemporary healthcare environment. A thorough inventory of health services should include a review of existing networks and relationships within the delivery system. In an era of managed care and negotiated contracts for health services, the existence of networks and relationships has taken on added importance. The significance of such situations cannot be overestimated and organizations must take the influence of these arrangements into consideration in their planning efforts.

An important aspect of this analysis involves referral relationships. As relationships have become more important, they are being increasingly emphasized in the strategic planning process. In fact, it can be argued that patients will utilize a provider in the future because of existing relationships, rather than the traditional approach of relationship development *following* utilization. The existence of networks, integrated delivery systems, and other relationships within the community should be fully addressed during the strategic planning process.

State-of-the-Organization Report

At this stage of the planning process, it is usually worthwhile to present a state-of-the-organization report. The nature of the report will depend upon many issues that have been raised earlier, focusing on those of relevance to the organization.

The state-of-the-organization report should include the following sections summarizing the data collection up to this point:

- Overall societal/healthcare/service trends
- Market area delineation
- Market area population profile
- Market area population health characteristics
- Current position of the organization/product
- Customer profile
- Competitive situation
- Other likely future developments affecting the organization

This status report should include the strengths, weaknesses, opportunities, and threats identified during the analysis. It should include an "issues statement" based on the results of the analysis to this point. The mission statement and the original assumptions should also be revisited at this juncture.

The state-of-the-organization report represents an opportunity to frankly describe the state of the organization. This allows all parties to "get on the same page" and to develop consensus with regard to the assumptions. This is the launching point for subsequent plan development.

Developing Strategies

This is an excellent point in the process to consider strategies. A strategy involves a generalized approach to be taken to the challenges of the market. At the organization level, the choice of strategy is critical. The strategy establishes the tone for subsequent planning activities and, in effect, sets the parameters within which the planners must operate. Examples of strategies that might be adopted by organizational planners included the following:

- *Dominance strategy* whereby the number one player in the market opts to focus on maintaining this position
- *Second fiddle* strategy in which the "runner up" in the market concedes this second fiddle status and plans accordingly
- *Frontal attack* strategy in which the organization decides to take on the market leader or major competitors head on

- *Niche* strategy in which the organization concedes it cannot be involved in the competition for the mainstream market, but instead concentrates on niche markets based on geography, population groups, or selected services
- *Flanking* strategy in which the organization "outflanks" the competition by entering new markets, cultivating new populations, or offering fringe products

These are only some examples of the types of strategies that might be adopted, and the options are essentially unlimited. A complex plan may involve more than one strategy, in fact. For example, a hospital may concede a second-tier position as a general hospital while actively striving to control major niches within the market.

Developing the Strategic Plan

The effort up to this point provides the foundation for the actual development of the plan. If the initial work is properly carried out, the planning process should flow smoothly, at least from a technical perspective.

Setting the Goal(s)

The goal or goals that are established should reflect the information that was provided in the state-of-the-organization report and should be in keeping with the organization's mission statement. Goals tend to be relatively general in nature and lack the specificity of objectives and other components of the plan. They identify an ideal state that will serve as the target for future development. For a national medical products company, the goal may be to establish the firm as the low-cost provider of a certain product. For a local health services provider, the goal may involve positioning the organization as a niche player to take advantage of certain market opportunities. For the purveyor of a specific service, the goal may be to become recognized as the provider of choice for a certain segment of the market.

The number of goals to be established depends on the complexity and size of the organization and the nature of the issues at hand. If the focus is narrow, a single goal may be appropriate. On the other hand, the complexity of many healthcare organizations mandates the establishment of multiple goals. Goals may be established, for example, specific to particular service lines or units within the organization.

Setting Objectives

Objectives refer to the specific targeted processes that support goal attainment. To many, these represent the "tactics" that support the strategies. Objectives for a strategic plan are stated in such terms as follows: The hospital's orthopedic practice will recruit a sports medicine specialist within the next 12 months (in support of the stated goal of expanding the organization's orthopedic product lines). For every goal a number of objectives are likely to be specified, with four or five objectives not being unusual. Multiple objectives are common since it is likely that action will be required on a number of different fronts in order to attain a specified goal.

As the planning team establishes objectives, any barriers to accomplishing the stated objectives of the organization should be considered, and these must be identified and assessed. The extent to which these barriers can be overcome must be determined. In the case of insurmountable barriers, an objective may have to be eliminated. It may be found, for example, that a lack of physical therapy personnel represents a potential barrier to expanding the organization's outpatient rehabilitation program. If it can be determined that there is, in fact, an untapped source of physical therapy staff, this may be diminished as a barrier. In another case, it may be found that the objective of expanding medical staff privileges at the other hospital in town is being thwarted by a competing practice that is well established at that hospital. This may turn out to be an insurmountable barrier.

Prioritizing Objectives

The prioritization of objectives becomes an important step in the process. There is no one procedure for prioritizing objectives, and the approach is likely to vary with the situation. However, some level of consensus must be developed beforehand in the process in order to systematically consider priorities. There are a number of questions that might be asked in this regard and these are spelled out in Chap. 6.

The challenge is to identify on the front end the criteria that are the most important for prioritization purposes. It may even be necessary to utilize different sets of criteria within one planning initiative due to the nature of the project. The process is also likely to result in the elimination of some objectives that are deemed less important once the criteria are applied.

The possibility of unanticipated consequences arising from the meeting of any of the objectives should also be considered. For each objective it is important to specify the likely consequences of carrying it out. This should involve both the intended consequences and potential unintended consequences. Virtually every action taken is going to result in negative consequences. While these cannot be eliminated, conceding their existence is the first step toward minimizing their impact.

For example, if the stated objective is to open an outpatient surgery center in the shadow of a competing hospital (in support of the goal of expanding surgical market share), both the intended and unintended consequences of meeting this objective should be considered. The intended consequences would include increasing outpatient surgical volume (thereby improving market share), increasing surgical revenue, capturing some of the competitor's patients, providing an additional site for staff physicians to operate, and establishing a presence in "enemy" territory.

On the other hand, the potential unintended consequences might include transforming a passive competitor into an active one, offending members of the competing hospital's medical staff, drawing patients away from existing surgical facilities while not attracting new patients, and so forth. Too often the positive aspects of the situation are examined in isolation from the negative consequences that could result from the actions.

Specifying Actions

The specification of the actions to be carried out is a critical step in the process. Having determined what should be done, it is necessary to indicate how it will be done. For each of the objectives that have been identified, a set of actions must be specified. In virtually every case, numerous actions must be performed to achieve an objective. These actions take a wide range of forms, from assuring that postage is available to support a direct mail initiative to developing a strategic partnership as a means of reaching an objective.

If the objective of a specialty practice is to recruit and deploy a new sports medicine physician in a satellite office within 12 months, a number of actions must be carried out. These include identifying a recruiting firm, allocating funds for recruitment costs, setting up an internal screening committee, determining compensation terms, identifying a site for the new office, furnishing the new office, and so forth. Many of these actions imply a certain sequence and this is a point at which the original project plan might be further refined to specify the sequencing of the action steps (Box 9.2).

Box 9.2: Case Study: A Strategic Plan for a Faith-Based Clinic Network
Christ Community Health Services (CCHS), a faith-based clinic network recognized as a federally qualified health center (FQHC), operates six clinics in a middle-sized southern city. Clinic leadership initiated a strategic planning process in order to update the existing 5-year plan that was set to expire the next year. In addition, CCHS administration felt an urgency to move forward aggressively in light of changes that were taking place within the healthcare environment.

(continued)

Box 9.2 (continued)

Clinic leadership established a planning team that included key clinic employees (administrators, clinicians), board members, and representatives of the patient population. Team members were instructed to "think outside the box" and develop a plan that would prepare the organization for the environment of the future.

The planning team established four overarching goals to guide future development. A number of objectives were established for each goal. Objectives were prioritized and action steps generated for each objective. The overarching goals are listed below with objectives enumerated for one of the goals for illustration purposes. For one of the objectives actions steps were identified. Although space does not allow the complete presentation of the components of the plan, the material presented below offers a glimpse of what the fully developed plan would look like.

The following overall goals were established:

Overall Goal 1: Develop and implement a "population health" model as a framework for marshaling community-wide support for community health improvement.

Overall Goal 2: Position CCHS as a "wholistic" program that leverages existing clinical resources while marshaling nonmedical resources for whole-person health and an integrated mind/body/spirit approach.

Overall Goal 3: Establish a "healthy start" philosophy/practice that permeates all aspects of CCHS operations and programs, taking a proactive (rather than reactive) approach to all endeavors and emphasizing healthcare rather than sick care.

Overall Goal 4: Expand the patient pool and the volume of services provided by CCHS to a level that will support the further expansion of CCHS facilities in its service area.

For Overall Goal 1, a rationale and the following objectives were established:

Overall Goal 1: Develop and implement a "population health" model as a framework for marshaling community-wide support for community health improvement.

Rationale: Although the Memphis/Shelby County population is becoming healthier overall, there is a limit to the impact that clinical medicine can have. There is evidence that we are becoming sicker as a society even in the presence of state-of-the-art care. In order to advance community health status an approach that considers the social determinants of ill health and addresses the root causes of ill health is required.

Objective 1: Assign a staff person (or independent professional if funding is available) to oversee the development and implementation of the population health model within (TBD) months.

(continued)

Box 9.2 (continued)

Objective 2: Develop a population health model that involves the marshaling of multi-sector resources for collective impact as a framework for population health improvement within (TBD) months.

Objective 3: Identify the sectors to be involved (and the concomitant social determinants) and recruit participants for implementing the population health model within (TBD) months.

Objective 4: Seek funding from and/or partnerships with local and national funders (including social impact funding) to support this innovative approach to community health improvement over (TBD) months.

For Objective 1 under Overall Goal 1, the following action steps were identified:

Objective 1: Assign a staff person (or independent professional if funding is available) to oversee the development and implementation of the population health model within (TBD) months.

Action Step 1: Identify the responsibilities of the person assigned to oversee the development and implementation of Overall Goal 1.

Action Step 2: Identify the characteristics desired in the person assigned to oversee development and implementation.

Action Step 3: Identify the resources required to support staff assigned to development and implementation.

Action Step 4: Identify potential candidates among existing CCHS staff.

Action Step 5: In the absence of potential internal candidates, identify options for external resources.

Action Step 6: Contract with the person charged with developing and implementing the population health model.

The material presented here does not represent the totality of the strategic plan but it does provide examples of goals, objectives, and action steps.

Implementing the Plan

An implementation plan is required to transform recommendations into actions. The planning process creates a road map; now the organization has to use it to get where it wants to go. It is at the implementation stage that the process often breaks down. The fact that "the last plan is still sitting on the shelf" generally reflects a failure of implementation rather than any flaw in the plan itself. The transition from planning to implementation involves a hand-off from the planning team to the management team. It also requires implementation at several different levels and by different divisions within the organization. The implementation plan is likely to require significant change in many aspects of the organization, including management processes, information systems, and corporate culture.

Steps in Implementation

In order to approach plan implementation systematically, both a detailed project plan and an implementation matrix should be developed. The implementation plan as initially described in Chap. 6 depicts the logical process that must be followed in order to carry out the objectives of the strategic plan. The fact that the process now shifts from the planning team to the organization's managers makes a well-thought-out implementation plan imperative. And, again, the need to coordinate various units within the organization further mandates a detailed approach to implementation.

An implementation matrix can be developed, laying out who is to do what and when they are to do it. The matrix should list every action called for by the plan, breaking each action down into tasks, if appropriate. For each action or task the responsible party should be identified, along with any secondary parties that should be involved in this activity. The matrix should indicate resource requirements (in terms of staff time, money, and other requirements). The start and end dates for this activity should be identified. Any prerequisites for accomplishing this task should be identified at the outset (and factored into the project plan). Finally, some milestones should be identified that allow the planning team to determine when the activity has been completed. (See Chap. 6 for an example of an implementation matrix.)

Requirements for Implementation

The resource requirements from the implementation matrix should be combined to determine total project resource requirements. For most strategic plans there will be a number of factors to consider. The amount of *capital investment* necessary to support implementation must be determined. Similarly, during startup and subsequent periods of operation the amount of *operating funds* that will be required must be determined. The implementation plan should indicate any *facilities* that will be required along with any *equipment* needs. In addition, the *human resource* requirements for the initiative should be determined. This refers to both existing internal personnel requirements and additional requirements. *Information system* requirements must be specified and their development coordinated with other information management initiatives. Any changes in *governance or management* will need to be specified, along with anticipated *marketing* needs.

When this process has been completed, the total resource requirements of the project will be identified for the first time. It is not until this point that the burden that must be borne by the various units of the organizations becomes clear. The extent of the requirements may have to be addressed in relation to available funds and any other fiscal constraints.

Means of Implementation

The means used to implement the plan will invariably involve various departments and units, and the impact of the project on them should be considered at this point. Processes that transcend departmental boundaries are likely to be controversial and, as with many types of change, resistance is likely to be exhibited.

Both direct and indirect means of implementation can be utilized. The direct means of implementation have been addressed to a certain extent through the development of the implementation matrix and the identification of resource requirements. Indirect means might include making changes in *physical facilities*, modifying the nature of *communication* within the organization, or taking *symbolic actions* that provide psychological support for the operationalization of the plan.

In many cases, the corporate culture will have to be modified for successful plan implementation. If a planning mindset does not already exist within the organization, this will have to be incorporated into the culture. If the culture emphasizes strict organizational divisions, a new way of thinking may have to be introduced in order to implement the strategic plan across divisional lines.

Evaluating the Effectiveness of Planning

The means for evaluating the success of the strategic planning initiative should be built into the planning process. This is important to those involved in the process, as well as to any parties that may be assessing the value of the planning initiative. For example, grant makers and funders will usually want to know how many people were reached and served by the initiative, as well as whether the initiative had the community-level impact it intended to have. At the community level, community groups may want to use evaluation results to guide them in decisions about their programs, and where they are putting their efforts. At the organization level, decision makers need to determine the effectiveness of the efforts in order to make midcourse adjustments. Individuals throughout the organization deserve to know how effective the planning initiative was in order to determine if their efforts in support of it were justified.

Evaluation techniques focus on two types of analysis: process (or formative) analysis and outcome (or summative) analysis. The former evaluates systems, procedures, communication processes, and other factors that contribute to the efficient operation of a program. Outcome evaluation focuses more on end results or what is ultimately accomplished. Process evaluation essentially measures efficiency, while outcome evaluation measures effectiveness.

Evaluation should involve ongoing monitoring of the strategic planning process, including benchmarks and/or milestones for assessment along the way. This will require the clarification of the objectives and goals of your initiative. As noted in

Chap. 6, the evaluation process should address planning and implementation issues, the extent to which objectives were achieved, the impact of the process on participants, and the impact on the organization's constituents.

Data collection and benchmarking are extremely important for measuring progress and quantifying benefits accruing to the community or to the organization. Documenting the process of community or organizational change is an ongoing task that should occur on a regular basis. (See Box 9.3 for a discussion of plan evaluation in the physician practice setting.)

Box 9.3: Evaluating the Effectiveness of Strategic Planning: The Medical Group Model

The challenges facing a physician practice have never been greater than they are today. Practice management has become increasingly complex and now calls for a range of skills beyond those usually available to any one person. Apart from the stresses of day-to-day operations, physician-managers and administrators are increasingly being confronted with questions like the following: Where will the practice be tomorrow, next month, or at the end of the year? What must the practice do to adapt to changing reimbursement patterns? What are the implications of changing demographics within the market area?

Given these types of question, there is pressure, on the one hand, to forge a long-term plan for the practice; on the other, there is concern with the immediate future. These are not unrelated issues, however, in that the immediate future impacts the 5-year plan. Because the planning process helps the group identify itself, it forces the members within the group to "buy into" the plan, and, most importantly, it allows the group to focus on the process for allocation of its scarce resources.

Before a practice can develop a plan it must understand the internal and external issues facing the group. For example, how does the world perceive the group? What are the practice's strengths, weaknesses, opportunities, and threats? Planning should give the practice the ability to circumvent obstacles while maintaining forward momentum toward a recognized goal.

Some of the short-term issues that face medical practice physicians and administrators today include:

- The operational effectiveness and efficiency of their practice
- Satisfaction levels of patients and referring physicians
- Organizational responsiveness to patients
- Effective billing and accounts receivable processes
- Clinical outcomes monitoring
- Compliance and accounting audits
- Marketing management

(continued)

Box 9.3 (continued)

The challenge for today's physician-manager is to address these disparate issues through a coherent plan that works for the group, its patients, its employees, and the countless other entities that interact daily with the group. This involves coordinating internal processes (like patient flow) with external processes (like marketing initiatives).

A strategic plan developed by a physician practice must be focused on meeting the needs of its customers, even more so than many other healthcare organizations. There are certain critical indicators of success that are shared by the better performing medical groups. In these medical groups, the patient flow process was analyzed from the time the patient made the initial phone call for the appointment until the last piece of paper was filed in the medical record of the patient's chart. A critical element in the success model derived from this analysis was the satisfaction of the patient with the flow.

The typical medical group thinks in terms of designing systems that streamline internal processes. This "internal" flow issue is related to "external" expectations on the part of the patient. In the better performing practices, the level of patient satisfaction is given equal weight with financial success. In addition to streamlined patient management processes, other factors identified as critical for superior patient satisfaction include hours of operation, scope of services provided by the group, quality of care provided by the physician and the staff, quality of communication between the physician/staff and the patient, quality of communication between the physician back to the referral source and to the insurance company, and quality of patient education offered by the group.

The lesson to be learned from these "best practices" is that, for practices to survive and thrive in the future, they must structure the practice to meet or exceed the needs of patients. The strategic plan determines the "interventions" required to create a system that meets the needs of the practice's customers. Once these interventions are in place, it is critical that the tools for evaluating their effectiveness be available.

The practice's performance review must measure the effectiveness of communication between the patient and the physician and the support staff, evaluating whether the quality of care provided by the physician and staff met the needs of the patient, and evaluating the level of responsiveness of the group overall to the needs of the patient. The most direct way to evaluate the effectiveness of the practice's strategic plan is through a benchmarking system. This involves evaluating practice performance on a monthly, quarterly, or semiannual basis and subsequently developing action plans to improve performance. All medical groups are in a constant state of dynamic motion, and the practice should evaluate its situation and modify its processes to be more responsive to our internal and external environment on an almost daily basis.

Simply defined, a benchmark is an operating performance standard. It is an indicator of the relative strength or weakness of an organization at a departmental or cost accounting level. Typical benchmarks include such items as number

(continued)

Box 9.3 (continued)

of days in accounts receivable, net fee-for-service collection percentage, new patient referrals, overhead percentage, and ratio of full-time nonphysician employees to full-time physicians. The only way to evaluate how well the practice is doing is through a comparison with some standard or benchmark.

Although it may be interesting to compare experiences with those of Dr. Smith in a different medical specialty with a different number of physicians operating in his facility, such comparisons are of limited value. A practice must compare its operations to physician groups in the same medical specialty and of comparable size. Then and only then can we meaningfully specify performance at the 25th, 50th, 75th, or 90th percentile. Once that comparison is made, it is possible to state quantitatively that the practice is at a given point on the continuum and ranks in the specified percentile in terms of overall performance. This can be thought of as a monthly report card.

Benchmarks should only be considered as a guide; the actual benchmarks used in a practice must be developed based on the size of the practice, practice location, and specialty. Any benchmark used to measure the effectiveness of your practice must:

- Be clearly understood by the staff and the physicians in the practice
- Be agreed to by the group, the physicians, and the employees
- Be trackable with data generated by the practice's systems
- Provide results that can be communicated to the participants
- Be a cause of celebration and rewards when targets are met

The benchmark system will generate baseline data that can be presented to the group to assist in its overall planning efforts. There can be no question about the effectiveness of the interventions called for in the strategic plan, if there are clear benchmarks against which they can be compared.

Needless to say, all of the activities described above require access to the necessary data, and another characteristic of the best medical groups is that they have adequate information processes in place. Quality data equates to better decisions.

Internal productivity reports and external benchmark survey data can also be used to provide meaningful feedback to physicians concerning their own level of productivity. Physicians can be paired with an "administrative partner," a nurse team leader, or department manager to review monthly reports. As a result, practicing physicians can remain well informed about their performance and the impact it has on the department, particular clinic site, or group as a whole.

Ultimately, productivity will hinge on the ability of the practice to coordinate the range of internal processes with external considerations. Practices that fail to interface these "two sides of the coin" will be at a disadvantage in a competitive healthcare environment. Having a well-thought-out plan in

(continued)

The Strategic Plan: A Moving Target

While it may be convenient to conceptualize the strategic planning process as a
discrete activity with a beginning and an end, this is not realistic in most situations,
particularly in today's healthcare environment. Planning should not be considered
as a discrete activity in any case but should be merged with the other functions of
the organization. Strategic planning in particular, with its emphasis on the external
environment, should involve a process that is tied in with the operation of the healthcare organization. Rather than being an end in its own right, any plan should serve
as a launch point for subsequent planning activity.

The strategic plan also represents a moving target due to the volatility of the
healthcare environment. There was a time when healthcare organizations could
expect a little breathing room between one major development in the healthcare
arena and the next. For example, Medicare might have made a significant change in
its reimbursement practices and little more would happen in this regard for a couple
of years. Today, dramatic change comes fast and furious. For this reason, it is likely
that the strategic plan will be modified before it is even completed. Developments
related to reimbursement, technology, provider relationships, and managed care can
occur almost overnight. The planning process must be flexible enough to take into
account fast-breaking developments in the environment.

A final factor to consider is the dynamics of the planning process itself. As the
planning team carries out its activities, it will be in constant contact with various
components of the organization. This interaction will involve the exchange of information, the solicitation of ideas, and the posing of potential strategies. Remembering
that the value is in the planning and not in the plan, it is not uncommon for many of
the plan's ultimate recommendations to be implemented before the plan is finalized.
The ideas and proposals that are developed, as well as suggested changes in operational aspects, are often adopted by various parties within the organization at a
faster pace than others. In fact, there are likely to be few original ideas developed
during the strategic planning process; most of them have already been thought of by
organizational personnel. The plan, however, provides the impetus for acting on
some of these ideas, as well as validation of their worthiness and permission to
move forward.

The plan may be modified many times before it is finalized. In fact, it may be best
if it is never finalized. If it is properly constituted, the process and the plan both
should be able to adapt to the changes that occur during the planning process. In this
sense, the plan teaches the organization to swim rather than simply throwing it a life
preserver.

Further Reading

Bryson, J. M. (2018). *Strategic planning for public and nonprofit organizations: A guide to strengthening and sustaining organization achievement.* Hoboken, NJ: Wiley.

Martin, B. (2018). *Strategic planning in healthcare: An introduction for health professionals.* New York: Springer.

Sheldon, A., & Windham, S. (2002). *Competitive strategy for healthcare organizations.* Frederick, MD: The Beard Group.

Zuckerman, A. (2012). *Healthcare strategic planning* (3rd ed.). Chicago, IL: Health Administration Press.

Chapter 10
Marketing Planning

Introduction

While marketing planning is well established in other industries, it is a relatively new function in healthcare. Until the 1980s, healthcare providers typically did not engage in formal marketing activities, thereby obviating the need for marketing plans. While some sectors of the industry such as insurance, pharmaceuticals, and medical supplies have a long history of marketing planning, organizations involved in patient care were slower to become involved in marketing activities. The introduction of competition in the 1980s, probably more than any other factor, drove the need to systematically approach the market for health services. Now, the contemporary healthcare environment demands that virtually all healthcare organizations have a marketing plan. Indeed, provisions in the Affordable Care Act (ACA) mandate that not-for-profit hospitals develop plans for addressing shortcomings in the care provided in their service areas, an endeavor that implicitly involves a marketing component.

Marketing planning may be defined simply as *the development of a systematic process for promoting an organization, service, or product.* This straightforward definition masks the wide variety and potential complexity that characterize marketing planning. Marketing planning can be limited to a short-term promotional project or comprise a component of a long-term strategic plan. It can focus alternatively on a product, service, program, or organization.

The Nature of Marketing Planning

Marketing plans share many of the characteristics of other types of plans discussed in this book. At the same time, marketing planning is distinguishable from those along a number of dimensions. Of all the types of planning discussed, marketing

© Springer Science+Business Media, LLC, part of Springer Nature 2021   247
R. K. Thomas, *Health Services Planning*,
https://doi.org/10.1007/978-1-0716-1076-3_10

planning most directly relates to the customer. While other types of plans may reference "patients," "clients," or "consumers," marketing plans are single minded in their focus. The emphasis on "promoting" in the definition above assumes that the organization or service is being promoted to someone. Whether the customer is the patient, the referring physician, the employer, the health plan, or any number of other possibilities, the marketing plan is built around someone's needs.

Because of this orientation, the marketing plan is probably the most externally oriented of any of the plans discussed. Although a concern for internal factors does exist (and "internal marketing" may be a component of many marketing plans), the marketing plan focuses on the characteristics of the external market with the objective of influencing change in one or more of these characteristics.

The marketing planner initially obtains much of the same information on the internal characteristics of the organization that would be done, say, for strategic planning purposes. At the same time, the marketing planner has information needs above and beyond those required in other planning scenarios. A more in-depth understanding of the organization's products and services and the manner in which customers are processed is required. Detailed information on existing marketing activities is needed. The same information will typically be required on competitors in the market area.

Marketing planning is often, although not always, shorter in scope than other types of planning. In many cases, the desired outcomes in marketing planning are more immediate. Few strategic plans are expected to reach their goals in a matter of months, but a focused marketing plan may include the expectation that objectives (e.g., awareness of a new service) be met within 6 months or less.

The shorter time frame reflects the fact that marketing planning is typically more narrow in its focus than other types of planning. In fact, the marketing plan is often a subcomponent of the strategic plan or the business plan. Although marketing plans geared toward changing the image of an organization are understandably broad, many marketing initiatives involve a particular product or service. As such, they are very focused and relatively narrow in scope.

One final, and important, difference relates to the manner in which outcomes are evaluated. While strategic plans are evaluated on the success of the plan in positioning the organization vis-à-vis its environment, the intent of most marketing plans is to effect change in consumer knowledge and/or behavior. Thus, the evaluation process is likely to measure changes in consumer awareness and attitudes or, even more concretely, through the monitoring of changes in volume, sales, revenues, or market share.

Although marketing planning is often seen as a stand-alone activity, it should be in keeping with the organization's overall strategic initiatives. Thus, the objectives of the marketing plan should correspond with those outlined in the strategic plan. A marketing plan should be an inherent component of any formal business plan as well. Even if established relationships exist with customers for an existing product, a marketing plan is required; a plan is even more important if new customers are being sought or new services being introduced. In fact, potential investors reviewing a business plan are not likely to give much credence to the business proposition in the absence of a marketing plan.

Marketing planning is typically not a component of community-wide planning, although it would be inappropriate to contend that it be totally excluded from planning at the community level. In fact, there has been growing conviction that many of the goals of public sector organizations operating within the community cannot be met without the benefit of a well-crafted marketing plan. The use of "social marketing" is becoming increasingly accepted by not-for-profit healthcare organizations. The fact that *everyone* needs to market has been evidenced by the emergence of numerous "how to" marketing books published for not-for-profit organizations. (See Box 10.1 for a discussion of social marketing.)

Box 10.1: Marketing Planning for Social Marketing

"Social marketing" is a form of marketing that is performed frequently within the healthcare field. While a variety of different definitions might be applied to social marketing, it typically refers to marketing by a not-for-profit organization—quite often a government agency—with the intention of promoting a program designed to bring about some type of social change. It is more likely to promote a cause than a particular service or product. It attempts to bring about social change through influencing the behavior of groups of individuals. At the same time, it is more targeted to the community than it is to the individual. In this regard, it attempts to influence public opinion in order to bring about some benefit to the general population.

Not surprisingly, the organizations involved in social marketing are those that are mandated to improve health conditions through programs geared toward society as a whole. These include public health departments (e.g., promoting prenatal care), government agencies (e.g., promoting seat belt use), and voluntary associations (e.g., anti-smoking campaigns). These programs utilize the mass media to promote their respective causes.

The development of a social marketing program involves the same marketing planning process that would accompany the marketing of a product or service. The marketing planner would examine the societal trends that are contributing to the issue being addressed and determine what factors play a role in the development and spread of the condition. This research component was applied in the campaign to combat AIDS, for example, by identifying the distribution of HIV and AIDS within the population, determining its cause, identifying the affected populations, and determining the means of transmission. This information provided the foundation for the development of a social marketing program as one means of addressing the AIDS epidemic.

As with any planning process, a goal was formulated—in this case, reducing the spread of HIV. The objectives that were identified in support of this goal included reducing the number of new cases during a specified time period, increasing awareness of the dangers of AIDS among at-risk populations, providing information and referral resources for the affected and at-risk populations, and encouraging behavior change among high-risk populations.

(continued)

Box 10.1 (continued)

The marketing planning process also involved identifying any barriers to the achievement of these objectives. These included such factors as ignorance as to the nature of the disease and its spread, fear on the part of those who might be affected, and the stigma associated with the disease.

The social marketing plan utilized the information to develop marketing initiatives aimed at the achievement of these objectives. A particular message was formulated and certain media were selected for the delivery of the message. The campaign involved the use of public service announcements on billboards, in print media (e.g., newspapers, magazines), and in electronic media (e.g., radio, television). It also involved community outreach programs in areas where high-risk populations were likely to be concentrated. These programs provided information for those at risk and encouraged the behavior changes necessary to combat the epidemic.

The social marketing initiative also involved a component geared to the general public. This component publicized the risk factors associated with the spread of HIV but, at the same time, attempted to demythologize AIDS and reduce misconceptions the general public had about the condition. Part of this campaign was intended to reduce the stigma associated with HIV and AIDS, thereby encouraging at-risk and affected populations to more readily present themselves for testing and treatment.

While social marketing was not the only approach used to combat HIV and AIDS, the efforts of various agencies contributed to the reduction of infection within the target population. Social marketing contributed to the successful management of HIV within the initial target population, a population that was receptive to these types of marketing initiatives.

By the beginning of the twenty-first century, however, HIV had spread to new populations in the United States. No longer concentrated among white gay males, it began to spread rapidly among African-American and Hispanic populations and among heterosexual populations. These new populations may not be as receptive as the original affected population to social marketing. At the very least, a different message and different media are likely to be required to address the AIDS epidemic among these hard-to-reach populations.

Marketing planning is one of the few planning activities that may actually have a departmental "home" within the organization. Many large healthcare organizations have formal marketing departments, and this unit provides a base for the development of marketing plans. Strategic planning, on the other hand, tends to be more organization-wide and typically does not have a departmental base. Business planning activities tend to occur throughout the organization and not be restricted to any department. Thus, it is not unusual for a large healthcare organization to have more in-house expertise related to marketing planning than it does for other types of planning.

Organization vs. Service Marketing

Marketing planning typically focuses on either the organization or a product or service offered by the organization. With organization-focused marketing, the intent is typically to promote the overall image of the organization. This may involve increasing awareness, creating a more positive image, clearing up misperceptions, or generally promoting the organization within the community. As such, this type of marketing is more general in its approach than marketing that focuses on a specific product or service.

The goals and objectives in marketing the organization will be relatively broad, as will the target audience. The intent is to convince essentially everyone that this is the best hospital, cardiology practice, or health plan. Thus, the approach used is likely to resemble traditional mass marketing more than the target marketing that has become common in recent years. The time frame involved in marketing planning for the total organization is likely to be fairly lengthy relative to service marketing, as changes in attitudes and perceptions cannot be affected overnight.

Finally, outcomes are evaluated much differently for organization-wide marketing than for the marketing of a specific service or product. Even though sales volume, revenues, profits, and other objective indicators may be considered as outcome measures, the real test is the extent to which the marketing initiative has resulted in increased name recognition, greater consumer awareness of its programs, higher ratings relative to its competitors, and/or more frequent selection by consumers as the provider of choice.

The process of marketing a product or service has essentially the opposite characteristics. The image of the organization is a secondary issue, since the objective is to make the public aware of a specific product or service. Or, in the case of an existing service, the intent will be to distinguish it from that of competitors and make it appear more desirable to consumers. The goals and objectives are, thus, much narrower and much more concrete. The target audience is also much narrower. Promotions geared for the general public would be a waste of resources and are not likely to achieve the desired effect. Not everyone is a candidate for the birthing center, even though obstetrical care is a fairly widespread need. The more specialized a service is, the more targeted the marketing must be.

Of course, it does not hurt if the organization's name is on the product or service—especially if it has positive brand recognition. On the other hand, the successful promotion of quality products or services may serve to burnish the organization's brand.

While all planning activities should be time delimited, marketing plans are often obsessive in this regard. Clear-cut target dates are virtually always included, since the content of marketing campaigns is often time sensitive. There may be some slack in a strategic plan's timeline for an objective related to increasing market share, but a marketing plan that calls for the establishment of consumer awareness prior to the opening of a new clinic does not allow much margin for error.

The outcomes in marketing a service will typically be measured in terms of sales, revenues, and profits. This is not to say that enhanced awareness, increased consumer preference, and other more subjective measures are not important. Ultimately, however, a marketing plan designed for a product or service is going to be measured in terms of concrete results.

Obviously, the approach to marketing planning is going to vary depending on the focus of the project. A lot depends on whether the plan is generated for a new organization or service or for an existing one. In the former case, the intent of the marketing plan would be to create awareness, generate initial business, and establish a customer base. Thus, approaches to acquiring customers will be different from those used at a later stage to retain them. Since little may be known about the actual characteristics of prospective customers, general promotional principles are utilized.

For an existing organization or service, the intent may be to enhance or improve the organization's image. On a more concrete level, the objectives may include changing existing customer behavior, such as convincing customers to switch to the organization or service from a competitor or encouraging the customer to consume more services. Since information on existing customers is available, the approach here focuses on capitalizing on this knowledge to derive as much business as possible from existing clients. This knowledge can also be used to expand the customer base to new clients.

When hospitals and other healthcare organizations first began formal marketing in the 1980s, much of the effort went into image advertising that promoted the overall advantages of the organization. These image campaigns were very expensive and generally did not accomplish their objectives. It was not unusual—and still is not—for a hospital to be top of mind with the public and be rated as best on all important dimensions, but still not be the facility of choice at decision time. This is because many other factors than those addressed in a marketing campaign are likely to influence the individual's choice of hospital (even if they have a choice at all).

These initial attempts at marketing the organization fell well below expectations. Not only an improved image (if that, in fact, did occur) did not necessarily translate into increased business, but also the hospitals that were most conspicuously involved in this type of advertising often generated considerable negative backlash due to their apparent extravagance.

Today, most advertising by health services organizations focuses on products or services. This is in keeping with the national trend in other industries to back away from an all-things-to-all-people approach and focus on specific products and specific target audiences. Thus, instead of General Hospital touting its virtues, you might find highly targeted campaigns promoting its outpatient surgery program, its home health agency, or its newly acquired lithotripter. Box 10.2 offers an example of marketing planning for a hospital.

Box 10.2: Implementing a Marketing Plan

Since the 1980s, many hospitals have adopted the service line management concept long established in other industries. Service line management appeared attractive to hospitals looking for ways to become more agile, move closer to their customers, strengthen relationships with physicians, become more profitable, and move beyond cost cutting and reengineering to develop more innovative and effective ways of serving their patients.

A service line is a tightly integrated, overlapping network of semiautonomous clinical services and a business enterprise that bundles needed resources to provide specialized, focused care and value to a patient population. The most common service lines include cardiovascular services, orthopedics, rehabilitation, women's services, children's services, and oncology services. Service lines can be virtual in that all components may not be under one roof; some services are horizontal and cross departments and disciplines. A service line may be created around a business that is already well established, or the concept may be used to focus on a new service or niche.

The product line concept was developed by organizations in other industries—most notably Procter & Gamble, General Electric, and General Motors—to decentralize decision-making; make strategic planning more effective; improve cost management and productivity; improve communication and collaboration; and, most importantly, help its product line management teams better understand the needs of their customers. The product line management concept emerged in the healthcare industry in the 1980s as an organizational effort to deal with prospective reimbursement, a tight economic environment, declining revenues, and intense competition—all of which drove the need for improving the way hospitals did business. In healthcare, this concept has probably been carried furthest by pharmaceutical companies that organize their business enterprise by product lines.

Many of the gains from service line management were erased with the emergence of managed care and other innovative financing structures in the late 1980s. Although many hospitals maintained their service line orientation throughout the 1990s, the concept was latent and reemerged only around 1997, when hospitals began to renew their patient focus. This revitalized service line management model defines a hospital's clinical services; allocates organizational resources—human, financial, and strategic—to these service lines; and clearly assigns accountability for performance to a service line leader.

The service line platform integrates clinical and support services on a matrix management grid to create horizontal integration of clinical services along a traditional continuum of care along with the vertical integration of support services. Also built into this platform are education and wellness programs, retail models, business development tactics, and a strong focus on physician relationships—all with an increased emphasis on creating enhanced quality and value for patients.

(continued)

Box 10.2 (continued)

Because the service line is sensitive to its costs and operational dynamics, its customers, and its competition, hospitals and health systems are able to decentralize accountability for strategic, operational, and financial performance from the corporate or executive office to the clinical service line. This shift in accountability to the service line maximizes hospital capacity by focusing on the best use of space and resources and provides more flexibility in managing growth.

Whether the service line concept is an effective approach to healthcare strategy development is still open to debate, and little hard evidence of the merits of this approach exists. Service line management does facilitate the marketing of services in many ways, and the close relationship between operations and marketing that can develop is an advantage.

Around 2005 another wave of interest in service line management in healthcare emerged (Litch 2007). This renewed interest reflected a growing emphasis on quality control, integrated services, and physician collaboration. From a marketing perspective, the growing need to establish an advantageous market position appeared to drive the revival.

The significance of service lines to customers is not clear. Ideally, service lines are designed to address consumer needs, but most consumers probably think about healthcare as a continuum of services that extend across clinical lines, not in terms of vertical silos of care. As service lines become more entrenched in healthcare, a better understanding of their meaning for consumers should be established.

Source: Reprinted with permission from Thomas, R. K. (2020). *Marketing health services* (4th ed.). Chicago: Health Administration Press.

Who Needs Marketing Planning?

There are few organizations in healthcare today that cannot benefit from marketing planning. Most, in fact, are finding it a prerequisite for survival in an increasingly competitive environment. Although some hospitals, physician groups, and other organizations involved in direct patient care have been involved in marketing since the 1980s, growing numbers have developed significant marketing expertise today.

Some private sector for-profit and not-for-profit organizations, however, have a long history of marketing and, hence, marketing planning. The nation's pharmaceutical companies stand out in this regard, especially since the pharmaceutical industry is reputed to spend a greater proportion of its budget on marketing than any other industry. Other components of the industry that have a longer history in marketing and promotions include insurance companies and distributors of medical supplies and equipment. Marketing on the part of insurance plans took on a new dimension with the passage of the Affordable Care Act.

Part of the residual resistance to marketing is a function of misperceptions as to what constitutes "marketing." Even today, many health professionals think strictly of advertising when the issue of marketing is raised. Most of them do not realize that they have been involved in marketing for most of their careers; they just did not recognize it as such. Physicians who frequent clubs where other physicians are members or send a follow-up note to a fellow physician after a referral or agree to serve as the physician for the high school football team are all involved in marketing activities. The challenge for marketers has been to demonstrate the scope of marketing and to fit existing activities within that framework.

The Marketing Planning Process

Planning for Planning

The same notion of planning for planning applies here as it does with any other type of planning. Before the actual planning can commence, the spade work must be done with regard to the marketing framework (e.g., the relationship to the strategic plan), the identification of key players, the establishment of a marketing mindset, and so forth. These activities will vary depending on whether marketing planning is envisioned at the organization level or on behalf of a specific product or service.

The situation for marketing planning is somewhat different from that for most other types of planning. A planning structure is often already in place in the form of marketing staff and a procedure for developing marketing initiatives. Unlike strategic planning, for example, the lead planner is not going to have to recruit key members of the planning team *de novo* in order to start the planning process. It may be that additional resource persons are brought into the mix to develop the marketing plan for a new service line, for example, but this involves adding to the existing planning structure rather than starting from scratch.

Stating Assumptions

The stating of assumptions at the outset and throughout the planning process is important in marketing planning. For example, a major assumption in marketing planning may relate to the type of image that the organization wants to convey. There is a big difference between presenting the image of an aggressive, profit-seeking enterprise driven by hard-bitten business principles as opposed to the image of a humble community-based organization intent on serving the needs of the population. Other assumptions might relate to the type of approach or appeal that is to be considered.

Assumptions should be stated with regard to the potential consequences of the marketing initiative, and this is a situation in which marketing planning is unique. In today's reimbursement environment, for example, a healthcare provider does not want to attract all potential consumers for a product or service. The organization wants to attract those who can be reasonably expected to pay. At the same time, it should not appear that the provider is deliberately excluding certain classes of patients. This delicate balance plays a role in the development of assumptions.

The nature of the assumptions made at the outset reflects the extent to which a product or service is already in the market and has some level of awareness and utilization. In addition, the extent to which marketing activities are already underway will affect the assumptions that are made.

Initial Information Gathering

To the extent that a healthcare organization already has a marketing function in place, it may be unnecessary to perform many of the tasks associated with initial information gathering. The marketing staff will typically have already examined most aspects of the environment as part of their ongoing market research activities and, at most, some updating of information on certain aspects of the environment will be necessary. In the case of a newly formed marketing department or the introduction of outside marketing resources, it may be necessary to carry out the type of comprehensive gathering of background information described in previous chapters.

The data collection process begins by gathering general background information on the organization through a review of any materials that have been prepared on the organization and on the particular product or service. Simply determining the attributes of the organization and/or its services may not be adequate for marketing planning, however. The planner really needs to know the extent to which the organization or service is different and the extent of these differences.

In a large organization such as a hospital, the marketing staff is not likely to be familiar with all services, especially if they had not been heavily marketed in the past. New services are frequently added by a hospital, and some existing services may be marketed for the first time. These situations are likely to call for additional background information gathering.

This review of materials should be accompanied by interviews with knowledgeable individuals within the community, both inside and out of the medical establishment. A general understanding of the external market should be developed during this phase of information gathering as well.

Not surprisingly, much more emphasis is placed on identifying and assessing existing marketing activities in the marketing planning process than in other types of planning. An early step typically involves inventorying marketing resources and determining the extent to which current marketing activities relate to the proposed project. It is easy to overlook ongoing marketing activities (especially if they are not labeled as such), but duplication of effort should be minimized. At the same time, the possibility of marketing activities operating at cross purposes needs to be avoided. (A classic example would be the hospital that was promoting its emergency room as the place for *all* unscheduled health problems while marketing its urgent care network as an alternative to emergency room care.)

As part of this process, potential barriers to the planning initiative should be identified. Individuals or organizations that are clearly resistant to any planning process will surface, although the development of a marketing plan may not be nearly as "intrusive" as that for a strategic plan. Immutable patterns of behavior should be identified, particularly if internal marketing is to be involved. Supporters of services within the organization that may be considered in competition could become an issue, for example. The director of the emergency department (ED) may not react favorably to a marketing campaign meant to direct patients away from the ED to urgent care centers affiliated with the hospital. While some barriers can be surmounted, others might not be. These understandings become a part of the assumptions that drive the process.

Environmental Assessment

The first step in the formal data collection process here as elsewhere involves an environmental assessment. If the marketing planning focuses on the organization, the environmental assessment is likely to be broader than if it focuses on a specific product. Although marketing planning should involve an evaluation of the environment at all levels as would be done for other types of plans, the effort expended may not be as great due to the narrower focus of many marketing initiatives.

Obviously, a lot depends on the nature of the organization that is involved in marketing planning. A national organization that seeks a truly national market— e.g., a pharmaceutical company developing a direct-to-consumer marketing initiative—will probably perform an analysis involving substantial detail at the national level. On the other hand, a home health agency that is licensed to practice in a single county is not likely to need much detail with regard to national trends in order to develop a marketing plan. Regardless of the type of organization, the question should be this: What external constraints are likely to affect this organization and what can be found out about them?

An added dimension related to marketing planning involves the collection of data on similar initiatives in other markets. The planner should be able to incorporate information about marketing approaches that have and have not worked when similar organizations or services were being marketing in other contexts.

As part of the environmental assessment, broad *social trends* should be analyzed and their implications for the market area considered. These societal trends should include demographic trends, economic considerations, lifestyle trends, and particularly shifts in attitudes. Many trends discussed elsewhere have implications for marketing planning, and, in many ways, marketing planning is more sensitive to changing societal patterns than are certain other types of planning.

Lifestyle trends are likely to be more important when it comes to marketing planning than for other types of planning. An example of changing lifestyles involves the health and fitness consciousness that characterizes many segments of the American population. The fitness movement that began in the 1980s has created an unprecedented demand for health clubs, health food, athletic goods, and sports medicine. It has not been uncommon, in fact, for a marketing plan to focus on the fitness-related attributes of a product or service that was never intended as a fitness aid.

Even changes in *consumer attitudes* at the national level may have implications for local communities. The increasing diversity characterizing many communities suggests a divergence in lifestyles. This creates the challenge of marketing to subgroups with varying attitudes, interests, and preferences.

More open consumer attitudes have also led to the overt marketing of historically controversial products and services. Until recently, for example, few healthcare organizations would openly market products for the treatment of erectile dysfunction or advertise "morning after" pills for induced abortions. Now, with more liberal attitudes in evidence, clever advertisements attract attention to organizations and their services, with advertisements for medication for erectile dysfunction now commonplace.

The same type of analysis should be applied to *health industry trends* to determine what developments are likely to affect the local community. The emergence of hospital service lines in the 1980s, for example, influenced the marketing agenda. Further, a major marketing effort has been introduced by health maintenance organizations seeking to capture the indemnity insurance market. The establishment of the health insurance "marketplace" under the Affordable Care Act served to restructure established insurance marketing efforts. Trends like these have profound implications for marketing planning.

Of particular importance in marketing planning is the *industry or product life cycle*. A new product that is being introduced will be approached differently from an existing product that is struggling to differentiate itself. Both will be approached differently from an established product that is nearly at the end of its life cycle.

Regulatory, political, and legal developments should all be considered. Regulations enacted by a variety of governmental and nongovernmental agencies may set constraints on marketing activity. The political environment also has both direct and indirect implications for marketing planning. There is no doubt that the marketing plan for hospital chain Columbia/HCA took a different turn in the mid-1990s after its activities came under federal scrutiny. Legal activities at the national, state, and local levels also have implications for the local healthcare system. For example, marketing activities that could be thought to illegally encourage referrals or other questionable activities would be a consideration here.

Developments in the area of *technology* can exert a major influence on the nature of the healthcare system. Not only should the marketing planning team be familiar with the technology surrounding a given service or product, but it must also be familiar with other technologies in the field. Promoting an organization's new procedure as cutting edge may be inappropriate if hundreds of other hospitals are already performing this procedure. It is also important to be aware of any technological developments on the horizon that may affect the positioning or perception of the product being marketed.

The passage of the Affordable Care Act in 2010 represented the most significant effort to "reform" the healthcare system in many decades. Its primary focus was insurance industry practices that were considered detrimental to healthcare consumers. The Act created healthcare insurance exchanges and put certain restrictions on insurance industry practices. Its provisions implicitly called for regular community health needs assessments on the part of not-for-profit hospitals and the development of plans for addressing any identified gaps in community services. Addressing gaps in services is likely to require an intensive marketing effort.

Reimbursement patterns may be influenced by all levels of government as well as by private sector third-party payers. Anticipated developments in reimbursement must be taken into consideration in marketing planning. To the extent that consumers with the ability to pay for the service are important, the reimbursement situation within the market must be considered. The marketing initiative, in fact, is likely to be tailored to appeal to a particular payer category. If price is an issue, information on the availability of insurance benefits is important.

Baseline Data Collection

Marketing planners place considerable emphasis on the characteristics of the organization. The planner must understand the nature of the organization and develop a feel for its "character." This is particularly true if an image campaign is envisioned for the total organization. But it is also true if a specific product is being marketed. For example, a relatively unknown service might be differentiated from that offered by competitors by pointing out the support available from an organization that already has a positive image in the community. This "halo effect" may be used to advantage if this in fact is the situation. Thus, a new progressive birthing center could be promoted partly on the basis of the clinical backup available from the large staff of specialists in the med/surg units and the fact that extensive neonatal intensive care services are available as needed.

The Internal Audit

In performing the internal audit, a number of different aspects of the organization should be examined for marketing planning. Among the components that are particularly relevant for marketing planning are the following:

Services/products. What are the services that are provided and/or the products that are produced? What are the characteristics of these services and products?

Customer characteristics. How many customers does the organization have and what are their characteristics? What are other demographic characteristics that are most pertinent? Where do patients reside and what is the "reach" of the organization? What is the case mix of current customers? What are the financial categories of the patient base?

Utilization patterns. What is the volume of services and products consumed by the organization's customers? How does this volume break down by product line or procedure?

Pricing structure. How is pricing determined for the organization's services and products? How does this price structure compare with that of competitors, the industry average? How price sensitive are the goods and services offered?

Marketing arrangements. What marketing programs are currently in place and how is marketing structured? What type and level of resources are available for marketing? Are there processes in place for internal marketing?

Locations. To what extent are operations centralized or decentralized? How many satellite locations are operated and how were these locations chosen? Are there markets that are not being served by existing outlets?

Referral relationships. How are customers referred to the organization? To what extent are there formal referral relationships?

The External Audit

The external audit in the marketing planning process involves the same steps described in earlier chapters for assessing the organization's environment. The process starts with an analysis of the macro-environment and progresses through the various levels down to the microenvironment. Broad social trends are reviewed and developments within the economy are analyzed for their implications for healthcare. Health industry trends are reviewed, with attention paid to developments in the regulatory and reimbursement arenas. The scope of the environmental analysis will be determined by the nature of the organization and the issues being considered. As noted below, the external audit for marketing planning addresses some additional dimensions.

Profiling the Market Area and Its Population

A logical first step in the marketing planning process is the identification and profiling of the market area to be considered. The market area could range from a very small geographic area served by a pharmacy, for example, to a national or even international market served by a pharmaceutical company. The "market" that is profiled should be in keeping with the geographic scope of the organization doing the planning.

There may be situations when the market area is not clear cut, and a certain amount of research may be required to identify the market that is to be cultivated. (See Chap. 9 for a discussion of the delineation of market areas.) In most cases, the market will be delineated by geography. Certainly, local healthcare providers will be restricted to a relatively circumscribed geographic area. On the other hand, the market may actually involve broad population segments and, except for national boundaries, may not be related to geography at all. Thus, a retail pharmacy mail order business may have a national market defined in terms of population characteristics that exist independent of geography.

The type of information required on the market varies with the nature of the project. The main categories of data that might be emphasized are listed below. The first type of data typically compiled is demographic data, including biosocial and sociocultural traits. At a minimum, the analyst would examine the population in terms of age, sex, race/ethnicity, marital status/family structure, income, and education. In the process, the situation with regard to insurance coverage is typically assessed.

The demographic analysis is often accompanied by an assessment of the psychographic characteristics of the market area population. Information on the lifestyle categories of the target audience can be used to determine the likely health priorities and behavior of a population subgroup. *Consumer attitudes* are another dimension of the population that is typically considered at this point. The attitudes displayed by consumers in a market area are likely to have considerable influence on the demand for almost all types of health services. At the organization level, the attitudes of a wide variety of constituents besides direct consumers must be taken into consideration. (Details of these characteristics are provided in Chap. 7.)

Of these various characteristics of the market area population, attitudes probably receive more attention from marketing planners than from other types of planners. While there may be interest in the demographic or psychographic characteristics of a population, marketing planners often view these primarily as clues to the attitudes of that population. Since the thrust of many marketing plans attempts to change attitudes, this category of information is critical and often requires primary research.

In situations in which the market is not closely linked to geography, data collection for the market profile will be addressed differently. For example, the market may be constituted of active, younger seniors or of women of childbearing age. In either case, the characteristics of the market will be determined initially independent of geography (except for the limitation of national boundaries). Thus, the characteristics of younger seniors or women of childbearing age will be identified in terms of the above dimensions and *then* linked to geography for the spatial dimension. Geographic areas with concentrations of young seniors or areas with concentrations of childbearing age women would subsequently be identified.

Market Segmentation

Of particular importance in marketing planning is the market segmentation process. Most marketing initiatives are going to involve target marketing in which subsegments of the population are singled out for cultivation. Market segmentation can take the following forms:

Demographic Segmentation

Market segmentation on the basis of demographics is the best known of the approaches to identifying target markets. The links between demographic characteristics and health status, health-related attitudes, and health behavior have been well established. For this reason, demographic segmentation is always an early task in any marketing planning process. Thus, demographically distinct subgroups are typically defined relative to various services and products.

Geographic Segmentation

An understanding of the spatial distribution of the target market has become increasingly important as healthcare has become more consumer driven. One of the implications of this trend has been the increased emphasis on the appropriate location of health facilities. The market-driven approach to health services has demanded that healthcare organizations take their services to the population, and the major purchasers of health services are insisting on convenient locations for their enrollees. Knowledge of the manner in which the population is distributed within the service area and the linkage between geographic segmentation and other forms of segmentation is critical for the development of a marketing plan.

Psychographic Segmentation

For many types of products and services an understanding of the psychographic characteristics of the target population is essential. The lifestyle clusters that can be identified for a population often transcend (or at least complement) its demographic characteristics. Most importantly, psychographic traits can be linked to the propensity to purchase various services and products, as well as to the attitudes, perceptions, and expectations of the target population. (See Box 10.3 for a discussion of lifestyles and the use of health services.)

Box 10.3: Lifestyle Segmentation Systems and Health Behavior

Lifestyle segmentation systems have been used for decades in other industries but have never received wide acceptance in healthcare. For the most part, healthcare provider organizations depended on physicians or health plans to channel patients to them. They, in fact, had little interest in the characteristics of their patients. In the new healthcare environment, however, there is growing interest in customer segmentation. The market has become much more consumer driven and individuals are taking a much more active role in healthcare decision-making. Today, growing numbers of health plans, health services providers, and other organizations are expressing an interest in customer segmentation and target marketing.

Lifestyle segmentation is also of interest to health planners and others who are interested in the distribution of healthcare phenomena within a population. Although variations in demographic and sociocultural characteristics serve to explain a lot of the differences found in health status and health behavior among various groups, there is growing evidence that lifestyle characteristics may actually transcend these standard dimensions for segmentation. Among the elderly, for example, it was customary to classify those over 65 into one monolithic category or at best three categories based on age breaks (e.g., 65–74, 75–84, and 85 and over). Lifestyle analysis indicates, however, that the 65–74 age cohort actually contains two or more lifestyle clusters that may have similar demographic traits but be different in terms of lifestyles. For this reason, medical sociologists must consider the lifestyle clusters that characterize the population under study.

The first lifestyle segmentation systems—also referred to as psychographic segmentation systems—were developed in the 1970s. This new approach to segmenting the population was developed in response to some of the perceived deficiencies in demographic profiling. Marketers had come to realize that people in the same demographic category may fall into different groupings based on lifestyle despite being very similar on paper. Lifestyle research discovered that within this demographic category there were various lifestyle categories that had a greater impact on consumer behavior than age did.

The best known early lifestyle segmentation system was developed by Stanford Research International (SRI) in the 1970s. It was called VALS for "values and lifestyle system" and inspired a variety of subsequent lifestyle segmentation systems. The VALS system never benefited from widespread use but three subsequent systems are widely used today. These are lifestyle segmentation systems developed by Claritas (PRIZM), Experian (MOSAIC), and CACI Marketing Systems (ACORN). While the various systems were built using similar methodologies, they differ in terms of the specific procedures utilized to create the categories.

(continued)

Box 10.3 (continued)

The concept behind all segmentation systems is the use of geodemographic data in conjunction with data on consumer behavior, attitudes, and preferences to establish distinct lifestyle clusters that cover the entire population. This allows researchers to classify healthcare consumers into distinct categories, each with its peculiar characteristics. Once the lifestyle segments have been identified for a population, it is possible to attach a broad range of characteristics to the respective categories.

The PRIZM developed by Claritas may be the best known system, primarily due to the clever names it has given its lifestyle categories. Individuals may be classified as, for example, "Patios and Pools," "Shotguns and Pickups," or "Executive Suites" among the 62 PRIZM clusters designated at the time. The PRIZM system is the only one that has been used extensively to date to link health characteristics to lifestyle clusters. This information, however, is proprietary and can only be obtained by becoming a client of the data vendor that developed the healthcare links to the various clusters.

U.S. MOSAIC is the latest version of the Experian lifestyle classification system. This system includes 71 lifestyle clusters grouped into 12 major categories. The naming scheme is somewhat more straightforward than for the PRIZM system, with the "Upscale Singles Category" including such clusters as "High-income urban singles in apartments" and "Urban, upper-mid-income seniors in apartments."

CACI's ACORN is an acronym for "A Classification of Residential Neighborhoods." A number of multivariate statistical methods were applied to create this system. CACI analyzed and sorted the country's 226,000 neighborhoods by 61 unique lifestyle characteristics, such as income, age, household type, home value, occupation, education, and other key determinants of consumer behavior. Next, market segments were created by a combination of cluster analytic techniques. The techniques were selected to produce statistically reliable solutions and to handle an immense amount of information. This process results in the assignment of over 220,000 neighborhoods to various lifestyle segments.

Health planners involved with the development of marketing plans are increasingly emphasizing the importance of lifestyles for both health status and health behavior. It is only natural to begin to link various health characteristics to the respective lifestyle clusters. As the value of lifestyle segmentation becomes more obvious to health services researchers, the range of health-related characteristics that are likely to be associated with the various lifestyle segments can be expected to grow.

Usage Segmentation

A common form of segmentation long used by marketers is now being applied to healthcare. The market area population can be divided into categories based on the extent of use of a particular service. In the case of urgent care center usage, for example, the population can be divided into heavy users, moderate users, occasional users, and nonusers. This information provides a basis for subsequent marketing planning that can be tailored differently, for example, for existing loyal customers and noncustomers.

Payer Segmentation

A form of market segmentation unique to healthcare involves targeting population groups on the basis of their payer categories. The existence of insurance coverage and the type of coverage are major considerations in the marketing of most health services. Health plans cover some services and not others, and this becomes an important consideration in marketing. For elective services that are paid for out of pocket, a highly targeted marketing approach is required. The payer mix of the market area population has now come to be one of the first considerations for many marketing planning activities.

Identifying Health Characteristics

The health characteristics of the population will be identified following the steps outlined in Chaps. 6 and 8. The emphasis, of course, will be on those dimensions that are relevant to the needs of the organization.

Fertility characteristics refer to the attributes and processes related to reproduction and childbirth, and the importance of these characteristics varies depending on the type of organization and the type of plan. The number of births as well as the characteristics of those births, along with the attributes of the mothers and fathers of the children, form the basis for fertility analysis.

A wide range of service and product needs revolve around childbearing, and childbearing also triggers the need for such down-the-road services as pediatrics and contraception-related services. The demand for treatment of the male and female reproductive systems and the heightened interest in infertility treatment are by-products of management of the reproductive process.

The level of *morbidity* within a population is a major concern for health services planners. Incidence and prevalence rates can both serve a useful planning purpose and both may be employed as part of a planning analysis, depending on the nature of the project. Incidence rates are utilized for acute conditions and prevalence rates for chronic conditions. Morbidity includes disability indicators along with measures of morbidity in terms of disease prevalence. To the extent possible, planners need to project rates of incidence and prevalence into the future in order to plan for coming developments.

The study of *mortality* examines the relationship between death and the size, composition, and distribution of the population of the market area. Organization-level planners typically have less interest in mortality analysis than those involved in community-wide planning, since the latter are more concerned with the overall health status of the community. Nevertheless, mortality data is always examined to determine what it can tell us about the health status of the community.

The emphasis in most marketing planning initiatives will be on the morbidity profile of the population. The incidence and prevalence of various health conditions will drive much of the planning activity. For most organizations, the demand for health services derived from this level of need is what drives the market. Planners are likely to be interested in both the level of morbidity and the utilization patterns that it generates.

Identifying Market Needs

Marketing planning differs from other types of planning in the sense that the research component of the planning process may determine the focus of the plan. In strategic planning, for example, the process is informed by the research findings, but it is not likely that the strategic direction of the organization is going to be radically modified as a result of the research. With market research, on the other hand, the intent may be to determine what the needs and desires of the market are quite independent of the services that the organization is already providing. It is not inconceivable that marketing research could result in a decision to develop a new service or a new business line that had not been previously considered. This is the hallmark of a market-driven industry; the organization does not simply sell what it has to offer, but it goes to the market to determine what the opportunities are.

Identifying Health Behavior

Health behavior can be defined as any action aimed at restoring, preserving, and/or enhancing health status. It involves such formal activities as physician visits, hospital admissions, and drug prescriptions, as well as informal actions on the part of individuals that are designed to prevent health problems and maintain, enhance, or promote health.

An appreciation of the nature of consumer behavior is much more important for marketing planning than for other types of planning. Since marketing is driven by consumer needs, an appreciation of the behavioral dimension of any target population is essential. It is ultimately this behavior that the marketing plan seeks to influence.

The following steps in the consumer purchase model should be taken into consideration in the development of a marketing plan (Hillestad and Berkowitz 1991). The point at which the target market is located in the consumer behavior progression will determine the focus of the plan.

Awareness. Awareness refers to the initial exposure of the target population to the product or service being marketed.

Knowledge. Knowledge refers to the point at which the potential consumer understands the nature of the product or service.

Perception. Perception develops at the point at which the consumer develops an opinion of the product or service.

Contract access. Contract access is a step unique to healthcare, in that many services or products will not be considered for purchase if the provisions of the consumer's insurance plan do not cover them.

Location. The geographic availability of a service may become a factor once a consumer expresses interest in the product or service.

Preference. Preferences develop at the point that the consumer expresses a tendency for one type of product or service (e.g., a podiatrist rather than an orthopedic surgeon) and/or decides between different providers of the same service (e.g., podiatrist A rather than podiatrist B).

Choice. This is the decision point at which the consumer eliminates other options and decides to buy a particular product or utilize a particular service.

Usage. This is the point at which the consumer actually buys the product in question or utilizes the service.

Satisfaction. The consumer subsequently displays some level of satisfaction with the product or service and this influences future utilization.

Advocacy. The successful marketing initiative will ultimately create an advocate for the product or service, thereby extending the impact to the initiative.

One other consumer dimension of importance to the marketing plan involves the bases on which consumers differentiate various services and products in the market. This might be thought of as the "hot buttons" characterizing the target market. It is important to determine if the target population is most interested in, for example, *quality* or *value* in a service. Or is it the case that, for a particular service, *location* or *convenience* is the most important consideration. In other cases, *price* may be a determining factor in consumer behavior.

The bases for differentiation may not be obvious from baseline data collection, and this is an area in which primary research may be required. Regardless of the effort required, this is critical information. This knowledge will not only shape the marketing strategy, but it has implications for product/service design, packaging, distribution, and pricing.

One other unique characteristic of healthcare that has implications for the marketing plan is the fact that the end user of a service may not be the ultimate target of a marketing initiative. In fact, healthcare marketers have identified a number of other categories of target audiences that are more important than the end user. For example, various categories of *influencers* have been identified. These could be family members, counselors, or other health professionals that encourage consumers to use a particular service. The role of various *gatekeepers* might also be considered. These could include primary care physicians, insurance plan personnel, discharge planners, and others who have responsibility for channeling consumers into certain services. Referral agents of various types are also a consideration.

Another category involves the *decision makers* who actually make choices for the consumer. These could be family members, primary care physicians, or caregivers who act on behalf of consumers for various reasons. Unlike other industries, there are many cases in which the person to receive the product or services does not make the decision. Doctors may decide what tests, treatments, and drugs should be administered. Insurance companies may guide patients to different providers or limit the types of services that are covered. Ambulance drivers may make the choice with regard to the emergency room to be used. Parents make healthcare decisions for their children and, in their later years, children make healthcare decisions for their parents.

Finally, there is a category of *buyers* of healthcare services that includes employers, business coalitions, and other groups that might indirectly control the behavior of consumers by determining which services they can and cannot utilize. In some cases, such as employers, they may be bearing most of the cost of healthcare for their employees, particularly if they are self-insured. A group of local (and in some cases national) businesses may leverage their patient volume by negotiating contracts with insurance plans. An accountable care organization might disrupt traditional health services patterns by creating new alliances. These "wholesale" approaches to arranging for healthcare delivery will be increasingly prominent players in the healthcare arena.

Competitive Analysis

The resource identification process takes the form of a competitive analysis in the marketing planning process. The focus will typically be on the organizations and the services that are likely to be in competition with the entity doing the marketing planning.

In actuality, competition takes place at two levels in the healthcare market. At the level of service provision, the content of the services provides a basis for competition. At the marketing level, however, the *perceptions* that exist within the target audience constitute another battleground for competition. In many ways, the battle for the "hearts and minds" of the customer is waged independently of the more substantive competitive activities.

The review of *facilities* in marketing planning will typically be restricted to those facilities that are directly applicable to the project. A facility competing in terms of a narrowly defined service may be interested only in those facilities that offer that service. Marketing planning for a full-service hospital, on the other hand, will require a very broad review of facilities. This would include not only the hospitals that compete with the facility, but also the variety of nonhospital organizations that compete in a particular market area with the hospital.

The same approach would be followed with regard to *products and services*. The programs and services to be analyzed will typically be those of immediate concern to the organization. The more complex the organization and the more comprehensive its services, the wider the net that will be cast in terms of competing programs and services.

Although a competitive advantage in terms of *equipment* is typically not thought of as a marketing angle, there are numerous examples in healthcare in which hospitals or other facilities compete directly on the basis of the technology they have to offer. If the technologies are comparable, the marketing challenge is to somehow differentiate, for example, one hospital's imaging capabilities from another's. In some cases, the technology may be truly unique (as with the first organization to acquire the latest laser technology for eye surgery). The marketing approach will be different in this case than it would if everyone's technology were comparable.

In many ways, healthcare organizations, particularly those involved in direct patient care, succeed or fail based on the characteristics of their *personnel*. Certainly in developing an image campaign, the qualities of the organization's personnel will be displayed. Even for a particular program or service, the presence of a "name" physician or access to the only retina surgeon in the market constitutes a basis for differentiation. The planner will want to determine the number, type, and characteristics of the personnel within the organization for these purposes.

The inventory of market area services should include a review of existing *networks and relationships* within the delivery system. This aspect of the research is particularly challenging, since no directories of "relationships" are likely to exist for the community. In an era of managed care and negotiated contracts for health services, the existence of networks and relationships has taken on added importance.

An important aspect of this analysis involves referral relationships, since much of the marketing plan research will focus on identifying sources of customers. The research should identify both existing referrers and non-referrers to the organization. It should also identify potential referral source types that are not already being tapped.

Inventory of Marketing Resources

Data collection for marketing planning includes a component related to the organization's existing marketing resources. This information indicates the resource base on which the marketing planner can build. This inventory includes information on the role of the marketing department within the organization and, more specifically, its role with regard to the service or product in question. The analysis should also determine the level of marketing expertise that currently exists within the organization. It is important to determine the extent to which marketing is built into the operation of the organization, with this information helping to determine the extent to which a marketing "mindset" exists.

Obviously, the planner needs to determine if there is an existing marketing plan and, if so, what its characteristics are. At the same time, any ongoing marketing evaluation activities should be identified. The nature and location of any marketing activities need to be determined.

Consumer Awareness

Of particular importance in the marketing planning process is the degree of consumer awareness that exists with regard to the organization and/or product under consideration. Information on awareness of and perceptions concerning competing organizations and their services and products is important as well.

This is an area where there is likely to be little existing information, unless a substantial market research process is in place. In the typical case, primary research will be required to determine the extent to which consumers are familiar with the organization or its products, the image held by consumers, the level of their knowledge, and the propensity to utilize various services. Similar data should be collected on consumer perceptions of competitors and their services.

It may be necessary to develop an understanding of the degree of awareness characterizing different segments of the market. A high level of awareness may exist among segments of the market area population that are not likely to be heavy users, while the segments with the greatest customer potential may exhibit a low level of awareness. The acquisition of this type of knowledge is likely to require primary research.

Market Share Analysis

The market share for the organization or the specific product or service is of particular importance in the marketing planning process. Although some effort may be required to determine the relevant market share in many situations, this information not only provides an indicator of the current position of the organization or service in the market but also serves as an important basis for evaluating the success of a marketing initiative.

If the organization is the focus of the marketing initiative, the market share the organization holds within the market area should be determined. Overall market share may not be as important, however, as market share for the various product lines or specialty areas. Certainly, the planner will want to know how the overall market share is split among the various programs. It may be less important to know that the hospital holds a 25% market share of admissions within the market area than it is to know that the share for obstetrics is 35% and for cardiology is 15%. Realistically, it is difficult to change overall market shares for hospitals in established medical markets. It makes more sense, then, to think in terms of the market shares characterizing component programs.

If a specific product or service is the focus, obviously the planner will want to determine the market share held by that product or service. If the service line is outpatient surgery, a first step is to determine the extent to which the surgery center controls the market. Again, it will probably be worthwhile to break this down into component procedures, since the overall outpatient surgery figure may not be very meaningful.

When dealing with national corporations, it is likely that the market shares they hold will be easily determined. Sales volumes for pharmaceuticals, medical supplies, and equipment are closely tracked, and market share data are likely to be readily available. However, determining the share held by a product or service at the local level may be more of a challenge.

Despite the difficulties, market share must be determined to the extent possible. This may require some primary research or, at the very least, some creativity in "massaging" available data in order to obtain the necessary information. The fact that market share is likely to be a critical benchmark for determining the effectiveness of a marketing plan mandates that every effort be made to establish the baseline market share and track it during the course of the marketing campaign.

The market share analysis is comparable to the gap analysis performed in community-wide planning and strategic planning. The "gap" is in effect the difference between the market share held by the organization or product and the overall market or volume for that product. Thus, a 25% market share indicates that the organization is failing to capture 75% of the potential business. It becomes important to analyze this 75% to determine how the rest of the market is divided up. If the other 75% is controlled by a single competitor, the marketing approach will be a lot different than if the remainder is divided among a dozen small players. Other considerations might include whether the competitors are small local players or large national concerns. Further, are these well-established organizations or are a lot of new players entering the market?

State-of-the-Market Report

At this stage of the process, it is usually worthwhile to present a state-of-the-market report. The nature of the report will depend upon many issues that have been raised earlier, including whether an organization or a product is being marketed, whether it is a new product being introduced or an old one that is being revived, and whether the target is existing customers or new ones.

The state-of-the-market report should include the following sections summarizing the data collection up to this point:

- Overall industry/product trends
- Market area delineation
- Market area population profile
- Market area population health characteristics
- Current position of the organization/product
- Competitive situation and market share
- Likely future developments

This status report should include the strengths, weaknesses, opportunities, and threats identified during the analysis. It should also include an "issues statement" based on the results of the analysis to this point. This is also the point at which the mission statement and the original assumptions are revisited to verify that the marketing direction is in keeping with the intent of the organization.

This is an opportunity to frankly describe the state of the market and the organization's position in it. This provides a means for getting all parties on the same page and confirming assumptions. This should be the launching point for subsequent plan development.

Developing Strategies

The strategy refers to the generalized approach that is to be taken to the challenges of the market. Strategies set the tone for subsequent planning activities and in effect set the parameters within which the planner must operate. The strategy that is chosen will influence the nature of the plan that is ultimately developed.

The development of strategies for marketing plans is often different from other types of plans in that the focus may be narrower, say, than for a strategic plan. However, it is likely that the general approach could be framed in terms of an educational initiative, a public relations rather than an advertising approach, a soft-sell vs. a hard-sell approach, and so forth.

Ideally, the strategy employed for a marketing initiative will support the organization's mission statement and reflect the strategies embodied in the organization's strategic plan. Thus, if the organization's strategy involves positioning itself as the "caring" organization, marketing initiatives should support this approach. Of course, there are occasions in which a particular marketing situation may call for a departure from the established approach. For example, a hospital that has been content to live in the shadow of a more powerful competitor and pursued a "we're Number Two" approach may develop a world-class program in a particular area and decide to take a much more aggressive approach in the marketing of this service than for the organization in general.

Developing the Marketing Plan

The effort up to this point provides the foundation for the actual development of the plan. If the initial work is properly carried out, the planning process should flow smoothly, at least from a technical perspective.

Setting Goals

The goal represents the generalized accomplishments that the organization would like to achieve through its marketing plan. The goal or goals that are established for the marketing plan should reflect the information that was provided in the state-of-the-market report. As in other planning activities, the goal should be in keeping with the organization's mission statement.

The number of goals to be established depends on the complexity and size of the organization, the nature of the issues at hand, and the type of planning being undertaken. If the focus is narrow, a single goal may be appropriate. On the other hand, the complexity of many healthcare organizations mandates the establishment of multiple goals.

The goal of the marketing plan would be stated in a form such as this: To establish Hospital X as the top-of-mind facility in the market area. Or, for a service-oriented initiative, it might read: To capture the market niche for occupational medicine.

Setting Objectives

Objectives refer to the specific targeted processes that support the attainment of marketing goals. Objectives must be developed in response to the major opportunities or problems identified and should represent potential solutions (or at least part of the solution) for these issues.

While goals are general statements, objectives are very specific. Objectives should be clearly and concisely stated. Any concepts must be operationalizable and measurable. Objectives must also be time bound, with clear deadlines established for their accomplishment. Further, objectives must be amenable to evaluation. This is particularly critical since the success of the marketing plan will typically be measured in terms of the extent to which objectives have been achieved.

For every goal a number of objectives may be specified, since it is likely that initiatives will be required on a number of different fronts in order to reach the specified goal. Any barriers to accomplishing the stated objectives of the system or the organization should be identified and assessed at this point. Marketing objectives are stated in such terms as follows: The proportion of the general population for whom Hospital X is top of mind will be increased from 10% to 25% within 6 months (in support of the stated goal of making Hospital X top of mind in the community).

Barriers to marketing objectives arise for a variety of reasons. Some of these such as a lack of resources or talent may be common for any type of plan. There are some types of barriers that are more or less unique to marketing planning. For example, there may be ethical or legal considerations associated with some types of marketing, including situations in which advertising may be prohibited for certain health professionals. There are also issues of appropriateness and taste that may be a consideration. It may be found, for example, that the educational level of the target audience is a barrier to introducing a new high-tech procedure or that a new procedure is considered "experimental" by the public, thereby making potential patients apprehensive.

Prioritizing Objectives

The prioritization of objectives may not be as important an issue in marketing planning as it is for some other types of planning. However, there needs to be some consensus developed beforehand in the process in order to systematically consider priorities if that becomes necessary. The challenge is to identify on the front end the criteria that are the most important.

One approach that might be used for prioritizing the objectives of a marketing plan involves the traditional "four p's" of marketing: product, price, place, and promotion. The decision could be made, for example, to focus on the product in the marketing initiative, at the expense of the price, place, and promotion. Thus, objectives that are most directly related to promoting the characteristics of the product would be emphasized. Or it might be appropriate to capitalize on the price advantage of the product, thereby encouraging an emphasis on objectives that focus on the pricing dimension.

Specifying Actions

The next step in the marketing planning process is the specification of the actions to be carried out. It is one thing to indicate what should be done, and it is another to specify how it should be operationalized. For each of the objectives that have been identified a set of actions must be specified. These actions take a wide range of forms, from assuring that postage is available to support a direct mail initiative to enlisting a celebrity spokesperson as a means of reaching an objective.

If the objective of a specialty practice is to raise awareness of its new sports medicine program, for example, a number of actions must be carried out. These may include selecting an advertising agency, allocating funds for marketing, "packaging" the program, aligning promotional referrers, and so forth. Many of these actions imply a certain sequence, and this is a point at which the original project plan might be further refined to specify the sequencing of the action steps.

The action steps developed for a marketing plan may be more standardized than those for other types of plans. It is likely that marketing initiatives are already underway (unlike a strategic plan that is being developed for the first time), and this type of activity may be frequently carried out by the organization. A reasonable understanding of the resource requirements is likely to have been previously established, and there may be parties that already have responsibilities that would be directed toward the planning initiative.

Implementing the Marketing Plan

Planning is ultimately only an exercise, albeit a meaningful one. The payoff comes in the implementation of the plan. The planning process creates a road map that the organization must use to get to where it wants to go. To a certain extent, planning is talk, but implementation is action.

Marketing planners also have the advantage that the hand-off from planning to implementation is likely to be smoother than it is for other types of planning. Indeed, the same parties are likely to be involved in both activities. This is in contrast to strategic planning, for example, in which the planning team transfer responsibility to management once the plan has been developed.

Steps in Implementation

In order to approach plan implementation systematically, it is important to develop both a detailed project plan and an implementation matrix. The project plan has been discussed elsewhere, and standardized approaches are likely to be in place for the implementation of a marketing plan.

The implementation matrix should list every action called for by the plan, breaking each action down into tasks, if appropriate. For each action or task the responsible party should be identified, along with any secondary parties that should be involved in this activity. The matrix should indicate resource requirements (in terms of staff time, money, and other requirements). The start and end dates for this activity should be identified. Any prerequisites for accomplishing this task should be identified at the outset (and factored into the project plan). Finally, some benchmark should probably be established that allows the planning team to determine when the activity has been completed. (See Chap. 6 for an example of an implementation matrix.)

Requirements for Implementation

The resource requirements from the implementation matrix should be combined to determine total project resource requirements. When this process has been completed, the total resource requirements of the project will be identified for the first time. The extent of the requirements may have to be addressed in relation to available funds and any other fiscal constraints.

Means of Implementation

In marketing, there are well-established techniques for implementing a marketing plan. The different approaches that might be utilized include advertising, public relations activities, and community outreach efforts, among others.

There are also decisions that must be made with regard to the specific marketing methods. The implementation plan can focus on a traditional media campaign with heavy advertising or it might emphasize direct marketing. On the other hand, perhaps internal marketing is the most efficacious approach to take. Or the situation may call for business-to-business marketing. If a media approach is chosen, the type of media to be utilized becomes an issue for the implementation plan. The techniques utilized will be dictated by the nature of the marketing initiative.

The Evaluation Plan

The notion of evaluating the planning project should be top of mind on the first day of the process and, in fact, should be built into the process itself. It should involve ongoing monitoring of the process, including benchmarks and/or milestones for assessment along the way. While the evaluation process is important for all types of planning processes, it is particularly important in marketing planning. Since the objectives of the marketing process are typically fairly focused, measures of marketing effectiveness are essential and often easy to perform.

Evaluation techniques focus on two types of analysis: process (or formative) analysis and outcome (or summative) analysis. Both of these have a role to play in the project. Outcome evaluation is particularly important for the marketing planning process. Changes in image or sales volume must be measured, and the success of the project is likely to be calculated in much more precise terms than it is for other types of planning.

Although evaluation techniques are often praised for their bottom-line objectivity, they are also useful in healthcare where it is not possible to place a dollar value on everything. Thus, cost-effectiveness analysis should take into consideration the non-tangible aspects of the service delivery process in its evaluation.

Revision and Replanning

As noted earlier, it is unlikely that a plan will be completed without being modified for one reason or another. This type of "on-the-fly" revision is inevitable in a rapidly changing environment. At the end of the planning period, it is important to reaccess the internal characteristics of the organization and the external environment. What developments have subsequently occurred that will affect the plan or the implementation of its provisions? What actions have been taken supportive of the plan that were not anticipated? Have there been developments that affect resource requirements? Have actions on the part of competitors affected the "strategic balance"?

The marketing approach chosen should be reviewed to determine if it is still the best approach in view of possible changes in the environment. The goals and objectives should be revisited to assure that they are still appropriate in the light of any changes in either the internal or the external environment.

References

Hillestad, S. G., & Berkowitz, E. N. (1991). *Healthcare marketing plans*. Gaithersburg, MD: Aspen Publishers.

Litch, B. K. (2007). The re-emergence of clinical service line management. *Healthcare Executive, 22*(4), 14–18.

Further Reading

Armstrong, G., & Kotler, P. (2014). *Marketing: An introduction* (12th ed.). New York: Pearson.

Bashe, G., & Hicks, N. (2000). *Branding health services*. Gaithersburg, MD: Aspen.

Berkowitz, E. N. (2016). *Essentials of healthcare marketing* (3rd ed.). Burlington, MA: Jones & Bartlett.

Berkowitz, E. N., Pol, L. G., & Thomas, R. K. (1997). *Healthcare market research*. Burr Ridge, IL: Irwin Professional Publishing.

Resnick, M. (2012). *Marketing public health: Strategies to promote social change*. Burlington, MA: Jones & Bartlett.

Thomas, Richard K. (2020). Marketing Health Services (4th edition). Chicago: Health Administration Press.

Chapter 11
Business Planning

Introduction

Business planning was introduced to healthcare in the 1980s when the industry was undergoing significant transformation. Due to increased competition and a more volatile environment, healthcare organizations needed to behave more like businesses, and this meant adopting business practices long common in other industries.

The adoption of business planning techniques was also given impetus by the entrance into healthcare of entrepreneurs from other industries during this same period. These newcomers may not have known much about healthcare, but they knew a lot about business. Old-line healthcare administrators found themselves at a disadvantage vis-à-vis these new competitors, and they had to adopt business planning principles in order to continue to compete.

Business planning can be simply defined as follows: *The systematic development of a plan for meeting a business objective.* The business plan establishes the outline for developing a project or business in terms of its potential for generating profit. The plan describes the what, when, who, where, why, and how of the business. If the plan is for a new business or product line, it describes the process to be followed in establishing the business plan. If it involves an existing business, it considers the organization's history and the manner in which the business will be developed in the future.

The Nature of Business Planning

While the business plan by definition has a specific purpose, it is increasingly seen as a tool for analysis and management. How better to assess the "health" of one's business than to work through the business planning process? How better to understand issues related to the management of the operation than through examining it within

© Springer Science+Business Media, LLC, part of Springer Nature 2021
R. K. Thomas, *Health Services Planning*,
https://doi.org/10.1007/978-1-0716-1076-3_11

the context of the business plan? The business planning process introduces the discipline and logical thought necessary for moving the business forward, in addition to laying out the road map for effective business development.

The business plan should be framed within the context of the organization's strategic plan. The objectives of the business plan should support the objectives of the strategic plan and be in keeping with the mission and goals of the larger organization. It should also be coordinated with other types of planning being carried out by the organization.

The business plan can be distinguished from strategic plans and marketing plans in one important way. The business plan is inherently conservative, even if it deals with an innovative service or product. While the strategic plan should be visionary and the marketing plan creative, these traits are generally not encouraged in a business plan. The bottom-line orientation calls for a sober approach to plan development.

Business planning is also distinguished from strategic planning in that the objective of the plan is typically foreordained. With strategic planning, the planning team may be starting out with a blank slate and, through the interaction of those involved, a planning agenda is developed. In most cases, there are few preconceived notions concerning the strategic direction the organization will take, and the strategic plan may look very different from what anyone had envisioned. On the other hand, the business plan is generally formulated to support a business concept that has already been conceived and now needs to be operationalized.

This implies that the business plan is relatively rigid compared to some other plans. However, plans can only go so far in anticipating unexpected developments, uncontrollable circumstances, and other complexities of the market. But like all plans, the business plan should be sensitive to potential developments that may require midcourse corrections. It should have the flexibility to adapt to changing circumstances without losing sight of the business objective.

Business planning is seldom applied in the community-wide planning process, since the nature of community-wide planning does not lend itself to this approach. However, healthcare organizations within a community should be encouraged to adopt business planning principles in their efforts to contribute to the objectives of the community-wide plan. Indeed, it is difficult to conceive of a community-wide plan being successful unless the business plans of major players are aligned.

When Should a Business Plan Be Developed?

It is difficult to imagine any healthcare organization operating in today's environment without a business plan of some type in place. Regardless of the competitive situation or the stage of development of the organization, a healthcare organization should have a business plan to guide its actions. The plan defines the organization in relation to its environment and its competitors. It establishes general planning objectives and provides a context in which business decision-making can occur.

Any time there is a need to analyze an existing business and determine its future direction, a business plan is necessary. A plan should also be developed whenever a decision is being made that impacts the business. This may involve the addition of a new service, the introduction of a new product, staff changes, or other actions.

Certainly any effort at initiating a new venture requires a business plan. This is especially true if the venture is a startup and has no history to guide it. Even if the new venture is being launched within an existing framework, a business plan for the new component is necessary.

Business plans typically are developed for either an internal or an external audience. Quite often business plans for existing organizations are developed to guide the overall direction of the organization or for the benefit of some subunit. If a new service or product is envisioned by the organization, a business plan may be developed to justify the initiation of this new line.

Increasingly, healthcare organizations are seeking outside funding for business development. This may be from traditional investment sources, venture capitalists, or even foundations. They may also be seeking funds from major donors. In every case, it is important to have a well-conceived business plan to present to the funding source.

Why Healthcare Is Different

Every discussion of planning so far has noted the uniqueness of healthcare. Business planning may be the situation in which healthcare is the most unique, and it is unique in a variety of ways. The mission of the healthcare organization is likely to be quite different from that of organizations in other industries involved in business planning activities. The mission may emphasize the charity or service orientation of the organization, rather than a bottom-line concern with profits. The mission is also likely to be more diffuse than that for organizations in other industries. A mission of "improving the health status of the community" is a lot different than the bottom-line-oriented missions of most corporations in other industries.

The objectives of the healthcare organization are also likely to be much more diverse than those of its counterparts in other industries. The hospital, with its myriad of functions and interests, is the epitome of the multipurpose organization. A business plan for an organization this complex must be able to consider a wide range of perspectives, especially when few of these components were established with an eye to the bottom line.

The constituencies of healthcare organizations are typically quite different from those of other industries. Although a growing number of healthcare organizations must be accountable to stockholders, most are more directly accountable to other types of constituencies. A public hospital may have to cater to politicians, consumer interest groups, vested interests in the medical community, and other entities.

A church-affiliated hospital not only has a board of directors to which it reports, but it may also be accountable to the denomination's leadership as well.

Healthcare organizations are also different in the sense that they are "required" in one way or another to provide comprehensive services. In other industries, an unprofitable product line can simply be eliminated. Hospitals and some other healthcare organizations, however, may feel that they cannot compete on equal terms unless they are comprehensive in their service offerings. For a hospital to drop an unprofitable obstetrical operation may have negative implications for other aspects of the operation. Indeed, state regulations may mandate the operation of the unit and eliminating it may not be an option.

Ultimately, the healthcare industry is still primarily not-for-profit in its orientation. The main objective is to provide a service needed by the community or to fill a gap in the organization's complement of services. If a business line is profitable, that is a plus. There is no other industry where an organization would knowingly enter into a business venture that has no prospect of being profitable.

This situation reflects, among other things, the intangible aspects related to the provision of health services. In many cases, the intent is not to make a profit on the specific business but to use a service line to support other aspects of the operation. Perhaps the best example involves the establishment of a network of urgent care clinics that will be marginally profitable at best, with the notion that 20% of the patients will be referred to the organization's specialists and 20% of these will end up being admitted to the organization's inpatient facility. The indirect benefits, in this case, are considered to be more important than any profits that would derive directly from the operation of the urgent care centers.

Expertise Required

Although some of the expertise necessary for developing a business plan will be available in-house to large healthcare organizations, many smaller ventures will not have the required capabilities. While much of the data collection process is similar to that for other types of planning, business planning requires much more detail on the financial aspects of the operation. This means that the planners must know the right questions to ask and then know how to interpret the information that is generated.

Business planning is also different in the sense that once financial data are collected, this information must be converted into a pro forma document and other financial statements that depict the likely future direction of the business initiative. This requires a certain level of skill that may not be readily available in all organizations. There are many sources of assistance for developing financial statements, and outside expertise may be required for the development of an effective plan.

Developing the Business Plan

The business plan is perhaps the most technical of the plans that are featured in this book. At the same time, it is probably the most straightforward. The components of the plan are highly standardized and much of the process can be reduced to a formula. In fact, computer software has been developed to support business planning more so than other types of planning.

The business plan should be a tool for setting the direction of the company over the next several years and indicate the action steps and processes needed to guide the company through this period. With a well-thought-out plan, the organization can better anticipate future situations and deal with them proactively.

Planning for Planning

Planning for planning is somewhat different for the business plan than for most other types of planning. In general, the organizational phase involves identifying and enlisting the various parties appropriate for and necessary to the development of a plan. In the case of a business plan, the ultimate goal will have been established prior to initiation of the planning process. Whereas the strategic planner may ask "What are the financial dimensions involved in creating this vision for the future?" the business planner will ask "What do we need to do to introduce the new service?" The end point is predetermined, and the planning process serves to demonstrate the feasibility of reaching that goal and provide the means for completing the steps required for its achievement.

Today, it has become common in hospitals to expect managers in various departments to justify their requests for staff, programs, equipment, or other resources in terms of business considerations. Subunits are increasingly expected to submit business plans to justify their requested resources while at the same time contributing to the organization-wide business planning process. This is sometimes carried to the absurd point of making a business case for the purchase of a desktop computer. For the most part, however, business planning is left to the organization's business planners (although they are likely to carry some other title), and relatively few of the organization's staff will have regular involvement in the business planning process. Key individuals may be involved as necessary, especially in that any activity being planned is likely to overlap or interface with activities in other departments. And, certainly, appropriate experts from within or without the organization will be utilized as appropriate.

Initial Information Gathering

Initial information gathering should begin with a review of any available organizational materials. These would include publications produced by the organization such as annual reports, press releases, and marketing materials. It may even be appropriate to review the "resumes" of management and key clinical and technical personnel. Other potential sources of information include any reports filed with regulatory agencies, grant proposals, and certificate-of-need applications. Certain internal documents, such as executive committee minutes, planning retreat summaries, and evaluation studies may also be useful. Of course, detailed financial statements for several previous years should be reviewed.

Unless this is a truly unique initiative, information on the experiences of other organizations should be readily available. Business practices are standardized enough that it should be possible to capitalize on the experiences of those organizations. Financial analysts in healthcare have more access to examples to emulate than do those developing strategic or marketing plans.

The *major issues* should be identified, particularly as they relate to the business side of the organization. In the case of a business plan, the information sought through this initial research will center around the project being contemplated. This will involve an analysis of the *organizational structure* for the existing or proposed program. This involves a review of the division of labor, the chain of command, and the internal communications channels.

The *key players* in the organization should be identified through this process and, when appropriate, any influentials external to the organization as well. Some key players are obvious, such as those in formal positions of authority. Other critical participants may be those who are positioned to have access to critical information. The business plan particularly requires identification of management capabilities and other personnel resources, since these will be critically reviewed by those considering the proposal.

This stage of the process should also identify the key constituents of the organization. Constituents may include patient groups, referring physicians, employee benefits managers, insurance plan representatives, politicians, and any number of other categories of constituents. If it is a publicly held company, the board of directors and its shareholders represent constituents of some importance.

The initial information-gathering process for the business plan is not likely to be as comprehensive as it is for most other types of plans. The plan by definition is much more focused and there is no need, for example, to identify the issues affecting the organization above and beyond those that relate to the planning effort. The financial "bean counters" involved in this process may not have the requisite knowledge in some of these areas and are likely to require input from staff in other departments.

Profiling the Organization

The initial information gathering should allow the planner to develop a sense of what the organization is and which business it is in. The products or services of the organization need to be clearly defined for the business plan, since these will be its focus. The resources available for carrying out the business plan must be identified in more detail and earlier in the process than for, say, strategic plan development. Similarly, the customers for these products or services must be identified in order to tailor the plan to their needs.

In some cases, the business proposition may be clear-cut (e.g., the feasibility of renovating an existing clinic); in others (e.g., establishing a new service line), the process may be open ended and require more resourcefulness on the part of the business planner.

The stating of assumptions at the outset and throughout the planning process is important in business planning. Any number of assumptions might be made with regard to the market, consumer behavior, competition, and many other aspects of the environment or the organization. In particular, assumptions must be made that justify the financial statements that are developed. Assumptions should be stated with regard to the potential consequences of the business development initiative.

The nature of the assumptions made at the outset reflects the extent to which a product or service is already in the market and already has some level of awareness and utilization. In addition, the extent to which related business activities are already underway will affect the assumptions that are made.

Baseline Data Collection

As with other types of planning, both internal and external analyses are likely to be performed.

The Internal Audit

The "internal audit" as described in Chap. 8 is used in business planning to collect most of the necessary data on the organization. The intent of the internal audit is to determine who does what within the organization, when and where they do it, how they do it, and even why and how well they do it.

The internal audit will require access to a wide range of internal data describing operations, staffing, finances, physical plant, policies and procedures, information systems, and any other relevant aspect of the organization and its operation. The internal audit may even require the use of primary research methods to obtain certain information.

A more thorough assessment of the organization is likely to be performed for the business plan than in other types of planning. This is not only important for the sake of the planning effort, but to the extent that outside funding sources are to be involved, the financial condition of the organization will be critical. Considerable emphasis is placed on the current management of the organization, and detailed data on its capabilities, experiences, and traits are likely to be required. This should include information on the combined skills and experience, integrity, industry contacts, and previous experience in working together on the part of management. (It has been purported, in fact, that investors base 60% of their decision to fund a project on the characteristics of the management team that is to be involved.)

The business plan obviously goes much further than other types of plans in compiling financial data on the organization. Detailed statistics on the organization's past financial experience and its current financial status will be required. This will include balance sheets, profit and loss statements, and cash flow statements. Any unusual situations related to the organization's finances should be clearly explained.

Detailed information on sources of revenue will be required on the organization; for most organizations this will be fairly straightforward. For a hospital, however, specifying distinct sources of revenue is much more complex. In some cases, personal financial statements and tax returns may be required of the owners, if outside investment is being considered.

If the project represents a startup operation or a new product line for an existing organization, the management team may not be in place. These situations require an indication of the management skills that will be available to the project. External funding entities will probably want to see letters of commitment, in fact.

The business plan also goes further in examining the personnel of the organization and their characteristics. The availability of the appropriate staff to carry out the business plan will be a consideration, as will access to additional personnel if a new initiative is being considered. Access to consultants and specialists in key areas will be a factor as well.

The legal status of the organization needs to be specified, along with the ownership structure. Whether the organization is for-profit or not-for-profit will often make a difference in the process. For for-profit organizations, its legal status (e.g., partnership, corporation) will be a consideration for potential investors. At the same time, the ownership structure will provide information on the resources available to the organization on the one hand and on potentially contentious stakeholders on the other. For this reason, one of the first questions asked by external funding sources typically has to do with the organization's owners.

Any existing contracts with clients should be identified and the prospects for continued relationships determined. The extent to which these contracts can be leveraged into new business for the proposed project will often be a consideration. For example, the proposed business line may be in direct response to requests from existing customers and converting them to the new service may be almost automatic.

Fortunately, a great deal of the required information is likely to be readily available. Much since much of what is required involves standard business reporting, and many of these reports should be routinely generated. Contemporary accounting software can generally accommodate the additional requirements of the business plan.

The External Audit

The external audit for the business planning process involves the same steps described in earlier chapters for assessing the organization's environment. The process starts with an analysis of the macro-environment and progresses through the various levels down to the microenvironment. Broad social trends are reviewed and developments within the economy are analyzed for their implications for healthcare. Health industry trends are reviewed, with attention paid to developments in the regulatory and reimbursement arenas.

In the case of business planning, a great deal of emphasis is likely to be placed on the industry analysis. An overview of the industry (or more likely the relevant industry segment) will be required. For example, if a hospital is considering entering the long-term care market, background information on both the hospital industry and the long-term care industry will probably be required. The overview should consider trends in the industry, including its stage in the industry life cycle. (See Box 11.1 on industry life cycle analysis.)

This overview should also pay particular attention to reimbursement trends and technological developments. Changes in reimbursement patterns arc frequent and being able to anticipate likely changes can mean the difference between the success or failure of a business enterprise. Technological advances can quickly make a product or service obsolete on the one hand or open up business opportunities on the other.

> **Box 11.1: Industry and Product Life Cycles**
> Regardless of the type of planning being initiated, an understanding of the stage of the industry or product life cycle is critical. For strategic planning initiatives, for example, the life cycle state that characterizes the relevant segment of the industry should be considered. If the organization is primarily involved in providing inpatient services, an appreciation of the point in the industry life cycle where inpatient services can be placed is required. If a business plan is being developed for a specific procedure, the point in the life cycle where this product resides must be determined.
>
> The position in the industry or product life cycle has numerous implications for planning activities. It is likely to influence the packaging of service and products, promotional techniques, approaches to competitors, and relationships with other organizations.

(continued)

Box 11.1 (continued)

The first stage in the life cycle for an industry or product is the introduction or market development stage. At this point, a new product or perhaps an entirely new industry is emerging. Because the industry or product is likely to be innovative, most of the effort is directed toward creating awareness and cultivating "early adopters" in the market. At this stage, there are relatively few competitors, and products and services are not standardized. Entry into the market is relatively easy because there are few established players.

The second stage is the growth phase. At this point, the industry has become established, and the product or service has been accepted by the market. Expansion is rapid as new customers are attracted and additional competitors enter the arena. Products or services become increasingly standardized, although enhancements may continue to contribute to product evolution. Marketing planning at this stage emphasizes differentiation of the organization, product, or service.

During the third stage, the industry or product achieves maturity. At this point, most of the potential customers have been captured and growth begins to tail off. Because few new customers are available, competition increases for existing customers. Product features and pricing are highly standardized, and little differentiation remains between competitors. The number of competitors decreases as consolidation occurs among the various players in the market, and it becomes increasingly difficult for new players to enter the market. Marketing activities emphasize retaining existing customers and/or capturing competitors' customers.

At the final stage in the life cycle, the industry or product experiences a period of decline. The number of customers decreases as consumers substitute new products or services. There is typically a "shakeout" among industry players as the dominant competitors squeeze out the less entrenched, and other competitors adopt a different strategic direction. Competition among the remaining players for existing customers becomes even more heated. Because no innovations are being introduced and the customer base cannot be expanded, there is increasing emphasis among the remaining competitors on reducing costs in order to maintain profitability.

The industry overview should also consider competitors within the industry. Other organizations that are in direct competition with this particular product or service should be identified, as well as those that are offering different but competing products. The estimate of revenue potential especially should account for the impact of existing competitors. It is one thing to calculate the total potential revenue to be generated; it is another to determine the effective revenue possible.

With regard to the market in which the organization plans to compete, a market share analysis should be conducted. For an existing service, the organization's current market share should be determined, along with past trends in market share. To the extent this share can be disaggregated into components (e.g., demographic categories, payer types), the more useful the data will be. The analysis should consider the extent to which the organization might be able to capture additional market share.

For a new product or service, much of the emphasis will be placed on potential market share that can be captured. The identification of potential customers for the proposed business line is an important consideration. The size of the market should be determined and the capturable market share indicated. The extent to which existing relationships can be capitalized on should be determined.

Consideration should be given to whether the project will involve capturing market share from existing players or if new markets are going to be tapped through this business venture.

The current and anticipated positioning of the organization with regard to the market is an important consideration. More precisely, what is the business positioning of the proposed product or service? Whether the proposed business line represents an innovative service, an improved or less expensive version of an existing service, or a convenient alternative to what is currently in the market makes a big difference in the business planning process.

It is essential that the planning team get out into the market and talk to existing customers, potential customers, and industry experts. It will also be worthwhile to talk to healthcare colleagues offering similar programs in other markets. Third-party payers and potential referral agents should be contacted as appropriate. It is beneficial to attend trade shows, conferences, and professional association meetings to develop a better appreciation of what is transpiring in the market. Although the planning team may think it "knows the market," there are always going to be new developments that must be identified and evaluated.

State-of-the-Business Report

At this stage of the process, it is usually worthwhile to present a state-of-the-business report. The nature of the report will depend upon many issues that have been raised earlier, including whether the plan is for a stand-alone facility or for a component of an existing organization, whether a new operation is being contemplated or the modification of an existing program, and whether the target is existing customers or new ones.

The state-of-the-business report should have the following sections summarizing the data collection up to this point:

- Overall industry/industry component trends
- Market area delineation
- Market area population profile
- Market area population health characteristics
- Current position of the organization or service
- Competitive situation

• Likely future developments

This status report should include the strengths, weaknesses, opportunities, and threats identified during the analysis. This is an opportunity to frankly describe the state of the market and the organization's position in it. With the business plan, in fact, this is likely to represent a go/no go decision point. Assuming that the project will continue, this should be the launching point for subsequent plan development.

Project Planning

Project planning is an inherent component of the business planning process. In effect, the business plan is a project plan. More so than other plans, the business plan includes a month-by-month and year-by-year outline of the business development process. This will include staffing, expected expenses, and anticipated revenues for the time period being planned for.

Developing the Business Plan

The effort up to this point provides the foundation for the actual development of the plan. If the initial work is properly carried out, the planning process should flow smoothly, at least from a technical perspective. (See Fig. 11.1 for a depiction of the business planning process.)

Specifying Goals

The goal or goals that are established for the business plan should reflect the information that was provided in the state-of-the-business report. As in other planning activities, the goal should meet certain criteria before it is accepted. Chief among these is the goal's support of the organization's strategic plan and its compatibility with the organization's mission statement.

The number of goals to be established depends on the complexity and size of the organization and the nature of the issues at hand. However, with business planning there is likely to be a specific goal that reflects the focused nature of the project.

This phase of planning is somewhat different for business planning in the sense that, from the outset, the goal was likely to be clearly defined. This is in contrast to some other types of planning in which the goal may not be determined until well into the planning process. The emphasis in business planning is specifying how the organization is going to achieve predetermined goals.

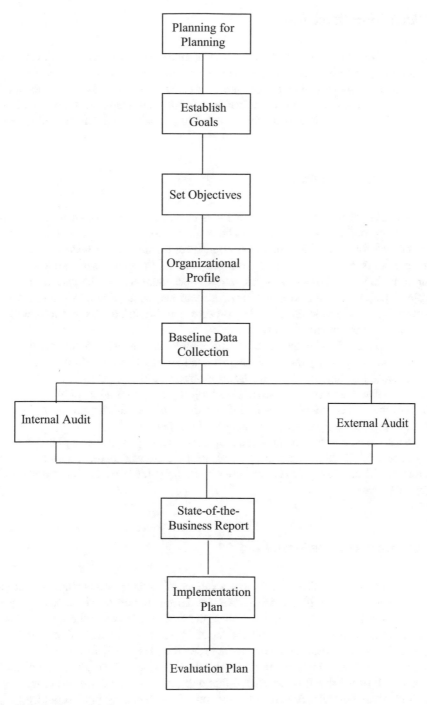

Fig. 11.1 Business planning process

Establishing Objectives

The objectives should be tied directly to the goal of the organization. For every goal a number of objectives may be specified. Four or five objectives are fairly common, although many more than that become unwieldy. Objectives are stated in such terms as follows: The hospital will hire a manager for the pain management unit within 3 months (in support of the stated goal of establishing a pain management product line).

Information Processing

The business plan differs from other plans in that it is not enough to collect and analyze appropriate data, and it must be further massaged to develop the information needed for the business plan. Obtaining past financial records is only one step. These figures must be converted into projections. Projected data are even more important in the case of a new organization. Since there is no organizational history, projections have to be developed based on various assumptions. While one set of assumptions will guide the planning process, another set of assumptions will be developed for the financial analysis.

A complete set of financial statements should be prepared to support the proposed project. Typically these will be extended 5 years into the future. These documents should include balance sheetsand profit and loss and pro forma statements, and pro forma. They should also include projections of staffing, capital investment, and any other activities that will impact the progress of the business venture. (Sample pro forma statements are included in Appendix C.)

To a great extent, the business plan represents an implementation plan per se, so that aspect of the planning process will not be discussed here. It should also be noted that the business plan will require a marketing plan as part of its overall development process.

Presenting the Business Plan

While other types of plans can follow a variety of formats, the business plan typically requires a standardized format. For that reason, an outline of the business plan is presented in this chapter. The length of the business plan and the level of detail depend on the nature of the project and the anticipated audience. A generalized plan may suffice in some cases, but considerable detail will typically be required. In most cases, it is probably appropriate to develop two versions of the plan. One of these contains all of the detail required and that will ultimately be reviewed *in toto* by a handful of individuals. A summary version of the business plan should also be developed that can be more widely circulated. Figure 11.2 illustrates a simplified risk analysis matrix that might accompany a business plan.

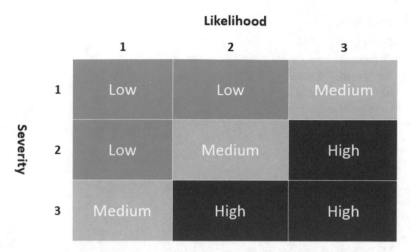

Fig. 11.2 Risk analysis

The following components should be included in the business plan:

- Overview/summary statement on the organization:

  - Present status
  - Strategic opportunities
  - Company thrust
  - Business strategies
  - Resource requirements
  - Expected benefits
  - Net cash requirements
  - Performance measures and milestones

- Description of the business or department:

  - Philosophy
  - Goal(s)
  - Corporate overview

      Corporate history
      Products/services
      Current customers
      Technology position
      Cost comparisons
      Operational resources

  - Strengths/weaknesses
  - Bases for competition
  - Key success factors
  - Competitive position

- Industry analysis:

  - Overview
  - Definition
  - Key growth factors
  - Industry life cycle
  - Competitors
  - Competing products
  - Financial measures

- Market analysis:

  - Overview of market/strategic opportunities
  - Market segmentation
  - Changes in demand/trends
  - Position in the market
  - Major customers/concentrations
  - Potential customers
  - Location(s)
  - Distribution capabilities
  - Pricing trends
  - Existing promotions/advertising
  - Competition
  - Promotional strategy (e.g., differentiation)
  - Market share and sales

- Strategic planning status

  - Overview of the plan
  - Plan assumptions
  - Long-term goals
  - Realistic assessment of strengths/weaknesses
  - Key performance indicators
  - Milestone schedule
  - Red flags
  - Company strengths to exploit
  - Weaknesses to overcome
  - Market opportunities to exploit
  - Risk analysis (see Fig. 11.2)

- Organization assessment:

  - Ownership structure
  - Management
  - Personnel
  - Consultants/specialists
  - Legal structure
  - Requirements in terms of permits, CON, regulatory agencies, licensure

- Financial data:
  - Sources of investment funds
  - Capital equipment
  - Real estate/insurance
  - Balance sheet
  - Profit and loss statement
  - Break-even analysis
  - Personal financial statements/tax returns

- Conclusions
- Appendices:
  - Resumes
  - Pictures of facilities, equipment, other pertinent tangible factors
  - Existing contracts, relationships
  - Market studies
  - Pertinent published materials

The Operational Plan

An important component of the business plan is the operational plan. Unlike the rest of the document, this component is primarily for internal use. The management team will use this for coordinating the efforts of corporate players in reaching the objectives set out in the business plan.

The operational plan incorporates components of the project plan and the implementation matrix discussed in other planning contexts. As such, it provides an indication of how the project will be carried out over the 5-year planning period. The plan is "operational" in the sense that it lays out the actual process of operating the facility, service, or program and not simply for its establishment.

Further Reading

Abrams, R. M. (1998). *The successful business plan: Secrets and strategies*. Grants Pass, OR: The Oasis Press (software available).

Jian Tools for Sales. (2003). *BizPlan Builder. Computer software*. Mountain View, CA: Jian Tools for Sales.

Chapter 12
Research Methods for Health Services Planning

Introduction

The significant role played by research in the planning process should be obvious from even a casual review of the preceding chapters. Much of the time and effort involved in planning can be attributed to the research activities that lead up to and support the planning function. Every type of planning requires some degree of research support. Even traditional types of organizational planning that are essentially introspective require some amount of spadework. For more externally oriented planning initiatives, extensive research activity is inevitably required. Without the appropriate knowledge base, the planning team will have little foundation for developing the plan.

The type and amount of research undertaken during the planning process are dictated by a number of factors, including the kind of plan being formulated, the nature of the organization, the available resources, and the intended use of the findings. A critical skill for the planner is the ability to determine the type and scope of research appropriate for a particular planning initiative.

In an ideal world, the research necessary to support planning would be an ongoing function within the organization. It is not practical to initiate discrete research projects from scratch to support every planning initiative. By the time most organizations can mount a data collection process, the planning period is likely to be over. However, with ongoing monitoring systems in place, it is possible to track changes in physician referral patterns, trends in admissions, or emerging market niches.

Because of the various aspects of planning that could come into play, this chapter can only serve as an introduction to the research activities that support planning. The resources listed at the end of the chapter provide some additional guidance.

© Springer Science+Business Media, LLC, part of Springer Nature 2021 297
R. K. Thomas, *Health Services Planning*,
https://doi.org/10.1007/978-1-0716-1076-3_12

Planning Research: Whose Responsibility?

Early in the planning process a decision must be made concerning the project's research requirements. Even the most basic type of planning research is likely to require certain skills, substantive knowledge, and familiarity with multiple methodologies and perspectives. In cases where the community or the organization does not have an ongoing planning effort, the requisite skills may be lacking. While a community may have certain research skills resident within various organizations, these resources may not be readily available to the planning team. There may, in fact, be resistance to any particular organization having a dominant role in this important function.

A major decision, thus, involves the assignment of responsibility for the research function. The range of research options includes performing all planning research in-house using internal resources, totally outsourcing the research process, and utilizing a combination of internal and external resources. The latter may involve performing some research functions in-house while outsourcing others. Another "compromise" approach might involve bringing in an outside consultant to coordinate the use of internal resources for the planning research. The option chosen will depend a great extent on the overall approach taken to the planning process. If the planning itself is being outsourced, the research activities would probably be carried out under that auspices. If the planning is being done totally in-house, it might be more practical to use internal resources. The corporate culture of the organization will also be a factor influencing the approach taken.

There are numerous advantages to bringing an outside expert into the research process, regardless of the level of internal capabilities available. An outside resource is likely to introduce a broader perspective than that held by those closely involved with the organization, in addition to having had experience with similar organizations. The outside consultant may have expertise in specialized techniques that are required for the project or may already have expensive resources (e.g., geographic information systems) that would otherwise have to be acquired. From a political perspective, the outsider may bring a measure of objectivity and neutrality that might not be available internally.

There are disadvantages to using outside experts as well. They can be very expensive and a certain level of sophistication is required in order to negotiate a reasonable contract. (Note that there are no small costs involved in carrying out research activities in-house, particularly if no dedicated function is already in place.) There may be situations in which such sensitive data is involved that outside access may be undesirable. Further, an outsider is an outsider and there may be aspects of the community or organization that are difficult to understand without having an insider's perspective. Ultimately, every organization will have to weigh the pluses and minuses of using outside resources for planning research.

The Approach to Planning Research

Planning research involves a number of distinct components that generally follow a certain sequence. With each component the intent is to collect data that can be converted into information that can in turn serve as the basis for identifying solutions. Raw numbers are of limited use until they are converted into meaningful information. Information is only beneficial if it can contribute to decision-making.

Within this general framework, the following functions served by the planning research process can be identified:

Describing

The first responsibility of the health services planner is to describe the community or the market under consideration. Description here refers to the development of a (usually) comprehensive profile of the target area being studied. It may be a population, a patient grouping, or any number of other appropriate targets for the analysis. The planner must develop an informed description of the chosen subject, taking into consideration the relevant dimensions of that subject.

Identifying

Typically, the description of a community or market is followed by the identification of distinct patterns or noteworthy attributes related to the target community or organization. These phenomena may involve unserved or underserved populations, a service niche that is not being addressed, a lack of certain equipment, or a variety of other conditions. Identifying patterns and attributes takes description a step further and extracts from the numerous possibilities within the typical market the meaningful options (and threats) within that context.

Comparing

An important step in the processing of data collected during research is the comparison of findings to relevant benchmarks. Depending on the plan, this may involve comparing one population to another, one health indicator to another, or one hospital to another. Analysis of the health indicators for a community may involve comparisons with historical figures, with other comparable communities, with national averages, or with established benchmarks. Similarly, an analysis of the data collected on a community hospital may involve comparisons to the hospital's past performance, a competitor's performance, JCAHO guidelines, or a target set in the hospital's business plan. Through comparative analysis, the planner can begin to determine what the research findings *mean*.

Comparative analysis can be extended further in the research process when different options present themselves. A community may need to compare potential sites for a public health clinic. A healthcare organization may need to compare one market to another or one business opportunity to another. There are seldom going to be clear-cut choices in terms of appropriate services to be offered. The planner must be able to comparatively analyze the options, employing both quantitative and qualitative techniques.

Evaluating

It is seldom enough to describe a community or organization or to simply identify noteworthy patterns. The status of the community or organization must be evaluated based on relevant criteria. The comparative analysis above provides a basis for evaluating existing services, personnel, or market opportunities. The analyst's ability to assess whether a situation is favorable or unfavorable is critical for the planning activities that follow.

Ultimately, the planner must determine if a situation is "good" or "bad." If it is found, for example, that the community reports 5 hospital beds per 1000 population, this figure must be evaluated. If the national standard is 4 beds/1000, it could be concluded that, all things being equal, the community had overcapacity in terms of beds. If, on the other hand, the community was a regional medical center and drew patients from surrounding counties that lacked hospitals, a different "read" could be made on the statistics. This is where the skills of the planner start coming into play.

Monitoring

Planning research activities typically involves the monitoring of various phenomena. This may mean monitoring population trends in a potential target area, tracking changes in patient satisfaction, or measuring the impact of marketing initiatives on the consumer image of the organization. Especially to the extent that planning is an ongoing function, monitoring in some form is likely to be one of the responsibilities.

Interpreting

At a time when few sources of health data existed, decision makers were happy with any information they could access. Today, with access to data less of an issue, the emphasis is on the ability to interpret the massive amounts of data that have become available within the industry. The ability to analyze and interpret the data that have been collected (i.e., convert data into information) is what distinguishes a planner from a technician.

Recommending

The next step beyond interpreting the data involves recommending actions suggested by the planning research. This may even involve a go/no go decision or a choice among a number of different options. Increasingly, planning analysts are being asked to go beyond simply turning the numbers over to someone else for decision-making. The planning team is likely to expect the one answer they are looking for and not a lot of confusing options. The growing emphasis on generating recommendations reflects the shift from a technically oriented planning approach to a management-oriented approach.

Types of Research

The research component of the planning process is likely to involve a variety of methodologies, the choice of which is determined by the type of organization and the type of plan involved. In formulating the research design to support the planning effort, three general categories of research should be considered based on the type of information required. These three categories of research are *exploratory, descriptive*, and *causal.*

The goal of exploratory research is the discerning of the general nature of the problem or opportunity under study and the associated factors of importance. Exploratory research is characterized by a high degree of flexibility, and usually relies heavily on literature reviews, small-scale surveys, informal interviews and discussions, and a subjective evaluation of the data. Exploratory designs are typically used for initial information gathering at the outset of a planning initiative. The objective here is to gain insights into the planning context and gather information, even if anecdotal, that may inform further planning research.

Descriptive research involves the development of a factual portrait of the various components of the community or organization that are being examined. Market profiles, community assessments, and resource inventories are examples of the products of descriptive research. Any source of information can be used in a descriptive study, although most studies of this nature rely heavily on secondary data sources and survey research. Carefully designed descriptive studies are the bread and butter of planning research, and they provide the basis for any subsequent research that is performed. The bulk of the effort in planning-oriented data collection is geared toward descriptive studies, with no pretense of explaining the "why" of any of the observed findings.

Causal (or inferential) research attempts to specify the nature of the functional relationship between two or more variables in the situation under study. For example, a study of the relationship between place of medical training and physician referral patterns would probably involve an analysis of cause-and-effect relationships. A study on the market response to a promotional campaign would seek to isolate and identify the ways in which increased advertising, for example, fostered a rise in outpatient visits. Causal research designs typically infer relationships, since a direct causal relationship usually cannot be conclusively demonstrated.

Little of the planning-oriented research conducted in healthcare in the past could be characterized as causal research. Although causal research has contributed to an understanding of the motivation for consumer behavior in other industries, health services planning has a long way to go to arrive at this level of sophistication.

Steps in the Research Design Process

The planning research process can be conceptualized as a multistage endeavor. The exact number of stages varies from planning analyst to planning analyst and from problem to problem, but all research designs include certain basic elements. The process leads from the initial inquiry (e.g., is the management of eating disorders a service worth pursuing?) to the ultimate decision made by the organization (e.g., a pilot eating disorder program should be initiated). No two experts agree completely on the steps involved in the research process, and research that supports health services planning has unique characteristics that distinguish it from the process in other industries. The steps below represent the general order of activities in the research plan, although there is nothing sacred about the order in which they occur. The steps in the design process sometimes interact and often occur simultaneously. These steps should be modified as appropriate to suit the particular planning exercise.

Initial Information Gathering

In planning research, the first step typically involves developing a generalized understanding of the community or organization for which planning is occurring. For community-wide planning, a general knowledge of the community is clearly required. If a strategic planning initiative is being undertaken for an organization, a reasonable knowledge of the nature of the organization needs to be developed. For a marketing planning initiative, information on the product or service is required, as well as information on the market area. If it is a business planning initiative, a reasonable understanding of the financial operation of the organization is necessary.

A review of the existing literature is an obvious place to start the research process. "Literature" is used here in a very broad sense. In traditional research this typically refers to the professional journals in which the field's conventional wisdom is codified. Unfortunately, health services planning has yet to develop a body of comparable professional journal resources. (In fact, the term "health planning" was virtually absent from the industry literature during the 1980s and early 1990s.) The literature for health services planning will include not only standard journals but also newsletters, government reports, technical papers, professional meeting presentations, annual reports, and publications of professional associations.

Today, planners can gain access to the Internet for literature reviews and other sources of relevant information. Most bibliographic databases can be accessed through the Internet and any number of other sources—some of them quite serendipitous—can be uncovered by accessing the Internet. Another type of electronic "literature review" involves the growing volume of e-mail exchanges among the informal network of health professionals. An increasing amount of health-related data is becoming available via cyberspace with the Internet is becoming a standard research tool.

Identifying Issues

Issue definition is an important step in the planning research process. Unless the issues are properly defined, the information produced by the research process is unlikely to have much value. In planning research, the "problem" is likely to be defined in terms of a process or the specific issues related to a process. The scope of the research is thus much broader and diffuse than it is in other types of research projects.

Isolating the relevant issues becomes an important early task in the research process. Planning initiatives are typically triggered by a crisis or a concern of some type. The "iceberg" effect can often be found, in that the apparent issue is simply the tip of the iceberg and suggests that there are other, perhaps more serious, underlying concerns. It is also often the case that the problem posed by the party initiating the process may be quite different from the "real" problem. This is part of the art of planning research, with the planner being able to examine the situation and determine the nature of the underlying issues. A more precise statement of the issues may imply a very different research problem from the initial statement.

Developing the Research Plan

As in any research process, a carefully thought-out research plan must be developed. The initial information gathering stage should provide a guide to the types of data that will be required. The nature of the planning initiative will also dictate certain research requirements. Thus, a community-wide plan will typically require a broader range of data than an organization-level plan; a strategic plan will involve a broader research scope than a technology plan; research on the competitive situation will be more important for a business plan than for a community-wide plan; and so forth.

The nature of the planning initiative will determine the objectives of the research plan, and various action steps will specify the effort required. The categories of data to be considered, the means of collecting the relevant data, the indicators to be utilized, and the analytical techniques to be employed, among other attributes, are included in the research plan.

The research plan specifies the sequence in which various research efforts are to be carried out, the responsible party(s), the resources required, and the time frames involved. The plan should also specify the "products" that are expected from the research effort.

Specifying the Analytical Approach

Data are useful only after they have been analyzed. Data analysis involves converting a series of observations, however obtained, into descriptive statements and/or inferences about relationships. The types of analyses that can be conducted depend on the nature of the sampling process, the measurement instrument, and the data collection method. It is at this point that raw data are converted into information that supports the planning process.

Since most planning research is essentially descriptive, the same attention is unlikely to be paid to the analytical methods as in more basic research. Nevertheless, it is important to visualize the types of output that the research is expected to generate and specify the analytical approaches that provide the desired outcome.

A variety of different analytical approaches can be utilized, with the choice being dictated to a great extent by the type of plan. Virtually all plans will involve a demographic analysis, but the use of epidemiological analysis, for example, may be more appropriate for community-wide planning than for organization-level planning. Examples of useful analytical techniques are presented later in this chapter.

Research Resource Allocation

Once the research plan has been developed, the planner must estimate resource requirements. The requirements are time, money, and personnel. If the research is to be conducted in-house, resources can be broken down into direct expenses (e.g., to hire additional interviewers) and "in-kind" contributions such as staff time, office space, and supplies. Time refers to both the time needed to complete the project and the time commitment required of personnel. The financial requirement is the monetary representation of the personnel time, computer time, and material requirements. In addition, the opportunity costs incurred by those participating in planning-oriented research must be calculated to the extent possible.

If an outside consultant or resource is to implement the process, the determination of costs must be calculated differently. The consultant will typically present a proposal that includes cost estimates for performing the requisite research. The planning team will work with the consultant to determine the nature of the process and the division of labor between internal staff and consulting staff.

Project management tools like the program evaluation review technique (PERT) and the critical path method (CPM) offer useful aids for estimating the resources needed for a project and for clarifying the planning and control process. PERT involves dividing the total research project into its smallest component activities, determining the sequence in which these activities must be performed, attaching a time estimate for each activity, and presenting them in the form of a flowchart that allows a visual inspection of the overall process. The time estimates allow planners to determine the critical path through the chart.

Data Collection

Data collection involves the actual process of acquiring the raw data that will be converted into the information needed for the planning analysis. The data collection process can take a variety of forms but will typically involve both primary data collection and use of secondary data. Secondary data are virtually always collected first because they are likely to be readily available without much in the way of additional expense. Primary research is likely to be used when certain types of data cannot be acquired through secondary research.

Planners obviously have a variety of techniques to choose from for data collection. In considering the alternatives available for any project, each approach has its own unique advantages and disadvantages. And, in using any one of these approaches, there are special concerns which the researcher must address and be cognizant of to ensure that the data collected will be reliable and valid.

It would be a rare project that did not involve the use of both primary data and secondary data. For example, in collecting data to support planning for a new health service, an analyst may (1) examine hospital records for information relating to past introductions of similar services (secondary data); (2) conduct a set of interviews to determine current consumer attitudes about the service (primary survey data); and (3) conduct a pilot study in which consumer reception of the proposed service is measured (primary experimental data).

Since an unlimited amount of data on an infinite number of topics can be collected, the planner must ensure that any data collected are relevant to the issues at hand. In particular, care must be taken to assure that the data collected is "actionable." Some things may be interesting to know, but, if they do not contribute to the process, they may not be necessary. Specifically, the planner should list the questions that need to be answered by the end of the study and structure the data collection process accordingly. Further, the potential use for any information to be collected should be determined in advance.

Methods for conducting primary research are discussed later in this chapter. Sources of secondary data are described in Chap. 12.

Data Analysis

Data analysis involves the processing, manipulation, and analysis of the data collected through the means specified in the research plan. A variety of techniques for statistical analysis can be applied, although the descriptive nature of most planning research mitigates against the use of sophisticated analyses. Basic statistics will typically suffice for most planning analyses.

On another level, however, there are a number of analytical approaches that could be utilized that contribute to the interpretation of the data. For example, the health services planner should probably be familiar with the techniques utilized in demographic analyses, the methods developed by epidemiologists, and approaches to evaluation analysis. Several of these techniques are described later in this chapter.

Drawing Conclusions

The main objective in analyzing the data that have been collected is the generation of conclusions related to the planning issues. The conclusions drawn will rely heavily on the analysis step described above. Properly chosen analytical techniques should generate useful findings.

Conclusions may be drawn at various levels in keeping with the tiered approach as described in the discussion of the environmental assessment. There are likely to be conclusions drawn concerning the national situation, the state level, and the local market. At another level, conclusions can be drawn that are very specific to the planning study. These may relate to findings concerning market share, utilization trends, or changing market characteristics.

These conclusions should provide the basis for subsequent planning activities. Some of them, in fact, become a part of the assumptions that have been stated and restated throughout this process.

Formulating Recommendations

The formulation of recommendations is a relatively new role for the researcher, but one that is likely to grow in significance. Historically, planning research was seen as a technical support function. The researcher's role was to turn over numbers to administrators and they would make the appropriate decision.

As planning issues have become more complex and research methods more sophisticated, planners are increasingly asked to offer recommendations. Rather than providing the decision maker with three objectively compared options for review, the analyst is likely to be asked to indicate the best choice among the three given the results of the various analyses.

Primary Data Collection Methods

Virtually every planning study is going to require the collection of primary data. There are always going to be situations when the desired information is simply not available. This is particularly the case in an industry undergoing the rapid and dramatic changes that characterize healthcare today.

The major advantage of primary data is that the information is collected for the particular problem or issue under investigation, making the data more directly relevant and current than most secondary data. Another major advantage is that primary data collection allows the organization to maintain the proprietary nature of the information collected. Conducting primary research also gives the planner control over the types of information elicited, rather than having to rely on questions asked by another party perhaps with quite different intentions.

Primary data collection, however, has some disadvantages. The collection of primary data can entail significant costs and require an extended period of time to complete. The administration of primary research also requires some fairly sophisticated skills that may not be available within the organization.

When initiating primary research activities, the means of data collection must be determined. The "right" data collection method depends on a number of factors. There are many alternative methods to choose from in conducting such research (Creswell 1994). Several commonly used methods—both quantitative and qualitative—for collecting primary data are described below. (Box 12.1 compares qualitative and quantitative approaches to research.)

Box 12.1: Bringing Back Qualitative Data

For much of the last half of the twentieth century, the importance of quantitative data eclipsed that of qualitative data in healthcare as it did in other fields. Researchers and administrators became enamored with surveys in particular. Because there was a substantial body of knowledge related to survey research, it was relatively easy to conduct virtually any kind of study that involved interviews of patients, their families and friends, healthcare professionals, and physicians. Indeed, there were even those who argued against any use of qualitative data, claiming that such information was "soft" and the process lacked scientific rigor.

By the end of the century, however, the use of qualitative data had become increasingly common, even in the healthcare industry. It became standard practice for healthcare providers to conduct focus groups and other interviews. Observation for data collection and content analysis for examining the data were increasingly used to supplement quantitative approaches. New software designed for the analysis of qualitative data furthered these efforts.

This renewed interest in qualitative research reflects to a certain extent the growing willingness of researchers to concede the shortcomings of strictly quantitative research in healthcare. There are numerous subjective dimensions to the experience of illness and the operation of the delivery system. Further, many aspects of healthcare simply cannot be understood without the use of qualitative methods.

As healthcare entered the twenty-first century, researchers and planners recognized the value of both qualitative and quantitative methods, and the importance of using these methods in tandem was being increasingly appreciated. Surveys in healthcare are no longer limited to close-ended questions that restrict responses. Open-ended questions are frequently employed and the answers subjected to qualitative analytical techniques. In data-driven healthcare organizations, continuous collection, monitoring, and analysis of both types of data is a standard procedure.

The research required to support the planning process should involve both quantitative and qualitative techniques. Planners must be able to coordinate the two types of data collection and analysis to successfully implement the research component of the planning process.

Observation

Observational research involves techniques in which the actions and/or attributes of those being studied are observed either by another individual or through a mechanical recording device such as a video camera. Information is not so much elicited from the subjects as it is observed. Data collection by means of observation is performed according to specified rules based on stated objectives.

Before observation can be used in planning research, three minimum conditions must be met. First, the data must be accessible via observation. Motivations, attitudes, opinions, and other "internal" conditions cannot be readily observed. On the other hand, behavior in a waiting room, for example, can be observed and recorded. Second, the behavior must be repetitive, frequent, or otherwise predictable. Finally, an event must be of relatively short duration. Thus, we are usually restricted to observing activities that can be completed in a relatively short time span, such as clinic visits or segments of activities with a longer time span.

Observational methods are typically used in planning research when data cannot be obtained through interviews or from secondary sources. This approach is particularly useful when a process is being analyzed. For example, a hospital might place a trained observer in its waiting area to observe the admitting process. Observers might track individual emergency patients from their initial encounter in the admitting area through their examination in the emergency room. Some organizations use a "professional shopper" program to improve the organization's ability to perform this type of observational research. By actually going through the admissions process, for example, these simulated patients may obtain more information about the process than any other method would yield.

Observational techniques are characterized as either participatory or nonparticipatory. In participatory observation, the researcher becomes part of the group or activity that is being observed. Participant observation allows the observer to analyze the group, situation, or process as an "insider." Also, by becoming part of the group, the impact of the observation process on behavior hopefully is minimized. However, the participant observer typically cannot take notes or otherwise record the observations that are being made. Thus, the observer must rely on memory for the recording of observations at a later date. The greatest concern, of course, relates to the possibility of the observer's mere presence altering the behavior of those being observed.

Nonparticipant observation involves a situation in which the researcher is detached from the individuals, situations, or processes that are being observed. In some cases, the observer may view the subjects from afar or, in more controlled environments, through the one-way mirror of an observation booth. The advantage of this approach is that the process typically does not affect the phenomena being observed, since the subjects do not know they are being observed.

One disadvantage of observational research is that the researcher is not in a position to control the variables under study, either physically or statistically. Further, observational data are difficult to quantify. There are likely to be a small number of observations, and the open-endedness of the information collected typically does not lend itself to quantitative analysis.

Although observational data are useful in observing what people do, they cannot address *why* people behave in the way they do. Thus, it is often necessary to supplement observational research with personal interviews or some other form of data collection to determine the motivations underlying the observed behavior.

In-Depth Interviews

In-depth (or one-on-one) interviews typically involve one respondent and one interviewer. The in-depth interview is of value when the respondent must be probed regarding his/her answers. Complicated questions, or questions that do not lend themselves to simple dichotomous responses, often require personal interviews. The interview does not necessarily follow a defined set of questions that must be asked in a predetermined order, but probes and questions as necessary to elicit the required information.

In-depth interviews are sometimes referred to as "key informant" interviews. They typically last 30–45 min but can last several hours. There is latitude within the interview to ask *ad hoc* questions, follow up on responses that appear worthy of further exploration, and generally elicit the best information possible within this research framework.

In-depth interviews appear to be the most useful in situations where more superficial data collection techniques will not work. These include situations in which extensive probing is required, where the subject matter may be very complicated, confidential, or sensitive, or the group influence (e.g., in the focus group setting) may be a distraction.

Ostensibly, in-depth interviews can be conducted with anyone presumed to have knowledge of a particular topic. However, in healthcare in-depth interviews are usually carried out with key informants who possess a particular set of knowledge (e.g., technical innovators); have a broad perspective for the issues (e.g., hospital administrators); are in a position to be familiar with the perspectives of a large number of people (e.g., human resource manager); or are likely to hold influential opinions (e.g., hospital medical staff members).

It is difficult to imagine undertaking any planning initiative within a healthcare organization without including in-depth interviews with key informants. One of the initial tasks is to identify the problems or opportunities being faced by an organization. In-depth interviews provide an excellent setting for this type of problem/ opportunity identification. In fact, such interviews are typically used as a basis for constructing the survey forms that are used in subsequent quantitative research.

Personal interviews have some limitations. This method requires skilled interviewers, and even then there is potential for bias on the part of interviewers or misrepresentation on the part of respondents. There is also the danger of "experts" going off on a tangent. A physician-respondent on a "soapbox" may be difficult to rein in.

Group Interviews

In recent years one of the most popular qualitative research techniques in healthcare has been the group interview. Group interviews can be fairly structured, as in the case of *focus groups*, or more informal, as in the case of *naturally occurring groups*. Focus groups consist of a group of people who are assembled to discuss a particular topic of interest under the direction of a professional moderator. The objective is to have people express their feelings or views on a range of interests. Naturally occurring groups in healthcare might include all persons working the same shift in a particular department or the families and friends of patients admitted to a hospital.

Focus groups can be used for several purposes. For example, information from focus groups might be used in the construction of a survey instrument. A second frequent use of the focus group is in needs assessment. For example, a hospital might want to better understand the type of programs or services they could provide that would be valuable to referral physicians.

Focus groups are often used to test ideas for new programs or services. For example, an orthopedic medicine group might conduct focus groups among parents of youth between the ages of 6 and 18 years to assess the feasibility of establishing a pediatric sports medicine program.

Another valuable use of focus groups is in examining the underlying meaning of survey results. Often, in conducting a quantitative survey, the organization examines the response and finds, for example, that 50% of the emergency room patients thought the service was unsatisfactory. A focus group among emergency room users might help reveal the reasons behind the quantitative findings.

As with any research methodology there are advantages and disadvantages to focus groups. The advantages of focus groups include:

- The synergy created by the group environment
- The ability to probe for additional information or follow unexpected directions
- Relatively low costs
- Short data collection and analysis time spans
- The richness of the data collected
- Direct input from consumers or patients

While the advantages of a focus group are several, it is also important to recognize the real limitations which exist for this technique. Some of these include:

- Lack of control of variables
- Inability to use quantitative analytical techniques
- The usual drawbacks involved in qualitative data analysis
- Group variations due to small "samples"
- Potential moderator bias
- An inability to generalize the results

The focus group method would never be used as the primary tool for planning research. It does serve, however, to provide useful insights that can contribute to a formulation of the issues and the development of subsequent research activities. As such, it is a useful supplement to the other types of research employed.

Survey Research

Many, if not most, planning projects will involve some survey research. Survey research can take one of the three common forms: mail-out surveys, personal interviews, and telephone interviews. Computerized interviews and online surveys are also becoming common. Each of these forms of survey research is described below.

Mail Surveys

Mail surveys are a common method of administering sample surveys. Mail surveys involve the development of a survey instrument, the identification of an appropriate sample of respondents, and the mailing of survey forms to the sample. Returned survey forms are analyzed according to predetermined analytical techniques.

Mail surveys have the advantage of being a relatively inexpensive way to collect data. Typically, costs involve the reproduction of the survey form and the postage to send and return it. Mail surveys also provide anonymity to the respondent and eliminate potential interviewer bias. Mail is also an efficient way to contact individuals who are dispersed over a large geographical area. For this reason, mail surveys are often used in healthcare to collect patient satisfaction data.

While mail surveys have these advantages, there are several disadvantages to this data collection method. Response rates to mail-out surveys are often low. The instruments are self-administered, leaving the items open to interpretation on the part of the respondent. "Turnaround" time may be lengthy, and the short time frames characterizing much marketing planning, for example, may preclude the use of this method.

Personal Interviews

A second method of surveying individuals involves personal (or face-to-face) interviews. An individual interview is a valuable way to collect data when the respondent must be probed regarding his/her answers. Complicated questions or questions that require explication on the part of the interviewer can best be handled in a face-to-face situation. In contrast to the in-depth interview, these interviews are relatively short, involve a larger number of respondents, and require that those interviewed are representative of the population being studied. Personal interviews also require a lower level of interviewing skills and less substantive knowledge of the topic than in-depth interviews.

In planning research, the focus is often on specific audiences. For this reason, on-site interviews are often conducted. The waiting rooms of clinics, emergency departments, and other healthcare facilities offer such an opportunity. This survey approach has become popular in recent years since it has the advantage of face-to-face interviewing without the expense of the door-to-door canvassing involved in community surveys.

There was a day when community surveys were routinely conducted, but they are much less common today. With the community survey, a sample of households is selected and an interviewer or a team of interviewers contacts individuals in their homes for the interviews. Today, the costs involved in community surveys have become nearly prohibitive. Further, the perceived danger involved in sending interviewers into various neighborhoods has made many research organizations reluctant to use this approach. At the same time, it is difficult to find respondents at home during much of the day, and potential respondents are increasingly reluctant to open their doors to strangers.

In terms of cost, personal interview is the most expensive of the survey approaches. Trained interviewers are required, and all travel costs for interviewers must be considered in the budget. Another drawback besides the cost is the potential for interviewer bias. Untrained interviewers may condition responses by their reactions to answers or by their mannerisms, or they may fail to accurately follow the wording of a survey.

Telephone Interviews

The third common survey technique involves the telephone interview. While there have been increasing complaints from consumers about the intrusive nature of telephone surveys, this methodology still offers many advantages. Telephone interviews represent a quick way to acquire information. Using multiple interviewers in a telephone interview bank, considerable data can be acquired in a short time frame. If the interviewers have some "hook," a high response rate can generally be obtained. Telephone interviewing allows for a reasonable degree of probing by the interviewer. On the other hand, while it is often difficult for a respondent to terminate a personal interview, terminating a telephone interview is easy.

There is an inherent sampling bias with telephone interviews in that they require the respondent to have a telephone. While telephone ownership is high in this country, certain areas or populations may have significantly lower telephone ownership than the national average. Low-income populations and racial and ethnic minority groups, in particular, have lower than average levels of telephone installation. Further, cellphone numbers are generally not listed

Increasingly, people are requesting unlisted telephone numbers, making the phone directory, always a questionable sampling frame, even less useful. One method to address this problem uses computerized programs to perform a random digit dialing sequence working from the prefixes utilized in an area and generating the last four digits randomly. Still another approach involves randomly selecting numbers listed in the telephone directory or other directories and systematically adding or subtracting one from the last digit. (See Dillman (1978) for the definitive reference on the effective administration of mail and telephone surveys.)

Computer-assisted telephone interviewing (CATI) has become increasingly common among survey researchers, and inexpensive software has made this technology available to most interviewers. A CATI system involves a survey workstation in which the telephone interviewer enters answers to survey items directly into the questionnaire programmed into the system. The responses are automatically entered into the computer and typically directly into the database to be utilized for analysis. The intelligence built into the software application can "flag" out-of-range answers, adjust subsequent questions based on earlier answers, and automatically lead the interviewer through a series of branching questions.

Computerized Interviews

Computer-based interviews have become increasingly popular as software has become more user friendly, and the general public has become more comfortable with computers. In computerized interviewing, the computer presents the survey items to the respondent on the screen in very much the same form it would take on a printed interview questionnaire.

On-site computerized interviewing is being utilized in more and more healthcare settings. The most frequent use to date is for collecting patient satisfaction data. After a clinic visit, for example, a respondent may be asked to sit down at a computer station and "fill out" the questionnaire that is shown on the screen. The more user-friendly systems allow the user to touch the appropriate response on the screen. Others may instruct the interviewee to strike certain keys on a keyboard.

This on-site approach to data collection has the advantage of capturing the information at a time when it is top of mind. It allows researchers to obtain responses from virtually every patient rather than relying on a sample. The provision of information is easy for the respondent and the computer-assisted system often has the ability to modify itself during the course of the interview, edit the responses, and even perform analysis. Computerized interviewing saves time and resources and eliminates much of the paper involved in survey research. The results of the surveys can typically be obtained in hours if not minutes.

The disadvantages of this approach are that the survey must be relatively short, survey items must be very simple and completely clear, and patients must be willing to cooperate, especially if they suffer from computer phobia. There is always the fear the patients may resent being asked to go to this extra trouble, especially if they are not feeling well or they have just paid a large fee. In addition, some analysts feel that patient satisfaction responses are not valid unless they have had some time to "age"; they would contend that surveys conducted, for example, 2 weeks after the visit are more valid than those conducted at the time of the visit.

Some researchers have begun to administer surveys via the Internet, and the high level of Internet penetration for the general public has made this medium increasingly popular. Assuming that the target population is "wired," data collection via the Internet is convenient and inexpensive. A growing proportion of consumers are completing surveys on their smartphones. To date, this approach works best in the case of an existing network of customers, an advisory board, or other groupings that may already be linked by electronic mail, rather than for general consumers. As penetration rates increase and consumers become more familiar with this data collection approach, the use of the Internet for survey research will undoubtedly increase.

Analytical Techniques

As data have become more widely available in healthcare, some of the emphasis has shifted from data collection to data analysis. Unanalyzed data is essentially useless and must be processed and interpreted to turn it into information. There are a number of analytical methods that are available for this purpose, and some of the more important ones are described below.

Demographic Analysis

The use of descriptive demographic data is clearly a cornerstone of planning research in healthcare as in any other industry. The researcher must be conversant with the numerous variables considered under the heading of demographics, be able to access them, and be able to apply them to research in an intelligent way.

The need for demographics, however, does not end with basic descriptive demographics. Market analysts must be familiar with the three demographic processes that contribute to change in both population size and composition. These processes are fertility, mortality, and migration. Each of these has an associated body of statistical techniques that the analyst should be familiar with. These three processes account for much of the dynamics that characterize healthcare markets.

There are also a number of more advanced demographic techniques that should be considered. The planning analyst should be familiar with procedures for *cohort analysis*, since this is so important to an understanding of future changes in health services demand. The analyst should also be familiar with *standardization* techniques, since these are important in comparing markets. *Contextual analysis* is becoming increasingly important as an approach for understanding health behavior.

It is also appropriate to consider population estimates, projections, and forecasts under the heading of demographic analysis. The analyst must be familiar with the techniques used to generate such "synthetic" data, since these are important in any planning research. Further, the underlying techniques also are important since the time may come when the analyst is called upon to generate custom estimates or projections. (See Box 12.2 for a discussion of estimates, projections, and forecasts.)

Box 12.2: Estimates, Projections, and Forecasts

Almost all analyses conducted by health services planners, of necessity, involve the use of estimates, projections, and/or forecasts. In many cases, actual data do not exist related to the service area or healthcare activity under study, and demand or utilization estimates are required. The inherently futuristic nature of planning calls for the frequent use of projections and forecasts. Also referred to as "synthetic" data, each of these types of data calculations has different characteristics and different uses.

Estimates involve the calculation of statistics for a current or past time period. Estimates of population are common, but estimates could also be made of the incidence of a health condition or the amount of health service utilization. Estimates typically involve the extrapolation or interpolation of actual data (e.g., census data) for two or more known time periods. The starting point for most planning analyses is the current population, patient pool, or even the level of demand and, quite often, these figures have to be estimated. A variety of techniques are used to generate estimates, and many commercial data vendors have built substantial businesses preparing estimates of population and/or health services demand.

Projections involve estimates of population or some other quantifiable phenomenon for some future period. Planning ideally focuses on future conditions, so some method must be employed to develop a picture of the future. Projections by their nature reflect past trends and carry them forward into the future. Analysts generating projections may simply extrapolate a trend into the future or may apply adjustments based on known or potential developments in the area for which the projection is being made. In other words, a known trend would be modified based on assumptions about the future in this case. As with estimates, a number of different methods are used to generate projections and, again, commercial data vendors are heavily involved in synthetically producing projections of future populations or other phenomena of interest to health planners.

Forecasts resemble projections in that they offer an estimation of conditions for some future point in time. Forecasts, depending on the methodology used, may or may not rely heavily on historical trends. The distinguishing characteristic of forecasts is that they attempt to take likely future developments into consideration. For this reason, there is more of a subjective dimension to the formulation of forecasts relative to projections. The forecaster is likely to try to anticipate future developments that will affect the size of the population or the level of demand, perhaps quite independent of any prior developments. Econometric models are often used to generate forecasts rather than projections because of their tendency to incorporate a number of variables that are thought to reflect future developments. The lack of relevance of past trends for future developments in healthcare has encouraged an increasing number of analysts to generate forecasts.

Epidemiological Analysis

Epidemiology is the medical specialty concerned with the distribution of disease within the population. As definitions of health and illness have evolved, epidemiology has taken on a broader meaning that includes virtually any factor that is related to the incidence of disease. The subdiscipline of social epidemiology has emerged to address the increasingly important relationship between social conditions and health status (Dever 1991).

Epidemiology has developed its own set of analytical techniques, many of which have relevance for health planning research. Some of the techniques discussed elsewhere were developed by epidemiologists. The procedures for calculating incidence and prevalence rates came out of this field, and many of the indicators utilized in fertility and mortality analyses came out of this tradition. Such advanced analytical techniques as life table analysis and survival analysis can be attributed to epidemiologists.

Epidemiological analysis is particularly useful in profiling a service area or population, particularly from the perspective of public health. The growing interest in population-based healthcare and the revival of concern in public health over the resurgence of communicable diseases will assure that epidemiological methods remain important in health planning research.

Spatial Analysis

Spatial analysis is a concept developed by geographers that focuses on the spatial relationships among phenomena within the environment. This approach goes beyond the simple mapping of data (which is certainly important for descriptive purposes) to the calculation of statistics based on the distribution of cases on the map (Plane and Rogerson 1994). The spatial approach improves on nonspatial representation because it takes into account the proximity or isolation of the phenomena under study.

Geographic information systems (GIS) have been developed for use by planners that assist in the performance of spatial analyses. GIS software can be used to describe and analyze the geographic distribution, for example, of diseases or persons at risk for developing certain health conditions. It can be used to target population segments and select sites for treatment programs or facilities. The software allows the data to be visualized and facilitates analyses of geographic and longitudinal variation. This approach has a lot in common with epidemiological techniques, since one of the main applications of GIS systems is in the study of epidemiological phenomena. Concerns over the threat of bioterrorism have further raised the interest in spatial analysis as applied, for example, to the geographic dispersion of a biological pathogen.

Spatial analysis can be utilized to generate a variety of map types. The choice depends on the issues under study and the type of analysis being performed. GIS software has the ability to link two or more mapped variables and perform statistical analysis. Indeed, accessibility analyses on available health services, made possible by GIS software, have become a standard technique in planning studies. GIS software includes the ability to "geocode" data to a specific latitude and longitude. This means that, for displaying phenomena on maps, the exact location can be plotted.

Although spatial analysis is becoming increasingly important with the introduction of low-cost, user-friendly geographic information systems, this method requires a certain level of specialized skills. Medical geographers and others who have experience in spatial analysis in healthcare are rare and it is likely to be a while before this method is in widespread use.

Evaluation Analysis

Evaluation analysis has a long history outside of healthcare but is now beginning to find a growing number of health-related applications. Evaluation techniques can be utilized in a number of ways in healthcare. They can be utilized to evaluate a particular program or service (both retroactively and prospectively). They can be utilized to evaluate various marketing activities, and to a lesser extent they can be utilized to evaluate a market. The most effective use of evaluation in healthcare is probably related to feasibility studies and business planning. Various evaluation techniques (e.g., cost/benefit analysis) can be used for the planning of new programs.

In their broadest application evaluation practices are designed to (1) provide a basis for decision-making and policy formulation; (2) assess and evaluate progress; (3) monitor and manage programs; and (4) generate information for improving programs. As such, evaluation analysis can serve as a valuable component for any planning study.

Evaluation techniques focus on two types of analysis: process (or formative) analysis and outcome (or summative) analysis. The former evaluates systems, procedures, communications, and other factors that contribute to the efficient operation of a program. Outcome evaluation, on the other hand, focuses more on end results. Process evaluation essentially measures efficiency, while outcome evaluation measures effectiveness.

Evaluators are increasingly thinking in terms of "impact evaluation." While outcome evaluation focuses primarily on what was accomplished by the end of the project period, impact evaluation looks at what changes occurred as a result of the project. Thus, the scope of evaluation is expanded to attempt to identify any significant changes that have occurred as a result of the project.

Although evaluation techniques are often praised for their bottom-line objectivity, they are also useful in healthcare where it is not possible to place a dollar value on everything. Thus, cost-effectiveness analysis can take into consideration the nontangible aspects of the service delivery process in its evaluation.

SWOT Analysis

The SWOT analysis has become an increasingly common technique for assessing the position of a healthcare organization within its market. It can also be utilized to assess the overall characteristics of a community's health system. The SWOT analysis involves an examination of the *strengths*, *weaknesses*, *opportunities*, and *threats* relative to the community or the organization.

In the case of community-wide planning, it would be normal to identify the strengths of the community's healthcare system overall, as well as particularly effective or well-developed programs or facilities. Weaknesses within the community's healthcare system would be identified in the same manner. Opportunities may take the form of service niches that could be addressed, new sources of insured patients, or potential collaborative projects. Threats may take the form of system under-capacity or overcapacity, declining reimbursement for "public" patients, or overly aggressive competition among the players. In the case of the organization, the SWOT analysis will involve both internal and external audits.

The SWOT analysis should include input from the quantitative research that is being conducted as well as from the interviews that are administered. Because the strengths, weaknesses, opportunities, and threats that are identified will guide further development of the plan, it is important that consensus be reached on these attributes before proceeding with the planning process.

Gap Analysis

A "gap analysis," as the name implies, assesses the gap between the needs of a population and the existing resources for meeting those needs. Thus, this form of analysis involves assessing the needs of the population, identifying the services or other resources available to meet those needs, and then determining what the unmet needs (or the gaps in services) are. In the case of organization-level planning, the process may involve specifying some ideal state (e.g., a 25% market share) and determining the gap between this target and the current reality. Thus, gap analysis can be utilized to assess the gap between where an organization is and where it wants to be.

The gap analysis is frequently used in performing community assessments. The community's healthcare needs are compared to the services available, and unmet needs are subsequently identified. These needs may be expressed in terms of some global rating or linked to specific programs (e.g., there are ample specialists in the community but a shortage of primary care physicians). This same approach can be applied by private sector organizations and this technique, under various guises, serves as the starting point for much strategic decision-making.

A supply and demand analysis is an example of a gap analysis utilized in healthcare. An example of such an analysis involves the community's physician supply. In the typical case, the level of physician need for a particular community or population is determined, preferably in terms of specialty categories. The next step is to determine the existing supply of physicians in the community or otherwise serving the target area. It then becomes a simple matter of comparing the demand for physicians with the current supply to complete the analysis. The analysis should identify the extent to which surpluses or shortages of physicians exist on a specialty-by-specialty basis. The conclusions of the analysis serve as a guide for planning physician services. Gaps can be identified in terms of personnel, as in the example above, facilities, services, equipment, funding, and a variety of other types of resources.

"What-If" Analysis

The "what-if" analysis has become an increasingly important analytical technique as the ability to model processes using computers has become more widespread. The approach involves a low-level simulation technique in which the components of a particular model are adjusted to determine the likely impact throughout the model. Thus, "what if" we manipulate the hospital admission? How will that impact revenues or occupancy rates?

What-if models can range from quite simplistic to highly complex. Fortunately, many what-if scenarios can be modeled using a spreadsheet on a personal computer. A market analyst might be asked, for example, to estimate the impact of offering a service at varying fee levels. A what-if scenario could be modeled using a spreadsheet or financial analysis software to determine the impact of different fee schedules. Obviously, a great deal of information is needed for what-if analyses, and the analyst must fully understand the process being modeled for this to work. However, a well-constructed, what-if model can be very useful to the planning analyst.

References

Creswell, J. W. (1994). *Research design: Qualitative and quantitative approaches*. Thousand Oaks, CA: Sage.
Dever, G. E. A. (1991). *Community health assessment*. Gaithersburg, MD: Aspen.
Dillman, D. A. (1978). *Mail and telephone survey: The total design*. New York: Wiley.
Plane, D. A., & Rogerson, P. A. (1994). *The geographical analysis of population*. New York: Wiley.

Further Reading

Aday, L. A. (1989). *Designing and conducting health surveys*. San Francisco, CA: Jossey-Bass.

Berkowitz, E. N., Pol, L. G., & Thomas, R. K. (1997). *Healthcare market research*. Burr Ridge, IL: Irwin Professional Publishing.

Curry, L., & Nunez-Smith, M. (2014). *Mixed methods in health sciences research: A primer*. Thousand Oaks, CA: Sage.

Forister, J. G., & Blessing, J. D. (2019). *Introduction to research and medical literature for health professionals*. Burlington, MA: Jones & Bartlett.

Mackridge, R., & Rowe, P. (2018). *A practical approach to using statistics in health research: From planning to reporting*. Hoboken, NJ: Wiley.

Ozdenerol, E. (2017). *Spatial health inequalities*. Boca Raton, FL: CRC Press.

Chapter 13
Information Sources and Data Management

Introduction

The health services planner seeking data to support the planning process is presented with something of a paradox. The healthcare industry generates a wealth of data, but large portions of this bounty are inaccessible to planners. Unlike other industries, healthcare has never developed national clearinghouses for bringing industry data into a central repository. When data are available, they often suffer from a lack of standardized reporting format, thus limiting the comparability of much of the data from site to site or from time period to time period. Since health-related information is often internally generated by a private healthcare organization, potentially useful health data sets may be unpublished, proprietary, and/or difficult to interpret.

In recent years the demand for health-related data has grown dramatically. Historically, interest in health data was limited to organizations involved directly in patient care, a few for-profit components of the system (e.g., insurance, pharmaceuticals), and certain government agencies. Today, a wide variety of other organizations both inside and outside of healthcare now require health-related data for an expanding number of uses. Insurers, employers, benefits managers, policy makers, consultants, and a variety of other interests increasingly seek health-related data for their planning needs. Healthcare providers who made minimal use of available data just a few years ago now aggressively seek a wider range of data for a growing number of applications within the organization.

Data on the external environment have become increasingly important as strategic, business, and marketing planning have become more common in healthcare. Despite this, however, the healthcare industry still lags behind other industries in the collection and dissemination of market-related data. The local orientation and autonomous nature of many healthcare organizations have impeded data sharing. Much important information lies buried in government reports, organizations databases, and proprietary research documents that are inaccessible to most of the

© Springer Science+Business Media, LLC, part of Springer Nature 2021
R. K. Thomas, *Health Services Planning*,
https://doi.org/10.1007/978-1-0716-1076-3_13

healthcare community. Increasingly, the health planner's ability to access, manipulate, and interpret these external data means the difference between the success and failure of a planning initiative.

Today's healthcare environment demands improvement in the quality, quantity, and specificity of the data used for planning purposes. In response to these needs, the amount and variety of health-related data have been greatly expanded. Organizations in both the public and private sectors have begun generating new data sets. More importantly, efforts are underway on the part of various entities, particularly within the federal government, to make existing data more accessible and affordable for the healthcare community. The ability to post data online in electronic format has contributed substantially to this effort.

The primary purpose of this chapter is to outline the categories of data required for various planning initiatives, describe the ways in which they are generated, and indicate sites where they might be accessed. In view of the growing number of types and sources of health-related data, this chapter cannot present an exhaustive discussion of this topic. It should, however, direct the reader to the most important sources of data for health planning. While many of the information sources discussed in this chapter have been introduced in specific contexts earlier in the book, important characteristics of these sources—such as frequency of release, geographic specificity, and methodological limitations—are presented here.

A number of the data sets described here are not what most users would consider health-related data. However, health-related data can be a large umbrella in that much of what affects the health industry does not result directly from health-related events. Beginning in the 1990s, there was an increase in the demand for data thought in the past to be unrelated to healthcare, including data on such topics as employment, housing, and crime. Therefore, this discussion has been expanded to include data sets that reflect the more general environment affecting healthcare-related activities.

Data Dimensions

The data being considered for use in planning activities can be categorized along a number of different dimensions. By categorizing data along these dimensions, some organization is introduced into the data management process. Some of the most important dimensions are addressed in the sections below.

Community vs. Organizational Data

As noted throughout this text, the compilation of health data can be approached at two different levels, the community level and the organizational level. The former involves the analysis of community-wide health data, whether the "community" is the nation, a state, a county, or a planning district. This macro-level approach has historically been associated with public sector planning activity. Community-level data focus on top-of-the-organization statistics as opposed to detailed internal data for organizations. The emphasis is likely to be on overall patterns of health service delivery and on dominant practice patterns than on the details of the operation of various organizations. Thus, community-level data will provide the planner data on such phenomena as patient flow into and out of the service area, levels of overcapacity or under-capacity affecting the area's health facilities, and adequacy of various types of biomedical equipment within the service area.

At the organization level, data analysis focuses on the characteristics and concerns of specific corporate entities such as hospitals, physician groups, and health plans. The organization-level approach is more typical of the private sector in healthcare. The emphasis is likely to be on the details of the organization's operation vis-à-vis the activities of competitors and other healthcare organizations within the market area. There is interest in the overall pattern of system operation only to the extent that it affects the particular organization. For example, the specialty physician practice is primarily interested in the details of competing specialty practices (e.g., patient volume, market share, procedures performed) rather than more general data on the health service area.

Internal vs. External Data

Community-wide and organization planners alike will require the use of data on both the internal environment and the external environment. While it has been natural for healthcare organizations to turn first to internal information sources, data on the external environment have become increasingly important. Data related to the external environment are sometimes difficult to locate and access but, relative to internal data, are more available to the public. The healthcare organization's ability to access, manipulate, and interpret external data sets is increasingly the difference between success and failure.

Internally generated data represent a ready source of information at the organization level. Healthcare organizations routinely generate a large volume of data as a by-product of their normal operations. These include data related to patient characteristics, utilization patterns, referral streams, financial transactions, personnel, and other types of information that almost always have a demographic dimension. To the extent that these data can be extracted from internal data management systems, they serve as a rich source of information on the organization and its operation. (This chapter will, however, focus on sources of external data, since these are the data sets to which the health planner is most likely to have access.)

Data on the internal characteristics of the organization typically include information on patient characteristics, utilization trends, staffing levels, and financial trends, among others. Internal data are usually compiled through an *internal audit*. The internal audit typically includes analysis of the organization's structure, processes, customers, and resources. The internal audit may compile data generated through standard reports generated by the organization's data management systems (e.g., patient activity reports), but additional "runs" are often required in order to generate the desired information. Few data management systems within healthcare organizations were set up with the generation of data for planning in mind and many are too inflexible to produce custom data sets. In these cases, the internal audit is likely to require some primary research. (More detail on the internal audit is provided in Chap. 8.)

Most of the data collection effort on the part of health planners will be directed toward external data. As healthcare providers, in particular, have become more market driven and the emphasis has shifted to strategic planning, business planning, and marketing planning, the interest in external data of all types has grown. And, of course, the primary concern of the community-wide planner is external data since virtually all of the data is "external" to the planning entity.

While the types of planning specified above all require some level of internal data, strategic, business, and marketing planning are primarily external in their orientation. They all must address the external environment in which they are to operate. They need to take into consideration national, state, and local trends in healthcare delivery, financing, and regulation. They need to be aware of developments in the local market that will affect their initiatives. They particularly need to have an understanding of the characteristics of other healthcare organizations within the market area, especially those that may compete with them. Much of this chapter is devoted to an understanding of the types and sources of external data.

Primary vs. Secondary Data

Another useful distinction is also made between primary data and secondary data. Primary data collection involves the use of surveys, focus groups, observational methods, and other techniques for the stated purpose of obtaining information on a specific topic. Secondary data refers to data gathered for some other purpose besides planning, marketing, or business development but that is nevertheless of value in the formulation of strategy and policy.

This chapter focuses on secondary sources of data rather than primary research. Primary research requires a much more detailed treatment than can be afforded in this framework and is better addressed in a research methodology context. Also, primary research activities are usually focused narrowly on specific issues facing an organization at a particular time under certain conditions. While the value of primary research has become well established within healthcare as evidenced by the growing number of patient satisfaction surveys and focus groups being conducted, these activities usually generate proprietary data that are not likely to be disseminated outside the sponsoring organization.

Geographic Level

Another dimension of health data that should be noted is the geographic dimension. Health planners are likely to operate at different levels of geography depending on the type of plan and the type of organization involved. The Centers for Disease Control and Prevention, for example, may think in terms of national level data and examine morbidity trends for the entire US population. Similarly, a pharmaceutical company with a national market may also examine data at that level. Realistically, though, healthcare is primarily a local concern and most organizations require data at a level much lower than the national level.

Community-wide planners are likely to require data for a fairly restricted service area (e.g., a county or group of counties), but they need it at a relatively high level of granularity in order to make distinctions between various parts of the community. Thus, they may collect data at the census tract level, which is the smallest unit of geography for which extensive data are likely to be available. State health planners, on the other hand, are more likely to be concerned about county-level data, since these are essentially the administrative building blocks for the state. Sub-county data are likely to involve more detail than state-based planners require.

The type of organization and the nature of the service area will determine the level of geography at which the organization-level planner functions. A large specialty group is likely to draw patients from a wide geographic area covering several counties; in this case, the county is probably the best unit for data collection. A family practitioner in a solo practice is likely to serve a fairly circumscribed service area that exists within a particular county. In this case, the ZIP Code may be the level at which data would be collected and analyzed.

The choice of geographic unit for the analysis is important not only because of its implications for the service area under study, but also because different types of data are available for different geographies. For many types of information, the county may offer the most extensive range of data and, generally, the smaller the unit of geography, the less the data available. While use of the ZIP Code or census tract as the unit of geography may allow for more precise delineation of the service area, access to certain types of data becomes more limited. Thus, there is likely to be a trade-off related to the specification of the service area and the types of data that are available.

Temporal Dimension

One other dimension of data that needs to be taken into consideration is the temporal dimension. Health professionals typically think in terms of current data—that is, data that relate to the present time frame or, at least, to the immediate past (e.g., the last set of lab tests). The nature of healthcare focuses the practitioner on the present and, hence, the interest in information management systems that can provide "real-time" access to data.

From a planning perspective, current data are important but, in some ways, are less important than future data and even historical data. The value of current data rests with its ability to provide a baseline against which past and future figures can be compared. "Future" data refers to data that describes conditions at some point in the future. By definition, planning is future oriented, and effective planning requires insights into the future of the healthcare environment. Since actual future data do not exist, efforts must be made to generate projections of future conditions relevant to the community or the healthcare organization. Increasing emphasis is being placed on the production of "synthetic" estimates of future populations, service demands, and utilization patterns. The growing interest in predictive modeling among health plans and other care managers is encouraging the development of techniques for predicting future trends.

Planners routinely collect historical data on the community or the organization. To a great extent, the planning process relies on the ability to extrapolate past trends into the future. Thus, historical patterns of population growth, hospital admissions, and disease prevalence can provide the basis for predicting future trends. It could be argued that, since healthcare continues to change dramatically, the past is not a good predictor of the future. While there is considerable merit in this position, it would be reckless to not consider the trends that led up to the current situation for the community or the organization.

Data Generation Methods

The methods for data collection discussed in this chapter are divided into four general categories: censuses, registration systems, surveys, and synthetically produced data. Censuses, registries, and surveys are the more traditional methods of generating data supportive of health planning activities, although synthetically produced statistics such as population estimates and projections have become standard tools for most planning analyses.

Censuses

A census of the population involves a complete count of the persons residing in a specific place at a specific time. The U.S. Census Bureau (within the Department of Commerce) conducts an enumeration of population and housing every 10 years (the decennial census) and the 2010 enumeration was the twenty-third decennial census. A lesser known enumeration of business units, or an "economic census," is conducted every 5 years.

Although a census theoretically includes a complete count of the population, it is increasingly difficult to strictly apply this term to the decennial census conducted in the United States. While the U.S. Census ostensibly counts every resident, it falls short of a true census in two aspects. First, every decade a certain segment of the population is missed in the enumeration, resulting in some level of "undercount." While the undercount is typically less than three percent, its mere existence creates myriad problems. This undercount tends to be concentrated among certain segments of the population, resulting in a situation in which members of some groups have a greater chance of being enumerated than members of others. This has significant implications, since the results of each census are used as the basis for redistributing congressional seats and allocating government funds. Because of the undercount, the publication of initial census figures every 10 years produces a spate of lawsuits related to the accuracy of the census itself and, with the 2000 census, it led to congressional intervention into the determination of the "official" count.

The second factor diminishing the enumeration's value as a census is the fact that the "long form" is no longer administered to a sample of the nation's households. The short form currently in use only collects data on the age, sex, race, ethnicity and relation to householder. Users of census data should become knowledgeable about the validity of the figures, especially when small geographic units are being studied.

The infrequent administration of the census is another source of problems. In a society where rapid change is common, collecting data at 10-year intervals has its shortcomings. As time elapses after the census year, the usefulness of the data is diminished. Nevertheless, commercial data vendors and other organizations that generate population estimates and projections continue to use these "dated" data as their baseline for calculations. This practice opens the door for potential miscalculations for which the magnitude might not be known.

The census collects data on the number of persons residing in each living unit (e.g., house, duplex, apartment, or dormitory) and the characteristics of those individuals. Information once collected via the census long form is now obtained through the American Community Survey (ACS). The ACS collects additional data for individual household members on marital status, income, occupation, education, employment status, and industry of employment. There are also questions about the dwelling unit in which the respondent lives, including information on the type of dwelling unit (e.g., apartment or duplex), ownership status, value of owned house, monthly rent, age of dwelling unit, and a number of other housing characteristics.

Health-related items are noticeably absent from the census, since very few have been mandated for collection through legislative action. Other government agencies, as will be shown later, have a much more significant role in the collection of health-related data than does the Census Bureau.

The value of the census to health planners clearly rests with its demographic data. These data have direct application to the performance of market analyses and indirect applications as input into models for generating prevalence and demand estimates.

Although the census is only conducted every 10 years, the Bureau maintains the capacity for generating population estimates and projections on an ongoing basis. These figures may not be as detailed as some commercially produced ones—e.g., they are only calculated down to the county level—but they are broken down in terms of age, race, income, and other important variables. These data are increasingly being made available by the Census Bureau via the Internet.

Census data are made available by the Census Bureau for virtually every formally designated geographic unit in the United States, and this is a clear advantage of census data over some other types of data. Statistics generated by the census are disseminated for states, counties, ZIP Codes, metropolitan areas, and cities. Data are also published for specially designated areas created by the Census Bureau, including census tracts, block groups, and blocks. The Bureau offers free and relatively user-friendly online access to its data sets, and most census data can be accessed through the American Factfinder feature of the Bureau's website.

The modern economic census was initiated in 1954 and is conducted every 5 years (currently in years ending in 2 and 7). The census covers businesses engaged in retail trade, wholesale trade, service activities, mineral industries, transportation, construction, manufacturing, and agriculture, as well as government services. The information collected through the economic census includes data on sales, employment, and payroll, along with other, more specialized data. These data are available for a variety of geographic units, including states, metropolitan areas, counties, and places with 2500 or more residents.

While it may appear that these data are unrelated to health issues, the economic census actually compiles a lot of data on healthcare business. All businesses are assigned a code using the North American Industry Classification System (NAICS). Aggregated data on businesses within the NAICS catvegories that involve health-related activities (e.g., physician practices, pharmacies, medical laboratories) are available from this source. There is no other all-inclusive source that will indicate the number of hospitals, pharmacists, and chiropractors, for example, that are located in a particular area. As with the population and housing data, the Bureau is increasingly distributing data from the economic census in electronic form.

Registration Systems

A second method of data collection that generates data useful for health planners is represented by registration systems. A registration system involves the systematic compilation, recording, and reporting on a broad range of events, institutions, and individuals. The implied characteristics on a registry include the regular and timely recording of the phenomenon in question. Most of the registration systems relevant to this discussion are sponsored by some branch of government, although other types of registration systems will be discussed below as well.

The best known registration activities in the United States are those related to "vital events," including births, deaths, marriages, and divorces. However, other registries can prove valuable, especially when examining changes in the level and types of health services required by a population. These include registration systems sponsored by the Centers for Disease Control and Prevention (CDC), the Social Security Administration (SSA), Medicare, and the Centers for Medicare & Medicaid Services (CMS), among others.

A variation on registries that is finding increasing use in health-related research is "administrative records." Administrative records systems are not necessarily intended to be registries of all enrollees or members of an organization or group but a record of transactions involving these individuals. Thus, the list of all Medicare enrollees would constitute a registry, but the data generated by virtue of Medicare enrollees' encounters with the healthcare system would be under the heading of administrative records (since not all Medicare enrollees would use services during a given time period). Data sets made available by the federal government on Medicare activity involve administrative records that are useful for a number of purposes. Some examples of useful registries are described below.

Vital Statistics

The tracking of vital statistics in the United States involves data collection on births, deaths, marriages, and divorces and, in some jurisdictions, induced abortions. The collection of data on vital events is initially the responsibility of the local health authority. Health departments at the county (or county equivalent) level are charged with filing certificates for births and deaths. These data are forwarded to the vital statistics registry within the respective state governments. The appropriate state agency compiles the data for use by the state and transmits the files to the National Center for Health Statistics (NCHS). NCHS has the responsibility of compiling and publishing vital statistics for the nation and its various political subdivisions. (See Box 13.1 for a description of the National Center for Health Statistics.)

Box 13.1: The National Center for Health Statistics
The National Center for Health Statistics (NCHS) is considered by many to be the Census Bureau of healthcare. As a division of the Centers for Disease Control and Prevention (CDC), NCHS performs a number of invaluable functions related to health and healthcare. For almost 40 years the Center has carried out the tasks of data collection and analysis, data dissemination, and development of methodologies for research on health issues. The NCHS also coordinates the various state centers for health statistics.

Part of the Center's responsibilities includes the compilation, analysis, and publication of vital statistics for the United States and each relevant subarea. This is a massive task, but the results provide the basis for the calculation of

(continued)

Box 13.1 (continued)

fertility and mortality rates. These statistics, in turn, provide the basis for various population estimates and projections made by other organizations. The compilation and analysis of data on morbidity are another important function, and the Center has been responsible for the development of much of the epidemiological data available, for example, on chronic disease and AIDS.

In addition to the data compiled from various registration sources, the Center is the foremost administrator of healthcare surveys in the nation. Its sample surveys are generally large-scale endeavors that fall into two categories: community-based surveys and facility-based surveys. Perhaps the Center's most important survey is the National Health Interview Survey (NHIS), through which data are collected annually from approximately 49,000 households. The NHIS is the nation's primary source of data on the incidence/prevalence of health conditions, health status, number of injuries and disabilities characterizing the population, health services utilization, and a variety of other health-related topics. Surveys that involve a sample from the community include the Medical Expenditure Panel Survey (MEPS), the National Health and Nutrition Examination Survey (NHANES), and the National Survey of Family Growth (NSFG). Another survey, the National Maternal and Infant Health Survey (NMIHS), involves a sampling of certificates of birth, fetal death, and infant death.

One of the newer surveys has become the most important source of information on the increasingly important topic of ambulatory care. The National Ambulatory Medical Care Survey (NAMCS) samples the patient records of 2500 office-based physicians to obtain data on diagnosis, treatment, and medications prescribed, along with information on the characteristics of both physicians and patients. Important facility-based surveys include the National Hospital Discharge Survey and the National Nursing Home Survey.

The data collected through NCHS studies are disseminated in a variety of ways. Much of the information is disseminated as printed material. The Center's publications include annual books such as *Health, United States* (the "official" government compendium of statistics on the nation's health), and publications such as *Vital and Health Statistics*. Data from NCHS surveys are available in a variety of formats. The NCHS sponsors conferences and workshops offering not only the findings from the Center's research but also training in its research methodologies. NCHS-generated data sets are being made increasingly available via the Internet and can be accessed at www.cdc.gov/nchs.

From the perspective of a health data user, there are other resources that the Center can offer. By contacting the appropriate NCHS division, it is possible to obtain detailed statistics, many unpublished, on all of the topics for which the Center compiles data. Center staff are also available to help with methodological issues and provide that "one number" that the health data analyst might require. In short, the NCHS is a service-oriented agency that provides a number of invaluable functions for those who require data on health and healthcare. Much of the information required for the US system to adapt to the changing healthcare environment, in fact, will be generated by the NCHS.

Standard birth certificates capture data on the time and date of birth, place of occurrence, mother's residence, birth weight, pregnancy complications, mother's pregnancy history, mother and father's age and race (ethnicity in selected states), and mother's education and marital status. Data elements available from the standard death certificate include age, race (ethnicity in selected states), sex, place of residence, usual occupation, and industry of the decedent, along with the location where the death took place. In addition, data are collected on the immediate and contributing causes of death and on other significant health conditions.

Birth and death statistics are regularly reported in federal government publications and, now, via the Internet (http://www.fedstats.gov). The compiled statistics are typically presented based on both the place of occurrence of the event (e.g., the location of the hospital) and the place of residence of the affected individual. Considerable detail is provided in the reports for a wide range of geographic units including states, MSAs, counties, and urban places. Data for other geographic areas may be available through state and local government agencies. Yearly summary reports are produced and published by the NCHS, though monthly summaries are also available through the monthly vital statistics reports. Virtually all NCHS reports and data sets are in electronic format.

Vital statistics reports are also made available by most state governments and most local health departments. Although basic data will always be reported by these agencies, the format, detail, and coverage vary from state to state and county to county.

CDC Disease Surveillance

The CDC has been involved in disease surveillance activities since the establishment of the Communicable Disease Center in 1946. Surveillance activities now include programs in human reproduction, environmental health, chronic disease, risk reduction, occupational safety and health, and infectious diseases. The purpose of the surveillance system is to provide weekly provisional information on the occurrence of diseases defined as "notifiable" by the Council of State and Territorial Epidemiologists (CSTE). To this end, the CDC maintains a number of registries on various disease categories.

Notifiable disease reports are received by the CDC from 52 US jurisdictions (Washington, D.C., and New York City report separately) and 5 territories. The number of diseases and conditions reported is quite large. The list of monitored diseases includes, among others, anthrax, botulism, cholera, diphtheria, food-borne disease, leprosy, mumps, and toxic shock. Statistics on notifiable diseases are published weekly by the CDC in *Morbidity and Mortality Weekly Report* (MMWR) and compiled in an annual report published by the agency. The CDC is now providing a growing amount of information via the Internet.

Because of the historical focus of the CDC on communicable diseases, chronic diseases are generally not officially tracked as part of the public health agenda. This situation creates a serious void in the ability to monitor the chronic conditions that now account for the bulk of morbidity within the US population. Although our knowledge of these conditions has been advanced through survey research on the part of the NCHS, information derived from sample surveys limits our understanding of the epidemiology of chronic conditions and, thus, the system's ability to monitor their prevalence. As a result, the CDC and other agencies are currently exploring possibilities for improving capabilities for identifying and monitoring chronic conditions.

Health Personnel

Registries constitute the main source of data on many categories of health personnel. Most health professionals must be registered with the state in which they practice. In addition, most belong to professional associations whose rosters become *de facto* registries. Like other registries, the registration of healthcare personnel involves the regular and timely recording of persons entering a given profession. Registries of health personnel—either government or professional—require constant updating, making them more prone to error than certain other types of registries.

The federal government is the primary source of registry data on health personnel at the national level. The U.S. Department of Health and Human Services (DHHS) is responsible for collecting and disseminating data on the status of health personnel in the United States. These requirements have led to the establishment of registries for various categories of health professionals. DHHS also generates projections of the future personnel pool for selected categories of professionals. In addition, the listing of health professional shortage areas maintained by the Health Resources and Services Administration within DHHS is often of use to health planners. This database tracks the counties, communities, and special populations (e.g., Indian reservations) that report less than the recommended number of primary care physicians. In addition, the Centers for Medicare & Medicaid Services maintains detailed registries of many types of health professionals that receive reimbursement under federally sponsored health programs.

State governments often represent more direct sources of information on health personnel than federal agencies, since the various states have the primary responsibility for the licensing and monitoring of virtually all health professions. As part of their administrative activities, they necessarily establish registries for specific categories of health personnel. The databases created at the state level for physicians, nurses, physician assistants, and other categories of health personnel are typically up to date. However, the detail provided and the usefulness of the data collected for planning, marketing, and business development purposes vary widely from state to state.

Other major sources of health manpower data include the American Medical Association (AMA) physician master file; medical, osteopathic, dental, and nursing school enrollment data; the American Academy of Physician Assistants master file; the American Dental Association dental practice survey; the Inventory of Pharmacists; and licensure information from the National Council of State Boards of Nursing and various accrediting bodies and professional associations serving the allied health profession (e.g., laboratory technicians, dietitians, physical therapists).

State licensure agencies maintain databases on health professionals registered in the respective states. While this information is often available to the public, mere registration in a jurisdiction does not necessarily indicate an active practice. Further, these databases are likely to include only the barest of data required to carry out the mandated functions of the licensing agency. Specialty boards and other organizations also maintain registries on their members or certification recipients. While this information is often available in printed directories, the availability of the actual databases varies.

Many local organizations have begun to develop and maintain personnel databases for their particular service areas. Since most healthcare markets are local, national databases are of limited usefulness. Business coalitions have led the way in support of database development in many local markets.

Commercial data vendors maintain databases of physicians and other personnel, and some of these are comparable to the more traditional databases maintained by the professional organizations and government agencies. Data vendors may identify emerging professions or "marginal" practitioners that do not have an association base or are not tracked by the government. Other vendors repackage data from government organizations or association sources and resell the data in modified form.

Health Facilities

The federal government is the major source of nationwide data on health facilities. The National Master Facility Inventory (NMFI) is a comprehensive file of inpatient facilities maintained by the NCHS. The institutions included in this NCHS data collection effort are hospitals, nursing homes and related facilities, and other custodial or remedial care facilities. The NMFI is kept current by periodically adding the names and addresses of newly established facilities licensed by state boards and other agencies. Annual surveys are used to update information concerning existing facilities.

The facilities databases established by NCHS include data on facility size, personnel, admissions, discharges, services offered, type of ownership, and type of certification. These data are available through various published reports and much of this information is obtained initially from professional associations and processed by the NCHS or some other federal agency. CMS is now making available a set of data files on health facilities and other providers of care. Its "Provider of Services" files include every provider that has filed claims with Medicare.

Arguably, the nation's most complete hospital registry is maintained by the American Hospital Association (AHA). Data are compiled annually on the availability of services, utilization patterns, financial information, hospital management, and personnel (American Hospital Association 2003). The database is continuously updated through an ongoing survey of the nation's hospitals. These data are available for a variety of geographic units (including regions, divisions, states, counties, and cities). They are available in the form of published reports and via the Internet. Some of the information is reprinted in secondary sources such as the *County and City Data Book* and *Health, United States*. Certain commercial data vendors have also established hospital databases. Solucient, one of the nation's largest health data vendors, produces an annual profile of hospitals based on its database.

Since most health facilities are licensed by the state, information is usually available from the state agency charged with that responsibility. Increasingly, local organizations such as planning and regulatory agencies and business coalitions maintain facilities databases. For facilities other than hospitals, some private data vendors have begun collecting and disseminating data. There are now vendors selling data on health maintenance organizations, urgent care centers, freestanding surgery centers, and a variety of other types of facilities.

Mental Health Facilities

An inventory of mental health organizations is maintained by the Center for Mental Health Services (within the DHHS) and is updated every 2 years. The agency publishes periodic reports on the status of mental health services in the United States, although the format varies from edition to edition. Additional information can be obtained from the Center's website (http://www.samhsa.gov/cmhs/htm).

Since many mental health services are administered by state governments, the respective state agencies represent a source of mental health statistics, although the data provided vary in terms of accessibility, content, and format. While rather detailed statistics have become available on ambulatory care services for physical illness, this is not the case for mental illness. Some limited data on mental health outpatient activity may be available through reports filed by comprehensive community mental health centers.

Surveys

Sample surveys are frequently used to supplement data from other sources. A sample survey involves the administration of an interview form to a portion of a target population that has been systematically selected. The sample is designed so that the respondents are representative of the population being examined. This allows conclusions to be drawn concerning the total population based on the data collected from the sample.

The federal government is the major source of survey research data related to healthcare. Primarily through the NCHS, the federal government maintains a number of ongoing surveys that deal with hospital utilization, ambulatory care utilization, nursing home and home health utilization, medical care expenditures, and other relevant topics. The National Institutes of Health and the CDC also conduct surveys, although more episodically, that generate data of interest to health planners. Some of the more useful sample surveys for health demographers are discussed in Box 13.2.

Box 13.2: Federal Sources of Survey Data

The combined agencies of the federal government represent the nation's largest data collection force. Led by the National Center for Health Statistics (NCHS), federal agencies conduct a variety of surveys on health-related issues. The sections below describe a sample of these federal survey activities that have particular relevance for healthcare planning.

The *National Health Interview Survey* (NHIS) is an ongoing national survey of the noninstitutionalized civilian population in the United States. Each year, a multistage probability sample of 49,000 households are interviewed. The data gathered are quite detailed and include demographic information on age, race, sex, marital status, occupation, and income. Information is compiled on physician visits, hospital stays, restricted-activity days, long-term activity limitation, health status, and chronic conditions. Recently, questions regarding AIDS knowledge and attitudes have been added to the survey. Food nutrition knowledge, smoking and other tobacco use, cancer, and polio are also subjects sometimes addressed.

The *National Health and Nutrition Examination Survey* (NHANES) is a survey conducted by the NCHS, Centers for Disease Control and Prevention (CDC). This survey has been designed to collect information about the health and diet of people in the United States. NHANES is unique in that it combines a home interview with health tests that are done in a mobile examination center. Tens of thousands of interviews are conducted annually and, during a 12-month period, examinations are performed on some 5000 of the interviewees. The survey collects information on physical health status, dental health, and nutrition. Data are used to determine cholesterol levels, trends in obesity, and other health characteristics of the population.

The *National Hospital Discharge Survey* (NHDS) is a continuous nationwide survey of inpatient utilization of short-stay hospitals. All hospitals with six or more beds reporting an average length of stay of less than 30 days are included in the sampling frame. A multistage probability sampling frame is used to select hospitals from the National Master Facility Inventory and discharge records from each of the hospitals. The resulting sample has ranged from 192,000 to 235,000 discharge records. Information is collected on the demographic, clinical, and financial characteristics of patients discharged from short-stay hospitals.

The *National Ambulatory Medical Care Survey* (NAMCS) is a nationwide survey designed to provide information about the provision and utilization of ambulatory health services. The sampling frame is office visits made by

(continued)

Box 13.2 (continued)

ambulatory patients to physicians engaged in office practice. A multistage probability sampling frame is used to select physicians from the master files maintained by the American Medical Association and the American Osteopathic Association. A sample of the records of these physicians for a randomly assigned 1-week period are then examined. Recent samples contain about 35,000 records. Data regarding the age, race, ethnicity, and sex of the patient are gathered, along with the reason for the visit, expected source(s) of payment, principle diagnosis, diagnostic services provided, and disposition of visit.

The *National Survey of Long Term Care Providers* (NSLTCP) is a periodically conducted national survey of nursing and related care homes, their residents, their discharges, and their staffs. Last administered in 2018, data are collected using a two-stage probability design. Once facilities are selected, residents and employees of each facility are sampled. Six separate questionnaires were used to gather data in the most recent survey. The first addresses characteristics of the facility and involves an interview with the administrator or a designee. The second focuses on cost data and is completed by the facility's accountant or bookkeeper. Information on the current and discharged residents is obtained by interviewing the staff person most familiar with the medical records of the residents. Additional resident data is gathered using telephone surveys of the resident's families. Full-time and part-time employees, including nurses, complete a nursing staff questionnaire. This data set includes approximately 1400 facilities, 5100 discharges, 3000 residents, and 14,000 staff records.

The *National Home and Hospice Care Survey* (NHHCS), last conducted in 2013, involves the collection of data from a sample of home health agencies and hospices. Patient questionnaires are administered to the various agencies and information collected on the demographic and health characteristics of the patients served by these agencies.

The *National Survey of Family Growth* (NSFG), last administered in 2017, involves a survey of approximately 10,000 women aged 15–44 years. The survey collects data on factors affecting birth and pregnancy rates, adoption, and maternal and infant health. Specific characteristics that are examined include sexual activity, contraception and sterilization practices, infertility, pregnancy loss, low birth weight, and use of medical care for family planning and infertility.

The *Medical Expenditure Panel Survey* (MEPS) was initiated in 1996 as a replacement for previous surveys focusing on expenditures for health services. Co-sponsored by the Agency for Healthcare Research and Quality (AHRQ) and the NCHS, MEPS is designed to generate data on the types of health services Americans use, the frequency with which they use them, how much is paid for these services, and who pays for them. In addition, MEPS provides information on health insurance coverage.

Box 13.2 (continued)

The *Behavioral Risk Factor Surveillance System* (BRFSS), sponsored by the CDC, was initiated in 1995 to collect information on the health behavior and lifestyles of the US population. Over 90,000 persons respond to the survey annually. The survey includes data collection on such timely items as smoking, alcohol and drug use, seat belt use, and obesity, as well as other factors that might contribute to one's health risk profile.

In the area of behavioral health, the Center for Mental Health Services (CMHS) conducts an annual survey of mental health organizations and general hospitals that provide mental health services. These surveys collect data on the characteristics of all providers of behavioral health services and on the characteristics of the patients served. Other related surveys include samples of patients admitted to various treatment programs.

The *Current Population Survey* (CPS) is the Census Bureau's mechanism for gathering detailed demographic data between the decennial censuses. Since 1960, the sample size has ranged from 33,500 to 65,500 households per year. Data are collected on many of the items formerly included in the census of population and housing (e.g., age, race, and education). Questions are included on some health issues and on fertility issues that have implications for healthcare. Of particular interest to the healthcare industry are the data on health insurance coverage for the US population. These data were the basis for recent estimates of the size of the population that lacks health insurance.

This review does not exhaust the list of government sources of data relevant to health planning, but only provides a sampler. Publications of the federal National Technical Information Service (NTIS) provide a good starting point for finding other relevant databases and, of course, the NCHS website (www.cdc.gov/nchs) provides links to most of these surveys.

There are also a few surveys sponsored by commercial data vendors that contain data useful for health planning. These organizations sponsor nationwide surveys every year or two that may include as many as 100,000 households. Through these surveys, data are collected on health status, health behavior, and healthcare preferences. Certain market research firms collect health-related data as part of their consumer surveys and public opinion pollsters may also collect data on health and healthcare. Some of the data collected in this manner are considered proprietary and are generally not available except to clients. Other vendors make data available for purchase to the general public.

Public opinion polls are often overlooked as sources of certain types of data. Methodologically sound opinion polls are constantly being conducted by research organizations of various types. While the sample sizes are relatively small, opinion polls can provide insights into developing national trends. For example, the shift in the perception of home healthcare as an inferior alternative to hospital care to a perception of the home as the preferred setting for care was first identified through opinion polls.

Synthetic Data

Synthetic data refers to figures that are generated in the absence of actual data by using statistical models. Synthetic data are created by merging existing demographic data with assumptions about population change to produce estimates, projections, and forecasts. These data are particularly valuable given that census and survey activities are restricted because of budgeting and time considerations. Since there is a large and growing demand for information for years between the administration of the census, the production of synthetic data has become a major business. Since no actual data are available for future points in time, any such data must be produced through synthetic means.

The demand for synthetic data is being met by both government agencies and commercial data vendors today. Within the federal government, population estimates for states, MSAs, and counties are prepared each year as a joint effort of the Census Bureau and the state agency designated under the Federal-State Program for Local Population Estimates (FSCPE). The purpose of the program is to standardize data and procedures so that the highest quality estimates can be generated.

Overall, the Census Bureau produces 30 different series of projections for each year. The Bureau provides relatively detailed population estimates for the current year and projections as far as 50 years into the future down to the county level. Most states also generate population estimates and projections that are available through state agencies.

A number of commercial data vendors have emerged in recent years to supplement the efforts of government agencies. Data generated by these vendors have the advantage of being available down to small units of geography (e.g., the census block group) and they are often provided in greater detail (e.g., sex and age breakdowns) than government-produced figures. They also offer the flexibility to generate estimates and projections for "custom" geographies (e.g., a market area) that government statistics do not have the ability to do. The drawback, of course, is that some precision is lost as one develops calculations for lower levels of geography and for population components. However, the ease of accessibility and timeliness of these vendor-generated figures have made them a mainstay of health services planners.

There is an ongoing debate over the quality of the synthetic data available. Users are demanding the most current data possible and, in an effort to serve the market, the question of quality has sometimes become a secondary concern. Users of synthetic data should develop knowledge of the methodologies utilized and the quality of the data used for baseline purpose.

A major category of synthetic data involves estimates and projections of health services demand. Since there are few sources of actual data on the use of health services and projections of future demand are often required, a variety of approaches have been developed for synthetically generating demand estimates and projections. The general approach involves applying known utilization rates to a current or projected population figure. To the extent possible, these figures are adjusted for, at a minimum, the age and sex composition of the target population. Utilization rates generated by the NCHS are the basis for most such calculations and the demographic data are likely to be obtained from a variety of different sources.

Commercial data vendors have led the way in the development of demand estimates and projections. Some vendors have developed calculations for the full range of inpatient and outpatient services, although these are often available only to established customers. Other vendors can provide selected data on, for example, the demand for a particular service line.

A somewhat different type of synthetic data is generated by the Bureau of Labor Statistics (within the U.S. Department of Labor). The Bureau maintains data on all occupational categories within the economy, including healthcare occupations. As part of the Bureau's responsibilities, it produces projections on the size of various occupational categories in the United States for 10–15 years into the future. Six projection models are generated, each containing a number of variables reflecting different scenarios reflecting changes in the total labor force, aggregate economy, industry demand, and industry employment, among other factors. Three sets of employment projections are created based upon differing sets of assumptions. Of interest here are the various categories of health-related occupations (e.g., dentists, physicians and surgeons, and therapists by specialty) and supportive occupations (e.g., dental and medical assistants, as well as nurse's aides). In recent years, health professions have been prominent among the occupations with the greatest projected growth. Data on occupational categories are available from the Department of Labor through regularly published reports and, increasingly, via the Internet.

Data Sources for Health Planning

There are numerous sources of data for health planners available today and the number of sources continues to grow. The sections below group these sources into four main categories: government agencies, professional associations, private organizations, and commercial data vendors. It should be noted that the "products" available from these sources fall into two categories: (1) reports that summarize the data and (2) the actual data sets themselves. Historically, data access was essentially limited to summary tables provided by the organization, agency, or vendor. Today, however, there is a trend toward providing the entire data set for use by health planners and other health data users. In reviewing the sources that follow, this distinction in format should be kept in mind.

Although the sources presented in each section refer to the agencies and publications responsible for the specific data set being discussed, numerous compendia exist that users should find quite useful. Box 13.3 describes the more important of these compendia.

Box 13.3: Compendia of Health Data

There is currently no national clearinghouse for data on health and healthcare in the United States. This makes identifying and acquiring needed data a challenge for health planners. There are, however, a few "compendia" of health data that might prove useful for many purposes. While no one of these publications provides all of the data a planner is likely to need, they offer a reasonable starting point. Not only do they compile specific data on certain topics, but they can also often direct the reader to the origin of the data and other useful resources.

The best known of the compendia of health-related data is entitled *Health, United States*. This work is published annually by the National Center for Health Statistics (NCHS) and includes data gathered from NCHS and many other sources. The publication includes data on health status, health behavior, health services utilization, healthcare resources, healthcare expenditures, and insurance coverage. These data are available mostly at the national level, although some state and regional data are available.

A companion publication, *Mental Health, United States*, is published less frequently than *Health, United States* but represents the primary source of data on behavioral healthcare. The statistics are based on data collected by the Center for Mental Health Services.

Another more specialized compendium is also published by the Centers for Medicare & Medicaid Services (CMS). Simply referred to as *Data Compendium* (with the publication year presented as part of the title), this book brings together data on Medicaid and Medicare. The data presented are drawn primarily from CMS files, although data from sources outside the agency are also included. The information compiled by CMS is presented only at the national level, with some data reported at the state level. No data are presented for sub-state levels of geography.

Since demographic data are so important to health planners, it is worthwhile to mention some compendia that focus on this type of data. The *County and City Data Book* is published every 2 years by the Census Bureau and includes over 200 separate items for each county and 134 items for each city of 25,000 or more persons. Data of interest to healthcare analysts include population statistics, vital records, and hospital, physician, and nursing home statistics, as well as certain insurance data.

The *State and Metropolitan Area Data Book* is published by the Census Bureau every 4 years and contains 128 data items for each state, 298 variables for each MSA, and 87 variables for each MSA's central city. *County Business Patterns*, prepared by the Bureau of the Census, provides a comprehensive count of the various healthcare businesses operating in each US county.

The *Statistical Abstract of the United States* is published every year by the Census Bureau. The *Abstract* contains detailed data for the nation as a whole for 31 different subject categories (e.g., vital statistics, nutrition), as well as data for states and metropolitan areas. Most states publish a statistical abstract that includes comparable data for that state and its counties and cities.

Government Agencies

Governments at all levels are involved in the generation, compilation, manipulation, and/or dissemination of health-related data. The federal government, through the decennial census and related activities, is the world's largest processor of demographic data. Other federal agencies are major managers of data for the related topics of fertility, morbidity, mortality, and migration statistics.

The federal government is a major generator of health-related databases. Through the NCHS, the CDC, the National Institutes for Health, and other organizations, a large share of the nation's health data is generated. The Bureau of Health Resources (DHHS) maintains a master file of much of the health data compiled by the federal government entitled the *Area Resource File* (ARF). Other federal sources outside of health-related agencies, such as the Bureau of Labor Statistics (e.g., health occupations) and the U.S. Department of Agriculture (e.g., nutritional data), create databases of supporting data. The number and variety of databases generated by federal agencies are impressive, but the variety of agencies involves means that databases vary in coverage, content, format, cost, frequency, and accessibility.

State and local governments are also major sources of health-related data. In fact, research on health data users indicates that various state agencies are their primary source of data for planning, marketing, and business development. State governments generate a certain amount of demographic data, with each state having a state data center for demographic projections. Vital statistics data can often be obtained in the most timely fashion at the state level, in fact. States vary, however, in the types and quality of data they generate. University data centers may also be involved in the processing of demographic data. Local governments may generate demographic data for use in various planning functions. City or county governments may produce population projections, while county health departments are responsible for the collection and dissemination of vital statistics data.

Professional Associations

Various associations within the health industry represent another source of health-related data. Chief among these are the AMA (and related medical specialty organizations) and the AHA. There are also other organizations of personnel (e.g., American Dental Association) and facilities (e.g., National Association for Home Care) that maintain databases on their members and on activities related to the organization's membership. These databases are typically developed for internal use but are increasingly being made available to the outside parties.

A number of organizations have been formed in recent years that focus specifically on health data, while others have established formal sections that deal with health data within their broader context. The National Association of Health Data Organizations (NAHDO), for example, brings together disparate parties from the public and private sectors who have an interest in health data. The National Association of County and City Health Officers (NACCHO) has become very active in terms of access to health data for local planning purposes. The Health Information and Management Systems Society (HIMSS) is one of the largest organizations that is addressing this issue as a collateral consideration to data management systems issues.

In recent years, many professional associations have made an increasing amount of information on their members available to the research and business communities. Not only do such organizations have an interest in exchanging information with related groups, but they also have recognized the revenue generation potential of such databases. Some of these databases include only basic information, while others offer a wealth of detail.

Private Organizations

Many private organizations (mostly not-for-profit) collect and/or disseminate health-related data. Voluntary healthcare associations often compile, repackage, and/or disseminate such data. The American Cancer Society, for example, distributes morbidity and mortality data as it relates to its areas of interest. Some organizations, like Planned Parenthood, may commission special studies on fertility or related issues and subsequently publish this information.

Many organizations repackage data collected elsewhere (e.g., from the Census Bureau or the NCHS) and present it within a specialized context. The Population Reference Bureau, a private not-for-profit organization, distributes population statistics in various forms, for example. Some, like the American Association of Retired Persons (AARP), not only compile and disseminate secondary data but are also actively involved in primary data collection, as well as the sponsorship of numerous studies that include some form of data collection.

Commercial Data Vendors

Commercial data vendors represent a fourth category of sources of health-related databases. These organizations have emerged to fill perceived gaps in the availability of various categories of health data. These include commercial data vendors that establish and maintain their own proprietary databases, as well as those that reprocess and/or repackage existing data. Some specialized data vendors maintain databases on nursing homes, urgent care centers, and other types of facilities and make this information available in a variety of forms. Also included in this group are the major data vendors (e.g., ESRI Business Information, Experian) who do not necessarily create health-related databases but incorporate health-specific databases into their business database systems.

Because of the demand for health-related data, several commercial data vendors have added health data to their inventories, and a few health-specific data vendors have emerged. These vendors not only repackage existing data into more palatable form, but some also are developing their own proprietary databases. At least three vendors are conducting major nationwide health consumer surveys.

Health planners may want to consider some of the national consumer databases that have been developed in their search for data on the community. Experian and Acxion, to mention two, are national data companies that maintain data on virtually every household within the United States. While the information is used primarily by marketers seeking to target individuals and households with certain characteristics—an activity that planners may have reason to consider—the data repositories include substantial amounts of data on demographics, lifestyles, and consumer behavior.

Because of the increasing demand for health-related data, improvement in the quality, coverage, timeliness, and availability of such data has become a priority with many organizations. The federal government has taken a lead in the public sector through its efforts to make its extensive health-related databases and registries available to the research and business communities. Through its various programs, the federal government is supporting projects that involve the application of contemporary computer technology to the processing, manipulation, and dissemination of health-related data, an area in which healthcare lags far behind other industries. Commercial data vendors continue to develop proprietary databases and to repackage and distribute databases produced by government and/or association sources.

The Internet represents a major force for the delivery of health data. Although the focus was initially on consumer-oriented health information, data for use by health professionals have become increasingly available. Bibliographical and text files are already becoming available, and some healthcare organizations are transmitting patient data over the Internet. In the future, there is every reason to believe that data for health services planning, marketing, and business development will be widely available via the Internet.

Health Data Management

The expansion in the availability of health data has generated a problem of a different sort for those involved in health planning. This involves the challenge of managing and ultimately exploiting the growing mountain of data on health and healthcare. Some health databases are of such massive proportions that they have been put in the category of "big data." Early attempts at managing health data were primitive by any measure and focused almost entirely on such practical dimensions as patient billing. Data management was controlled by information systems technicians who were essentially isolated from the operation of the organization. If healthcare professionals were to harness the power of the growing volume of data and exploit it for planning, marketing, and business development purposes, a better technical solution was necessary.

During the early 1980s it was realized by some that the ability to manage this growing volume of data was going to be critical. Most other industries had already addressed this issue and had developed fairly sophisticated means of processing and analyzing industry data. Because of its peculiar characteristics, the healthcare industry lagged well behind other sectors of the economy in terms of information management.

The widespread use of computer opened the door for more efficient data management. Bringing the power of the mainframe to the desktop, personal computers quickly transformed the data management environment. The transformation involved more than technical capabilities, however, as it allowed the control of data management to shift back to the administrators and health professionals that ultimately utilized the data.

In the mid-1980s, as the health data industry expanded, computerized applications for managing this growing wealth of data emerged. Several companies introduced "desktop" marketing and planning systems designed to run on microcomputers. Many were patterned after those developed in other industries, but most of these could not survive the transition. Others developed healthcare-specific desktop systems and the major vendors emerged to serve primarily the hospital market. Today, health data management is increasingly being handled via the Internet.

The introduction of desktop market analysis systems made possible the transformation of marketing research from a slow, plodding process of questionable accuracy to a scientific, accurate, and expeditious activity. Proprietary analysis systems offered a number of advances over previous approaches to market analysis. Now, most of these capabilities can be provided online. Internet-based data management systems can produce standardized or custom reports, tables, graphics, and maps pertinent to any application. They have the capability to import data sets in a variety of formats and to incorporate them easily into existing applications. The Internet offers a framework for integrating data from various sources and various federal agencies have committed to making their data accessible via the Internet.

Another important consideration with regard to the management and analysis of data for health planning is the growing importance of geographic information systems (GIS). Spatial analysis, in its various forms, has always been an inherent aspect of the community assessment process. At the same time, epidemiological fieldwork includes spatial analysis as a basic analytical technique. The introduction of high-performance, low-cost GIS applications has contributed greatly to the use of spatial analysis in health-related research. The power of mainframe-based spatial analysis has been brought to the desktop by applications such as MapInfo and ArcView, and even unsophisticated computer users can now generate complex maps. The opportunity for advanced spatial analysis is available to those that require it. Further advances in GIS applications are likely to make these systems even more important for health demographers in the future. The ability to process, manipulate, and disseminate health-related data has improved tremendously due to the advances that have occurred in computer technology. New developments in the areas of data warehousing, data standardization, and large-scale database management capabilities continue to improve the prospects for those requiring health data. Advanced techniques, such as artificial intelligence, fuzzy logic, and neural networks, are now being applied in the healthcare arena, and "predictive modeling" is coming into use by many healthcare organizations.

Ultimately, all of these developments reflect the changes that are occurring in the manner in which health data are being utilized. The demand for better data management and analysis capabilities is being driven by the new approach to health planning demanded by the changing environment. While being able to simply describe a situation in terms of data was a major breakthrough in the past, the new healthcare environment is calling for a much more proactive approach to the use of data. It is no longer sufficient to be able to describe a market area, for example, but the data must be used proactively for decision support and strategic planning.

Further Reading

American Hospital Association. *AHA guide to the healthcare field* (annual). Chicago, IL: American Hospital Association.

American Medical Association. *Socioeconomic characteristics of medical practice* (annual). Chicago, IL: American Medical Association.

American Medical Association. *Physician characteristics and distribution in the U.S.* (annual). Chicago, IL: American Medical Association.

Bureau of Health Professions, U.S. Department of Health and Human Services. Retrieved from http://www.hrsa.dhhs.gov/bhpr

Bureau of Primary Healthcare, U.S. Department of Health and Human Services, Washington, DC. Retrieved from http://bphc.hrsa.gov/

Census Bureau, U.S. Department of Commerce, Washington, DC (see in particular "American Factfinder"). Retrieved from http://www.census.gov

Census Bureau, U.S. Department of Commerce. *County business patterns* (annual). Washington, DC: U.S. Government Printing Office.

Census Bureau, U.S. Department of Commerce. *Information on the North American industry code system*. Retrieved from http://www.census.gov/epcd/www/naics.html

Center for Medicare and Medicaid. Retrieved from www.cms.gov

Center for Mental Health Studies, U.S. Department of Health and Human Services, Washington, DC. Retrieved from http://www.samhsa.gov/cmhs/htm

Centers for Disease Control and Prevention, U.S. Department of Health and Human Services, Atlanta, GA. Retrieved from http://www.cdc.gov

Centers for Disease Control and Prevention. *Morbidity and mortality weekly review* (weekly). Atlanta, GA: Centers for Disease Control and Prevention.

Experian Business Services. Retrieved from www.experian.com

Health Resources and Services Administration, U.S. Department of Health and Human Services, Washington, DC. Retrieved from http://www.hrsa.dhhs.gov

National Center for Health Statistics, U.S. Department of Health and Human Services, Hyattsville, MD. Retrieved from http://www.cdc.gov/nchs

National Center for Health Statistics. *Health United States* (annual). Washington, DC: U.S. Government Printing Office.

Chapter 14
The Future of Health Services Planning

Introduction

At the end of the second decade of the twenty-first century health services planning appears to have entered a new era. Today, health professionals in both public and private settings are increasingly performing planning-like activities even though they may be called something else. Integrated delivery systems are being formed, private and public entities are coming together to address community issues, and community-wide attempts to collect and share health-related data are being initiated. After almost three decades "in the closet," the "p" word is once again being said out loud.

The reasons for this renewed interest in health planning are complex and reflect the changing nature of the healthcare system itself. The factors encouraging this newfound focus on planning include (1) an emphasis on local, community-based approaches to health issues; (2) the perceived failure of "market" approaches; (3) identified deficiencies in public health; (4) the "excesses" that have characterized the private sector; (5) the costs of providing health services under current conditions; and (6) the perceived ineffectiveness of the healthcare system overall. Combined, these factors are driving the search for a new health planning paradigm.

Virtually all of the developments that have occurred make a planning approach in healthcare increasingly important. The paradoxical nature of just a few of the developments reflects the growing need for planning. Who would have ever thought that hospital administrators would be desperately trying to empty beds, providers would be avoiding sick people, clinicians and administrators would be aggressively trying to limit utilization of services, nonclinical personnel would be making "clinical" decisions, and patients would be increasingly perceived as "customers"? These developments clearly indicate a healthcare world turned on end, and the paradoxes they represent have gone a long way toward fostering renewed interest in health services planning.

© Springer Science+Business Media, LLC, part of Springer Nature 2021
R. K. Thomas, *Health Services Planning*,
https://doi.org/10.1007/978-1-0716-1076-3_14

Fueled by these developments, the paradigm shift from an emphasis on "medical care" to an emphasis on "healthcare" received substantial notice at the end of the twentieth century. This shift, involving an expansion of the notion of health into a qualitatively different concept and the broadening of the notion of healthcare to include a wide range of services and behaviors never before considered, seemed to hold promise in the face of a faltering system. This new paradigm inspired a number of "movements"—holistic healthcare, patient-centered care, primary care medical homes, and disease management, to name a few. Yet despite all of the smoke surrounding the new paradigm, there has been very little fire in terms of improving community health.

The new paradigm was not effective in improving population health because it continues to treat health conditions as the problems. It has become increasingly clear that most health problems represent *symptoms* of some deeper issue rather than being the problems themselves. Members of populations who would be clearly considered "sick" by traditional standards often conceptualize health and illness differently from those making the assessment. The public may point to a different set of health problems from those conventionally identified by health professionals, with members of the public often classifying nonmedical problems as medical problems—citing poverty, lack of housing, and lack of access to healthy food and open space among others.

The "inconvenient truth" that emerges from these realizations is that our healthcare system—really, any healthcare system—is not up to the task of improving community health in today's environment. The emphasis remains on treatment and cure rather than prevention, maintenance, and enhancement. The focus on acute conditions still lingers despite the predominance of chronic conditions. When one considers the reasons that people present themselves for treatment we find a mismatch between the skills displayed by the practitioner and the problems presented by the patient. Perhaps less than half of patients present with a physical health problem, with large portions exhibiting emotional, psychological, or addiction issues; dietary or nutritional issues; or some other nonmedical problem.

At the same time, it has become increasingly clear that our society's health problems are being driven by factors that are outside the purview of the healthcare system. In reality, these forces—which are all apparent to health professionals by now—impact groups of people as much as individuals. Poverty does not affect individuals one at a time nor does a toxic environment. The extreme health disparities that have been observed are not a reflection of individual morbidity but of unfavorable health status at the group level.

The New Community Health Planning

While the renewed interest in health planning might be viewed as a revitalization of the comprehensive health planning of the 1960s and 1970s, it is not appropriate to think of contemporary health planning in the same light. Just as the medical care model of the 1960s and 1970s does not represent an appropriate construct for today's healthcare environment, the traditional approach to health planning has little place in today's healthcare world.

What is it about this new planning approach that is different? Why are we not doomed to repeat our past mistakes? A major difference involves the revision of major assumptions regarding health and healthcare. The assumptions underlying the new approach to health planning include the following:

- Healthcare is not simply concerned with the treatment of disease.
- Well people should be the focus of any system of healthcare and keeping them well a primary concern.
- Community health status is not defined by the sum of individual health statuses but is an independent attribute of the community.
- The utilization of health services is not an accurate indicator of actual health services need.
- The utilization of health services can only be partially controlled through restrictions on facilities and services.
- Healthcare cannot be addressed in isolation from other systems in society.
- Healthcare should be measured in terms of quality not quantity.
- The existing delivery system requires significant restructuring in order to be effective.

The passage and implementation of the Affordable Care Act (ACA) of 2010 opened up new opportunities but also introduced new threats. This reality has required planners to develop new strategies. Before the ACA, for example, health plans catered mostly to employers or businesses that provided insurance benefits to their workforce. Today, health plans are marketing directly to individuals and households, who receive incentives under the ACA to have medical insurance coverage. Importantly, provisions of the Affordable Care Act mandate that not-for-profit hospitals conduct regular community health needs assessments. At the time of this writing, the future of the ACA remained uncertain. The elimination of any provisions of the ACA would have significant implications for the healthcare system and for healthcare consumers.

Shifting Emphases

This changing approach to community health planning is reflected in the variety of "shifts" that are occurring within healthcare, shifts that for the most part encourage a planning-oriented environment. These include shifts in the system's conceptual framework, in the scope of healthcare, and in the actual delivery of services. Some of the more important shifts in evidence are outlined below.

From disease control to health management. The traditional approach to health planning mirrored the healthcare system of the day with its emphasis on treatment and cure. It perpetuated the notion that the healthcare system was not activated until an illness or injury occurred. The new health planning focuses on well people rather than sick ones, and reflects the notion that it is easier to keep someone healthy than it is to cure them after they are sick.

From healthcare in isolation to integrated health management. Traditional health planning did not interface with other types of planning, there was no coordination with other institutions or systems in society, and nonclinical issues were felt to have no bearing on health status and health behavior. The more holistic approach of the new health planning involves interfaces with all institutions and emphasizes multi-sector collaboration for collective impact.

From a reactive stance to a proactive stance. The approach to traditional health planning typically represented a reaction to developments that had already occurred in the healthcare arena. Much of the effort was intended to redress wrongs and correct defects in the system. The new health planning, while not ignoring past and present issues, attempts to proactively address anticipated future developments.

From a formalistic orientation to a pragmatic orientation. Because of federal sponsorship, the traditional planning approach exhibited a formal/legal dimension that in many ways handcuffed those involved in planning activities. Rigid guidelines were passed down that were often paid lip service and then ignored in the implementation. The new health planning emphasizes a pragmatic approach that is tailored to the needs of the particular community or organization.

From maintaining control to providing direction. Traditional planning took a legalistic approach in an effort to regulate the operation of the system. Regulations often became the technique of choice for controlling the system. This created an inflexibility that, of necessity, led to a focus on very narrow goals. The new approach emphasizes providing direction for the development of a self-correcting system rather than trying to control its various components.

From nominally comprehensive to broadly comprehensive. To refer to traditional planning as "comprehensive" is to refer to a burger as a four-course meal. Ostensibly, health planning took all aspects of the healthcare delivery system into consideration and, in all fairness, probably did include what was considered the totality of the system at the time. In general, nonclinical aspects of healthcare were not taken into consideration and, importantly, the patient/consumer dimension was not emphasized.

From a public-only approach to public/private cooperation. Traditional community health planning was something that government agencies carried out and, to many, had little to do with the real world of patient care. While private sector healthcare organizations may have tried to influence or even control the process, most felt like it was not about them. The new planning approach is about everyone. Widespread participation is being called for, and the success of these efforts will depend on the extent to which an interface between community-wide and organization-level planning and between public sector and private sector organizations can be affected.

From a narrow constituency to a broad constituency. Despite mandated calls for community involvement in the planning process, any meaningful intercourse inevitably involved a handful of vested interests. It was believed that the operation of the process would directly affect only a few parties and, as implemented, this was probably true. The new planning recognizes a much wider range of interests. Even planning at the organization level is increasingly taking the per-spectives of various groups outside the organization into consideration.

From a utilization-based approach to need-based approach. The essence of health-care in the past was embodied by the notion of service utilization, so utilization levels became a proxy for both demand and need. The new health planning theo-retically, at least, begins with a realistic view of the true prevalence of health problems and predicates planning decisions on that basis. In this view, utilization patterns should represent a response to the true healthcare needs of the popula-tion rather than a phenomenon existing seemingly independent of other factors.

From narrowly defined outcomes to broadly defined outcomes. Under the traditional planning paradigm, outcomes were narrowly defined either in terms of the health status of individuals or compliance with bureaucratic mandates (e.g., no more than four hospital beds per 1000 population). The new approach focuses more on community-wide outcomes such as improved health status and improved access to services. Indeed, reimbursement arrangements are increasingly rewarding pro-viders on the basis of outcomes.

From impact on facilities/services to impact on population outcomes. The yardstick in traditional planning for measuring success was the impact that the process had on the inventory of facilities and services. The extent to which these were added or not added to the service complement was the measure of planning effective-ness. There was a clear disconnect between the technical application of planning methodologies and the actual impact the actions had on the community's health status. The question in the future will not be how it was done, but what was the impact of any action on the health status of the population.

While each of these shifts has important implications in its own right, taken together they represent a major reorientation for the healthcare arena. This is clearly a situation that demands efficient change management processes, and the planning process provides the foundation for addressing change. The need for a revitalized planning approach has been recognized by various parties, and increased financial support is slowly emerging.

Federal agencies like the Healthcare Resources and Services Administration (HRSA) within the U.S. Department of Health and Human Services have begun supporting planning initiatives through various programs. If not directly supporting planning activities, other programs are providing funds to improve the healthcare infrastructure to allow for more effective planning, through improvements in infor-mation technology and data availability, for example. National foundations like the Robert Wood Johnson Foundation are funding initiatives that involve a community planning component. Professional associations like the American Hospital Association have developed software applications to support community planning. While these developments still represent relatively isolated events, they do provide evidence of a slowly developing surge of interest in health planning.

Because of the failure of the late-twentieth-century healthcare to solve our healthcare problems, there is growing interest in the concept of population health among health professionals, policy analysts, and government agencies. As an approach that assesses health from a population rather than a patient perspective, it represents an opportunity for developing a better understanding of the health status of populations—whether they are patients or not—and an innovative approach to improving community health status. The concept is still evolving and the term "population health" has been used very inconsistently. Healthcare providers claim that they are using a population health approach to more efficiently manage their patients; consultants have rebranded themselves as population health experts to capitalize on this trend; and vendors claim to be able to support their clients' population health needs. Yet, it is clear that when one looks beneath the surface there is widespread misunderstanding of the concept at best and outright misuse of the term at worst.

Population health involves an assessment of the health status of a population that uses aggregate data on nonmedical as well as medical factors to measure the totality of health and well-being of that population and leverages this information for the improvement of community health.

As a verb, population health refers to an approach to improving health status that operates at the population level rather than the individual (or patient) level. The approach focuses on social pathology rather than biological pathology and involves the "treatment" of conditions within the environment and policy realms in addition to the provision of clinical services to individual patients. While an underlying assumption is that a population health approach aims to improve health status by focusing on the healthcare needs and resources of *populations* not individuals, it does not rule out specific patient-based medical treatment but views healthcare as only one component of a health improvement initiative.

> *Population health, v.*, An approach to improving community health status that focuses on populations rather individuals and addresses the root causes and structural impediments of ill health rather than exclusively focusing on treating the symptoms/conditions of individuals.

The application of the population health model can be explored at two different levels—a microlevel view that considers population health as it relates to the delivery of care and a macro-level view that considers population health from a societal perspective. At the microlevel one approach might be to identify individuals at high risk and intervene to reduce their risk. At that level the life circumstances of individuals and households are emphasized. At the macro-level the approach might involve reducing the average risk level for the total population by initiatives or policies addressing the social determinants of health. At that level social determinants of health are emphasized. Going forward every health planner must be familiar with this emerging paradigm. More and more organizations—public and private—are buying into the population health model, and it is expected to have a major impact on health services planning going forward.

The New Organizational Health Planning

Planning at the organization level does not seem to be undergoing the same degree of change as community-wide planning. However, organization-level planning does appear to be gaining momentum. Planning has become an increasingly important function within all types of healthcare organizations, although the "p" word itself may not always be used. It is becoming increasingly difficult to find any health professional, in fact, who has not been involved in some type of planning activity.

Many of the developments in healthcare that have encouraged community-wide planning are also contributing to the interest in planning within healthcare organizations. Pressure to contain costs, be accountable, demonstrate effective outcomes, and efficiently manage data are as important for private sector healthcare organizations as they are for public health entities. In fact, in many ways they are more important given the increasingly competitive healthcare environment.

On the other hand, there are some important differences in what is happening at the two different levels of planning. At the organization level, for example, the implications of not planning are often immediate and disastrous. This reflects the fact that a rapidly evolving healthcare environment demands the ability to expeditiously make decisions in response to market developments. Another difference evinced by organization-level planning is the focus on the consumer. The fact that organization-level planning has become market driven means that the behavior patterns and attitudes of consumers take on new meaning within the planning context. The costs involved in a wrong decision are certainly another consideration facing planners at the organization level.

One final difference that might be noted between community-wide and organization-level planning is the involvement of large, national corporations in the healthcare "space" occupied by many organizations. These organizations, which are often for-profit, are likely to have experience in various types of planning that a local organization might not have. The ability to plan from a national perspective sets organization-level planning apart from more community-based health planning initiatives.

Many components of the healthcare industry have progressed through the stages of the industry life cycle to the point of maturity and beyond. Perhaps the most outstanding example of this phenomenon relates to traditional inpatient care. As is typical of a mature industry entering decline, organizations that provide hospital services find that few new patients or population groups are demanding the service, most of the desirable patient groups have been captured, and relationships between providers and consumers are typically well established. There are few new major breakthroughs in treatment, the major players are becoming consolidated, and profit margins are becoming leaner. Since there are few new customers, the emphasis is on retaining existing customers and extracting as much from them as possible.

The purveyors of hospital-based care and certain other services are faced with an environment that calls for a particular planning approach. The needs of organizations that are mature or in decline are much different from those experiencing growth. Therefore, the planning approach must be tailored to the organization's position within the life cycle and its particular market. Planning for an approach that emphasizes "maintenance" is much different from planning for one that emphasizes expansion.

A parallel phenomenon reflects the emergence of new growth markets within healthcare. Healthcare might be likened to an air mattress to the extent that a reduction of services in one area is invariably offset by an increase in services in another. When an area is depressed, another tends to rise up. As certain segments of the industry have declined in importance, other segments have emerged. New services and products, as well as the repackaging of existing services and products, are frequent developments within the industry. Further, new organizational structures and innovative relationships are continually evolving.

Developments of this type in healthcare today are almost too numerous to mention. Some are fairly specific and include therapeutic techniques like laser surgery and other forms of microsurgery, new drug offerings, and various nutritional regimen that are being promoted. Others may involve emerging systems of care such as the various alternative therapy techniques that are being offered. Some of these may even involve repackaging existing services in a more contemporary guise. This would include the repackaging of subacute care, rehabilitation services, and home healthcare as "post-acute care." In many cases, this means converting a mature or declining service into a new business line.

Health planners at the organizational level must become knowledgeable about *population health management*. This approach applies the principles of population health (discussed in Chap. 4) to the management of a defined group of patients, employees, insurance plan members, or consumers. The intent is to manage utilization of services and control costs.

Population health management takes a proactive approach to increasing the efficiency of provider organizations for addressing the demands of the new healthcare environment. This approach emphasizes quality over quantity, prevention over treatment, group outcomes over individual patient outcomes, and, importantly, keeping people well rather than treating them after they become ill.

Although the changes in planning at the organization level have not been as radical as they appear to be in the community planning arena, there is one area in which this shift appears to be more dramatic. This involves the long-overdue change in the *mindset* of health professionals. Health professionals have been perhaps the most resistant of any group of professionals to the notion of planning. Yet, today, there is a growing conviction that planning should be an integral function of any healthcare organization.

Clearly the shift in focus from internally oriented types of planning to more externally oriented types has progressed significantly. The emphasis appears to be increasingly on strategic planning, marketing planning, and business planning, while less attention is devoted to facilities planning and operational planning. This trend is likely to continue as healthcare organizations become less tied to bricks and mortar and more dependent on relationships with other organizations.

Resource Availability

The improved availability of planning resources has contributed to the increased effectiveness of the planning efforts by health planners at both the community and organization levels. In retrospect, it is amazing that planning with any degree of effectiveness was even possible during the "golden age" of comprehensive health planning. Few people, inside or outside of healthcare, had much planning expertise. There was very limited data available with which to work, and virtually no applicable technology. Today, a number of developments are contributing to a more positive planning environment. Some of the major advances in planning support are described below.

Planning Expertise

At the inception of the comprehensive health planning act in the 1960s, planning as an art and science was not well developed. There were few individuals with the skill to develop a planning process and few models to emulate. Planning was only becoming established in other industries and, even here, these experiences did not translate well into the healthcare arena.

Today, planning methodologies, particularly at the organizational level, have become highly developed. In fact, other industries have progressed to a new level of sophistication while healthcare organizations are still struggling with the basics. Nevertheless, numerous tools are now available, and there is considerable expertise to draw upon. While much of this expertise has not been developed in a formal planning context, skills in research, analysis, project planning, marketing, and so forth provide a base on which to develop planning capabilities.

Data Resources

Traditional health planning emerged in a data-poor environment. This is not to say that healthcare organizations were not generating data, they were. However, the data that were generated tended to be proprietary for the most part and inaccessible to planners or the general public. There was little in the way of national databases, and federal and state governments were decades away from making their data readily available.

Today, not only do we have access to many more databases than we have had in the past, but we also have detailed data on utilization and costs heretofore unavailable. Although gaps still exist with regard to certain types of data, the availability of most types of data has increased dramatically. Organizations in both the public and private sectors have begun generating new data sets. Moreover, efforts are underway by various entities, particularly the federal government, to make existing data more accessible and affordable for the healthcare community.

Technology Resources

Traditional health planning emerged in an environment with virtually no technological support. These early initiatives predated the widespread use of computers by nearly 20 years. Without computers there could be no database management systems and no geographic information systems. In fact, until the 1980s, maps were still typically colored by hand.

If only the basic technological capabilities available today are considered, this alone would carry planning to a new era. Inexpensive, user-friendly geographic information system software has made the creation of sophisticated maps relatively easy. These basic technological capabilities are now being supplemented with data warehousing and other data integration capabilities, online analytical capabilities, advanced financial management capabilities, and a wide range of software development resources that have carried this process light years beyond even the twentieth century.

Financial Acumen

The approach to the financial component in healthcare in traditional health planning was superficial at best. Only now are we beginning to gain an understanding of the costs of providing care and to develop adequate financial analysis capabilities. Driven primarily by the changing reimbursement environment, healthcare organizations have been forced to develop a much more in-depth understanding of costs than at any time in the past. The notion that it was impossible to truly cost out healthcare has been discarded, and sophisticated approaches to cost accounting have been developed.

The Convergence of Community and Organizational Planning

One trend that is likely to influence the future of health planning is the convergence of community-level and organization-level planning. It has already been observed that public health agencies are being expected to apply a more private sector orientation to their tasks and that private sector organizations are adopting techniques from public health to address the needs of their enrolled populations. While these activities do not constitute the actual convergence of these two distinct approaches, they do suggest the existence of much more commonality than in the past.

Some of the areas of commonality that are emerging include an interest in community assessment and the health status of the total population (rather than only patients), a more proactive approach to addressing the needs of the medically indigent, and a growing emphasis on health promotion and health education. The "community" is increasingly being defined as the "customer" by both public and private organizations. To the extent that planning is occurring, at both levels it appears to be adopting an outside-in approach.

This convergence is also evidenced by the establishment of public/private initiatives to address a variety of health issues, including many, such as housing, drug abuse, and violence that have historically been considered outside the healthcare arena. For these purposes, representatives from such sectors as housing, education, criminal justice, and transportation among others are becoming involved. This collaboration has extended to the sharing of health-related data and there are now numerous attempts to establish community health information networks underway.

The New Health Planner

These developments in planning call for a new type of health planner and a new skill set. This does not mean simply adding contemporary quantitative techniques to traditional approaches but it really involves the adaptation of a different mindset from that of the traditional planning approach of the 1960s and 1970s. The planning concept at that time involved a narrow technical approach that emphasized the mechanical and quantitative aspects of planning. It was also an approach that isolated planning from implementation.

This is not to say that the skills that were important in the early days of health planning are no longer important, they are. These skills must be supplemented by different types of skills that are more appropriate for the new planning paradigm. The traditional planning approach—indeed all planning activities—requires analytical skills, an attention to detail, precision, timeliness, and follow-through. A complete familiarity with the steps involved in the planning process will always be important.

The new planning paradigm calls for a higher order of skills to supplement these basic technical skills. These new demands reflect the changes that have occurred in the nature of planning. The planning process is becoming much more system oriented and involves a much wider range of stakeholders than the traditional approach. Health services planners—in both the public and private sectors—must be able to think much more conceptually, possess qualitative as well as quantitative skills, and be able to work successfully in multiple settings. The new planner must be politically astute, be able to demonstrate leadership, carry out negotiations, and facilitate the planning process.

Unlike the lockstep planning environment of the past, the new planner must be able to live with ambiguity and demonstrate flexibility and creativity. It is one thing to perform calculations to determine if there is an oversupply of hospital beds; it is quite another to develop a plan for the creative reuse of an abandoned hospital building. This calls for broad experiences on the part of the planner and a grounding in the real world. After all, health services planning is increasingly business planning.

Skills are also required in technical areas such as information management and financial analysis. With regard to the former, a grounding in technology is not so important—the technology rapidly changes—but an appreciation of information management issues is critical. Every plan in the future is going to have a financial component, so a working knowledge of financial analysis, third-party reimbursement, and managed care negotiations will become increasingly important.

Communications skills will become more important than ever. The planner as facilitator will be required to make a case in written and oral form. As the role of the planner expands and the emphasis becomes more qualitative, the importance of communications skills increases.

The highly circumscribed role of the planner under the traditional planning paradigm is giving way to a much broader role that is essentially without limits. It can be argued, in fact, that by virtue of being a planner, no aspect of the system or organization is off-limits. The technical support function of the planner is being replaced by one of facilitator. This is being expanded by increased demands for decision-making on the part of the planning team. The responsibilities will be further expanded as planners are increasingly urged to take part in the implementation process.

Further Reading

Deloitte. (2019). *The health plan of tomorrow.* Retrieved from https://www2.deloitte.com/content/dam/insights/us/articles/4920_Health-plans-of-the-future/DI_Health-plan-of-tomorrow.pdf

Harvard Business Review. (2018). *The future of healthcare.* October digital edition. Retrieved from https://hbr.org/insight-center/the-future-of-health-care

International Journal of Quality in Healthcare. Retrieved from https://academic.oup.com/intqhc/article/30/10/823/5253761

The George Washington University. (2019). *How we can expect the healthcare industry to change in the future.* Retrieved from https://healthcaremba.gwu.edu/blog/how-we-can-expect-the-healthcare-industry-to-change-in-the-future/

Appendix A: Community-Wide Planning Examples

A Statewide Planning Initiative

Overview

The materials that follow offer a realistic example, albeit hypothetical, of a community-wide planning process. The state of Columbia (the newly added 51st state) was embarking upon its initial statewide health plan. Since the state had no previous experience with health planning, the process had to be established from the ground up. The initiative was to be spearheaded by the newly formed Office of Health Planning and Development (OHPD) within the state Department of Health.

Planning for Planning

The first step in the planning process was to establish the mission for this component of the Department's activities. In this case, the mission was established by the state Department of Health in consultation with the governor's office and other relevant state agencies. The mission as formulated was as follows: The Office of Health Planning and Development will establish a comprehensive plan for the coordination of all public and private healthcare organizations in the state with the intent of providing accessible, high-quality care to all of the state's citizens.

The next step involved establishing a planning team for carrying out the mission. A process was established by OHPD for soliciting recommendations for planning team participants. Guidelines were provided to assure that representatives of all stakeholders were included. Membership was to include not only health professionals but also adequate representation by consumer groups and patient advocates. It also called for the inclusion of "neutral" individuals who possessed technical expertise in the areas of healthcare administration, information management, clinical areas, and public health, among others. The staff of OHPD was to provide technical support for the project.

© Springer Science+Business Media, LLC, part of Springer Nature 2021   361
R. K. Thomas, *Health Services Planning*,
https://doi.org/10.1007/978-1-0716-1076-3

An outline of the planning process was developed that indicated the procedures that would be followed, the roles of the various participants, and a time frame for completing the plan. This outline would serve as the basis for the project plan that would ultimately be developed.

Initial Information Gathering

The information-gathering process began with the compilation of existing materials on healthcare in the state. Since this was the first planning initiative, little planning-specific material was expected to be available. However, the Department of Health had begun reporting vital statistics, collecting utilization data from hospitals, and compiling inventories of various health professionals. This information served as a starting point for data collection and as a basis for identifying data gaps that would be filled during the intensive research phase.

The next step was to conduct interviews with a wide range of key informants who held a perspective on various aspects of the system. A general outline for information gathering was established, with the intent of identifying the key issues and the most pressing health-related needs. Representatives of the various government agencies that were involved in any way with healthcare were included. In addition to Department of Health staff, these informants included representatives of the state mental health agency, the alcohol and drug bureau, the traffic safety bureau, the environmental protection office, the Department of Children's Services, the insurance regulation office, and the Medicaid office. The information from these informants was supplemented by representatives of local health departments.

Additional interviews were conducted with representatives of private sector healthcare organizations. These included representatives of the major general and specialty hospitals, allied health personnel, and alternative therapists. Professional organizations were represented by spokespersons for the statewide hospital association, nursing home association, home health association, medical society, and dental society. Interviews were conducted with representatives of the two medical schools in the state, as well as officials with selected nursing schools.

Interviews were conducted with representatives of voluntary associations and consumer groups. Either the statewide office or the most active of the chapters of the Cancer Society, Heart Association, and other voluntary organizations were tapped for information. Consumer groups representing the mentally ill, the disabled, the elderly, and other relevant groups were interviewed. Interviews were also conducted with representatives of the business community, including the Chamber of Commerce, major employers, and local business coalitions.

Once these interviews were completed and the information compiled, it was possible to begin identifying the issues and considering the direction that the planning initiative would take. The issue that appeared to be the most pervasive centered on the lack of access to basic primary care services, particularly for residents of rural areas and impoverished urban areas, although most of the population was at some disadvantage in this regard. Within this context, the specific issues that were identified included teenage and out-of-wedlock pregnancies, the unmet needs of the severely mentally ill, and chronic disease management for the growing elderly population. Many additional issues were identified and all would be further explored during the research process.

Stating Assumptions

As the planning team began to compile information, it formulated the assumptions that would drive the planning process. Since this was a new initiative, there were no explicit assumptions in place. The following assumptions were initially stated, with the notion that they would be revised as appropriate as the process progressed.

1. There are no preconceived notions concerning the goals of the plan or the form that any solution should take.
2. It will be possible to obtain cross-agency cooperation from the various agencies of relevance for the planning process.
3. Private sector organizations will gladly offer input but may be less willing to effect radical changes.
4. The business community is behind the process and is willing to provide a wide range of support services.
5. A lack of adequate information management capabilities is likely to be a major barrier to data collection and processing.
6. Any successful plan implementation will require the support of certain powerful consumer advocacy groups.

Baseline Data Collection

The first step in the formal data collection process involved an environmental assessment. Although the focus was to be restricted to the District of Columbia for planning purposes, it was still important to consider national trends that might have implications for developments at the state level.

Broad societal trends were analyzed and their implications for the local environment considered. These societal trends included demographic trends, economic considerations, and lifestyle and consumer attitude trends. The same type of analysis was applied to healthcare industry trends to identify any developments that are likely to affect the local community. These included trends in healthcare financing, changing organizational structures within the delivery system, and introduction of new treatment modalities.

Regulatory, political, and legal developments were reviewed for their implications for the community and affected organizations. At the state level itself, a number of initiatives were being considered by various agencies and by the state legislature that would have implications for the issues being addressed in the planning process.

Developments in the area of technology were reviewed, including medical and surgical treatment modalities, pharmaceuticals, biomedical equipment, and information management.

National trends in reimbursement were reviewed and the implications for the state considered. Of particular importance were trends in managed care and in government-sponsored insurance programs. The emergence of managed care within the state had already influenced both practice patterns and provider relationships. Potential changes in either the Medicare or the Medicaid programs needed to be considered for their impact on the provision of health services within the state.

This review of the social, political, economic, and technological trends affecting the environment provided a starting point for subsequent background research and a context in which additional knowledge could be framed.

Profiling the State's Population

In profiling the population to be affected by the plan, it was initially assumed that the state's boundaries appropriately delineated the geographic unit for planning purposes. While this was generally the case, it was found that three health service areas in the state actually crossed state lines. These "irregularities" had to be taken into consideration for planning purposes.

The characteristics of the state and its resident population were determined through the environmental assessment. The main categories of data that were collected are listed below:

- *Demographic Characteristics*

    - Age distribution
    - Sex distribution
    - Racial/ethnic distribution

- *Sociocultural Characteristics*

    - Marital status
    - Household characteristics
    - Income distribution
    - Educational level
    - Occupational characteristics
    - Industry characteristics

- *Psychographic Characteristics*
- *Insurance Coverage*
- *Attitudes*

    - Perceptions
    - Preferences
    - Expectations

The data necessary for environmental assessment were obtained from various state agencies, from secondary sources like the Census Bureau, and from commercial data vendors that offer population estimates and projections and psychographic profiles. A general profile of insurance coverage was pieced together using data from various sources. Ultimately, however, primary research had to be conducted to develop better data on insurance coverage and consumer attitudes.

Determining Health Status

The next step in establishing a baseline involved an examination of the health status of the community and the target populations identified. Information was collected on fertility patterns within the community, the target population's morbidity characteristics, and its patterns of mortality. Some data on all three of these categories were available from county health departments, and this information was supplemented by data from the state health department. Fertility and mortality data were relatively easy to acquire since these data are officially compiled by the health department.

Morbidity data, on the other hand, was more difficult to obtain. Except for the collection of data on certain notifiable diseases by the health department, there was no systematic source of data on morbidity. This data gap was approached from a couple of different angles. The first involved the collection of data from those organizations that were most heavily involved in serving the state's population. Data that indicated the types of diagnoses characterizing their patient populations and the types of procedures performed on their clients were obtained from the public hospital and the health department. Information was also available from some of the community-based clinics and mental health centers that serve this population. These steps provided some actual data from which to begin to understand the morbidity profile.

A second approach involved obtaining data from the National Center for Health Statistics that indicated, based on national survey data, the types of health conditions that would characterize populations with various attributes. This survey data could be used to estimate the morbidity profile of the target population. By looking at prevalence rates for the population with certain racial, income, and age characteristics, it was possible to develop a "proxy" profile of the population's morbidity status. Selective information was also available on indicators of morbidity at the state level from various national sources. Indicators of obesity and cholesterol levels, for example, were available from various federally sponsored surveys.

Health status indicators were subsequently developed that allowed comparisons with various standards. For example, the infant mortality rate was compared to that for other comparable states, to the national average, and to the standards set out in the Healthy People 2020 initiative. The same process was followed for such other relevant indicators as mortality rates, premature and low-birth-weight births, and teenage pregnancy.

A critical step here was to convert indicators of health status into health service needs. The prevalence of certain conditions could be directly converted into some measure of need; in other cases, the conversion was more indirect. Ultimately, however, the planning team was required to estimate the types and characteristics of the health services required by the state's population in the future.

Health Behavior

The next step in the process involved determining the level of activity for a broad range of health behavior. The following types of formal health behavior were reviewed as part of the research:

- *Inpatient Admissions*

    - Hospital admissions
    - Nursing home admissions
    - Residential treatment center admissions
    - Mental health facility admissions

- *Outpatient Visits*

    - Hospital outpatient visits
    - Hospital emergency room visits
    - Physician office visits
    - Other clinician office visits
    - Urgent care visits
    - Diagnostic center visits
    - Surgicenter visits
    - Mental health center visits

- *Other Service Utilization*

    - Home health visits
    - Physical therapy treatments
    - Alternative therapy visits

- *Procedures Performed*
- *Prescriptions Written*

Informal types of health behavior were also reviewed, although there was considerably less "hard" data on these activities. Some state-level data were available from national sources on a number of factors such as seat belt use, dietary patterns, and patterns of smoking and alcohol use. Certain other data were available from state records, including information on the use of prenatal care and the level of childhood immunization.

This information was supplemented by primary research that involved a sample survey of the state's population. This survey collected data on health status characteristics and health behavior. In addition, it obtained data on the attitudes, perceptions, and expectations of the state's population.

Community Resources Inventory

For a statewide comprehensive planning effort such as this, a wide range of resources needed to be identified and inventoried. These included, at a minimum, healthcare facilities and equipment, healthcare programs and services, health personnel, and financing options. Examples of the components of each category that were identified include the following:

- *Healthcare Facilities*

  - Hospitals
  - Nursing homes
  - Physician offices
  - Community clinics
  - Nonphysician clinical offices
  - Residential treatment centers
  - Assisted living facilities (and other residential units for seniors)
  - Mental health facilities
  - Home health agencies/hospices
  - Urgent care centers
  - Freestanding diagnostic centers
  - Freestanding surgery centers
  - Specialty treatment centers (e.g., pain management)

- *Healthcare Equipment*

  - Biomedical equipment
  - Information technology
  - Emergency services equipment

- *Health Personnel*

  - Physicians
  - Nurses
  - Nurse clinicians, physician's assistants, and other physician extenders
  - Dentists
  - Optometrists
  - Podiatrists
  - Chiropractors
  - Mental health professionals

- Rehabilitation therapists (e.g., physical therapists, speech therapists)
- Clinical support personnel (e.g., radiology technologists)
- Administrative support personnel (e.g., medical records technicians)
- Alternative therapists

• *Programs and Services*

- Inpatient programs/services
- Hospital outpatient programs/services
- Ambulatory care programs/services
- Long-term care services
- Community-based services
- Home health services

• *Funding Sources*

- Commercial insurance (including managed care)
- Medicare (including Medicare HMOs)
- Medicaid
- Other federally funded programs (e.g., Veterans Administration)
- State funding sources (e.g., mental health services)
- Local funding sources (e.g., public hospital subsidy)

• *Networks and Relationships*

- Formal hospital alliances
- Integrated delivery systems
- Provider networks
- Chain-operated facilities (e.g., hospitals, nursing homes)
- Contractual relationships

This process resulted in the establishment of the first inventory of healthcare resources in the state, thereby serving an important purpose in its own right. This information was incorporated into a computerized database that would allow for ongoing updating and enhancement as the planning process continued. This inventory was invaluable for the next step in the process, the assessment of the healthcare situation across the state.

Assessing Health Status and Healthcare Resources

At this point, a gap analysis was conducted to determine the extent of the mismatch between identified health problems and the resources available. The healthcare needs of the population identified were compared to the types, levels, and characteristics of the resources available across the state. Thus, the number of hospital beds required for the population was compared to the number of beds in operation. The number of physicians needed in various specialty categories was compared to the existing physician pool. The level of behavioral health needs was compared to the behavioral health resources available, and so on for each category of need.

It was important to not only examine the existing relationship between needs and resources, but also to project this relationship into the future. If the need for a certain service was decreasing, the future availability of that service should be considered. More importantly, if the need for a service was increasing, the extent to which the services available were also increasing became an issue. In this case, it was found, for example, that the need for services related to the AIDS population and the Alzheimer's population was increasing rapidly, with every indication that these needs would continue to grow in the future. In contrast, there had been only limited expansion in the resources available to meet these needs, and this shortfall had to be considered in the planning process.

Summarizing the Preliminary Analysis

Enough information was now available to present a state-of-the-state report to the various stakeholders. This report included a comprehensive description of the community environment, a status report on key organizations, and a report assessing the overall status of the community or market area. This status report also included the strengths, weaknesses, opportunities, and threats identified during the analysis.

The major conclusions derived from the analysis to this point included the following:

- The health status of the state's population could be considered "normal" overall.
- On the other hand, there were a number of indicators for which the state deviated negatively from national averages.
- A number of subgroups could be identified that were well below accepted standards for health status.
- A number of issues existed that required immediate attention.
- Private sector healthcare resources were highly developed (to the point of experiencing overcapacity).
- The public sector was poorly developed statewide; in fact, the "safety net" appeared to be deteriorating.

These generalized conclusions were supported by specific details for each category of healthcare issues. These conclusions became the basis on which subsequent plan development was founded.

Developing the Plan

The effort up to this point provided the foundation for the actual development of the plan. If the initial work was properly carried out, the planning process should flow smoothly, at least from a technical perspective.

A mission statement that had been developed at the outset was reviewed. This step represented an opportunity to clarify the mission of the organization before moving forward with the planning process.

Setting the Goal(s)

Since planning was being conducted for the entire state, a number of goals were identified by the planning team. Separate goals were developed for each of the following areas:

- Primary care access
- Reproductive health
- Chronic disease management
- Behavioral healthcare
- Lifestyle education
- Elder care
- HIV/AIDS management

A number of additional goals were considered, and it was determined that this first effort at a state plan should focus on those issues considered the most pressing.

Each of the goals was clearly stated. As an example, the goal related to reproductive issues was stated as follows: To create an environment that fosters quality reproductive health for all segments of the state's population.

Setting Objectives

For every goal a number of objectives were specified. The objectives for the goal for reproductive issues just stated included the following.

- To reduce the infant mortality rate from a state average of 12/1000 live births to 9/1000 within 5 years
- To reduce the proportion of births that are premature from 18% to 12% within 3 years
- To reduce the proportion of births that occur to adolescents from 13% to 9% within 3 years
- To reduce the proportion of births that occur out of wedlock from 32% to 20% within 3 years

In each case, any barriers to accomplishing the stated objectives were considered. In this case, it was found, for example, that a lack of educational programs on sexual activities available to junior high and high school students would be a significant barrier to reducing teen pregnancies. This was considered a barrier that could be addressed, so the objective was retained.

Prioritizing Objectives

Since it was not possible to achieve all of the identified objectives within a reasonable time period, the prioritization of objectives became necessary. A set of criteria were agreed upon to help determine the order of priority. Among the selected criteria were the following:

- What are the most urgent issues—issues that will bring about dire consequences if they are not resolved?
- What are the pivotal issues—issues that contribute most directly to the mission and goals?
- Which objectives will provide the greatest return for the planning "investment"?
- Which objectives can be achieved quicker, easier, and less expensively than others?
- Which objectives will result in the most visible and most tangible results?
- Which objectives will have the most lasting impact and/or can maintain themselves over time?
- Which objectives will involve multiple benefits if they are achieved?

With these criteria in mind, it was possible to review the numerous objectives and prioritize them in the implementation plan. The unanticipated consequences of meeting the various objectives were discussed, and any potentially negative consequences were addressed. Few negative implications were identified but, in the case of reproductive health, there was some concern raised with regard to aggressive efforts at birth control within certain minority populations.

Specifying Actions

Once the objectives were identified, the next step was to specify the actions necessary for carrying out the objectives. For each objective a number of action steps was identified. For the objective of reducing infant mortality, for example, the actions that were identified included the following:

- Develop a promotional campaign encouraging good health practices during pregnancy
- Develop school-based programs that teach healthy lifestyles before, during, and after pregnancy
- Develop materials to be distributed to organizations, clubs, and other groups that interface with high-risk women
- Develop financial incentives and disincentives that discourage additional births to unmarried women
- Develop a monitoring system to assure that all pregnant women obtain adequate nutrition during pregnancy

Implementing the Plan

As is often the case, plan implementation turned out to be a greater challenge than plan development. Although the OHPD had the authority to carry out certain actions and to influence the actions of some other entities, it did not have much leverage with most private sector healthcare organizations. Thus, in developing the implementation plan, the focus was on those activities over which OHPD was likely to have the most control.

The first step in plan implementation involved the development of a project plan. The project plan originally developed for the planning process was extended to include the implementation phase. It indicated the sequence of events that must occur and established the critical path for the achievement of each objective.

Further, an implementation matrix was developed using a spreadsheet that laid out who was to do what and when they were to do it. The matrix listed every action called for by the plan, breaking each action down into tasks. For each action or task the responsible party was identified, along with any secondary parties that should be involved in this activity. The matrix indicated resource requirements (in terms of staff time, money, and other requirements) and the start and end dates for each activity. Finally, benchmarks were established that allowed the planning team to determine when the activity had been completed.

Means of Implementation

Two important considerations in preparing for plan implementation dealt with the need for more effective internal communications and the need to present a coordinated effort to address issues in the statewide healthcare environment. A major component of implementation involved the development of internal communication mechanisms among various state agencies. This included agencies directly involved with health issues and those that had some indirect involvement (e.g., traffic safety, drug abuse). The intent here was to assure that all parties had adequate information on needs and resources and that information flowed freely from one component of state government to the next.

This implementation plan relied heavily on the information systems within state government. It came as no surprise, however, that the current information management system could not adequately support this initiative. This led to the initiation of a feasibility study on cross-departmental information systems that would serve a number of purposes besides communicating on healthcare issues.

The other implementation initiative involved developing more formal relationships with agencies outside of state government, including private sector providers. This was to begin with a period of general discussions or a "get-to-know-you" phase, followed by more formal attempts at data sharing and coordination of activities. The ultimate goal was to develop a statewide system of public/private care that assured that no gaps existed in the provision of services to any segment of the population.

The Evaluation Plan

During the early stages of the planning process, an evaluation plan was outlined that involved both process and outcome evaluation. The project's technical support staff constantly monitored the activities that were occurring and submitted regular reports on the extent to which the process was on schedule and the various processional benchmarks were being met.

The objectives that were established during plan development were used as the ultimate outcome criteria, and the extent to which these objectives were met would be the final measure of success. However, since most objectives called for a 3–5-year time frame, it was important that the team's success in meeting intermediate targets be assessed. Thus, the technical staff used the project plan and the implementation matrix as the basis for evaluating interim progress. This ongoing evaluation not only provided a regular source of information for those involved in planning but also encouraged those charged with carrying out the various steps to act in an expeditious manner.

Revision and Replanning

It is unlikely that a health plan will be completed without being modified in one way or another. This type of "on-the-fly" revision is inevitable in a rapidly changing environment. There will always be developments that occur subsequently to the initiation of planning that will affect the plan or its implementation. Additional information may become available during the course of the plan. Various parties may take actions in anticipation of the plan that have implications for the process and plan implementation. Developments may occur that affect resource requirements.

Ideally, each component of the planning process should be revisited with these concerns in mind. All assumptions should be reviewed along with the mission statement. Baseline data should be updated to account for the time lapse since the planning process was initiated. The strategy chosen should be reviewed to determine if it is still the best approach in view of possible changes in the environment. For example, has the collaborative strategy selected failed due to unanticipated turnover on the part of key officials? The goals and objectives should be revisited to assure that they are still appropriate in the light of any changes in either the internal or the external environment.

The process should have the flexibility to adapt to developments that occur during the course of plan development and implementation. Planners must remain open to these developments and realize that planning is an iterative process that will be constantly reshaped by a wide range of factors.

A Community Health Planning Initiative

Overview

Metro County Government has established a Department of Health Policy (DHP) that is charged with coordinating the provision of primary care to the medically indigent population within the county. In order to carry out its mission, a plan of action was required. DHP staff initiated a process that would allow for the development of a comprehensive approach to meeting the healthcare needs of the community's medically indigent. Since "medically indigent" was defined in the DHP mission statement as those enrolled in the Medicaid program, those without any form of health insurance, and those whose insurance does not provide an adequate level of coverage, these populations were the target for the planning initiative.

Planning for Planning

The first step in planning for planning was to identify the various public sector agencies that were involved in the provision of health services to the medically indigent. Key individuals involved with these organizations were identified and tapped for participation. Any organizations within the private sector that were providing health services to the medically indigent were also identified. These included hospitals that provided a significant level of charity care, community-based health clinics, and major community mental health centers, among others. Community physicians who serve a primarily indigent population were identified as well.

DHP established a planning task force that involved representatives of the above groups. Two DHP staff persons were assigned to provide technical support to the task force. An expert on health services research in the community was identified and engaged as a consultant to provide external oversight to the project. The task force reviewed the DHP mission statement, established an outline of the process to be followed during the planning initiative, made initial assignments to subcommittees, and laid out a tentative timetable for the planning process.

Initial Information Gathering

Although some preliminary information had been collected prior to establishing the task force, another phase of information gathering was initiated once the task force was in place. The task force itself was a good place to start, since it represented the key stakeholders with regard to the medically indigent. Interviews with task force members identified many of the key issues and provided the foundation for developing an outline to be used in interviewing other members of the community.

It was discovered in this initial round of interviews that (1) certain key public officials had not been included, (2) there was more private sector involvement in dealing with this population than originally thought, and (3) several of the truly vulnerable populations were not represented on the task force. Steps were taken to obtain input from representatives from each of these categories in order to round out the task force's understanding of the issues.

The initial data-gathering process also involved a review of existing reports, studies, and previously prepared technical papers. The public hospital and the health department had both utilized consultants at various times in the past, and these reports were obtained. Financial audits had been performed on most of the key organizations at one time or another, and this information was obtained as well. The health department had applied for numerous grants, and the data included in these applications was very useful. Information was obtained from several certificate-of-need applications that the public hospital had filed with the state. The local university had, through its healthcare administration program, carried out a number of studies on this population that also provided useful background information.

At the same time, efforts were made to identify any existing databases on the local health system in general and on the medically indigent population in particular. The availability of data from the public hospital, the county health department, the publicly operated nursing homes, and other local healthcare organizations was determined. Any data resources maintained by local universities were identified, along with data available from community-based clinics and mental health centers. The local offices of the Medicaid program, the Food Stamp program, the state welfare agency, and the state nutritional program were contacted for information. Statewide agencies such as the Department of Health, the Department of Children's Services, the environmental monitoring agencies, and other relevant agencies were contacted to determine the types of data they could make available. Data from these sources were collated, processed, and analyzed by the task force's technical staff.

Numerous conclusions were drawn from this initial round of information gathering. It was determined that the task force did not adequately represent the various stakeholders in the process, and it was subsequently expanded. It was determined that the process was going to be seriously hampered by a lack of solid data on the target population, and additional resources were allocated for primary research. It was also determined that there were between three and five organizations that accounted for the management of most of the medically indigent, and that these organizations should be the focus of the planning initiative.

It was also possible to state some basic assumptions at this point, some of which were derived from the preliminary conclusions above.

- There appear to be adequate resources available to meet the basic needs of the medically indigent, but these resources are not efficiently employed.
- Information management capabilities must be put into place for the process to be effective.
- Private sector organizations are not likely to play a meaningful role in planning for the needs of the medically indigent.

- State and federal regulations and actions that are beyond the control of the local community will be a major factor in the ability to plan for this population.
- The most effective course of action will be to focus on the key organizations that serve the target population.

These assumptions would, of course, be revisited throughout the process, but they allowed some initial parameters to guide the planning initiative to be set. The task force was now in a position to initiate more formal data collection activities.

Baseline Data Collection

The first step in the formal data collection process involved an environmental assessment. Since this was a local initiative, conditions and developments at the national and state level were less important than they might be for other types of planning. Nevertheless, the task force required knowledge of various trends at the national and state levels.

Broad societal trends were reviewed and their implications for the local environment considered. These included demographic trends, economic considerations, lifestyle trends, and consumer attitude trends. Health industry trends were analyzed to identify any developments that were likely to affect the local community. These included trends in reimbursement and changing approaches to public sector delivery systems.

Regulatory, political, and legal developments were of particular importance, since the majority of the citizens for whom planning was taking place were Medicaid enrollees. At the federal and state levels, likely regulatory developments had to be considered. Of particular importance were reimbursement trends for Medicaid services. It was also important to identify any trends in federal or state funding for targeted populations (e.g., the homeless, the working poor) that might have implications for the local planning initiative.

This review of the social, political, economic, and technological trends affecting the environment provided a starting point for subsequent background research and a context in which additional knowledge could be framed.

Profiling the Service Area and Its Population

The characteristics of the community had to be determined as part of the environmental assessment. The analysis initially focused on the total community and then targeted the medically indigent. The categories of data that were collected are listed below:

- *Demographic Characteristics*

    - Age distribution
    - Sex distribution
    - Racial/ethnic distribution

- *Sociocultural Characteristics*

  - Marital status
  - Household characteristics
  - Income distribution
  - Educational level
  - Occupational characteristics
  - Industry characteristics

- *Psychographic Characteristics*
- *Financing Characteristics*

  - Payer categories
  - Insurance coverage

- *Attitudes*

  - Perceptions
  - Preferences
  - Expectations

Most of this information was obtained from secondary sources of data. Census Bureau data were used to develop a demographic and sociocultural profile of the community in general and the affected population in particular, supplemented by data generated by commercial data vendors. Data on the payer mix of the resident population was pieced together from a variety of sources to provide a general picture of the population's distribution among the commercial insurance, government insurance, and uninsured categories. This same process was repeated for the areas of the city that were characterized by concentrations of the medically indigent. As this process unfolded, the planners realized that there were significant gaps in existing knowledge with regard to the characteristics of the medically indigent.

Even at this early stage, some conclusions could be drawn relevant for the planning process. First, the location of the medically indigent population was found to be changing; it was becoming less concentrated and more spread among the "normal" population. Second, it was found that the medically indigent did not have the stereotypical characteristics historically associated with this population; they were much more like the general population than had been thought. Third, it was found that the extent of medical indigence was much more widespread than originally thought, particularly when it came to the working poor who had neither private insurance nor Medicaid.

Determining Health Status

The next step in establishing a baseline of knowledge was to examine the health status of the community and the target population. Information was collected on fertility patterns within the community, its morbidity characteristics, and level of mortality. Some data relevant to all three of these categories were available from the county health department, and this was supplemented with data from the state health department. Fertility and mortality data were relatively easy to acquire since these data are officially compiled by the health department.

Morbidity data, on the other hand, were more difficult to acquire. Except for the collection of data on certain notifiable diseases by the health department, there was no systematic source of data on morbidity. This situation was approached from a number of different angles. The first involved the collection of data from those organizations that were most heavily involved with this population. Data were obtained from the public hospital and the health department that indicated the types of diagnoses characterizing their patient populations and the types of procedures performed on their clients. Information was also available from some of the community-based clinics and mental health centers that serve this population. This provided some actual data from which to begin to understand the mortality profile.

A second approach involved obtaining data from the National Center for Health Statistics that indicated, based on national survey data, the types of health conditions that would characterize populations with various attributes. This survey data could be used to estimate the morbidity profile of the target population. By looking at prevalence rates for a population with certain racial, income, and age characteristics, it was possible to develop a "proxy" profile of the population's morbidity status.

A third approach involved the administration of a sample survey within the target population. Respondents from over 500 households were interviewed in an attempt to gain a more "grassroots" understanding of the health problems faced by this population. This primary research understandably slowed down the planning process but turned out to provide invaluable data for the project.

Some other approaches were attempted but with limited success. Mortality data was reviewed to determine if the cause of death might be a useful indicator of morbidity in the population, but this turned out to be unfruitful. An attempt was made to obtain data from the state Medicaid files on the encounters reported for the target population. This turned out to be such a complex process that it was abandoned.

The data collection process on health status offered some additional conclusions to help guide the planning process. First, the target population was not nearly as outside the mainstream of medicine as conventional wisdom held. Most of the medically indigent did have access to basic medical care. The working poor without insurance or Medicaid were the exception; they seemed to have limited access to care. Second, the type of problems characterizing this population were little different from those of the general population. Third, it was reconfirmed that many of the health problems that exist reflect the presence of non-health factors in the environment. Health problems stemming from housing conditions, nutritional factors, crime, violence, and drug abuse were much more significant within this population.

Health Behavior

While general patterns of health behavior were identified, the research focused on those indicators of health behavior most relevant for the target population. The following types of health behavior were considered in the research process:

- *Inpatient Admissions*

  - Hospital admissions
  - Nursing home admissions
  - Residential treatment center admissions
  - Mental health facility admissions

- *Outpatient Visits*

  - Hospital outpatient visits
  - Hospital emergency room visits
  - Physician office visits
  - Other clinician office visits
  - Urgent care visits
  - Diagnostic center visits
  - Surgicenter visits
  - Mental health center visits

- *Other Service Utilization*

  - Home health visits
  - Physical therapy treatments
  - Alternative therapy visits

- *Procedures Performed*

The same sources of data were employed as for health status. Data on utilization were obtained from the public hospital, the health department, and the community-based clinics that maintained good records. In this case, data were also obtained from private sector providers, particularly hospitals, to determine the health behavior patterns of the medically indigent within the context of the overall community. The data collected through the sample survey were invaluable in this regard, since they revealed a great deal about the services that the medically indigent utilize and why they use them. Again, proxy data was applied based on NCHS surveys in order to round out the profile of service utilization.

One of the major findings from this research was that the medically indigent were more like the general public in their utilization patterns than was originally believed. Most preferred to use private physicians when they could, and there appeared to be declining dependence on strictly public sources of healthcare. The differences that were found in health behavior (e.g., the higher use of emergency rooms) reflected access issues more than preferences. A second finding from the primary research confirmed the contention that this population was much less focused on prevention than the general population. While their aspirations were similar to those of the general population, their concern with personal health behavior appeared to lag behind.

Community Resources Inventory

A number of categories of community resources needed to be identified and inventoried. These included healthcare facilities and equipment, healthcare programs and services, health personnel, and financing options, among others. Examples of the components of each category that were identified included the following:

- *Healthcare Facilities*

  - Hospitals
  - Nursing homes
  - Physician offices
  - Community clinics
  - Nonphysician clinical offices
  - Residential treatment centers
  - Assisted living facilities (and other residential units for seniors)
  - Mental health facilities
  - Home health agencies/hospices
  - Urgent care centers
  - Freestanding diagnostic centers
  - Freestanding surgery centers
  - Specialty treatment centers (e.g., pain management)

- *Healthcare Equipment*

  - Biomedical equipment
  - Information technology
  - Emergency services equipment

- *Health Personnel*

  - Physicians
  - Nurses
  - Nurse clinicians, physician's assistants, and other physician extenders
  - Dentists
  - Optometrists
  - Podiatrists
  - Chiropractors
  - Mental health professionals
  - Rehabilitation therapists (e.g., physical therapists, speech therapists)
  - Clinical support personnel (e.g., radiology technologists)
  - Administrative support personnel (e.g., medical records technicians)
  - Alternative therapists

- *Programs and Services*

  - Inpatient programs/services
  - Hospital outpatient programs/services
  - Ambulatory care programs/services
  - Long-term care services
  - Community-based services
  - Home health services

- *Funding Sources*

  - Commercial insurance (including managed care)
  - Medicare (including Medicare HMOs)
  - Medicaid
  - Other federally funded programs (e.g., Veterans Administration)
  - State funding sources (e.g., mental health services)
  - Local funding sources (e.g., public hospital subsidy)

- *Networks and Relationships*

  - Formal hospital alliances
  - Integrated delivery systems
  - Provider networks
  - Chain-operated facilities (e.g., hospitals, nursing homes)
  - Contractual relationships

All of these components were important in one way or another, and almost any one of them could have a substantial impact on the system. In particular, the extent to which they were available to the medically indigent had to be determined.

Assessing Health Status and Healthcare Resources

Once the community's needs and resources had been identified and inventoried, they could be evaluated. A number of approaches were considered for performing this assessment, and a gap analysis technique was selected for the initial assessment. The needs of the target population that had been identified were compared to the services available. As a result of this process a number of gaps were identified. These included the following:

- The number of practitioners required to serve the medically indigent population was much greater than the current supply of providers.
- The providers primarily serving the medically indigent were poorly located with regard to the current residential distribution of this population.
- The service complement offered by public sector providers serving this population was not appropriate for the current needs of the population.
- The traditional models for serving this population (e.g., public health, educational) were no longer in keeping with its needs.
- Access to care, not the ability to pay for it, was the major impediment.

To further assist in the analysis, a health status index was developed for the entire community. Using a number of different indicators of health status, an index number was developed for each ZIP Code and each census tract within the county. The health status index allowed the quantification of the level of unmet needs characterizing various parts of the community. It also served as a basis for determining priorities and, eventually, for evaluating the success of the planning initiative.

Summarizing the Preliminary Analysis

Enough information was now available to present a state-of-the-community report. This report included a comprehensive description of the community and the medically indigent population. This status report also included a review of the local system's strengths, weaknesses, opportunities, and threats identified during the analysis. It included an "issues statement" based on the results of the analysis to this point.

A number of conclusions could be reached at this point, and they informed subsequent planning activities. These conclusions included the following:

- The medically indigent population was currently much different than it was in the past.
- The characteristics of the medically indigent were changing, and the population displayed few of the stereotypical traits generally associated with this group.
- The location of the medically indigent was changing over time, resulting in a mismatch between the locations of service providers and concentrations of the medically indigent.
- The medically indigents were becoming more similar to the general population over time in terms of their health-related characteristics.
- Many of the more serious issues related to the medically indigent involved newly emerging ethnic populations that were not being integrated into the healthcare system.
- A lack of access was the major impediment to obtaining adequate care, not finances, transportation, knowledge, or any of the other traditional explanations.
- While the resources available to this population are not totally adequate, a more coordinated system could stretch existing resources much further.
- It will be increasingly important to take health services to this population, both in social and geographic terms.

At this point planners considered the importance of developing a strategy that would guide the rest of the planning process. It was decided that an integrated delivery system approach would be utilized in an attempt to create efficiencies in the provision of health services to this population. This would involve the integration of various public health functions under one umbrella and the development of critical linkages with private sector providers. Further, it was determined that a heavy outreach component must be included in order to take health services to the population and, at the same time, identify individuals or groups that are falling through the cracks in the system.

Developing the Plan

The effort up to this point provided the foundation for the actual development of the plan. The original mission statement of DHP was reviewed, and it was felt that the approach being taken was in keeping with that mission.

It was now possible to consider the appropriate goal or goals for the organization. In this case, the goal involved the development of a delivery system that assured that all segments of the medically indigent population had adequate access to basic healthcare.

A number of objectives were established subsidiary to this goal. These objectives included the following:

- Establishing an integrated public health delivery system within 2 years
- Affecting a redistribution of existing public sector services to more appropriate locations within 2 years
- Establishing a comprehensive database of the community's medically indigent within 1 year
- Developing a mechanism for implementing an aggressive outreach program to this population within 2 years
- Developing an outreach program targeting specific ethnic populations within 1 year
- Formally incorporating participation by at least one of the major private sector providers within 1 year

As the planning team established the objectives, barriers to accomplishing the stated objectives were considered. The major barrier in this case related to the challenge of merging existing public health organizations involving very different cultures into an integrated system.

At this point, it became necessary to prioritize the objectives, since all could not be accomplished at the same time. Representative questions asked in setting priorities included the following:

- What are the most urgent issues—issues that will bring about dire consequences if they are not resolved?
- What are the pivotal issues—issues that contribute most directly to the mission and goal?
- Which objectives must be addressed as prerequisites for achieving other objectives?
- Which objectives will result in the most visible or most tangible results?
- Which objectives face the least barriers?
- Which objectives will involve multiple benefits if they are achieved?
- To what extent is there likely to be a negative response to the achieving of an objective?

The unanticipated consequences of meeting the various objectives were discussed and any potentially negative consequences were addressed. One major consequence that was considered was the reaction of private sector providers if the public sector became more aggressive in attempting to address health problems.

This was recognized as a concern but, given the seriousness of the health problems of the medically indigent, it was considered a risk that must be taken.

Once the objectives were identified, the next step was to specify the actions necessary for carrying out the objectives. For each objective a number of action steps were identified. For the objective of developing a database on the medically indigent, for example, the actions that were identified included the following:

- Acquire data on clients from the key organizations that are involved in providing services to the medically indigent.
- Engage an information management consultant to assist in designing the database.
- Develop a community survey mechanism for identifying medically indigent individuals who might not appear in existing databases.

Implementing the Plan

DHP had limited authority to implement many of the objectives on its own. It would, instead, have to facilitate these activities through other players. In this case, considerable political manipulation was necessary in order to get implementation started.

The first step in plan implementation involved the development of a project plan. The project plan originally developed for the planning process was extended to include the implementation phase. It indicated the sequence of events that must occur and established the critical path for the achievement of each objective.

Further, an implementation matrix was developed using a spreadsheet that laid out who was to do what and when they were to do it. The matrix listed every action called for by the plan, breaking each action down into tasks. For each action or task the responsible party was identified, along with any secondary parties that should be involved in this activity. The matrix indicated resource requirements (in terms of staff time, money, and other requirements) and the start and end dates for each activity. Benchmarks were established that allowed the planning team to determine when the activity had been completed.

The Evaluation Plan

During the early stages of the planning process, an evaluation plan was outlined that involved both process and outcome evaluation. The project's technical support staff constantly monitored the activities that were occurring and submitted regular reports on the extent to which the process was on schedule and the various processional benchmarks were being met.

The objectives that were established during plan development were used as the ultimate outcome criteria, and the extent to which these objectives were met would be the final measure of success. However, since most objectives called for a 3–5-year time frame, it was important that the team's success in meeting intermediate targets be assessed. Thus, the technical staff used the project plan and the implementation matrix as the basis for evaluating interim progress. This ongoing evaluation not only provided a source of constant information for those involved in planning, but also encouraged those charged with carrying out the various steps to act in an expeditious manner.

Revision and Replanning

It is unlikely that a health plan will be completed without being modified in one way or another. This type of "on-the-fly" revision is inevitable in a rapidly changing environment. There will always be developments that occur subsequently to the initiation of planning that will affect the plan or its implementation. Additional information may become available during the course of the plan. Various parties may take actions in anticipation of the plan that have implications for the process and plan implementation. Developments may occur that affect resource requirements.

Ideally, each component of the planning process should be revisited with these concerns in mind. All assumptions should be reviewed along with the mission statement. Baseline data should be updated to account for the time lapse since the planning process was initiated. The strategy chosen should be reviewed to determine if it is still the best approach in view of possible changes in the environment. For example, has the collaborative strategy selected failed due to unanticipated turnover on the part of key officials? The goals and objectives should be revisited to assure that they are still appropriate in the light of any changes in either the internal or the external environment.

The process should have the flexibility to adapt to developments that occur during the course of plan development and implementation. Planners must remain open to these developments and realize that planning is an iterative process that will be constantly reshaped by a wide range of factors.

Appendix B: Selected Planning Case Studies

A Case Study in Strategic Planning

Overview

Southern NeuroScience Center (SNC) is a major specialty practice in the southeastern United States that includes nine neurologists and neurosurgeons. With 55 employees, SNC represented a major business operation. The organization had been highly successful in the traditional healthcare environment but was concerned about its positioning for the future direction of healthcare. SNC had never developed a strategic plan but was now faced with a number of important issues that required some type of framework for decision-making.

Although SNC was the dominant provider of "neuro" services in its market (roughly one-fourth of the state), it faced minor but persistent competition from a few other well-established neuro specialists in the community. Further, it was constantly faced with the prospect of national organizations entering the market. SNC was concerned that it had outgrown its existing market area and would be unable to increase its market share in the future. The organization had also made some decisions in previous years that needed to be revisited in the light of new developments in the environment.

The key decision makers in SNC realized that they would require outside resources in order to develop a strategic plan. They did not have the expertise for such an undertaking in house, and there were a number of competing agendas that needed to be isolated from the planning process. SNC already had a relationship with an organization that had performed a financial analysis for them, and this organization was engaged to prepare the strategic plan.

© Springer Science+Business Media, LLC, part of Springer Nature 2021
R. K. Thomas, *Health Services Planning*,
https://doi.org/10.1007/978-1-0716-1076-3

Initial Information Gathering

The initial steps in the planning process involved preliminary interviews with the practice manager, the business manager, the managing physician, and a representative from both the neurology and neurosurgery components of the organization. The practice manager was identified as the liaison with the consultant. This stage also involved acquiring and reviewing any information that was available on the organization. This included any materials for public distribution (e.g., promotional materials), annual reports, internal documents such as executive committee minutes, any planning reports or analysis that had been previously performed, and the *vitae* of all the organization's physicians.

This initial stage of information gathering provided an overview of the organization and its position within the market, an indication of the key players within the organization, and some notion of internal decision-making and communications.

This process also served to identify the key issues as seen from the perspective of those interviewed and as suggested by a review of existing materials. Some of the issues that were identified at this stage were declining physician revenues despite increasing workload; continuous agitation between the neurologists and neurosurgeons; an unsatisfactory compensation formula for physician partners; gaps in certain clinical areas; and unproductive and/or poorly located satellite offices. Additional issues were identified, and all of these were considered for future analysis. Potential internal barriers to the planning process were also identified at this time.

A general outline of the planning process was developed in conjunction with the practice manager, and this was presented to the SNC executive committee. This document served as the starting point for the planning process, with the assumption that it would continue to be modified as the process unfolded.

The organization did not have an official mission statement, beyond its intention to provide quality neurological care to the community. It was agreed that a more definitive mission statement would be formulated in the course of the process.

Initial assumptions were also formulated to create some basic parameters for the process. It was assumed, for example, that a joint neurology/neurosurgery practice was the form the organization should take; current relationships with hospitals and other providers were appropriate; little expansion could take place within the current market area; and there were no effective competitors within the market area. It was further assumed that managed care would continue to grow in significance, and major local employers would play an increasingly active role in the management of their employees' health insurance. All of these assumptions, of course, were open to revision as the planning process proceeded.

Baseline Data Collection

With this background, it was possible to begin collecting detailed data on the organization and its environment. This process began with an internal audit of the practice and its operations. In addition to previously acquired documents, the consultants obtained detailed financial statements, medical staff policies, personnel policies, and other documents that might provide insights into the organization.

Another round of interviews was conducted involving all of the SNC physicians, the department heads of each of the six departments, and two other individuals who were thought to be particularly knowledgeable about the organization.

A full-scale internal audit was then performed that included a detailed financial analysis, an organizational analysis, a patient profile, and an employee survey. The audit also examined the services that were being offered, the pricing for these services, and the locations at which these services were being provided. It further determined existing utilization patterns for all services and identified trends in these patterns. The customers for the practice were profiled along a number of different dimensions, and referral relationships were identified and assessed. The characteristics of practice personnel were reviewed, and all internal processes were identified and evaluated. Current marketing activities were inventoried.

The operations analysis component of the internal audit involved a review of patient flow and paper flow. It also reviewed internal processes for managing services and for communications. Information systems were reviewed, as were the processes for billing patients and collecting fees.

The internal audit took approximately 3 weeks to perform. Each of the items mentioned above included a number of subtopics. The consultants worked closely with business and clinical personnel in order to develop this information.

The initial findings from the internal audit were presented as an interim report to the SNC executive committee. Even at this early stage, there were a number of conclusions that could be drawn from the research. Some examples of the conclusions included the following:

- The neurosurgeons felt that the neurologists were not carrying their load but were being compensated as if they were.
- There was limited communication among the various clinical components and a number of misperceptions had emerged.
- None of the physicians was satisfied with the existing compensation formula.
- The existing organizational structure reflected the historical situation but was not appropriate for the new healthcare environment.
- While SNC employees were satisfied overall, there were certain important areas of concern that were affecting morale and productivity.
- There were certain procedures that were not being performed to the extent they should have been.
- There was no internal marketing program in place, resulting in frequent patient complaints and public relations problems.

The external audit began with a review of societal trends that were likely to have implications for the practice and/or its market. Demographic trends were reviewed, particularly as they related to the neuro specialties. Trends in lifestyles and consumer attitudes and expectations were considered. The overall economic outlook was examined, since upturns or downturns in the economy may affect utilization and payment capabilities. These same factors were examined at the state level as well.

This planning initiative took place during the period when the current administration was seriously considering healthcare reform legislation. Attention was paid to the potential impact that the enactment of various reform provisions would have on specific components of healthcare, including neurology and neurosurgery.

Health industry trends were carefully reviewed, again with an eye for their impact on the neuro specialties. Of particular interest were the implications of managed care for the reimbursement of neuroscience services. Trends in rehabilitation care were another area of interest to the practice, as was the controversy over back pain treatment.

An analysis of national trends in reimbursement was also considered crucial. This involved a review of reimbursement trends by commercial insurance carriers and, as noted above, managed care plans. Proposed changes in Medicare coverage and reimbursement were also an important topic. Changes in workers' compensation reimbursement and the provision of rehabilitation services also had to be considered. Although there were few state programs that would significantly impact a neuro practice, any state or local developments along these lines were identified.

Recent and emerging technological developments that would impact the provision of neurology and neurosurgery services were identified and evaluated for their implications for the practice.

A thorough analysis of the practice's market area was subsequently undertaken. Beginning with a review of secondary data sources, a complete demographic profile of the market area was established. Available sources of data were also used to determine the health status of the population and its patterns of health behavior. These characteristics of the general population were compared to the characteristics of the practice's patients.

Despite the availability of a reasonable amount of secondary data, the specialized nature of neurological care meant that somewhat less information was available than might have been for more common specialties. For this reason, this project relied more heavily on primary research than many similar planning initiatives might. There were a number of groups for which surveys were conducted. These included the following:

- The practice's patients
- Competitors' patients
- Referring physicians
- Nonreferring physicians
- Major employers (especially benefits managers)
- Key health plans (including managed care)

Personal interviews were also conducted with selected hospital administrators and other key informants who might have an opinion on SNC or neurological specialties.

A thorough competitive analysis was undertaken as well. This involved the identification and evaluation of all potential competitors with the practice. In this case, the numbers were few and competitors were easily identified. These competing specialists were profiled in terms of practice characteristics, personal demographics, specialty areas (if any), practice volumes, and case mix.

As a result of the primary research conducted, there was also considerable qualitative information available on competitors within the market area. This turned out to be a valuable exercise and revealed that the potential for serious competition was less salient than originally believed. It was found, for example, that the only competing group of any size was in the process of splitting up, that the major individual competitor was planning to leave the area, and that certain other neurologists and neurosurgeons were being forced to limit their practices because of impairments or personal circumstances. This was a useful information for the formulation of the plan.

A final component of the research was a locational analysis. Most of SNC's office-based services were developed at the primary site, and most of the hospital care was administered at the market's largest hospital. The practice had maintained three satellite locations for at least 2 years, and the appropriateness of these sites needed to be reviewed.

It was ultimately concluded that the location of the main office was appropriate and that the hospital relationship was favorable (although other options were not ruled out). It was further determined that two of the satellite operations were not appropriately sited, while one of them was.

Once the market data had been collected and reviewed, a SWOT analysis was performed. This technique was used to identify the strengths and weaknesses of the practice, the opportunities that existed for the practice in its market area (and beyond), and the threats and potential threats found in the market area or as a result of national trends.

The findings from the internal and external audits were reviewed first with the practice manager and the managing physician and, subsequently, with the executive committee. After a review of the findings with the key participants, a strategic planning retreat was scheduled.

The planning retreat—involving all nine physicians, the practice manager, and the business manager—was conducted by the consultants. They presented a review of the research methodology and a summary of the findings. A state-of-the-practice report was provided that summarized "who SNC was and what it was doing." The organization's strengths and weaknesses were outlined, and a report on its position within the market was presented. The major issues, as identified during the data collection process, were reviewed and discussed. Opportunities that existed for the organization were outlined, along with threats that might exist.

Developing the Plan

This information provided the basis for formulating the strategic plan. The process started with the specification of the primary goal for the organization. The goal that emerged from the planning retreat read as follows: To become the premier neuroscience practice in the southern half of the state. Once this goal was established, a strategy was adopted. The proposed strategy called for an aggressive program of expansion that involved the addition of new services and staff and the development of a decentralized network of service outlets.

With this goal and strategy in mind, a number of objectives were established in order to support their achievement. These objectives included the following:

- Increase the number of staff physicians from 9 to 15 over a 3-year period.
- Add sports medicine as a product line within 1 year.
- Open one new satellite office per year over the next 3 years.
- Add unique, state-of-the-art diagnostic technology over the next year.
- Immediately restructure the governance of the practice to support the type of aggressive initiative being proposed.
- Establish a major presence at a second local hospital within 1 year.

An additional objective that fell into a different category was identified during the planning retreat. This involved a revision of the compensation arrangements for practice physicians. It was agreed that this issue would be addressed independently of the strategic planning process.

The next step was to review the barriers that might exist with regard to any of the objectives. The only serious barrier that was identified involved the relationship with the second local hospital. Upon additional information gathering, the consultants found that a poor past relationship with the hospital would be a major impediment to closer ties. Further, the one group that represented any form of competition for SNC was very much in favor at this hospital. This objective was eliminated from the list.

Similarly, the consequences of meeting the various objectives were considered, both positive and negative, intended and unintended. There were few negative implications for any of the objectives that could be identified. Admittedly, some toes would be stepped on as the practice expanded into other market areas and added new services. This was to be expected and all parties agreed that, in the current competitive environment, ruffled feathers were inevitable. The bottom line called for an aggressive approach that could not take the narrow interests of competing practices into consideration.

The planning team then addressed the prioritization of the remaining objectives. Based on the agreed-upon goal and strategy, the highest priority was given to increasing the size of the physician staff to 15 and to setting up additional practice locations. The remaining objectives became second-tier objectives.

For each objective, a number of actions were specified. For the objective related to staff expansion, for example, the following actions were identified:

- Establish a screening committee to review all applicants.
- Budget funds for the recruitment process.
- Identify the specialties that are to be recruited.
- Engage a recruitment firm to begin the search.
- Prepare office space for the new physicians.

Implementing the Plan

Once action steps had been identified for all of the objectives, an implementation matrix was created. For each of the dozens of actions that had been identified, the matrix specified the following:

- The primary responsible party
- Other responsible parties
- The effort in terms of time anticipated
- A deadline for completion
- The necessary resources
- Any prerequisites

This matrix essentially determined who was to do what, at what time, and how they were to do it. This was a critical step in the process, without which it was unlikely that many of the actions would have been carried out in a timely fashion. The preliminary implementation matrix developed at the planning retreat was carried back to be finalized by the practice manager and the managing physician.

The last step in the process carried out at the planning retreat was the creation of a 10-year future scenario for the practice. Given the plan laid out during the session, participants were asked to contribute to the creation of a vision for the future practice. The scenario should envision who would be involved, where the practice locations would be, the types of services that would be offered, and so forth. In the end, the planning team had essentially "invented" the future for SNC. In carrying out the plan that had been developed, they would be responsible for making this scenario an actuality.

The final step in the planning process involved the evaluation component of the project. Using the implementation matrix as the basis, a mechanism was established for tracking the progress of plan implementation over the 3-year time period it covered.

A Case Study in Marketing Planning

Overview

SouthCoast Institute, a rehabilitation hospital with a historical focus on inpatient services, desired to expand its outpatient capabilities in response to various developments within the environment. This new direction would require considerable reorientation of the staff toward an outpatient mind set, as well as the establishment of a number of new services.

Among the options for new services was the development of an aquatherapy program to supplement the services currently provided to rehabilitation patients. An aquatherapy program would expand the capabilities of the existing program and make physical therapy possible for a wider range of patients. Since Medicare and most commercial health plans provided reimbursement for aquatherapy services, the program should be a source of additional revenue. It would further serve to differentiate SouthCoast Institute from other providers of rehabilitation services. While aquatherapy services would be utilized by the Institute's hospitalized rehabilitation patients, the intent was to bolster the fledgling outpatient program and attract other clients who were not involved with the hospital's inpatient rehabilitation program.

The decision to develop and market an aquatherapy program was one result of a major strategic planning initiative that was being carried out by SouthCoast Institute. Many of the organizational issues had been handled within the context of the ongoing strategic plan. A planning team was already in place, and a planning framework had been established. The aquatherapy initiative was incorporated as a component of the overall implementation plan. It remained for the staff to develop and implement a marketing plan to support the development of this new program.

Initial Information Gathering

The initial steps in the information-gathering process involved collecting background data on existing aquatherapy programs. Data were compiled on the types of procedures and services offered by most programs, types of patients typically served, reimbursement prospects, and so forth. A general notion of what was involved in operating an aquatherapy program was developed.

At the same time, a preliminary internal information-gathering process was carried out. This focused on the potential for developing the program within the confines of the existing rehabilitation therapy framework. The analysis examined the availability of personnel to provide aquatherapy services, potential for training additional staff, existing equipment and additional equipment needs, and, perhaps most importantly, attitude of the medical staff with regard to this service.

The internal information-gathering process uncovered a certified aquatherapist on staff who could serve as the product-line champion. There was also a pool of physical therapy aides who, with minimal additional training, could support the aquatherapy program. Although the hospital did not have a therapy pool, existing plans for renovating the rehabilitation facility included the construction of such a pool, along with a regulation-size exercise pool. Further, the medical staff who were primarily involved in referring patients to the Institute were generally supportive and, in some cases, enthusiastic about the prospects of aquatherapy.

Baseline Data Collection

These positive findings set in motion the formal data collection process, starting with data on the market potential for this service within the Institute's market area. The number of potential customers, in fact, turned out to be much greater than anticipated. Potential sources of referral were identified and subsequently interviewed concerning their interest. Local health plans were contacted to determine their willingness to reimburse for this service, and aquatherapy programs in other markets were identified and contacted for their input.

Several secondary target audiences were identified that, while contributing no major revenue streams, would increase utilization of the pools and perhaps contribute to some fixed costs. These included community groups, swim teams, social service programs, and even a "commercial" audience of water aerobics customers who could be expected to pay a fee for use of the facility. Employees of the Institute were also queried with regard to their interest in using these facilities as part of the employee fitness program.

A competitive analysis was conducted, and it was determined that no medically supported aquatherapy was being offered within the community. Options for interim use of existing area pools were explored, and a suitable temporary site was identified for piloting the program. Preliminary financial statements were prepared to provide an estimate of the potential profitability of the service.

When the potential barriers were examined, few if any were found to exist. The only barrier identified was a lack of knowledge about aquatherapy in the community (even among some medical practitioners). No inherent resistance was identified from any segment of the community.

Developing the Plan

With this background data indicating significant potential for a successful and profitable service, the planning team set a goal of establishing the Institute's program as the premier aquatherapy program in the region. In terms of strategy, the team decided that an approach that emphasized education and relationship-building was appropriate. The intent was to stay away from aggressive advertising and flashy promotions.

In support of this goal, the following objectives were established:

- Create and implement a comprehensive internal marketing program for aqua-therapy within 6 months.
- Directly contact all potential referrers outside the Institute and its affiliates within 6 months.
- Recruit and train a marketing/liaison person to work with the aquatherapy program on a full-time basis within 6 months.
- Identify and contact within 6 months all community groups that might poten-tially benefit from the standard swimming pool and the aquatherapy pool.
- Integrate aquatherapy services into the sports medicine and occupational medi-cine programs within 1 year.

With these objectives in mind, a number of actions were identified. The follow-ing marketing-related actions were included:

- Create promotional material for distribution to potential referral agents.
- Set up meetings with relevant internal parties (including medical staff) to explain the program.
- Identify an appropriate person to train for liaison with the community.
- Identify any appropriate external targets for promotional and educational activities.

The fact that the program was new and unique in the area guided the develop-ment of the marketing plan. The appropriate message to be delivered was formu-lated and the means of spreading it were determined.

In keeping with the educational/relationship-building approach, the marketing mix focused on low-key promotional activities and avoided high-profile media tech-niques. For internal marketing, the plan included a newsletter, internal publications, a flyer in each Institute employee's paycheck, posters, special information sessions for staff and referring physicians, and a videotape to explain the program. For exter-nal audiences, the plan called for a newsletter, press releases (and other media cov-erage as appropriate), print advertising (probably limited to the *Yellow Pages*), limited electronic media (for the grand opening), videotape, exhibits (e.g., schools, health fairs), and public presentations (support groups, medical society, voluntary health associations).

An implementation plan was developed as part of the marketing plan that identi-fied the resources needed, required financial commitment, responsible parties for the various tasks, and timelines for all activities. The SouthCoast program director was given primary responsibility for implementing the plan. The physical therapist with the aquatherapy certification would assist the program director.

An evaluation procedure was put into place to assess the progress of the program. Since it was a startup operation, it would be easy to track the volume of services uti-lized. The plan also called for a pretest and posttest to be administered to referral agents to determine the extent to which they were made aware of the program. Satisfaction surveys were to be developed for administration to patients and referrers. The extent to which the program generated secondary benefits in the community (e.g., with com-munity groups, schools, swim clubs) would be tracked and periodically reported.

A Case Study in Business Planning

Overview

A clinical psychologist had formulated an innovative program for the treatment of certain types of eating disorders. The program represented a unique approach and appeared to have substantial potential in the healthcare marketplace. The program's approach was predicated upon the fact that many cases of eating disorders could be attributed to a history of sexual abuse.

In order to initiate the program, external funding would be required. A business plan was developed as a basis for seeking investors and as a means of guiding project development. The following sections represent an abbreviated version of the business plan, since the full text would be inappropriately long for appendix material.

Eating disorders are an increasingly prevalent health condition in the United States. They were labeled the "disease of the 1980s" but the estimated size of the problem continued to grow through the 1990s. Research now indicates that between 3% and 10% of the female population in the United States is affected by anorexia or bulimia at any one time and perhaps as many as 40% over their lifetimes. It is further estimated that 30% of college women suffer from some form of eating disorder and that 10% of high school girls are anorexic. The exact prevalence is difficult to determine, however, since many individuals suffering from eating disorders, especially men, are reluctant to admit their condition. However, even at the lowest identified rates, there are an estimated one million women in the United States suffering from an eating disorder at any given time.

Similarly, sexual abuse is also prevalent in the United States. Recent studies have shown that one out of every three women will have been abused by the time she reaches adulthood. As with eating disorders, there may be many more cases of undiagnosed sexual abuse. This is particularly the case with men in our society, among whom both of these conditions are more common than was thought in the past.

It now appears that there is a strong connection between eating disorders and a history of sexual abuse. An estimated one-fourth to one-third of adult females in the United States are thought to have suffered from childhood sexual abuse. Of individuals identified with eating disorders researchers and therapists report that from 50% to 90% have suffered from sexual abuse as children. Despite these startling figures, there are virtually no treatment programs that take the interrelationship between these two conditions into consideration.

The Proposed Program

This business plan describes a residential program that offers an innovative therapy approach for individuals suffering from eating disorders, sexual abuse symptomatology, or, typically, a combination of both. Many individuals may suffer from one or the other of these conditions (eating disorders or sexual abuse) but may not realize the connection with the other. Unless they enter a program such as this, the relationship between the two conditions may not be discovered.

A residential program offers a cost-effective alternative to traditional inpatient programs. Hospitalization for 6 weeks typically costs $30,000 or more. While some insurance programs will cover a portion of these charges, many do not. Individuals are often left owing large amounts. Not only would a residential program be less expensive than inpatient care, but it also promises to be more effective than existing hospital-based programs.

Program Goals

The mission of the proposed project involves the development of a demonstration program for the treatment of individuals with eating disorders that may be related to a history of sexual abuse. The following goals and objectives have been identified:

Short-Term Goals

Goal 1: To establish the innovative treatment program as a therapeutically and financially viable operation
Goal 2: To publicize this form of treatment in order to gain attention and support for the program

Long-Term Goals

Goal 1: To establish a residential therapy center dedicated to the effective treatment of individuals suffering from eating disorders and sexual abuse using an approach that is sensitive to the relationship between these two conditions
Goal 2: To refine our understanding of the linkage between eating disorders and sexual abuse and subsequently improve the therapeutic techniques available
Goal 3: To develop a foundation for promoting the concepts and techniques of this form of eating disorder therapy on a national basis and expanding the program on a franchise basis

Examples of objectives developed pursuant to the short-term goal of establishing the treatment program as a therapeutically and financially viable operation include the following:

- Acquire and adapt a suitable facility for initial services within 6 months.
- Identify and negotiate with potential staff to complement existing personnel within 3 months.
- Acquire all licenses, permits, and certificates within 3 months.

- Negotiate and finalize the contract for program management services within 3 months.
- Identify and contact the major sources of referrals to the program within 4 months.

The Potential Market

For planning purposes, it is assumed that the county in which the treatment center will be located is the primary market area. The surrounding medical trade area will be considered the secondary service area. The primary market area includes around 870,000 inhabitants. The metropolitan area (five counties) includes a million residents, and along with the remainder of the surrounding medical service area contains a resident population of approximately 2 million.

Since there is no consensus on the exact prevalence of either eating disorders or sexual abuse and even less precise prevalence figures on the two combined, it is difficult to generate precise market estimates. However, based on national figures for sexual abuse alone, it is estimated that in the primary market area there are over 38,000 females between the ages of 21 and 39 who have experienced sexual abuse as children. If one considers the population that is believed to be afflicted with eating disorders, another 5200 college-aged females fall into this category, along with nearly 5000 high school-aged residents. Thus, if only females in certain age groups who have experienced childhood sexual abuse and females in certain age groups who are thought to have eating disorders are counted, the potential market in the primary market area alone amounts to approximately 50,000 individuals. Viewed another way, if 20% of the female population aged 15–39 years had either an eating disorder or a history of sexual abuse, the potential market would equal 34,000 individuals. Based on a reasonable ratio of male to female prevalence, an additional 8000–10,000 males could be added to this number.

These approximations of the local market should be adjusted to reflect certain characteristics of the local population. Because of the expense of treatment for eating disorders, few people without health insurance or the ability to pay for treatment out of pocket can be expected to participate in the typical program. Further, non-whites historically have not been attracted to this type of program. To be very conservative, one might adjust the potential market to reflect the importance of low-income and/or nonwhite populations within the primary service area. In addition, the program may want to restrict its clients to certain age ranges and, for the residential program, to women. After adjustment, there should still be a market in the range of 25,000–30,000 patients.

It would not be unreasonable to add an additional potential patient population of 10,000 individuals (unadjusted for demographic characteristics) in the remainder of the metropolitan area and another 10,000 unadjusted potential patients from the medical service area outside of the primary market area. Thus, even if these figures turn out to be overstated, it is clear that an adequate market for this type of program exists in the market area.

Existing Treatment Approaches

Many professionals are beginning to realize that each eating disorder, as well as each patient, should be treated as a unique case. Outpatient treatment generally entails individual psychotherapy but may also involve the family, especially in the case of the younger patient. It is important that the underlying patterns of interaction are recognized and that the family accept help in changing them.

Hospitalization is usually required when weight loss has reached a danger level—about 25% or more below normal weight. In most cases, weight can be restored by a combination of psychotherapy and learning new eating behavior patterns. Weight gain alone will not solve the problem. The underlying issues must be dealt with; otherwise, quite often people with eating disorders comply with the hospital rules until they gain enough weight to be released and then immediately return to serious dieting and weight loss.

Although a number of weight management programs have been developed and marketed nationally, no nationwide effort exists with regard to eating disorders in general and the eating disorder/sexual abuse syndrome in particular. There are a few programs in the market area that purport to deal with eating disorders. However, eating disorder treatment is not highly developed, and no existing program emphasizes treatment that takes past sexual abuse into consideration. While a variety of programs offer treatment for sexual abuse, eating disorder syndromes are typically not targeted by these programs.

Currently, no inpatient program is operating within the market area, nor are there any residential treatment programs for these types of problems. The only inpatient program to be offered in the area was discontinued in the 1980s due to poor reimbursement for inpatient care. None of the existing outpatient programs appear to have captured a significant share of the market. It is difficult to assess the quality, acceptance, or success rate for the existing programs because they have operated sporadically with little follow-up on their patients.

Existing Financing Mechanisms

Historically, eating disorders have not been widely covered by insurers. Typically only the larger insurance carriers (e.g., Prudential, Equitable, and Metropolitan) have provided this sort of coverage and, when provided, it is almost exclusively through employer-sponsored plans. A review of existing practices has indicated very limited reimbursement locally for the treatment of eating disorders. Coverage for treatment of past sexual abuse is sometimes available, but reimbursement is often difficult to justify. Neither eating disorder treatment nor sexual abuse treatment is routinely covered under most health plans.

Hospital-based programs have had difficulty admitting patients for treatment of eating disorders because of the paucity of coverage. One approach has been to obtain a diagnosis of depression and use this as a basis for admission. Even so, it is unlikely that many health plans will cover inpatient care for these conditions in the future.

The reimbursement situation suggests that out-of-pocket payments will be the primary source of revenue for a program such as this. The financial analysis assumes that 80% of the program's revenues will come directly from patients and their families. This is fairly typical for programs of this nature and, considering the socioeconomic status of many of the affected, it is not unreasonable to anticipate an adequate market willing to pay out of pocket.

Discussions have been held with the major health insurance carriers in the market area, and there does appear to be general support for a cost-effective and efficacious program that would address eating disorders and their underlying causes. As it stands, insurers are often reimbursing enrollees for expensive stomach stapling surgery and/or other resource-intensive attempts at weight control. It appears that any evidence of success may open the doors to a greater willingness to provide insurance benefits for the program. The state Workers' Compensation program also appears to be another possible source of reimbursement, given the cost to employers of workers who suffer from these problems. This has been a source of coverage in other states, and the possibility is being explored with regard to this project.

Existing Referral Sources

Individuals follow a variety of routes in entering eating disorder treatment programs. The most common referral patterns involve primary care physicians who immediately recognize an eating disorder and/or sexual abuse problem and make a referral to an appropriate program (if they can find one). Often, primary care physicians attempt to treat such patients and, after limited success, refer them to a more appropriate resource. Mental health providers are another source of referrals. Many of them are not prepared to treat either eating disorders or sexual abuse and are willing to refer their patients to experts in these areas.

Many other referrals can be expected from counselors, social workers, and other professionals who come into contact with individuals experiencing these problems but who do not have the resources to manage the patients. Another large group of patients is expected to be self-referred. Many of these patients will have obtained treatment for their condition without any measurable improvement. These conditions are such that affected individuals will go to great lengths to obtain any treatment that holds promise.

The program director is well positioned to capitalize on the major sources of referrals. She is well known within the behavioral health community and has extensive contacts among both private and public providers of mental health services. She is also well connected within the physician community, not only through family members but also through previous services she has provided for referring physicians.

Program Structure

The proposed program would treat patients in a residential setting, rather than the traditional hospital setting. In the residential program, participants will stay for a period of 3 months followed up by 3 months of aftercare. Participants will be encouraged to receive ongoing support through Overeaters Anonymous meetings and/or incest survivor groups when appropriate. During the 3-month period of residence, patients will be encouraged to begin part-time work or attend school as they become ready.

Treatment includes individual counseling, group therapy, education seminars, behavior modification, meditation, family group therapy, exercise physiology, nutritional counseling, body image exercises, and psychodrama. All patients will be treated as unique individuals, each going through his/her own process of recovery. Because this treatment program has an emphasis on sexual abuse, it is important that this issue is handled properly.

Program Personnel

The residential program will be under the direction of a program director as well as a medical director. Clients entering the program will be assigned to a treatment team. The team will consist of a physician, a social worker, a psychologist, a nutritionist, and a nursing staff member. The treatment team will be responsible for developing a written treatment plan for each client.

Most of the initial staff are already involved with the program director at one level or another. The program could begin immediately with limited need to hire additional staff. However, potential staff members will be identified and held in reserve until their employment becomes necessary.

Marketing Plan

Much of the work on the initial marketing plan for the program has already been completed. This work includes refining the understanding of local, regional, and national demand; adjusting these figures for various modifying factors to arrive at the effective demand; identifying and evaluating existing potentially competing programs; determining the share of the market that could potentially be captured and relating that to the eating disorders program threshold for success; and collecting the additional data required to clearly delineate the market and the manner in which it is being served. This would certainly include a study of existing attitudes and perceptions of patients and potential patients with regard to existing programs and treatment approaches.

In recruiting clients, the priority would be placed on individuals who have insurance coverage for eating disorders. Secondarily, those with the ability to pay out of pocket for these services will be targeted. However, this emphasis is primarily to ensure the financial viability of the program and does not seek to exclude any individual in need of these services. As cash flow warrants, individuals with less ability to pay will be targeted by the program, with their expenses being subsidized by better paying patients or, alternatively, subsidized by outside funds.

A separate marketing plan component will be developed for each of the target populations, since the respective target markets require different approaches. The discussion of marketing mix will describe the different types of marketing appropriate for the various targets.

During the planning process decisions must be made with regard to the promotional mix that will be utilized. The use of a variety of approaches is envisioned, and the list of options must be refined and prioritized. The budget available for promotions will probably be a factor in the promotional mix and vice versa. The options currently being considered include the following:

- *Establishing Referral Relationships*

    - Medical/social services
    - Employers/employer alliances
    - Insurers

- *Community Outreach*

    - Public service announcements
    - Community presentations
    - Health fairs

- *Professional Participation*

    - Presentations at conferences
    - Displays at conferences

- *Direct mail*

    - Potential referrers
    - Individuals

- *Media Advertising*

    - Traditional print media
    - Radio
    - Television
    - Yellow Pages

- *Newsletter Production*
- *Video/Audiotape Production*

Regardless of the eventual promotional mix, a variety of promotional materials must be prepared. At a minimum, tasteful brochures must be developed. There should probably be at least two different brochures, one for potential referrers and another for individuals. This will entail some creative input and technical production expenses. A logo should be developed and thought given to stylistic factors that will be interwoven throughout the material.

The use of a marketing consultant will be necessary, at least in the early stages of program development, in order to contribute to marketing planning. A marketing consultant who specializes in healthcare has been identified to provide this support. It is also possible that the affiliated hospital will be able to provide some marketing support once the program is underway.

Resource Requirements

The appendix (not included) provides a detailed listing of the resource requirements necessary for startup and operations. This section covers information on facilities requirements, furnishings and equipment, personnel, materials and supplies, overhead costs, and marketing resources.

Legal Considerations

A number of legal issues must be dealt with in establishing and operating the residential treatment center. Although a state certificate of need is not required, a number of licenses and certificates are required by the state and local authorities. Further, issues related to patient confidentiality, malpractice, and liability considerations must be addressed.

An attorney with extensive background in this type of project will be involved from the idea's inception. He/she will continue to provide ongoing input in his/her areas of expertise as the project progresses.

Financial Analysis

Detailed financial statements are provided in the appendix (not included), including 5-year pro forma statements. These documents detail sources of revenue and expenses for startup and the first 5 years of operations. As indicated from this supplementary material, minimal market penetration could generate significant program volume. Even with pricing well below traditional inpatient fees, this represents a significant business opportunity.

Development Schedule

The appendix (not included) also includes a detailed project plan that outlines startup requirements and carries the program through the first 5 years of operation. The project plan includes detail on responsibilities, resource requirements, task sequencing, and benchmarks that will be used to measure progress.

Appendix Materials

The following sections are included in the appendix (but not reproduced here):

- Description of proposed facility (including floor plans)
- Resumes and qualifications of program director and other key personnel
- Qualifications of the management consultant
- Financial statements
- Project plan
- Detailed marketing plan

Appendix C: From Community Health Needs Assessment to Population Health Assessment

Community health needs assessments (CHNA) have historically been conducted by healthcare organizations in order to determine the health status of their communities. The CHNA represents a systematic method of determining the health status and unmet healthcare needs of a population and identifying the changes required to address these unmet needs. These assessments can take various forms and are typically conducted for strategic planning purposes. They involve both quantitative and qualitative approaches for determining priorities that must balance clinical, ethical, and economic considerations of need. CHNAs have primarily been conducted by government agencies and not-for-profit organizations although many for-profit organizations also find occasions to conduct a CHNA.

Now—at least for certain hospitals—conducting a CHNA is not an option as the Affordable Care Act requires not-for-profit hospitals to conduct a comprehensive assessment at least every 3 years. Even providers who have routinely conducted community health assessments are not likely to be in compliance with newly enacted provisions of the Act. Tax-exempt hospitals must demonstrate an understanding of the healthcare needs of the total community (even those segments that it does not serve), identify gaps in services (even those that it does not provide), and formulate a plan for addressing any gaps that have been identified.

As originally conceived, CHNAs have the following attributes (Wright et al. 1998):

- Health needs assessment is a systematic approach for ensuring that the health-care system uses its resources to improve the health of the population in the most efficient way.
- The CHNA involves epidemiological, qualitative, and comparative methods to describe the health problems of a population; identify inequalities in health and access to services; and determine priorities for the allocation of resources.
- The health needs to be assessed are those that can benefit from healthcare and/or from wider social and environmental changes.
- Successful health needs assessments require careful planning, adequate resources, and ability to integrate the results into the planning and implementation of programs aimed at community health improvement.

© Springer Science+Business Media, LLC, part of Springer Nature 2021
R. K. Thomas, *Health Services Planning*,
https://doi.org/10.1007/978-1-0716-1076-3

Ultimately, a health needs assessment provides the opportunity for:

- Describing the patterns of disease in the local population and the differences from regional or national disease patterns
- Learning more about the needs and priorities of their patients and consumers
- Highlighting the areas of unmet need and providing a clear set of objectives to work toward meeting these needs
- Deciding how to rationally use resources to improve the local population's health in the most effective and efficient way
- Influencing policy, interagency collaboration, and research priorities

Importantly, health needs assessments provide a method for monitoring and promoting equity in the provision and use of health services and addressing inequalities in health.

The Changing Context for Community Assessments

A number of developments have implications for the CHNA process and point to the need for a more contemporary approach to needs assessment. The US population being assessed is undergoing considerable change that may affect the assessment process. Among these developments are the continued aging of the population as the last of the baby boomers enter their senior years. The aging of the population, of course, has resulted in an increasingly female population. Perhaps even more significant is the increasing racial and ethnic diversity of the US population. Non-Hispanic whites are rapidly becoming a minority as various racial and minority groups—most notably Hispanics—outpace the white population in growth. This increasing diversity complicates the aging picture in that members of most racial and ethnic groups tend to be much younger than their non-Hispanic white counterparts. Families and households have been experiencing a second "demographic transition" as nontraditional households come to dominate and fewer Americans are getting married and even fewer are having children. The marital status/household configuration further reflects differences between the older non-Hispanic white population and the younger populations comprising various racial and ethnic minorities.

These changing population characteristics also presage a change in the characteristics of patients. Contemporary CHNAs must focus on *consumers* and not just existing patients, since community health improvement by definition requires total population coverage. Under the ACA mandate, hospitals must assess the health status and healthcare needs of their communities *in toto* and develop a plan for responding to identified gaps.

These developments have been accompanied by changes in the population's disease profile. The acute conditions of the past have been displaced by the chronic conditions that affect a more mature population. The "diseases of civilization" represent the predominant health problems today even to the point that young children are exhibiting health conditions restricted to the elderly in the past. Add to these recently identified "diseases of despair" that are contributing to the changing morbidity and mortality profiles.

Driving much of the change in patient characteristics and health problems is contemporary disease etiology. Few conditions today are a result of biological organisms or genetic factors. Instead, the primary etiological factors have become lifestyles and the vagaries of unhealthy physical and social environments. A major factor in this regard is the role played by the social determinants of health. It is increasingly conceded that observed health problems are really the symptoms of underlying social pathology—the true causes of disease. Thus, housing instability, food insecurity, polluted neighborhoods, unsafe communities, lack of education, and other "external" factors are blamed for the level of ill health.

The Emergence of the Population Health Paradigm

Because of the changes noted above and the failure of late-twentieth-century healthcare to solve our healthcare problems, there is growing interest in the concept of "population health" among health professionals, policy analysts, and government agencies. As an approach that assesses health from a population rather than an individual perspective, it represents an opportunity for developing a better understanding of the health status of populations—whether they are patients or not—and a more meaningful approach to improving a population's health status.

A two-dimensional definition of population health has been suggested to provide clarity to the discussion. Population health can be viewed as both an assessment of the health status of a population that uses aggregate data on nonmedical as well as medical factors to measure the totality of health and well-being *and* an approach to improving health status that operates at the population level rather than the individual (or patient) level by addressing the underlying causes of ill health.

This approach focuses on social pathology rather than biological pathology and addresses conditions within the environment and policy realms. While an underlying assumption is that a population health approach aims to improve health status by focusing on the healthcare needs and resources of populations not individuals, it does not rule out specific patient-based medical treatment but views healthcare as only one component of a health improvement initiative.

The application of the population health model can be explored at two different levels—a microlevel view that considers population health as it relates to the delivery of care and a macro-level view that considers population health from a societal perspective. At the microlevel one approach might be to identify individuals at high risk and intervene to reduce their risk. At the macro-level the approach might involve reducing the average risk level for the total population by initiatives or policies addressing the social determinants of health.

A population health assessment uses population-based indicators to describe, prioritize, and address specific health-related issues within economic, social, racial, environmental, or individual domains. It focuses on community-based solutions at the health system, environment/infrastructure, education, or policy level. Figure C.1 depicts the population health assessment model.

There is little agreement as to the attributes of the population health model, just as there is no consensus with regard to the term's definition. However, the following attributes—each with implications for planning—are thought to characterize the population health model.

Recognition of the social determinants of health problems. Social factors are powerful determinants of health status (and health services utilization). An emphasis on understanding the social determinants of health is critical to the population health model, and the importance of social pathology over biological pathology must be recognized. Depending on the source it could be argued that social determinants

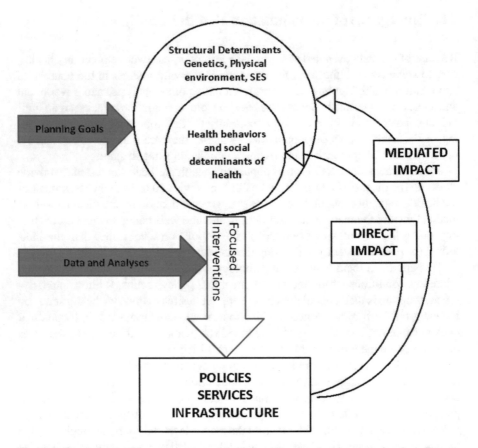

Fig. C.1 Population health assessment model. (Source: Reprinted with permission from Deprez, R., and C. Manchester (2018). "Population Health Assessment: Methods for Diagnosing and Fixing the Health of Communities," *Maine Policy Review* 17(7):51–59)

account for 40–60% of the variation in health status among subgroups of the population. If social factors are considered the root cause of observed health problems, any health improvement initiative should take these factors into consideration.

Focus on populations (or subpopulations) rather than individuals. Application of the population health model involves measuring the health status of the total population rather than simply assessing clinical readings for individual patients and combining them into an aggregate health status index. This assumes that populations exhibit attributes that are derived from the group's circumstances and not just the sum of individual attributes. It should be noted that meaningful subpopulations should be identified in order to focus on the social context characterizing targeted populations.

Shift in focus away from patients to consumers. As the healthcare industry was evolving in the late 1900s, "patients" came to be seen as "consumers." This trend was driven by baby boomers who wanted the benefits of quality care as patients coupled with the efficiency, convenience, and value that they had come to expect as consumers. This represented a significant conceptual leap for healthcare providers and moved the focus to potential patients (i.e., consumers) rather than only existing patients. This trend encouraged a more service-oriented, patient-centered approach and the introduction of "retail medicine."

Health status measured at the community level. A community-based (participatory) understanding of what the critical health issues are is a prominent feature of population health. While some argue that community health status represents the sum total of the health status of the individuals within the community, a population health approach would posit the existence of a state of health that exists independent of the health of the individuals who make up the population. This would explain the fact that certain communities exhibit persistent health problems over time regardless of who resides in the community. Even personal lifestyles might be thought to reflect the influence of the social groups with which the individuals are affiliated.

Geography as a predictor of health and health behavior. There is increasing recognition of the importance of the spatial dimension in the distribution of health and ill health. One of the most significant—and some would say disturbing—findings from decades of health services research is that both health status and utilization of health services vary in terms of geography. Where one lives is a powerful determinant of the kind and amount of medical care received. Rates for various procedures may vary by as much as a factor of 10, reflecting such conditions as local practice patterns, insurance coverage, availability of services, and consumer lifestyles. Now, it has been determined that one's ZIP Code of residence is the best predictor of one's health status and, by extension, health behavior.

Acceptance of the limited role of medical care. It has become increasingly clear that, while the cost of healthcare to consumers influences the amount of care consumed, there is no evidence that more care translates into better health. Indeed, a premise of the population health model is that health services make a limited contribution to the overall health status of the population. Indeed, as the US population consumes increasing amounts of healthcare resources per capita, our health status is not improving and may, in fact, be declining.

Innovative ways of measuring health status. The ways in which health status has historically been measured depend on indicators that have relevance for health professionals. Not surprisingly these indicators represent a biomedical bias. Any assessment of health status should reflect the perspectives of the community rather than those imposed externally by health professionals. The problems identified through community input are not likely to correspond with those recognized by the healthcare establishment. Even the public health department's criteria for assessing health issues may differ from those held by the general public.

Improvement in community health through collective impact. On the assumption that the healthcare system cannot improve the health of the population, the responsibility falls to the larger community. No one organization can have a significant impact on health status, especially in light of the variety of factors that are now known to influence health. Involvement by a wide range of community organizations—supported by but not led by the healthcare system—is necessary to create the collective impact that is required to "move the needle" when it comes to community health improvement. This includes involvement by representatives of the education, housing, economic development, criminal justice, and transportation sectors. Involvement on the part of government agencies related to policy making is also critical for the generation of the collective impact necessary to improve community health.

Similarities Between CHNAs and PHAs

There are a number of attributes that CHNAs and PHAs have in common. Both are comprehensive in their approach, including the entire population within the community and addressing the full range of health issues. Both recognize the importance of considering the total population while addressing relevant subpopulations and their attributes. The importance of disaggregating data and conducting analysis at the lowest level of geography possible is recognized by both. Similarly, both employ a broad notion of what constitutes health issues in that they attempt to assess not only physical but to the extent possible mental and spiritual health (although, admittedly, the population health assessment goes further in this regard).

To this end, both CHNAs and PHAs compile comparable data to establish a baseline for comparative analysis. This involves the collection of data on the demographics of the population (and relevant subpopulations), its morbidity characteristics, and its mortality patterns. Both types of assessment attempt to determine the health status of the population and do this using proxy variables to supplement direct measures.

CHNAs and PHAs both rely on the core sets of data that are thought to define health status and health behavior. These data are generated primarily through the efforts of local health departments on the one hand and through reporting of activities by healthcare providers on the other. Despite the deficiencies in both sources of data, they represent the primary options for obtaining data to define the attributes of a community's population. Both approaches also rely to a certain extent on synthetic data in that any plans should be future oriented. The only way to predict future health conditions and service demand is through the generation of projections for future years.

Both types of assessments involve an inventory of the health-related resources available to the population under study. Thus, an assessment is made of the available facilities, personnel, equipment, programs, and services within the community. With CHNAs the emphasis is more likely to be on the *quantity* of services rather than their *quality*, relying on availability rates to determine adequacy (e.g., ratio of primary care doctors to population).

Finally, both CHNAs and PHAs attempt to measure the utilization of services by community residents. The emphasis historically has been on the use of formal healthcare resources such as hospitals, clinics, and other sources of clinical or custodial care. Utilization rates for various types of resources have typically been calculated to determine the level of health behavior within the target population. However some attention is paid to informal and nontraditional types of health behavior, with the CHNA less aggressive in seeking out the elusive metrics for this type of health-inducing activity.

Both approaches ultimately employ gap analysis in order to assess the variance between identified needs and available resources. While any subsequent plans should consider the totality of issues related to the health of the community and the proposed responses, both pay particular attention to any shortfalls in resources or mismatches between the observed needs and the resources offered to address these gaps.

Differences Between CHNAs and PHAs

Despite the similarities that can be cited between CHNAs and PHAs, at the end of the day they represent qualitatively different approaches to the same task. There are conceptual differences between the two approaches and practical differences related to types and sources of data, analytical techniques, and importantly approach to improving community health.

Conceptual Differences

A critical distinction between CHNAs and PHAs is the fact that CHNAs focus on "sick status" while PHAs focus on "health status." The intent of the CHNA is to identify the conditions (e.g., mortality rates, morbidity rates) that indicate how unhealthy the population is. This standard approach is reflective of the medical model underlying it and the conviction that factors amenable to modification by the healthcare system should be the focus. PHAs, on the other hand, while not ignoring standard assessment metrics, seek to determine what is healthy about the population. Thus, community "health assets" are likely to be identified. What, for example, are the conditions that reflect positively on the health of the population? Even the most disease-prone population is likely to exhibit some positive attributes.

A defining feature of CHNAs is their emphasis on shortfalls in healthcare resources in the community. The reasoning is that the mere presence of formal healthcare services represents assets for the community. Yet, we now know that the presence of facilities and practitioners within a geographic area does not (1) assure access; (2) assure utilization if access is available; or (3) contribute to improving community health status if facilities are available and accessed. PHAs, on the other hand, are sensitive to health resources that, while not being noted by public health officials, are recognized by the community. These "health assets" may include social service programs, community development corporations, faith-based organizations, and community associations, to name a few. Even such unlikely "facilities" as barber shops and beauty salons may be considered health assets by community residents.

Of necessity, both approaches are limited by the data on health and health behavior that are available. Publicly available data are likely to be somewhat dated by the time they become available, and analysts are used to using mortality data that is 2 or 3 years old or older. This is a problem for both CHNAs and PHAs. This is more of an issue for CHNAs than for PHAs, since CHNAs are more focused on developing a "snapshot" of the current situation that describes the population at a point in time, while the PHA is more future oriented in its approach. The PHA's emphasis on the social determinants of health enables a more prospective approach to the health status determination.

The difference is not limited to the type of data but reflects a basic difference between the two approaches. The CHNA is content to establish a current baseline based on somewhat weak data and project past trends into the future. While the PHA does not eschew this methodology, the conceptual approach is much different. Instead of extending past trends into the future, the PHA approach identifies factors in the current environment that are likely to have implications for the future. The emphasis is on the social determinants of health with the notion that current housing instability, food insecurity, unemployment level, and transportation access, among other factors, will be contributors to future health status. Thus, the PHA places more emphasis on factors in the environment and the extent to which they portend a healthy or unhealthy future for the affected population (resulting in a forecast rather than a projection).

Historically, CHNAs have been restricted to analyses for fairly large geographical units—usually at the county level but occasionally at the ZIP Code level. This has meant that a fairly broad brush is used to paint the picture of health status and health service needs. This limitation reflects the lack of public health data for lower levels of geography exacerbated by the fact that public health officials are reluctant to release data for smaller geographic units. Although there are situations in which the "community" corresponds with the county, a ZIP Code, or a grouping of ZIP

Codes, it has become well established that communities do not neatly follow formal geographic boundaries.

Those conducting population health analyses tend to be much more aggressive in delineating meaningful boundaries that reflect a coherent community. This approach is still faced with the lack of data for small geographic areas but, as shown below, the focus on the social determinants of health rather than traditional epidemiological data means that other types of data from nontraditional sources may be accessed in order to carry out a PHA. Thus, while mortality rates may not be available at or below the ZIP Code level, it is possible to identify housing conditions, food deserts, transportation access issues, crime rates, and other factors—including access to health services—for lower levels of geography. The employment of different types of data allows the disaggregation of large geographical units into meaningful sub-units for analysis.

From Top-Down to Bottom-Up

The traditional approach involves external "experts" using epidemiological data to assess the health status of the community. This means using its own criteria for the level of ill health in the population, rather than criteria applied by community residents. If community needs are ignored then there is a danger of a top-down approach to providing health services, which relies too heavily on what "outside experts" perceive to be the needs of the population rather than what they actually are.

It is doubtful that any member of a community being assessed indicated that the major health problems were high mortality from heart disease or cancer. They are more likely to identify some measure of morbidity (e.g., high "sugar," obesity) as culprits, but even more likely to indicate examples of conditions that affect everyday life such as food shortages, unhealthy housing, inability to buy drugs, substance abuse and addiction, or domestic violence. It should be noted that the indicators of health status involved in a bottom-up analysis are, on the one hand, easier to impact than, say, heart disease mortality rates, but on the other hand require a broader approach. For example, the healthcare system has virtually no impact on the level of obesity characterizing a population; this will require initiatives that address an unhealthy environment, lack of access to healthy foods, lack of access to open spaces and exercise options, and other nonmedical interventions.

Focus on Populations (or Subpopulations) Rather than Individuals

Application of the population health model involves measuring the health status of the total population rather than simply assessing the clinical readings (e.g., reduction of A1C, blood pressure) for individual patients and combining them into an aggregate health status index. Since regulators, payers, and other evaluators will increasingly reward healthcare providers for their effectiveness in managing groups of patients, consumers, or plan members, the social context characterizing targeted populations will become more important.

As noted above, health status and decisions made with regard to health behavior are not thought to be the result of individual volition but reflect the impact of the individual's social context, cultural milieu, and life circumstances. The population health model recognizes that improvement in personal health status needs to be addressed within the context of the social or community environment (i.e., the "roots" of health problems) in a manner that leverages group pressure for health improvement.

Improvements in Community Health Through Collective Impact

On the assumption that the healthcare system cannot improve the health status of the population, the responsibility falls to the larger community. No one organization can have a significant impact on community health status, especially in light of the variety of factors that are now known to influence health. Involvement by a wide range of community organizations—supported by but not led by the healthcare system—is necessary to create the collective impact that is required to "move the needle" when it comes to community health improvement. This includes involvement by representatives of the education, housing, economic development, criminal justice, and transportation sectors. Involvement on the part of government agencies related to policy making is also critical for the generation of the collective impact necessary to improve community health.

Addressing the Problems Not the Symptoms

As the impact of social factors on health status has become documented, the argument is increasingly being made that the health conditions exhibited by a population are not the *problems* per se but are *symptoms* of underlying problems. Thus, the morbidity levels exhibited by various populations are a reflection of the social determinants of health and illness that are, in effect, the true problems. The presence of disease can thus be seen as the manifestation of these underlying conditions. This perspective is supported by research that suggests that disadvantaged populations are likely to identify as "health problems" such factors as lack of food, inadequate housing, and unsafe streets.

Critics of the US healthcare system point out that we have been treating these symptoms while not addressing the true cause of the problems. Putting a Band-Aid on the wound is of limited usefulness if the underlying infection is not addressed, and an approach that addresses symptoms without affecting a true cure is clearly ineffective when it comes to improving population health. This explains the fact that there is no correlation between health resources expended and health status. Further, it is now acknowledged that better access to health insurance does not guarantee access to care ... and that access to care does not assure utilization of services.

Finally, utilization of services does not necessarily foster better patient outcomes and by itself clearly does not contribute to improved population health.

Acceptance of the Limited Role of Medical Care

It has become increasingly clear that, while the cost of healthcare to consumers influences the amount of care consumed, there is no evidence that more care translates into better health. Indeed, a premise of the population health model is that health services make a limited contribution to the overall health status of the population. Indeed, as the US population consumes increasing amounts of healthcare resources per capita, our health status is not improving and may, in fact, be declining.

Getting back to the focus on root causes, the CHNA views deficiencies in the healthcare delivery system as a major determinant of health status ... and the healthcare system as the principal force for addressing identified health issues. The PHA, on the other hand, tends to minimize the role of the formal healthcare system in either contributing to the problem or serving as a means to solve the problem. Over time, the impact of health services on health status has been diminished, contributing perhaps as little as 10% to the differentials observed. Further, there is little evidence to support the notion that more services mean better health and clear evidence that increased expenditures on health services do *not* lead to better health.

Different Health Status Definition and Measurement

Traditional approaches to assessing the health status of a population have relied primarily on epidemiological data (e.g., mortality, morbidity). While these indicators (particularly mortality) were meaningful in a past era of acute health problems, they have less salience for an environment dominated by chronic disease. Over the years, various attempts have been made to develop health status indices incorporating proxy indicators including demographic variables (e.g., poverty level, educational attainment). None of these attempts have been widely accepted and the tendency has been to fall back on easily accessible epidemiological data.

The ways in which health status has historically been measured depend on indicators that have relevance for health professionals. The ability to measure health status using top-down epidemiological data has been increasingly called into question for several reasons. First, these indicators represent a biomedical bias with their focus on epidemiological measures. But, a key measure, mortality, has become a less and less meaningful measure of health status, and traditional morbidity measures (e.g., prevalence of major chronic diseases) only tell part of the health status story. Importantly, these measures are imposed from the outside by health professionals and assume that the healthcare system represents the route to health status improvement.

Further, these measures do not reflect the perspective of representatives of the communities for which health status is being assessed. While the development of a more contemporary measure of health status is still a work in progress, it is clear that the situation demands incorporation of less commonly used but increasingly important morbidity measures such as oral health, behavioral health, addiction, and domestic violence. Further, the new conceptualization must rely heavily on measures of the social determinants of health such as housing stability, food security, environmental threats, and numerous other historically neglected metrics. Demographers clearly have a role to play in the development of a definition of health status for today's healthcare environment.

Any assessment of health status should reflect the perspectives of the community rather than those imposed externally by health professionals. The problems identified through community input are not likely to correspond with those recognized by the healthcare establishment. Even the public health department's criteria for assessing health issues may differ from those held by the general public.

Data Differences

Every development in healthcare over the past 25 years has increased the demand for more detailed, comprehensive, and timely data—not only for existing clients but also for the total community. Indeed, the Affordable Care Act mandates that not-for-profit hospitals conduct a health status assessment at least every 3 years that takes into consideration the health status and unmet needs to the total service area population and not just their own patients. Further, the scope of data required has continued to increase, beyond health data per se and the usual demographic attributes to nontraditional sources of data from the realms of social services, housing, education, criminal justice, and so forth.

To be effective, the population health approach requires an unprecedented and in-depth understanding of the attributes of the service area population. In addition, the ability to read between the lines and ferret out the true healthcare issues and the underlying causes of these issues is critical. An effective population health approach should allow the healthcare organization to successfully engage patients, employees, and consumers in the management of their own health. Part of this involves viewing health problems from the consumer's perspective. Health professionals are notorious for imposing their perspectives on groups within the population when it comes to their health. Yet, when consumers are asked what they see as the health problems most affecting their communities, their answers are likely to be much different from those assumed by the healthcare system. Indeed, the health problems identified may not even *be* health problems but may be such factors as domestic violence, toxic environments, or unsafe housing.

Of course, marshaling adequate data to support the population health approach is easier said than done. One ongoing challenge when it comes to implementing a population health approach is the weakness of the data infrastructure supporting the population health movement. The issues faced by those attempting to obtain health data from disparate sources and integrating them in a manner that supports efficient analysis and data mining are well known. The approach proposed above calls for even more robust resource and data management capabilities and the ability to incorporate non-health data into a workable repository that can be interfaced with health data. Any effort toward the implementation of a population health approach must be cognizant of the shortcomings that exist with regard to data management and subsequent barriers likely to hinder implementation.

Proponents of a population health approach have argued that analysts are accessing types of data that do not offer a true picture of health status. It is now recognized that data must be collected on a wide range of topics that historically have not been linked to the health of the population. The recognition of the social determinants of health status has opened the door to the acquisition of data on a wide range of topics historically ignored by healthcare organizations. While most analyses include data on the demographic and socioeconomic characteristics of the service area population, additional information is now required on the lifestyles of consumers, their social context and cultural milieu, and the life circumstances that have implications for health status and health behavior.

Even more radical is the notion that data must be collected on topics previously thought to have no implications for health status. Attributes like income, educational level, and employment status for the target population continue to be collected, but now data on the social and physical environment, availability of affordable and adequate housing, employment options and job training opportunities, access to affordable and healthy food, access to green spaces and recreational activities, access to transportation, and exposure to crime and violence are considered relevant. The significance of this type of information has been highlighted as it has become increasingly obvious that no level of medical care can overcome poverty, environmental threats, malnutrition, or a stressful environment.

Although the healthcare industry generates massive amounts of data, these data are often not accessible to those who need it. Hospitals and other providers of health services do, however, generate extensive amounts of internal data. The operation of such complex organizations invariably generates massive amounts of data on operations, utilization, clinical activities, finances, human resources, and other aspects of the operation. The computerization of most medical records has materially assisted the process of generating extensive data on the medical management of patients, their consumption of resources, and their contribution to the financial well-being of the organization.

Most healthcare organizations today recognize that internal data is only one side of the data coin. Increasingly, healthcare providers are seeking to acquire "market data" that provides insights into the world outside the organization's walls. Indeed, it is not possible to establish benchmarks, calculate market shares, or develop business plans among other activities without access to external market data. It has become well established within the industry that internal data in isolation is not very useful except for tracking internal activities. This process does not mean much, however, if there are no standards, benchmarks, or comparable data to measure against.

The emphasis on community data is a major plank in the population health platform, with hospitals now expected to place as much emphasis on consumers in general as they do on their own patients. Further, hospitals will not be allowed to rely exclusively on their own data but must demonstrate that they have accessed resources in the community. The ACA specifically mandates that the local health department be involved in the assessment along with other healthcare providers. It further specifies that any organizations inside or outside of healthcare be consulted to the extent they can provide insights into the needs of the general population. The extraction of information from organizations outside of the system and even organizations outside of healthcare further supports the need for a population health approach.

This leads us to the most radical of the aspects related to data collection: the emphasis on non-health-related data. Data must be collected on a wide range of topics that historically have not been linked to the health of the population. The recognition of the social determinants of health has opened the door to the acquisition of a data on a wide range of topics historically ignored by healthcare organizations. While most analyses include data on the demographic and socioeconomic characteristics of the service area population, additional information is now required on the lifestyles of consumers, their social context and cultural milieu, and the life circumstances that have implications for health status and health behavior. In keeping with the population health approach, this information is not collected for individuals per se but for groups within the population. So, it is not so important to know that John Doe has certain characteristics but that 100 John Does in ZIP Code 99999 have those characteristics in common.

Type of Recommendations

A final difference between CHNAs and PHAs relates to the types of recommendations that the respective approaches might generate, recommendations that reflect previously noted differences. CHNAs are more likely to frame recommendations within the context of the healthcare delivery system. Operating on the assumption that "more is better," there is a tendency to treat the healthcare system as a hammer and see any gap as a nail. Thus, the answer to most identified problems is more facilities, personnel, and/or services. The PHA, on the other hand, is more likely to recognize the limitations of the healthcare delivery system in addressing identified problems. While the judicious deployment of health resources within the community is certainly an objective, less faith would be placed in the ability of these resources to address identified issues.

CHNAs are more likely to turn to traditional public health initiatives as a major component of any efforts at amelioration. While many of these efforts to address the factors that affect populations are worthwhile, this still represents a health system solution to a non-health problem. Even then, many public health programs are geared toward changing individual behavior rather than influencing group behavior. The CHNA is more likely to recommend health education programs, for example, that attempt to change the behavior of individuals.

The PHA, on the other hand, is more likely to be focused on population-oriented solutions that take a "wholesale" approach to health problems rather than focusing on individuals. The focus of PHAs on the social determinants of health mandates a solution that attempts to address the root causes of health problems. Rather than focusing on specific health problems, the intent is to create a healthier overall environment. The assumption here is that people are not healthy because they receive good healthcare but because they are healthy enough to never need it.

Finally, while both CHNAs and PHAs recognize the importance of policies in establishing a context for community health improvement, the CHNA is more likely to limit its policy recommendations to the healthcare arena. The PHA, on the other hand, would take a broader approach to examine policies within a number of sectors of society. It is one thing to monitor pollutants in the environment and recommend mitigative actions (CHNA approach), and it is another to lobby for policy changes that would have a major impact on the release of pollutants in the environment (PHA approach). Policies related to spheres such as education, housing, criminal justice, transportation, and healthcare, among others, are more likely to be considered in the recommendations of a population health assessment.

Reference

Wright, J., Williams, R., & Wilkerson, J. R. (1998). Development and importance of health needs assessment. *British Journal of Medicine, 316*(1740):1310–1313.

Glossary

Access The ability of individuals or groups to obtain health services. Access may be influenced by service availability, as well as access to transportation, insurance, and other factors.

Accessibility analysis An analytical technique that determines the extent to which plan enrollees or members of the general population have geographical access to providers or other health services. Access in this analysis typically is measured in terms of geographic distance or drive time.

Accountable care organization A structure involving a group of voluntary providers collectively held responsible for the overall cost and quality of care for a defined patient population.

Activities of daily living (ADL) The tasks that individuals must perform in order to take care of themselves (e.g., dressing, toilet use). The level of disability characterizing an individual is often determined by the number of ADLs the individual can or cannot perform.

Acute condition A health condition characterized by rapid onset, usually short duration, and a clear-cut disposition (e.g., cure, death), typical of developing countries and younger populations.

Administrative records Data collected routinely during the course of operations by healthcare organizations or government agencies; certain national registries (e.g., Medicare) are based on administrative records.

Admission The formal placement of an individual into a hospital or other inpatient facilities, typically limited to episodes of care involving an overnight stay. The number of admissions is a commonly used measure of hospital utilization.

Admission rate For a healthcare market area, the number of patients admitted to a hospital in a specified year per 1000 population.

Adverse selection Situation in which a health plan experiences enrollment of a disproportionate number of individuals with a higher-than-average risk of utilizing services and thereby filing claims against the plan.

Affordable Care Act (ACA) *See* Patient Protection and Affordable Care Act (ACA).

© Springer Science+Business Media, LLC, part of Springer Nature 2021
R. K. Thomas, *Health Services Planning*,
https://doi.org/10.1007/978-1-0716-1076-3

Agency for Healthcare Research and Quality (AHRQ) A federally funded research institute that supports studies on the utilization of health services and the efficacy of various treatment modalities.

Age-specific rates The level of occurrence (per 1000, 10,000, or 100,000 population) of a phenomenon for specific age cohorts.

Alternative therapy An umbrella term that refers to a variety of therapeutic modalities (e.g., homeopathy, acupuncture, nutritional therapy) utilized by patients as alternatives to mainstream allopathic medicine. Increasingly referred to as complementary therapies.

Ambulatory care Any type of treatment that is provided to an "ambulatory" patient that does not require an overnight hospital stay. Also referred to as outpatient care.

Ambulatory Payment Classification (APC) The classification system developed by the Centers for Medicare & Medicaid Services for reimbursing services provided to outpatients. It is essentially the ambulatory care version of the diagnosis-related group system.

Area of dominant influence (ADI) The geographic territory covered by a particular form of media.

Assumption A fact or situation that is accepted as true, often without proof.

Attitude An individual's cognitive evaluations, feelings, or action tendencies toward some person, object, or idea.

Audit, external An assessment of the external environment of a health system or organization, involving a range of data collection activities on the market area and its population.

Audit, internal An assessment of the internal environment of an organization, involving a thorough analysis of operations, staffing, systems, policies and procedures, customer characteristics, and other factors that contribute to a description of the organization.

Average length of stay (ALOS) The number of days on average patients remain in a hospital or other institutions, calculated as the number of patient days during a period (usually a year) divided by the number of admissions during that period.

Baby boomers The segment of the US population (born between 1946 and 1964) that constitutes the largest cohort in the age distribution and exhibits characteristics that set it apart from older and younger age cohorts.

Bed day One patient filling one bed for one day. Used as a measure of service utilization.

Big data Refers to data sets (and their management) that are too large to be manipulated using traditional data analysis techniques; usually combining data from a variety of sources.

Birth certificate Standard form completed for each birth that takes place in the United States. Birth certificates are collected and processed by local health departments and ultimately submitted to the National Center for Health Statistics.

Break-even analysis A mathematical determination of the volume of revenue required to cover total costs of a good or service at a given price.

Business coalition A cooperative formed by businesses in a community in order to jointly negotiate with healthcare providers with the intent of containing health-care costs.

Capitation An arrangement whereby providers are paid a predetermined per capita fee for providing a specified range of services to a specified population.

Case analysis A technique used by epidemiologists to identify the incidence of specific health conditions within a population and track the progression of these conditions over time.

Case mix The combination of diagnoses that make up the distribution of cases treated by a particular provider (e.g., the proportion of cases that are obstetrical, cardiac, etc.). Alternatively, the overall characteristics (e.g., age, sex) of a group of enrollees for which a case manager is responsible.

Catchment area The geographic area from which a healthcare organization draws its patients or enrollees; sometimes formally designated for assigning patients to various providers.

Causal research Research that attempts to identify cause-and-effect relationships by means of specifying the functional relationships between two or more variables in a research study.

Cause of death The reason for the death of an individual entered on the standard death certificate and used in mortality analyses.

Census A data collection technique that involves obtaining data from the entire population.

Census block The smallest geographic area for which the Census Bureau collects and reports data during the decennial census. A census block is the square or other polygon that is formed by the streets that comprise the four (usually) sides of a block.

Census block group The aggregation of census blocks into groups for data analysis purposes; the lowest level of geography for which the American Community Survey provides data.

U.S. Census Bureau The federal agency within the U.S. Department of Commerce with responsibility for conducting the decennial census and a variety of other censuses and survey activities.

Census tract A geographic area established by the Census Bureau for the collection and reporting of census data; typically includes between 2000 and 4000 residents.

Centers for Medicare & Medicaid Services (CMS) The federal agency within the U.S. Department of Health and Human Services with the responsibility for managing the Medicare and Medicaid programs.

Centers for Disease Control and Prevention (CDC) The CDC is the federal agency responsible for monitoring various infectious diseases and tracking the course of any epidemic condition. The CDC is an important source of epidemiological data. It is the primary public health agency within the federal government with the responsibility for monitoring health problems and addressing identified issues; a major source of health data and the organizational home for the National Center for Health Statistics.

Certificate of need (CON) In many states, a certificate-of-need application must be filed in order to obtain approval for the establishment of a new health facility or an addition or change in services provided. The states that maintain CON programs vary widely in terms of the types of services provided and the provisions for CON regulations.

Chronic condition A health condition characterized by slow onset, lengthy progression, and a usually indefinite disposition, typical of modern, industrial societies and older populations.

Coding system A structure for classifying and recording medical diagnoses, procedures, and other events.

Cohort A segment of the population that is distinguished by a particular attribute—e.g., all people born in the United States between 1946 and 1951 or all American soldiers exposed to Agent Orange in Vietnam.

Cohort analysis An analytical technique that monitors the movement of cohorts of individuals over time.

Cohort effect The observed impact that certain experiences and conditions exert on a cohort of individuals as that cohort is monitored over time—e.g., the analysis of the baby boom cohort's adaptation to aging.

Collection, data Any one of a number of procedures (both primary and secondary) for acquiring the data required for the implementation of a research plan.

Commercial insurer A category of for-profit insurance plan that typically reimburses providers on a fee-for-service basis; often referred to as a private insurer to distinguish from government-sponsored health plans.

Communicable (or infectious) disease A disease caused by a microorganism that can be spread directly or indirectly from one person to another.

Community health assets Resources, organizations, and people within a community that might be considered as "health assets" by residents and may be overlooked by health planners.

Community health needs assessment (CHNA) A comprehensive, in-depth assessment of a community's population, health status, health-related issues, and unmet needs.

Community resources inventory The collection of information on the resources (particularly health resources) that are available to a community—including both formal resources and community health assets.

Community survey A type of sample survey conducted on the community at large, typically using households within the community as the sampling frame.

Community-based care The range of health services provided to individuals or families outside of formal institutional settings.

Competition The effort of two or more organizations acting independently to secure the business of the same customers.

Competitive analysis Research undertaken on the characteristics of a healthcare organization's competitors within a market area.

Comprehensive Health Planning Act The legislation that established the first formal health planning structure in the United States in 1966. This Act was replaced by subsequent health planning legislation in the 1970s. All federal support for health planning was eliminated in the early 1980s.

Consumer Any individual in the community that is a potential user of a healthcare organization's products or services.

Consumer behavior The consumer's pattern of consumption of goods and services.

Consumer engagement The process of identifying and profiling consumers and subsequently involving them in desired behaviors.

Corporate culture The values, beliefs, and attitudes that characterize an organization and guide its practices.

Cost/benefit analysis A form of analysis that identifies the benefits (both tangible and intangible) that will be derived from a project and compares the benefits to the costs involved in carrying out the project.

Covered lives Totality of individuals who are covered under an insurance plan (as opposed to the number of individuals who participate in the plan)—i.e., plan participants plus any covered dependents.

Crude birth rate (CBR) A simple measure of the level of fertility of a population based on the number of births per 1000 population; the CBR may be misleading since the denominator includes the total population and not just the population at risk.

Crude death rate (CDR) A simple measure of the level of mortality of a population based on the number of deaths per 1000 population; the crude death rate may be misleading since there are significant variations in death rate by age. Also referred to as the crude mortality rate.

Current Procedural Terminology (CPT) A coding system used by physicians to code procedures performed. This code is tied to the fees charged.

Customer A patient or other type of client that currently utilizes one or more of a healthcare organization's products or services.

Dartmouth Atlas A product of the Dartmouth Institute for Health Policy and Clinical Practice (formerly the Center for Evaluative Clinical Sciences) that involves the compilation and analysis of Medicare data for the study of health services utilization; access to extension data is available to online users.

Death certificate Standard form completed for every death that occurs in the United States. Death certificates are collected and processed by local health departments and ultimately submitted to the National Center for Health Statistics.

Demand (for health services) The combined healthcare needs and wants of a population that constitutes the volume and type of health services "demanded" by the population (which may or may not approximate utilization).

Demand management An approach utilized primarily by healthcare organizations to proactively control health services utilization by preventing subjects from over- or underutilizing services.

Demographics The numerical, biosocial, and sociocultural characteristics of a population that constitute its demographic composition.

Density, population An indicator of the density or sparseness of the population in a geographic area, usually measured in terms of persons per square mile or, in urban areas, per acre.

Dependency ratio An index that compares the number of "dependent" individuals within a population to the number of independent individuals that are expected to support them. The very young and very old are typically included among the dependent population.

Descriptive research Research that describes the population, market, or situation under study, but does not attempt to explain the patterns that are identified.

Diagnosis-related groups (DRGs) A system of categorizing diagnoses and/or procedures for hospital inpatients into groupings based on relative resource utilization and used as a basis for prospective reimbursement by the Medicare program.

Diagnostic and Statistical Manual of Mental Disorders (DSM) A coding system patterned on the International Classification of Disease that is utilized for classifying mental disorders.

Diagnostic test A clinical procedure that tests for the existence of pathology in an individual typically in response to previous indications of the existence of the pathology. This contrasts with a screening test that is routinely conducted in the absence of any indication of pathology.

Differentiation strategy A business development or marketing approach that attempts to distinguish one organization or product from its competitors in ways significant to consumers or to create the perception that there is difference, even if there is not.

Disability A condition (physical or mental) of individuals that limits their ability to carry out the activities of daily living.

Disability rate The level of incapacity within a population as measured by the number of cases of physically and/or mentally handicapped individuals, or by the level of restricted activity (e.g., school-loss days or work-loss days).

Discharge The official release of a patient after an episode of care at a hospital or other inpatient facilities involving at least one night in the hospital. The number of discharges is a frequently used indicator of the utilization level for a hospital.

Discharge rate The number of patients discharged from a hospital within a specified year per 1000 residents.

Disease A term used in a number of different ways but generally referring to a state of pathology within an individual organism.

Disease management An approach to patient care that emphasizes the long-term, continuous, and often comprehensive management of a patient's disease, rather than an episodic approach to the treatment of the condition.

Disease of civilization A term applied to chronic conditions that have arisen as a result of the modernization of society and reflect the impact of environmental factors and lifestyle on health status.

Disease of despair A newly coined term that refers to health conditions that arise as a result of social or economic conditions and reflect a state of "despair" on the part of affected individuals.

Diversification Process through which healthcare organizations diversify their service offerings beyond their traditional service complement. Hospitals frequently diversify by establishing outpatient facilities to serve different patient needs. Other healthcare organizations may diversify into unrelated areas (e.g., real estate, assisted living facilities) in order to expand their revenue base.

Durable medical equipment (DME) Biomedical and assistive equipment that is utilized in the provision of care for institutionalized, homebound, and ambulatory patients. Wheelchairs and hospital-type beds are examples of durable medical equipment.

Econometric model A projection methodology that generates forecasts based on the "best-fit" model utilizing a wide range of variables that are thought to contribute to future conditions.

Economic census An inventory of economic activity conducted every 5 years by the Census Bureau that compiles certain data for every business in the United States; the primary source of data on healthcare establishments.

Elasticity The tendency for the demand for health services to rise or fall in response to nonclinical factors (e.g., insurance coverage, consumer preferences).

Elective procedure A procedure that is not covered by insurance typically because it is not considered medically necessary (e.g., cosmetic surgery). A consumer may "elect" to have such a procedure performed if he/she is willing to pay out of pocket for the service.

Encounter Refers to one patient visit to a provider, usually regardless of the number of procedures performed.

Environmental assessment (or scan) The comprehensive compilation of data that describes the environment in which a healthcare organization or health system operates; the assessment could include information ranging from the local level to the national level depending on the nature of the assessment.

Epidemiologic transition A change in a population's epidemiologic profile—from acute to chronic health problems—as a result of aging, changing demographic characteristics, and lifestyles.

Epidemiological analysis An approach to the study of health phenomena that involves the relationship between individuals and their social environment and the distribution of health problems among various segments of the population.

Episodic care The traditional approach to the provision of health services in which each physician visit for each reason is considered a separate episode unrelated to any other episodes of care for that condition.

Estimate, population A calculated estimation of the population for a particular area or population category for some current or past time period.

Etiology In epidemiology, the cause or causes of an identified disease.

Evaluation analysis An analytical technique that involves the assessment of the effectiveness of the processes and outcomes associated with a program or service.

Exploratory research Preliminary (often informal) analysis that examines the general nature of the problem or opportunity under study and provides guidance for the development of more formal descriptive analyses.

Extrapolation A projection technique that graphically, mathematically, or statistically identifies a pattern in a number of periods of past utilization, and then extends that pattern into the future to predict utilization.

Federally Qualified Health Center (FQHC) A health facility recognized (and subsidized) by the Health Resources and Services Administration (HRSA) as a provider to services to underserved populations; most FQHCs provide primary care services but may include dental and behavioral health services.

Fee for service The traditional means of paying for healthcare in the United States whereby insurers or patients pay a separate fee for each service that a physician, hospital, or other provider performs. This is in contrast to a capitation arrangement in which the provider receives a specified amount of reimbursement for managing a range of services.

Fertility The reproduction experience of a population, most often expressed in terms of total births and/or birth rates.

Focus group A qualitative method of data collection that involves obtaining feedback from individuals in a group setting; typically involves 8–10 persons and a trained moderator following an interview guide.

Forecast A prediction of future reality, based on an examination of present or past reality together with judgment regarding how reality might change.

Full-time equivalent (FTE) The amount of labor that would represent one employee working on a full-time basis. The FTE unit is used to standardize labor force counts where different organizations utilize varying amounts of part-time labor.

Gantt chart A template for outlining a project plan and visually illustrating project flow and relationships between various plan components.

Gap analysis An analytical technique used to assess the gap between needs of a population and resources required to meet those needs, or between the current status of an organization and the position in which it would like to be.

Gatekeeper The person or organization that controls a consumer's access to health services. Traditionally, the physician has served as the gatekeeper for the system. Other gatekeepers such as health plan authorization personnel and discharge planners also play an important role in managing utilization in today's healthcare environment.

Geographic information system (GIS) Computerized application for performing spatial analysis and generating maps reflecting the analysis.

Goal A generalized statement indicating the desired position of an organization or health system at some point in the future.

Gusher analysis An analytical technique that identifies particularly promising market opportunities that are immediately available (although they may not have much long-term benefit).

Health A state of wellness whose definition depends on one's perspective. In the narrowest sense, health has been defined as the absence of disease and disability. In its broadest sense, it has been defined as a state of complete physical, social, mental, and spiritual well-being.

Health behavior Any action aimed at restoring, preserving, and/or enhancing an individual's health status; more broadly could include any action (positive or negative) that potentially affects one's health.

Healthcare A comprehensive approach to the management of health that reflects a broad notion of health and healthcare; healthcare is in contrast to the more narrowly defined medical care.

Health disparity The observed difference between various groups in society in terms of their health status and/or health behavior; disparities may also be noted in terms of the manner in which various groups are treated by the healthcare system.

Health impact assessment (HIA) The process of evaluating the health impact of a project or policy. HIAs are increasingly being required before the undertaking of any major development project or the enactment of various policies.

Health Insurance Portability and Accountability Act (HIPAA) 1996 legislation that limits access to and protects individuals' protected health information.

Health literacy The level of understanding exhibited by a healthcare consumer or population with regard to health and healthcare.

Health plan A generic term that applies to any type of insurance program that provides coverage for health services, including companies that self-insure their employees.

Health Professional Shortage Area (HPSA) Area designated by the U.S. Public Health Service that has a shortage of specified categories of healthcare providers.

Health promotion Any activity or system that is designed to proactively maintain, improve, or enhance the health status of individuals or populations. Health promotion generally includes both preventive care and lifestyle-related health behavior.

Health Resources and Services Administration (HRSA) The federal organization within the U.S. Public Health Service most directly involved in the development and funding of community-based health services.

Health service area The geographic area served by a healthcare provider. The federal government designates formal health service areas covering the entire United States for some of its data management activities.

Health service region Area designated by the federal government as being served by a medical community (as opposed to an individual organization).

Health status The overall condition of an individual or population in terms of its health; the level of morbidity characterizing a population; for planning purposes refers primarily to population health.

Health status indicator A measure of the relative health condition of a person or population, usually in the form of an index score and generated through self-reports or from statistics produced on the population in question.

Health/healthcare system A multifacility healthcare organization; also may refer to the overall healthcare system.

Healthy People 2020 An ongoing program of the Centers for Disease Control and Prevention that seeks to address identified health-related issues on a national basis. The HP2020 program identifies challenges and specifies goals and objectives for addressing these challenges.

Immigrant paradox The situation in which immigrants arriving to the United States exhibit better health than their countrymen already in the United States.

The health status of second- and third-generation immigrants tends to decline with longer residence in the United States.

Impact analysis A form of evaluation research that examines the ultimate, long-term impact of a project or development on the health of the community; outcome analysis focuses more on the immediate results of the project.

Implementation matrix The list of specific actions, tasks, or activities needed to accomplish goals and objectives.

Incidence The number of new cases of a disease, disability, or other health-related phenomenon recorded during a specified period of time, reported in terms of the number of cases per 100, 1000, 10,000, or 100,000 population.

In-depth interview Research technique involving (usually) one-on-one interviews with key informants that are lengthy and involve in-depth probing for information.

Index A composite "score" usually calculated from responses, on a survey, or the characteristics of a population that have been identified; the index score can then be compared to other respondents or populations.

Indigent care Health services provided at no cost to individuals who are considered "medically indigent"—i.e., they are not covered under any type of insurance plan. Such patients are not necessarily impoverished but they lack the ability to pay for health services.

Industry life cycle The process that an industry typically follows involving the emergence of the industry as a new phenomenon, a growth phase, a maturity phase, and a period of decline as the industry's functions are replaced by other industries.

Infant mortality rate (IMR) The number of deaths to infants under 1 year of age per 1000 live births during a specific time period (usually 1 year). Also referred to as the infant death rate.

Information Data that have been rendered meaningful by means of statistical analysis and interpretation.

In-migration The flow of new residents into a geographic area; technically, the newcomers must cross a county line to be considered in-migrants.

Inpatient Technically, any patient that spends at least one night (or 24 h) in an institution such as a hospital or residential treatment program. Traditionally, most patients requiring any significant type of care were admitted to a hospital as inpatients.

International Classification of Disease (ICD) The standard classification system utilized to categorize the universe of diagnoses and procedures utilized in contemporary medical science.

Interpolation An estimation technique for calculating estimates between two points in time for which data are available—e.g., if population figures are available for 1980 and 1990, an estimate for 1985 could be made through interpolation.

Interview, mail (out) A research technique that involves mailing out survey forms to respondents, who then return completed forms to the organization that mailed them or to some third party for analysis.

Interview, personal A research technique that involves face-to-face administration of a survey instrument.

Interview, telephone A research technique that involves the administration of a survey instrument over the telephone.

Key informant An interview subject chosen as a key source of information due to his/her position within the organization, his/her role as an opinion leader, or some other characteristic that makes the informant a critical source of information.

Length of stay (LOS) The number of days an individual remains in a hospital or other healthcare facility. The length of stay is an important consideration in utilization management.

Life circumstances The conditions (typically negative) that affect the everyday lives of individuals and households and influence both health status and health behavior; social determinants of health playing at the microlevel.

Life expectancy The length of life that can be anticipated for members of a population; the average number of years calculated based on the age of death for all population members.

Lifestyle The set of attitudes, values, preferences, and behavior patterns that distinguish subsets of the population from each other; often used interchangeably with "psychographic characteristics."

Lifestyle analysis An analytical approach that evaluates a population on the basis of the lifestyle characteristics associated with various subsets within the population; often used interchangeably with "psychographic analysis."

Limitation of activity A measure of disability that involves a determination of the ability of an individual to carry out various activities. Usually presented in terms of bed-restricted days, school-loss days, work-loss days, etc.

Living arrangement Used to describe the nature of household relationships as a supplement to marital status. Includes such categories as married without children, married with children, living alone, co-habitative relationship, and unrelated individuals living together.

Long-term care (LTC) Refers to any type of care for the elderly and/or disabled that involves ongoing institutionalized management of the patient whether or not medical care is necessary. Nursing homes are the traditional form of long-term care but various other types of long-term care facilities have become common.

Maintenance strategy A strategic approach adopted by healthcare organizations when the industry is in the mature phase of the life cycle. Since there is limited expansion occurring, the emphasis is on maintaining existing business and extracting as much benefit from it as possible.

Managed care A planned and coordinated approach involving positive and negative incentives for both enrollees and providers for "managing" the services received by a population enrolled in a particular health plan.

Marital status The official status of individuals in terms of marriage, typically including the categories of never married, married, divorced, widowed, and, sometimes, separated.

Market Any geographic area or population grouping that can be conceptualized as a source of potential customers.

Market area The targeted geographic area in which the primary market potential for a healthcare organization is located; often used interchangeably with "service area."

Market research A multistep process involving the systematic gathering and analysis of market data that assists an organization in developing strategies and making decisions.

Market segment A specific subset of a population that differs from other subsets in terms of their use of health services.

Market share The proportion of health services utilization that any single provider is able to capture in a given time period.

Marketing mix The combination of the "four Ps" of marketing—product, price, place, and promotion—characterizing the marketing activities of a particular organization or product line.

Marketing plan An outline of the methods and resources needed to achieve organizational goals with regard to a specific target market.

Marketing research The process by which the marketer acquires information to be used to identify and define marketing opportunities and problems; generate, refine, and evaluate marketing actions; and improve understanding of marketing as a process.

Maternal mortality A measure of the deaths that occur to women as a result of giving birth.

Matrix analysis An analytical technique that involves simultaneously examining the various possible outcomes that are associated with a combination of factors that are likely to influence an outcome.

Measurement The assignment of numbers to characteristics of objects, persons, states, or events according to pre-specified rules.

Median age An indicator of the average age of a population, whereby the median age represents that age at which half of the population falls below and half falls above.

Medicaid The federally sponsored and state-administered government insurance program for the low-income population in the United States. The Centers for Medicare & Medicaid Services (CMS) manages the program, with the characteristics of the program varying from state to state.

Medical care The provision of formal clinical services to individual patients; medical care reflects a narrow notion of health and healthcare in contrast to healthcare.

Medically indigent Individuals who for whatever reason do not have access to health insurance and/or are not able to pay for health service out of pocket. The medically indigent may not be poverty stricken but are "insurance poor."

Medically necessary A characteristic of a procedure or service provided under an insurance plan that reflects a clear medical need for the procedure or service. This is in contrast to elective procedures (e.g., cosmetic surgery) that nay be performed in the absence of medical necessity.

Medicare The federally sponsored insurance program that provides coverage for the elderly population in the United States. All elderly citizens are eligible for basic coverage, with certain additional coverage option. The Medicare program is administered by the Centers for Medicare & Medicaid Services (CMS).

Metropolitan statistical area (MSA) An official designation for a large concentration of population that includes a central city, a county, and its surrounding counties.

Migration The physical movement of individuals or groups from one location to another, typically with the intent of a permanent change of residence.

Minor civil division (MCD)/census county division (CCD) Sub-county geographical areas established by the Census Bureau as the basis for data collection and reporting when census tracts are not used.

Minor medical center *See* urgent care center.

Mission statement A short statement (usually one or two paragraphs) describing an organization's reason for being.

Model A statement (mathematical or otherwise) that specifies the conceptual relationship between two or more variables—e.g., a model may depict the manner in which healthcare decisions are made with a hospital.

Morbidity The level of sickness and disability within a population, usually expressed in terms of incidence and prevalence rates.

Mortality The level of death characterizing a population, usually expressed in terms of the number of deaths and/or death rates.

National Center for Health Statistics (NCHS) The "census bureau" of healthcare, the NCHS is the federal agency responsible for the collection, management, and dissemination of most national data on health and healthcare.

National Health Planning and Resource Development Act of 1974 Health planning legislation passed in an attempt to bolster existing health planning initiatives; emphasized the development of regional and community health planning councils.

Need In this context, need refers to the actual need for health services within a population as measured by the prevalence of clinically identifiable health problems. This is in contrast to wants and desires for health services that might characterize a population. Need should represent the baseline level of health problems affecting a population.

Niche strategy A strategic approach that focuses on identifying and exploiting one or more niche markets within a service area. Rather than offering a full range of hospital services, a hospital may elect to focus on certain segments of the market (e.g., eye surgery, foot surgery).

Niche, market A market opportunity, usually narrowly defined in terms of population, geographic location, or service category, that is not being exploited by mainstream providers.

Nondurable good A product used once or a few times and then disposed of.

Notifiable disease A disease whose presence must be reported to public health officials. Typically, an infectious disease, notifiable conditions are generally first reported to local health departments and this information is compiled nationally by the Centers for Disease Control and Prevention (CDC).

Objective A formally designated achievement to be accomplished in support of a goal that is specific, concise, and time bound.

Observation, nonparticipatory A form of observation research in which the observer is detached from the group or activity being observed and those being observed typically are unaware of the research taking place.

Observation, participatory A form of observation research in which the observer becomes a part of the group or activity being observed in order to collect information as an "insider."

Occupancy rate The percent of the beds in a hospital or other inpatient facility that are occupied by patients during a particular time period. The occupancy rate is an indicator of the level of utilization of a hospital, with occupancy for licensed beds and operational beds often calculated separately.

Office visit The standard measure for use of physician services and the typical "encounter" that is recorded to measure utilization of physicians and other services.

Operationalization Process for representing a concept in the form of a measurable variable. For example, "social class" is often operationalized for research purposes in terms of "median household income."

Opportunity cost The potential benefits to be derived from a project that are forfeited by virtue of turning attention to another project. Out-of-pocket payment reimbursement for health services provided by consumers who are not covered by insurance or for whom the particular service is not covered. Certain procedures are never covered by insurance and consumers who require these services must pay out of pocket.

Outcome In healthcare, traditionally referred to as the results of clinical treatment but has been expanded to consider the long-term results of an initiative on community health.

Outcome measurement A formal process for assessing the effectiveness of treatment and/or patient satisfaction with treatment results.

Out-migration The flow of residents out of a geographic area; technically, movers must move across county lines in order to be considered an out-migrant.

Outpatient An individual who receives any type of health service that does not require an overnight stay in a hospital or other inpatient facility. Similar to an ambulatory patient, although homebound patients would be considered outpatients but not ambulatory patients.

Over-the-counter drug (OTC) A drug that can be purchased from a pharmacy without a prescription written by a physician.

Panel survey A sample of respondents who have agreed to provide information for a research project over an extended period of time.

Patient Any individual who receives "formal" health services from a licensed healthcare provider. This does not include self-care since the individual has not been formally diagnosed.

Patient origin The source of patients for a health service based on place of residence (usually identified by ZIP Code).

Patient Protection and Affordable Care Act (ACA) Comprehensive healthcare reform legislation passed in 2010 that attempted to revamp existing health insurance arrangements and expand access to health insurance for Americans; ACA included a provision that mandated that not-for-profit hospitals conduct a community health needs assessment every 3 years.

Payer (or payor) *See* Third-Party Payer.

Pay-for-performance An innovative approach to reimbursement—spearheaded by the Centers for Medicare & Medicaid—that rewards providers based on quality rather than quantity.

Penetration The percentage of business captured by a health plan or plans, usually used in reference to managed care. For example, a managed care penetration rate of 20% indicates that managed care plans have enrolled 20% of the area's potential health plan enrollees.

Plan A systematic approach to specifying and striving after a future goal, typically involving the matching of existing resources with market opportunities.

Plan, business A systematic approach for reaching a specific business objective at some point in the future.

Plan, human resources A systematic approach for allocating resources to meet future needs for personnel.

Plan, implementation A systematic approach for carrying out the activities specified in a strategic plan or other type of plan. The overall plan typically defines what is to be done, while the implementation plan determines how it will be done.

Plan, marketing A systematic approach for utilizing a marketing initiative to reach some objective of the organization.

Plan, operational A systematic approach for maintaining operations and reaching some specified operations-related goal in the future.

Plan, strategic A systematic approach to positioning the organization in the market, utilizing existing resources to exploit market opportunities.

Plan, technology A systematic approach for evaluating, acquiring, and implementing appropriate technology for use at some point in the future.

Planning The process for developing a systematic plan for identifying and reaching some future goal.

Population at risk The total number of persons within a population that are at risk of a particular condition. For example, the number of persons at risk of childbirth would equal the number of fertile childbearing-age women within the population.

Population health An approach to improving community health status that focuses on populations rather than individuals and addresses the root causes and structural impediments of ill health rather than exclusively focusing on treating the symptoms/conditions of individuals.

Population health assessment An approach to community health needs assessment that emphasizes the health of the population and improves on the traditional comprehensive health needs assessment process.

Population health management The application of population health principles to defined populations (rather than the community) for purposes of utilization control and fiscal management.

Population pyramid A stacked bar graph visually depicting the age and sex composition of a specific population.

Population-based healthcare An approach to the provision of health services that focuses on the needs of the total population rather than the needs of individuals. Outcomes are measured in terms of improvement in overall health status rather than by individual clinical successes.

Predictive modeling A technique for projecting the nature of health problems and the demand for health services into the future utilizing known rates.

Preferred provider organization (PPO) A form of health plan that encourages the use of a specified network of providers in exchange for lower rates for plan enrollees. The PPO typically negotiates discounted rates with providers in the network, with the intent of passing these discounts to consumers in the form of lower premiums.

Prevalence The total number of cases of a disease or disability within a population at a specific point in time, reported in terms of the number of cases per 100, 1000, 10,000, or 100,000 population.

Prevention An approach to health maintenance that attempts to forestall the onset of health problems rather than treating them once they occur.

Preventive care Any activity intended to prevent disease and/or improve health status carried out prior to the onset of a health problem. Preventive care includes health education, screening, and various health behaviors (e.g., tooth brushing) that protect the individual from the onset of health conditions.

Price The dollar amount that a provider charges for a service provided, typically referred to as a "fee" in healthcare. This is distinguished from "cost" which refers to the provider's cost of providing the service.

Pricing strategy A strategic approach that attempts to capture customers and market share by offering a price advantage to consumers.

Primary care The provision of basic, routine health services including preventive services. The physicians typically involved in primary care are general and family practitioners, general internists, obstetricians, and pediatricians, although other types of providers (e.g., behavioral health therapists) may be thought to provide "primary" care.

Primary data Information collected specifically to address a particular research issue.

Product life cycle The process that a product or service might follow as it evolves—i.e., involving the emergence of the product or service as a new phenomenon, a growth phase, a maturity phase, and a period of decline as the product or service is replaced by other products or services.

Product line *See* Service Line.

Projection, population A calculated figure indicating the size of the population for a particular area or population category for some point in the future.

Promotion Any activity intended to promote an organization, service, or product. Promotion is considered an important component of marketing and can involve public relations, advertising, direct mail, and many other types of activities.

Proprietary data Data gathered by or generated by an organization for exclusive use internally by that organization.

Protected health information A patient's identifiable healthcare data, including physical and mental health status, treatment record, and insurance and payment information.

Provider An individual or organization that is licensed to provide health services, products, or equipment.

Provider network A group of providers that have been formally contracted to provide services to enrollees in a particular health plan; in many plans, enrollees are restricted to providers that belong to the network.

Psychographics Subjective information reported by people regarding their beliefs, feelings, attitudes, and behavior patterns; also referred to as lifestyles and utilized as a basis for predicting health behavior.

Public health The set of activities designated for public health agencies that include disease surveillance, health status monitoring, air and water monitoring, food inspection, registration of vital events, and control of infectious conditions.

Public relations The maintaining of communication and relationships with the general public, various constituents, and consumer groups. As a dimension of marketing, public relations involves press releases, public speaking, "infomercials," and other means of communicating with those outside the organization.

Purchaser (of health services) Any organization or individual that pays for health services that are provided. In common usage, purchaser has come to refer to "group purchasers" such as large employers and business coalitions that represent large numbers of covered lives and can negotiate with providers due to their purchasing power.

Qualitative research Inductive, subjective, and process-oriented research methods utilized to describe, understand, and interpret research issues.

Quantitative research Deductive and objective research methods primarily designed to identify relationships between variables.

Quaternary care Specialized services provided in large medical centers for complex conditions.

Rate The level of occurrence of a phenomenon per a specified number of persons—e.g., per 100, 1000, 10,000, or 100,000.

Ratio The proportion of a characteristic in relation to another characteristic. For example, a sex ratio of 95 means there are 95 males per 100 females.

Region, geographic Generally a geographic area the extends beyond any one political jurisdiction to create an internally consistent region of some type (e.g., Appalachia). Also, refers to officially designated regions into which the United States is divided by the federal government.

Regional Medical Program A federal program initiated in the 1960s that created healthcare regions nationwide for supporting the diffusion of healthcare innovation outside of the medical centers.

Registry The systematic recording and reporting of events or situations characterizing a population—e.g., a registry containing all reported cases of cancer within a specified area or all licensed physicians within a particular state.

Reimbursement The predominant approach in healthcare for paying for services in which providers provide the services and then request reimbursement from third-party payers.

Reported cases Individuals with health problems who have presented themselves to the healthcare system for treatment and were subsequently counted as a reported case. Symptomatic individuals who do not present themselves for treatment are not counted.

Research design A blueprint or framework that is followed in conducting research.

Research question A specific statement concerning components of a business problem or opportunity that drive the research process; research questions are referred to as hypotheses in more formalized research circumstances.

Respondent A person or other unit (e.g., household) that takes part in a survey research project.

Return on investment (ROI) The expected percentage profit that can be expected measured against the amount of resources that are invested in a project.

Risk The exposure that individuals or population groups experience with regard to various health problems. The risk of contracting AIDS, for example, varies with the types of behaviors in which an individual participates.

Risk analysis An actuarial process in which the anticipated utilization and resultant healthcare costs for a particular population or enrollee group are determined.

Rural area An area designated by the Census Bureau for data collection purposes that does not meet the minimum standards for an urban area. That is, the population is limited in size and contains no population concentrations of any significance.

Sample A subset of the population selected for inclusion in a survey.

Sample size The number of individuals or other units selected for inclusion in a survey based on specified rules for determining the number.

Sample survey A survey in which a subset of the population has been selected for participation in a study. The intent is to draw conclusions concerning the total population based on the sample of respondents that have been interviewed.

Sampling frame The list of the target population from which the sample will be drawn—e.g., all addresses in a particular community.

Satisfaction survey A survey that attempts to measure the level of satisfaction with regard to health services or health plans on the part of patients, family members, plan enrollees, or other categories of customers.

Scenario The hypothetical presentation of a situation that reflects the possible effects of a variety of factors on an existing situation.

Screening test A clinical test for the existence of pathology when there is no indication of existing pathology; this is distinguished from a diagnostic test that tests for a known pathology.

Secondary care A level of health services that involves moderate-intensity care and a moderate level of resources and skill levels. Secondary care is more complex than routine care but less intensive than specialized tertiary services.

Secondary data Data collected for some other purpose (such as routine administrative records) but used for some other research application. For example, census data collected for federal statistical purposes might be used for market research.

Segment A component of a population or market defined on the basis of some characteristic relevant to marketers.

Segmentation The process of dividing a population into meaningful segments for purposes of market analysis and strategic planning.

Segmentation, benefit The grouping of people based on the benefits (such as convenience or value) sought from a product or service.

Segmentation, demographic The grouping of individuals into market segments based on such demographic characteristics as age, sex, income, and race.

Segmentation, geographic The grouping of individuals into market segments based on location of residence or work.

Segmentation, psychographic The grouping of individuals into market segments based on lifestyle and attitudinal characteristics.

Segmentation, usage The grouping of individuals into market segments based on their level of utilization of a product or service. Segments may initially be identified as user and nonusers, with the users broken down into subcategories based on their level of usage.

Self-administered questionnaire Survey forms that are completed by the respondents with little or no input from survey administrators.

Self-pay A category of patients who pay for their healthcare expenses out of pocket as opposed to submitting insurance claims; also referred to as the uninsured.

Service area The geographic area from which a healthcare organization draws the majority of its customers; often used interchangeably with "market area."

Service line A business development approach that involves the identification of a vertical set of services (e.g., cardiac care) and the subsequent operation and marketing of the set of services as a business line.

Sex ratio An indicator of the relative proportions of males and females within a population; typically calculated in terms of the number of males per 100 females.

Significance, statistical The determination that a research finding reflects a statistical association and not simply a chance correlation.

Social determinants of health Characteristics of society that contribute to conditions of health or illness within a population, thereby mitigating the effects of disease pathology and genetics.

Social marketing An approach to effecting behavioral change in the general population through public relations, advertising, and other techniques.

Social media A variety of communication modes that use Internet technology to support innovative forms of interaction between people.

Socioeconomic status An indicator of an individual or group's position in the social structure based on such measures as income, occupation, and education.

Spatial analysis An analytical technique that involves the study of the spatial relationships between various phenomena—e.g., the analysis of the geographic distribution of physician offices.

Stakeholder Any individual, organization, or constituency that has a stake in the operation of an organization or a healthcare system. Formal stakeholders may be stockholders or other investors, while informal ones may include medical staffs, suppliers, consumers groups, and so forth.

Standardization A process through which dissimilar populations are statistically adjusted to allow for meaningful comparisons.

Strategy A generalized approach to positioning an organization relative to the market and its competitors in that market. The strategy provides one parameter in the development of a strategic plan.

Strategy map An approach to planning that systematically identifies needs, assets, and desired outcomes as a basis for intervention planning.

Survey instrument Questionnaires used in survey research are referred to as survey instruments.

SWOT analysis An analytical technique that involves the evaluation of a community's or an organization's strengths, weaknesses, opportunities, and threats.

Syndicated research A form of contract survey research in which a professional research firm conducts a survey and sells the results to interested parties in the area or, alternatively, the research firm enlists the front-end participation of area healthcare organizations in the development of the survey.

Synthetic data Population estimates and projections that are generated using statistical techniques and models. Synthetic data are distinguished from actual data collected by means of censuses and surveys.

Tactics The actions that are initiated in order to pursue a strategy within the context of a strategic plan.

Target marketing A marketing technique that focuses on specific market segments rather than the mass market.

Tertiary care Specialized health services for the treatment of serious health conditions that require specialized clinicians, sophisticated equipment and facilities, and substantial support services.

Third-party payer (payor) Any agency or organization that is responsible for reimbursing the cost of health services provided on the part of an insured individual. The provider delivers the service to the patient, with the insurer being the "third party" that pays for the care.

Trend analysis The longitudinal analysis of data for the purpose of identifying the presence or absence of consistency over time; a form of time series analysis.

Uncompensated care Health services provided to medically indigent populations that have no ability to pay for care. Uncompensated care is sometimes informally used to refer to any shortfall between charges and reimbursement for services.

Underinsured Individuals or groups in a population who are technically covered under some insurance plan but have such limited benefits or unfavorable copay or deductible provisions that they do not have adequate coverage.

Uninsured Individuals or groups in a population who are not covered under any insurance plan; in financial accounting also referred to as self-pay.

Universal coverage Situation in which an entire population is covered by a standard form of medical insurance.

Urbanized area A Census Bureau designation for a geographic area that meets specific requirements for being considered "urban." An urbanized area may or may not be incorporated, since designation is a function of the size and characteristics of the population.

Urgent care center A primary care resource designed to handle a limited range of health issues in a convenient, affordable manner that includes "after-hours" care; the intent is to provide episodic care to those who do not have a regular source of care or are unable to access their regular source.

Utilization (of health services) The number and type of health services actually used by a particular population, as opposed to the demand for services.

Utilization management Theoretically, the process of assuring that a patient receives the appropriate care at the appropriate time in the appropriate setting. In actual practice, utilization management is often seen as a means of restricting utilization in order to reduce costs.

Value-based reimbursement A method of payment wherein third-party payers reimburse healthcare providers based on documented improvement in patient health rather than the number of services rendered.

Variable A concept of interest in a research study, operationalized in a manner that will allow for statistical analysis.

Vendor, commercial data A private sector corporation that generates and disseminates data and/or software for data manipulation.

Vital statistics Data collected by government agencies related to "vital events"—e.g., births, deaths, marriages, divorces, and abortions.

Vulnerable population Any population segment within a population that is placed at inordinate risk of health problems due to health status, environmental factors, lack of insurance, marginality, and any number of other factors.

Walk-in clinic Term applied to primary care sites located in drug stores, department stores, or other nonmedical locations that offer limited services typically provided by a nurse practitioner.

Want, healthcare The desire for health services that are not necessarily driven by medical necessity and are considered wants rather than needs; most elective procedures are classified as wants rather than needs.

Years of potential life lost A measure of disability and premature death that is calculated in terms of the number of years that an individual would have expected to live (or to have quality of life) had it not been for disability or death. This is sometimes transformed into "productive" years of life lost.

ZIP Code An administrative district created by the U.S. Postal Service for the efficient delivery of mail. Although not originally intended as units for data collection and dissemination, ZIP Codes are often used as a basis for planning, and marketing studies.

Index

Printed in the United States
by Baker & Taylor Publisher Services